CW01667357

AQA GCSE

French

Foundation

Clive Bell, Eleanor Mayes, Michael Wardle, Tom Hockaday,
Jérôme Garnier, Sandrine Chein, Naomi Crookston

Published by Pearson Education Limited, 80 Strand, London, WC2R ORL.

www.pearsonschoolsandfecolleges.co.uk

Copies of official specifications for all Pearson qualifications may be found on the website: qualifications.pearson.com

Edited by Pearson and Newgen
Designed and typeset by Kamae Design
Original illustrations © Pearson Education Limited 2024
Illustrated by Beehive Illustrations (Adam Linley, Joseph Wilkins and Andrew Pagram) and Andrew Hennessey
Cover design by Kamae Design
Cover photo © Shutterstock/Martin M303

Audio recorded at Chatterbox Studios, London, with thanks to Rowan Laxton, Lilian Lorain Broca, Elea Lorain Broca, Ryan Ghoussainy, Jean-Baptiste Fillon, Katherine Pageon, Tamara Moreau, William Ghoussainy and Giselle Begley

Written by Clive Bell, Sandrine Chein, Naomi Crookston, Jérôme Garnier, Karine Harrington, Tom Hockaday, Eleanor Mayes and Michael Wardle

First published 2024

28 27 26 25 24
10 9 8 7 6 5 4 3 2 1

British Library Cataloguing in Publication Data
A catalogue record for this book is available from the British Library

ISBN 978 1 292 468778

Printed in the UK by Bell & Bain Ltd, Glasgow

Acknowledgements
We would like to thank Sarah Bleyer, Florence Bonneau, Pascale Collier, Barbara Cooper, Leah Cooper, Céline Durassier, Gillian Eades, Gemma Etienne, Sylvie Fauvel, Bill Finegan, Missy Finegan, Seth Finegan, Anne French, Jérôme Garnier, Anne Guerniou, Shirley Hockaday, Qasim Khalid, Louise Leportoux, Chris Lillington, Aaron McKenzie, Sheena Newland, Mario Rogic, Fabienne Tartarin, Jo Heaton and the central team at Northern Lights Learning Trust, and everyone else who has helped in the development of this course.

The authors and publisher would like to thank the following individuals and organisations for permission to reproduce photographs:

123RF: andreypopov 8, Valiza 21, Cathy Yeulet 27, Doodkoalex 36, Cathy Yeulet 39, cladanifer 42, peopleimages12 43, Andrey Armyagov 51, Cathy Yeulet 59, Seventyfour74 79, RUTCHAPOOM MUANGKAEW 82, Sergii Koval 82, stylephotographs 101, Olena Kachmar 108, zurijeta 109, Valerii Honcharuk 110, Pkazmierczak 110, bloodua 111, Ihorsw 139, Cathy Yeulet 140, Arnoaltix 141, Amisb 147, Frugo 159, Bloodua 160, Gioiak2 164, Piyawat Nandeenopparit 164, Stockee 164, Iakov Filimonov 182, Viktoriia Hnatiuk 182, freeprod 186, julief514 186, Stockyimages 189, Stockbroker 221, Scott Griessel 225; **10jourssansecrans:** Association 10 JOURS SANS ECRANS 6, 10; **Alamy Images**: Sergi Reboredo 14, Jacques Brinon/Associated Press 32, UrbanImages 32, JLPPA/ABACAPRESS.COM/Abaca Press 38, STANCA SANDA 42, Ulrich Doering 58, Boaz Rottem 66, FORGET Patrick/SAGAPHOTO.COM 106, Antonio Guillem Fernández 107, JOHN KELLERMAN 108, Christophe Boisvieux 110, Eskimo 110, Avalon/World Pictures 112, Elena Bobrova 112, Guichaoua 112, Johner Images 116, Wavebreak Media Premium 121, Nature Picture Library 134, Thornton Cohen 138, Abaca Press 141, Aleksei Isachenko 159, Jonathan Larsen/Diadem Images 189; **Brussels - Jean-Paul Rémy:** CREDIT (c) visit.brussels - Jean-Paul Rémy - 2017 14; **Camping Le Haut Village:** Camping Le Haut Village 106; **Céleste De Kervenoaël:** Céleste De Kervenoaël 41; **CIJF:** ©CIJF 6; **GAËLLE VANESSA PRUDENCIO E.I:** Gaëlle Prudencio/Capucine De Chocqueuse 32; **Getty Images:** Simon002/iStock Editorial/Getty Images Plus 6, staticnak1983/E+ 8, Thurtell/E+ 8, sturti/E+ 8, SeventyFour/iStock/Getty Images Plus 8, SDI Productions/iStock/Getty Images Plus 12, skynesher/E+ 13, Mark Leech/Offside 15, RichLegg/E+ 18, FG Trade Latin/E+ 24, Vesnaandjic/E+ 24, Andreas Rentz/Staff/Getty Images Entertainment 32, Stephane Cardinale - Corbis/Corbis Entertainment 33, Pascal Le Segretain/Staff/Getty Images Entertainment 33, Mark Hunt/DisabilityImages 34, RobertDodge/iStock/Getty Images Plus 34, FRANCK FIFE/Contributor 38, Marc Piasecki/Contributor 38, Edward Berthelot/Getty Images Entertainment 40, Dominique Charriau/WireImage 40, KAMPUS/iStock/Getty Images Plus 42, tirc83 48, Tony Anderson/Stone 61, Stuart Fox/Gallo Images ROOTS RF collection 63, Vladimir Godnik/fStop 64, Golser/E+ 66, Juanmonino/E+ 68, SolStock/E+ 74, ChiccoDodiFC/iStock 82, bhofack2/iStock 82, Cook Shoots Food/iStock 82, golero/E+ 84, blackCAT/E+ 85, Westend61 90, TatyanaGl/iStock/Getty Images Plus 90, Evrymmnt/iStock 90, Pablo Rasero/iStock/Getty Images Plus 90, adamkaz/E+ 90, DGLimages/iStock 90, Rockaa/E+ 92, BERTRAND GUAY/AFP 93, Julien Hekimian/French Select 93, ALLEKO/iStock 94, sbossert/iStock 94, Chris Schneider/500px 94, DianeBentleyRaymond/E+ 96, Andreas Kindler/Johner Images Royalty-Free 108, LeoPatrizi/E+ 108, Pavliha/iStock 108, Maremagnum/Corbis Documentary 108, SDI Productions/E+ 109, Johner Images/Johner Images Royalty-Free 110, Balate Dorin/iStock/Getty Images Plus 110, Nick David/Photodisc 117, Westend61 117, VikramRaghuvanshi/E+ 117, Lighthouse Films/Corbis 122, skynesher/E+ 125, Stas_V/iStock/Getty Images Plus 138, Yongyuan/E+ 138, Cavan Images/Cavan 141, Mgreen2007/iStock/Getty Images Plus 158, SrdjanPav/E+ 159, Walter Bibikow/Stone 161, Laurent/iStock Unreleased 161, SDI Productions/E+ 163, Westend61 163, Catherine Ledner/Stone 163, Phynart Studio/E+ 168, Murat Taner/The Image Bank 169, Giraudou Laurent/Moment 169, AlexKozlov/iStock Editorial/Getty Images Plus 169, kali9/E+ 182, Imgorthand/E+ 182, pixelfit/E+ 184, ozgurdonmaz/iStock/Getty Images Plus 185, FG Trade/E+ 185, ALAIN JOCARD/AFP 187, FG Trade/E+ 189, iStock/Getty Images Plus 189, boonchai wedmakawand/Moment 191, Hill Street Studios/DigitalVision 191, Sam Diephuis/Tetra images 199, miniseries/E+ 217, Kentaroo Tryman 224; **Gîte La Troglo à Plumes:** Troglo à Plumes, ©Gîtes de France Anjou 106; **MANGERBOUGER.FR:** Mangerbouger.fr 83; **Nicolas Leblanc:** Nicolas Leblanc 141; **Pearson Education Ltd:** Debbie Rowe 42, Jon Barlow 59, Studio 8 77, Handan Erek 86, Gareth Boden 113, Miguel Dominguez Muñoz 171; **Samaya Production:** Luxe Photographie/Samaya production 17; **Shutterstock:** Martin M303 6, Katatonia82 6, Abumuslim1 7, DenPhotos 8, Kaspars Grinvalds 8, New Africa 8, Adriaticfoto 11, Olga_Kuzmina 11, Nipa74 14, Christopher Chambers 15, Brocreative 15, Prostock-studio 24, Stuart Monk 24, Vane Nunes 27, Shutterstock 26, Nejron Photo 29, Raushan_films 34, Brostock 39, Spotmatik 39, Iryna Zhezher 42, Zurijeta 42, Rawpixel.com 48, Shutterstock 51, 10topvector 53, Pyzata 58, Shutterstock 59, Daisy Daisy 64, Prostock-studio 65, Angelika Jakob/imageBROKER 66, Prostock-studio 68, Anna Kraynova 72, wavebreakmedia 77, SpeedKingz 78, Casper1774 Studio 85, M_Videous 86, Zurijeta 86, SewCream 88, StevenK 90, Wazzkii 92, Ph.FAB 93, Zurijeta 98, Iakov Filimonov 101, 10topvector 103, Mila Supinskaya Glashchenko 108, Wavebreakmedia 108, David Hughes 108, Gonzalo Buzonni 108, Fasttailwind 108, Holbox 108, Olrat 108, CrispyPork 108, Gkuna 108, Viacheslav Lopatin 108, Gautier Willaume 109, Gautier Willaume 109, Samuel Borges Photography 110, VladKK 110, T photography 113, BIRYUKOVA EKATERINA 116, Ina Meer Sommer 116, AndriyShevchuk 118, wavebreakmedia 123, APIWAN BORRIKONRATCHATA 125, 10topvector 127, Saiko3p 136, Slavik_ua 136, T.Schofield 136, 2009fotofriends 137, PhotocechCZ 137, Rich Carey 138, Spwidoff 138, LanaElcova 138, chanasorn jele 138, efka 138, AYO Production 138, Julia Tsokur 138, Julia Kuznetsova 140, Serenity Images23 142, Bist 143, Kelvn 144, R_Tee 150, wavebreakmedia 153, Dusan Petkovic 153, 10topvector 155, Enrika Samulionyte 158, LuckyPhoto 158, Alexgo.photography 159, ASashka 159, Leonid Andronov 160, AJR_photo 160, Jacob Lund 160, Krakenimages.com 163, On_france 164, SHARIFUL RIFAT 164, Tracy Whiteside 167, Ekaterina Pokrovsky 169, Shutterstock 174, Krakenimages.com 175, Daniel M Ernst 177, Marko Zamrznuti tonovi 177, 10topvector 179, Bensliman hassan 183, Zoltan Katona 183, karamysh 186, Blue Titan 187, Diego Cervo 187, Insta_photos 189, Blend Images 189, Lucky Business 189, Shutterstock 189, SRStudio 196, fizkes 197, Tyler Olson 199, 10topvector 201, Pressmaster 210, Jacob Lund 213, Shutterstock 214, Shutterstock 216, Sam Wordley 217, GaudiLab 218, Space_Cat 219, Valmedia 221, Arsenii Palivoda 222, dekazigzag 225; **Village Flottant Pressac:** #levillageflottantpressac 106; **Yannis Richardt:** Yannis Richardt 40.

Text extract reproduced with permission from:
USAID: 134; **eurail.com/interrail.eu:** 182

Notes from the publisher
Pearson has robust editorial processes, including answer and fact checks, to ensure the accuracy of the content in this publication, and every effort is made to ensure this publication is free of errors. We are, however, only human, and occasionally errors do occur. Pearson is not liable for any misunderstandings that arise as a result of errors in this publication, but it is our priority to ensure that the content is accurate. If you spot an error, please do contact us at resourcescorrections@pearson.com so we can make sure it is corrected.

Table des matières

Table des matières

Module 7 *Mon petit monde à moi*

Theme 2: Popular culture
Theme 3: Communication and the world around us

Module 8 *Mes projets d'avenir*

Theme 1: People and lifestyle
Theme 2: Popular culture

Révisions

Speaking support

Module 1 Tu as du temps à perdre?

Fêtes et jeux

- Exploring events in the francophone world
- Using *aimer* + noun and *aimer* + infinitive

A 10 jours sans écrans

Qu'est-ce que c'est, les dix jours sans écrans?

Les jeunes passent dix jours sans télévision, sans portable, sans jeux vidéo et sans ordinateur!

Les parents, les professeurs et les organisations locales organisent d'autres activités:

du sport 

de la danse 

du théâtre 

de la cuisine 

de la musique 

sans	*without*
l'écran (m)	*screen*

B Tous les ans, c'est la Fête de la Musique le 21 juin

Plus de 120 pays participent à la fête.
Il y a des concerts dans plus de 1000 villes.

♪ On peut écouter toutes sortes de musique.
♪ On peut voir toutes sortes d'instruments.
♪ On peut voir toutes sortes de groupes.

le pays	*country*
participer à	*to participate, take part in*

C Les Jeux de la FRANCOPHONIE

Tous les quatre ans, c'est les Jeux de la Francophonie.

Plus de 3000 jeunes de 88 pays francophones participent aux Jeux de la Francophonie.

C'est le seul événement sportif et culturel international, en langue française, organisé pour les jeunes.

les jeux (m)	*games*
la Francophonie	*group of countries that have French as their main language*
seul(e)	*only, alone*
l'événement (m)	*event*

D Programme des Jeux de la Francophonie

Concours culturels

- la chanson
- la danse
- la littérature
- la peinture
- la photographie

Compétitions sportives

- le basket
- le cyclisme
- le football
- le judo
- le tennis de table

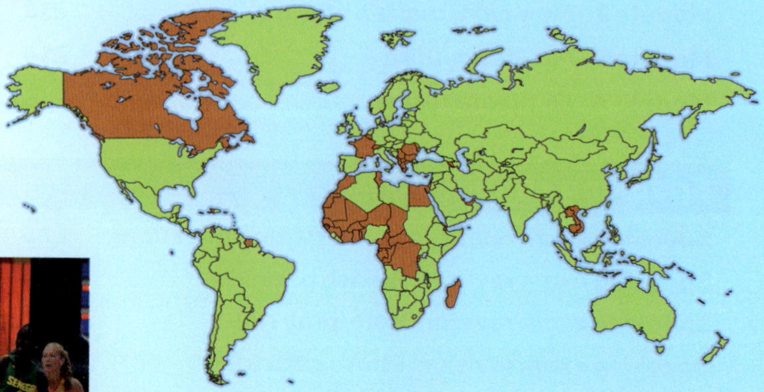

■ pays participants

le concours	*competition*
la peinture	*painting*

Écouter 1 **Listen and repeat these words. Pay special attention to the pronunciation of *é*.**

activit**é**s | **é**couter | id**é**e | int**é**ressant | jeux vid**é**o | th**é**âtre

> The letter ***é*** is a shorter sound than 'ay' in English.
> To pronounce it correctly, try grinning widely as you say it!

Écouter 2 **Read text A. Then listen. Is each person positive (P) or negative (N) about the *dix jours sans écrans* initiative? (1–3)**

Les dix jours sans écrans. À ton avis, c'est une bonne idée ou une mauvaise idée?

À mon avis, c'est …	🙂	une bonne idée. amusant. intéressant.
	🙁	une mauvaise idée. ennuyeux. nul.

je suis d'accord	*I agree*

Parler 3 **In pairs, give your opinion in French about *les dix jours sans écrans*. Pay attention to the sound *é* and the liaison.**

- *Dix jours sans écrans! À ton avis, c'est une bonne idée?*
- *À mon avis, c'est … Tu es d'accord?*
- *Oui, je suis d'accord. / Non, je ne suis pas d'accord. À mon avis, c'est …*

> In French words, the final consonants **-n**, **-s**, **-t** and **-x** are usually silent.
> However, if the next word begins with a vowel, the final consonant is pronounced. This is called a **liaison**.
> Listen and repeat the phrases:
> *dix jours sans écrans*
> *à mon avis*
> *C'est une bonne idée.*

Lire 4 **Read text B. Copy and complete the sentences below in English.**

1 The *Fête de la Musique* is every ___ on the ___.
2 More than 120 ___ take part.
3 There are ___ in more than 1 000 ___.
4 You can ___ to all kinds of ___.
5 You can see all kinds of ___ and ___.

Écouter 5 **Listen to and read text C. Note down in English <u>four</u> key facts about *les Jeux de la Francophonie*.**

Lire 6 **Read text D. Look up any unknown words. Copy and complete the grid in French with your own likes and dislikes from text D. Make sure you use the correct definite article (*le*/*la*/*l'*).**

Example:

J'adore … ❤❤	J'aime … ❤	Je n'aime pas … ✗	Je déteste … ✗✗
la danse	**le** tennis de table		

Écrire 7 **Translate the sentences into French.**

1 I love basketball.
2 I like playing football.
3 I don't like dancing.
4 I hate sport.

> **G**
> To express likes or dislikes, use *aimer* (to like), *adorer* (to love) or *détester* (to hate), followed by:
> - a definite article + a noun
>   *J'aime **le** basket.* I like basketball.
>   *J'aime **la** danse.* I like dancing.
> - a verb in the <u>infinitive</u>
>   *Je n'aime pas <u>jouer</u> au basket.* I don't like playing basketball.
>   *Je n'aime pas <u>faire</u> de la natation.* I don't like swimming.

1 Ma vie en ligne

- Talking about what you do online
- Using the present tense of regular *-er* verbs
- Discussing pros and cons

Écouter 1 **Listen and write down the letters of the activities in the order you hear them. (1–8)**

Qu'est-ce que tu fais en ligne?

la tablette	*tablet (computer)*

a Je télécharge des applis sur ma tablette.

b J'écoute des chansons sur mon portable.

c Je parle avec ma famille au Maroc, en Afrique.

d Je partage des photos.

e Je cherche des idées pour des activités.

f J'achète des vêtements.

g Je joue à des jeux contre ma meilleure amie.

h Je regarde des vidéos amusantes.

Lire 2 **Find and write down the <u>eight</u> regular *-er* verbs in exercise 1. List them like this:**

je télécharge (I download) → *télécharger* (to download)

Écouter 3 **Listen. For each speaker (1–4), note down in English:**

- what they do online
- how often they do it.

tout le temps	*all the time*
tous les jours	*every day*
souvent	*often*
parfois	*sometimes*
de temps en temps	*from time to time*

G

There are many regular *-er* verbs in French. They work like this in the present tense:

jou**er** (*to play*)	
je jou**e**	*I play*
tu jou**es**	*you* (singular) *play*
il/elle/on jou**e**	*he/she/one plays / we play*
nous jou**ons**	*we play*
vous jou**ez**	*you* (plural or polite) *play*
ils/elles jou**ent**	*they play*

envoyer (to send) changes **y** to **ie** in these forms:
*j'envo**ie*** *tu envo**ies***
*il/elle/on envo**ie*** *ils/elles envo**ient***

Page 20

Parler 4 **Read the dialogue with your partner, then create two new dialogues by changing the <u>underlined</u> details.**

- *Qu'est-ce que tu fais en ligne?*
- *<u>Je regarde des clips sur TikTok</u>.*
- *Est-ce que tu fais ça souvent?*
- *Oui, je fais ça <u>tous les jours</u>. Et toi? Qu'est-ce que tu fais en ligne?*
- *<u>J'écoute des chansons sur Spotify</u>. Je fais ça <u>souvent</u>. C'est <u>génial</u>!*

Listen and repeat the words. Say these as though they were one word:
Est-ce que (*tu*) ...? (sounds like *eska*) = **Do** (you) ...?
Qu'est-ce que (*tu*) ...? (sounds like *keska*) = **What** (do you) ...?

Use ***c'est*** + a masculine adjective to give simple opinions:
C'est amusant / génial / super!
C'est dangereux / mauvais pour la santé.

Écouter 5 **Listen and read. Is each statement below true or false?**

Internet: pour ou contre? La parole aux jeunes Québécois

Le pour

Malik
Internet, c'est génial! Il y a des applis pour tout – pour la musique et pour les jeux par exemple. J'adore ça!

Hugo
Pour les jeunes, Internet, c'est essentiel. On parle avec des amis, on écrit des e-mails, on envoie des messages.

Noémie
J'adore les réseaux sociaux comme TikTok et Instagram. Par contre, il y a des problèmes de sécurité.

Le contre

Alexia
Au Québec, les jeunes aiment passer du temps devant un ordinateur ou sur un portable, mais c'est mauvais pour la santé.

Omar
À mon avis, Internet, c'est dangereux. Il y a de fausses informations et de mauvaises images.

Karima
Je n'aime pas utiliser ma propre identité en ligne car il y a des risques.

1 Malik doesn't like using the internet.
2 Hugo thinks the internet is very important for young people.
3 Noémie thinks social networks can be unsafe.
4 Alexia thinks spending time online is good for you.
5 Omar thinks information online can be trusted.
6 Karima uses a different identity online.

on envoie (envoyer)	*we send (to send)*
passer du temps	*to spend time*
la santé	*health*
ma propre identité	*my real identity*

The following terms are often used to express contrasting points of view:
mais but
par contre on the other hand

Lire 6 **Re-read the text in exercise 5. Find the French for the phrases below.**

1 there are risks
2 apps for everything
3 social media
4 it's dangerous
5 fake news
6 it's bad for your health

Parler 7 **In pairs, take turns to read the sentences out. Give feedback on each other's pronunciation. Then listen and check.**

1 À mon avis, Internet, c'est une bonne chose.
2 J'adore jouer à des jeux en ligne.
3 Par contre, les jeunes passent souvent trop de temps sur un portable.
4 Il y a aussi des risques de sécurité.

Watch out for silent final **-e** (e.g. *chos***e**) and silent final consonants like **-s**, **-t** and **-x** (e.g. *jeu***x**). The verb endings **-e**, **-es** and **-ent** are also silent.

One exception is *Internet*, where the final **-t** is pronounced.

Words that are similar in English are usually pronounced differently in French, e.g. *Internet, risque, portable*.

Écrire 8 **Write a post about your online life for the web forum in exercise 5. Include the following bullet points:**

- what you do online
- how often you do it
- opinions
- good and bad points of the internet.

Je joue à des jeux contre mon ami. J'écoute de la musique sur mon portable. J'envoie des messages.	
Je partage Je regarde	des photos sur Instagram. des clips sur TikTok.
Je fais ça	souvent / parfois. tous les jours / tout le temps.
À mon avis, Internet est	génial / essentiel. dangereux / mauvais pour la santé.
Il y a	des risques de sécurité. de fausses informations.

2 Tu as une vie active?

- Saying what you do to stay active
- Using the present tense of irregular verbs
- Listening and transcribing in French

Écouter 1 **Listen and read. Write down the letters of the two activities mentioned in each text. Then translate the phrases in blue into English.**

bientôt	*soon*
être en ligne	*to be online*
s'il ne fait pas beau	*if the weather isn't good*
être membre de	*to be a member of*

C'est bientôt les 10 jours sans écrans

Qu'est-ce que tu fais comme activités, si tu n'es pas en ligne?

1 Manon
Normalement, **je fais du vélo** avec mon frère. S'il ne fait pas beau, on va à la piscine et **on fait de la natation**.

2 Enzo
Je suis très actif! **Je suis membre de l'équipe de handball** du collège et tous les week-ends, on a un match. Je joue aussi au tennis avec mes amis.

3 Ahmed
Toutes les semaines, **j'ai un cours de musique**. Je joue du violon et mon meilleur ami joue de la guitare. Parfois, **on va à des concerts**.

a

b

c

d

e

f

Lire 2 **Read the texts again. Note down in English with whom each person does an activity.**

Écouter 3 **Listen to Sarah talking about what she does to stay active. Note down in English (1–4):**

- the activities she does
- when she does them
- how often she does them.

G

The following key verbs are irregular in the present tense.

aller (*to go*)	**avoir** (*to have*)	**être** (*to be*)	**faire** (*to do/make*)
je vais tu vas il/elle/on va	j'ai tu as il/elle/on a	je suis tu es il/elle/on est	je fais tu fais il/elle/on fait

On means 'one', but can also mean 'we'. It takes the same part of the verb as *il/elle*.

Some French expressions use *faire* (to do/make) where 'to go' is used in English:

*faire **du** vélo*	to go cycling
*faire **de la** natation*	to go swimming

Page 21

Parler 4 **In pairs, imagine you have a no-screen day once a month. Make up your own conversation.**

- *Qu'est-ce que tu fais comme activités, si tu n'es pas en ligne?*
- *Normalement, je vais au centre sportif avec mes amis et on joue au basket. Et toi, qu'est-ce que tu fais?*
- *Normalement, je lis un livre mais parfois, je vais à la piscine avec ma sœur.*

Je joue	**au** basket / football / rugby	dans	l'équipe du collège.
	du piano / violon **de la** guitare / flûte		un groupe de musique.
Je fais	**du** sport / vélo **de la** cuisine / danse	avec	mon ami(e) / mon copain. ma famille / ma copine. mes amis/amies.
Je vais	**au** centre sportif / théâtre **à la** piscine / plage		
J'écoute	**de la** musique.		

Lire 5 **In pairs, look at the gapped sentences. Predict what sort of word could go in each gap.**

Look at the verb in each case. Does it tell you what they play or do, or where they go?

1 Je vais à la ___ avec mon ___.
2 Je fais du ___ avec mes ___.
3 Je joue au ___ dans une ___.

What do these words tell you? Is the missing word a person or a place?

What clue do these give you? Is the missing word something masculine, feminine, singular or plural?

Écouter 6 **Listen and fill in the gaps in the sentences in exercise 5.**

Remember, the final **-e**, **-s** or **-t** on French words is silent (unless the next word starts with a vowel), but it must be there when you write it!

Lire 7 **Read the texts and answer the questions in English.**

Est-ce que tu as une vie active?

Je ne suis pas très actif. Normalement, le soir, ma sœur et moi jouons à des jeux en ligne. Mais, comme c'est les dix jours sans écrans, je fais un effort et on va à la piscine. Après, je bois un coca avec ma sœur et on mange quelque chose ensemble. **Manu**

Généralement, le dimanche, je regarde des séries. Mais, pendant les dix jours sans écrans, je ne regarde rien. Je vais au parc avec mon chien. J'écoute toutes sortes de musique et je lis un bon livre. **Coralie**

faire un effort	*to make an effort*
toutes sortes de musique	*all sorts of music*

Who …
1 goes to the park?
2 usually plays games online?
3 is going to the swimming pool?
4 normally watches series on Sundays?

G
Negatives go around the verb:

*Je **ne** suis **pas** actif/active.*	I am **not** active.
*Elle **ne** fait **rien**.*	She does **nothing**. / She **doesn't** do **anything**.

Page 21

Lire 8 **Translate Coralie's text into English.**

G
These two verbs are irregular in the present tense:

boire (to drink)	*je **bois*** (I drink)
lire (to read)	*je **lis*** (I read)

3 Qu'est-ce que tu regardes?

- Talking about what you watch
- Forming and answering questions
- Preparing a role-play

Écouter 1 **Read the questionnaire. Listen and note down the answers that Marie gives to the survey. (1–5)**

Example: 1 *b*

1 Qu'est-ce que tu aimes regarder?
J'aime regarder …
a des séries ou des comédies.
b des émissions de sport.
c un peu de tout.

2 Quelle sorte de vidéos est-ce que tu regardes?
Je regarde …
a des clips de musique ou de danse.
b des vidéos de cuisine.
c des vidéos amusantes d'animaux.

3 Quand est-ce que tu regardes des vidéos?
Normalement, je regarde des vidéos …
a le matin, avant le collège.
b le soir, après les cours.
c quand j'ai du temps libre.

4 Comment est-ce que tu préfères regarder des films?
Je préfère regarder des films …
a chez moi, à la télé, ou en streaming.
b au cinéma.
c sur mon portable.

5 Avec qui est-ce que tu aimes regarder des films?
J'aime regarder des films …
a avec les membres de ma famille.
b avec mon meilleur ami / ma meilleure amie.
c tout(e) seul(e), dans ma chambre.

l'émission** (f) **de sport	*sports programme*
un peu de tout	*a bit of everything*
le temps libre	*free time*
chez moi	*at home, at my place*

G

To form questions, you can use a question word + *est-ce que* …

Qu'est-ce que tu aimes regarder?	What do you like watching?
Comment est-ce que tu préfères regarder des films?	How do you prefer to watch films?
Avec qui est-ce que tu aimes regarder des films?	With whom do you like watching films?

quel/quelle/quels/quelles + noun means 'which …?' or 'what … ?'.
It is an adjective and has to agree with the noun it refers to.

masculine singular	*feminine singular*	*masculine plural*	*feminine plural*
quel cinéma?	**quelle** série?	**quels** films?	**quelles** émissions?

Quelle sorte de vidéos est-ce que tu regardes? — What kind of videos do you watch?

Page 21

Parler 2 **In pairs, do the survey.**

- *Qu'est-ce que tu aimes regarder?*
- *J'aime regarder des émissions de sport. Et toi?*
- *Moi, j'aime regarder un peu de tout.*

qu is always pronounced 'k'.
c is also pronounced 'k' in front of the letters *a*, *o* and *u*.

Listen and repeat the words.
***qu**and, **qu**e, **qu**i, **qu**el, **c**ombien, **c**omédie*

Écrire 3 **Copy and complete the French translations.**

1 *With whom do you like going to the cinema?* ___ ___ est-ce que tu aimes aller au ___ ?
2 *When do you prefer to watch TV?* ___ est-ce que tu préfères ___ la ___ ?
3 *Which programmes do you watch?* ___ émissions ___ ___ tu regardes?

Lire 4 **Read the text. Find the French for the phrases below, choosing from the bold phrases in the text.**

J'aime regarder un peu de tout, mais **je regarde souvent** des émissions de télé-réalité. **Je finis** les cours à cinq heures, donc je regarde la télé le soir ou le week-end. **Je ne regarde jamais** de vidéos de cuisine parce que c'est trop nul!

Je préfère regarder des films toute seule, sur mon ordinateur. Cependant, **je vais** au cinéma tous les mois avec ma meilleure amie. **On choisit** un film d'action ou un film de science-fiction parce que c'est passionnant!

Amina

G

Regular *-ir* verbs like *fin**ir*** (to finish) and *chois**ir*** (to choose) work like this in the present tense:
*je fin**is***
*tu fin**is***
*il/elle/on fin**it***

Page 20

nul (nulle)(s)	*bad, rubbish*
cependant	*however*
passionnant(e)	*exciting, thrilling*

1 We choose
2 I go
3 I prefer to watch
4 I often watch
5 I finish
6 I never watch

Lire 5 **Re-read the text in exercise 4. Copy and complete the sentences below in English.**

1 Amina often watches ___.
2 She finishes ___, so she watches TV ___.
3 She never watches ___.
4 She prefers watching films ___ on her ___.
5 Amina and her best friend go to the cinema every ___.
6 They choose ___ or ___, because ___.

Écouter 6 **Listen and read, paying attention to how the underlined words are pronounced. Then read the dialogue with a partner.**

- *Qu'est-ce que tu regardes à la télé?*
- *Je regarde des émissions de télé-réalité.*
- *Quand est-ce que tu regardes la télé?*
- *Je regarde la télé le soir, après le dîner.*
- *Quelle est ton opinion sur les vidéos de cuisine?*
- *Moi, j'adore les vidéos de cuisine sur TikTok.*
- *C'est bien.*
- *Tu aimes aller au cinéma?*
- *Oui, j'aime bien aller au cinéma.*
- *Moi aussi.*
- *Décris-moi ton film préféré.*
- *Mon film préféré s'appelle Shang Chi.*

Lire 7 **Re-read the dialogue in exercise 6 and find three question words and two opinion phrases.**

Parler 8 **Prepare your answers to this role-play card. Then listen and respond to the teacher.**

- You are talking to your French friend.
- Your teacher will play the part of your friend and will speak first.
- You should address your friend as *tu*.
- When you see this – **?** – you will have to ask a question.

1 Say what you watch on TV. (Give **one** detail.)
2 Say when you watch TV. (Give **one** detail.)
3 Give **one** opinion on cooking videos.
? 4 Ask your friend a question about going to the cinema.
5 Describe your favourite film. (Give **one** detail.)

Use a full sentence (e.g. *Je regarde* ...).

Start with an opinion phrase (e.g. *J'aime*).

Use a full sentence to give a title or a genre of film.

You can use a time (e.g. *à huit heures*) or a time marker (e.g. *le soir*).

Remember that there are many questions you can ask about this.

4 Qu'est-ce qu'on va faire?

- Making plans to go out
- Using the near future tense
- Understanding and making invitations

Écouter 1 **Listen and read the times on the clocks.**

	à neuf heures		à neuf heures vingt-cinq		à dix heures moins le quart
	à neuf heures dix		à neuf heures et demie		à dix heures moins dix
	à neuf heures et quart		à dix heures moins vingt		à midi / à minuit

Écouter 2 **Listen to the voicemails (1–4). For each one, write:**

- the letter of the correct advert
- when they are going to do it (e.g. tomorrow morning, nine o'clock).

aujourd'hui	demain
ce matin	demain matin
cet après-midi	demain après-midi
ce soir	demain soir

Que faire en Belgique, pendant les vacances de la Toussaint?

A

B

C

D

les vacances de la Toussaint	*autumn half-term holiday (usually at the end of October)*

Lire 3 **Read the two text messages. Translate one of them into English.**

1

Aujourd'hui, je vais aller au centre commercial avec mon frère. On va faire les magasins. On va prendre le bus à deux heures et quart. Tu viens?

2

Demain après-midi, ma famille et moi, nous allons voir un spectacle de musique au parc. Tu viens avec nous? Nous allons partir à midi.

Tu viens? *Are you coming? / Do you want to come?*

G

You can use the present tense of *aller* (to go) + an **infinitive** to refer to the future. This is called the **near future tense**.

je vais	***aller*** *au parc*
tu vas	***prendre*** *le bus*
il/elle/on va	***jouer*** *au football*
nous allons	***visiter*** *le musée*
vous allez	***voir*** *un spectacle*
ils/elles vont	***partir*** *vers midi*

Page 22

Parler 4 **In pairs, turn the exercise 3 text messages into two voicemails. Read them out. Then create a new voicemail by changing the underlined details.**

Lire 5 **Read the chat. Fill in the gaps with the correct word from the box. There are two words you don't need. Then listen and check.**

Alex

Coucou! Demain, je **1** aller en ville avec des amis. Ça t'intéresse?

Peut-être. Qu'est-ce que vous allez **2** en ville?

On va faire les magasins. Après, on **3** manger quelque chose au café.

Qui vient aussi?

Théo et Lucie. Théo va **4** un cadeau d'anniversaire pour sa mère.

Vous allez partir à quelle heure?

On va prendre le bus à dix heures et **5** .

D'accord. Je veux bien, merci.

Génial! Ça va être **6** ! À demain, alors!

acheter
allons
amusant
faire
matin
quart
va
vais

Écouter 6 **Listen. Copy and complete the grid in English. (1–2)**

	Place / Activity	When	Time	Accepts? ✓ ✗
1				

pas de problème! *no problem!*

Ça t'intéresse?
Tu es libre?
Tu viens?

👍	👎
Oui, je suis libre. Ça m'intéresse. Je veux bien, merci. D'accord.	Non, désolé(e). Je ne peux pas. Je ne suis pas libre.

Le stade Roi Baudouin à Bruxelles

Le parc d'attractions Walibi près de Bruxelles

Écrire 7 **Imagine it's the start of the half-term holiday! Write a message to your friend about your plans for today and tomorrow. Include the following bullet points:**

- where you will go (*je vais aller en ville*)
- what you will do and when (*ma famille et moi allons voir un film à 15 heures*)
- which means of transport you will use (*on va prendre le bus à dix heures*)
- an invitation to your friend (*Ça t'intéresse?*).

Je vais On va Nous allons	aller	au musée	aujourd'hui. demain. ce soir. cet après-midi. à 9 heures.
	faire	les magasins	
	jouer	au foot / au tennis	
	acheter	un cadeau / un tee-shirt	
	partir		

5 Qu'est-ce que tu as fait?

- Saying what you did last weekend
- Using the perfect tense
- Pronouncing *é*, *er*, *ez* correctly

Lire 1 **Look at the pictures (a–i) and match each one to the correct caption (1–9).**

#Un Week-end Ordinaire

Qu'est-ce que tu as fait, le week-end dernier?

1 J'ai joué au foot sur la plage.
2 J'ai marché à la campagne.
3 J'ai bu un coca avec mes amis.
4 J'ai pris des photos.
5 Je suis allée au café avec ma famille.
6 On a mangé du couscous.
7 Je suis restée à la maison.
8 On a lu un peu.
9 On a regardé la télé.

On is sometimes used in French to say 'we'. *On* takes the same form of the verb as *il/elle*.

a

b

c

d

e

f

g

h

i

Lire 2 **Re-read the sentences in exercise 1. Then find nine different verbs in the perfect tense and translate them into English.**

Écouter 3 **Listen and note down the letters (a–i) of the activities each person did. Listen again and note in English when they did them. (1–4)**

samedi dimanche	matin après-midi soir

G

You use the perfect tense to refer to the past.
It is formed of two parts:

1 the auxiliary verb (part of ***avoir*** or ***être***)
2 the past participle.

You form the past participle of regular **-*er*** verbs like this:
chanter (to sing) → *chant**é***
*j'**ai** chant**é*** (I sang) *il/elle/on **a** chant**é*** (he/she/we sang)

The following verbs have an irregular past participle:
boire (to drink) → *j'ai **bu*** (I drank)
faire (to do/make) → *j'ai **fait*** (I did/made)

For verbs that take ***être***, e.g. *aller* (to go) and *rester* (to stay), the past participle must agree with the subject:
*elle **est** allé**e*** (she went) *on **est** allé**s*** (we went)

Page 22

Parler 4 **Read the tongue-twisters aloud. Pay attention to the pronunciation of the key sound in the tip box. Then listen and check.**

1 Mon footballeur pr**é**f**é**r**é** est Kylian Mbapp**é**.
2 Elle est all**é**e au caf**é** pour mang**er**.
3 Samedi derni**er**, je suis rest**é**e ch**ez** Chlo**é** et on a pass**é** une bonne journ**é**e.

é is pronounced the same as ***er*** and ***ez***.

Listen and repeat the words.
*mang**é*** *mang**er*** *mang**ez***

Écouter **5** **Listen and read what Mariama did over the weekend. Complete each sentence starter by writing the letter of the correct activity. Make sure that you put the activities in the order in which Mariama did them.**

Un week-end extraordinaire au Burkina Faso

Samedi dernier, c'était la Fête de la Musique dans notre capitale.

Il y avait un programme extraordinaire avec des concerts gratuits. C'était passionnant!

Pour commencer, je suis allée à un concert de Marko, un jeune chanteur de rap. J'ai adoré sa musique et on a chanté et dansé.

Ensuite, j'ai vu un concert d'Élue 111, qui est ma chanteuse préférée. Pendant le concert, elle a chanté toutes sortes de chansons. C'était vraiment génial!

Après, il y avait un concert de Teriya, un groupe africain, mais on n'a pas vu le groupe parce que c'était complet!

Finalement, j'ai acheté un poster, mais je n'ai pas acheté de tee-shirt car c'était trop cher.

J'ai passé un week-end parfait!

Mariama

extraordinaire	*extraordinary*
gratuit(e)(s)	*free (no cost)*
complet (complète)(s)	*full*

Élue 111

G

c'est	it is
c'était	it was
il y a	there is/are
il y avait	there was/were

1 First, ...
2 Then ...
3 Afterwards, ...
4 Finally, ...

a she bought a souvenir of the occasion.
b she saw her favourite singer.
c she missed seeing a band because the concert was full.
d she went to a concert where everyone sang and danced.

Écouter **6** **Listen and, for each speaker (1–3), make notes on each point below:**

a what they did last weekend
b what they didn't do
c whether a positive or negative opinion.

C'était	amusant / cher / complet. extraordinaire / génial. passionnant / sympa / nul.

G

In the perfect tense, negatives go around the part of *avoir* or *être*:

*je **n'**ai **rien** acheté*	I haven't bought anything
*on **n'**a **rien** vu*	we haven't seen anything
*je **ne** suis **pas** resté(e)*	I didn't stay
*il **n'**est **pas** allé*	he didn't go

Page 21

Parler **7** **In pairs, make up a conversation about last weekend.**

- *Qu'est-ce que tu as fait, le week-end dernier?*
- *Samedi matin, pour commencer ... Ensuite, / Après, / Finalement, ...*
- *Et dimanche?*
- *Dimanche, ...*
- *C'était comment?*
- ...

To create extended sentences, use:
- time expressions *samedi soir, dimanche matin*
- sequencers *pour commencer, ensuite, après, finalement*

J'ai	joué	au foot / au tennis	avec mes amis. avec ma famille.
	fait	les magasins	
	mangé ... acheté ... regardé ...		
Je suis	allé(e)	à un concert au restaurant	

Écrire **8** **Write a blog entry about a busy weekend. Include opinions and at least one negative.**

6 J'ai participé aux Jeux de la Francophonie!

- Taking part in an interview
- Understanding questions in the perfect tense
- Using two tenses together (present and perfect)

Lire 1 **Read the interview questions. Copy and complete the English translation of each one.**

1 **À quel âge** as-tu commencé à jouer au tennis de table?
 ___ *did you start playing table tennis?*

2 **Quand** as-tu participé aux Jeux de la Francophonie?
 ___ *did you take part in the Francophone Games?*

3 **Qu'est-ce que** tu as fait pour être prête pour les Jeux?
 ___ *did you do to be ready for the Games?*

4 **Est-ce que** tu as gagné aux Jeux de la Francophonie?
 ___ *you win at the Francophone Games?*

prêt(e) *ready*

Lire 2 **Read the answers below. Write the letter of the correct answer for each question in exercise 1. Then translate all the answers into English.**

Un grand succès aux Jeux de la Francophonie!

a J'ai participé aux Jeux de la Francophonie pour la première fois l'année dernière.

b J'ai fini en première position – j'ai gagné la compétition!

c Pour être prête, j'ai joué trois ou quatre heures chaque jour au centre sportif.

d J'ai commencé à jouer au tennis de table à l'âge de quinze ans.

j'ai participé	*I participated*
la première fois	*the first time*
à l'âge de	*at the age of*

Écouter 3 **Listen and check your answers to exercise 2.**

G

Questions in the perfect tense often use inversion.
The subject swaps places with the first verb, with a hyphen in between.
Tu as participé aux Jeux de la Francophonie. → *As-tu participé aux Jeux de la Francophonie?*

When there is a question word, it comes at the start of the question:
Quand *as-tu participé aux Jeux de la Francophonie?*

Inversion is not used with questions that start with *Est-ce que …?* or *Qu'est-ce que …?*

Page 23

Parler 4 **Read out the interview from exercises 1 and 2 with your partner. Make your questions sound like questions!**

Use **rising intonation** when you ask a question. Make your voice go up at the end.

Listen and repeat the question.
Est-ce que tu as gagné aux Jeux de la Francophonie?

Lire 5 **Read the text about the *Jeux de la Francophonie* (JDLF). Copy and complete the profile in English.**

Les JDLF, ce n'est pas seulement une compétition sportive, c'est aussi un concours culturel!

Je m'appelle Lucas et mon pays, c'est le Mali, en Afrique. Je suis chanteur et musicien.

J'ai commencé à jouer du piano à l'âge de huit ans. J'adore faire de la musique et j'écris tout le temps des chansons!

Tous les jours, je passe sept heures à mon piano, pour être prêt pour les Jeux de la Francophonie.

J'ai déjà participé aux Jeux, c'était il y a deux ans – j'ai chanté une chanson. Je n'ai pas gagné, mais j'étais content.

L'important n'est pas de gagner mais de participer!

Name: Lucas
Country:
Talent(s):
Started when?:
Preparation for contest:
Took part in JDLF when?
Success at JDLF?

L'important n'est pas de gagner mais de participer! *saying that means 'It's not the winning but the taking part that counts.'*

Lire 6 **Read the text again. Find at least <u>six</u> verbs in the present tense and <u>four</u> verbs in the perfect tense.**

il y a has two meanings:
1 there is/are *il y a un centre sportif*
2 ago *il y a deux ans* (two years ago)

Écouter 7 **Listen to the podcast and answer the questions in English.**

1 What country is Thomas from?
2 What sport does Thomas play?
3 At what age did he start playing?
4 When does he play?
5 When did he participate in the *Jeux de la Francophonie*?
6 Did he win?

Parler 8 **In pairs, create a podcast interview with a participant at the *Jeux de la Francophonie* (JDLF). Use details from one of the boxes below.**

Nadia – Belgium
basketball – started age 12
plays every day – sports centre
JDLF – last year – won

Ahmed – Senegal
dance – started age 7
dances in the evenings – school
JDLF – 3 years ago – 2nd place

Présent			
Tu es de quel pays?	Je suis	du Sénégal. de Belgique.	
Qu'est-ce que tu fais comme activité?	Je joue	au basket.	
	Je fais	de la danse.	
Quand et où est-ce que tu fais ça?	Je joue	au centre sportif	tous les jours.
	Je fais de la danse	à l'école	le soir.

Passé		
À quel âge as-tu commencé à pratiquer ça ?	J'ai commencé	à l'âge de ... ans.
Quand as-tu participé aux Jeux de la Francophonie?	J'ai participé aux Jeux	l'année dernière. il y a trois ans.
Est-ce que tu as gagné aux Jeux de la Francophonie?	J'ai gagné J'ai fini en deuxième position	aux Jeux.

Grammaire 1

The present tense of regular verbs (Unit 1, page 8 and Unit 3, page 13)

Regular *-er*, *-ir* and *-re* verbs form the present tense like this:

parl**er** (*to speak/talk*) → **parl-**
je parl**e**
tu parl**es**
il/elle/on parl**e**
nous parl**ons**
vous parl**ez**
ils/elles parl**ent**

fin**ir** (*to finish*) → **fin-**
je fin**is**
tu fin**is**
il/elle/on fin**it**
nous fin**issons**
vous fin**issez**
ils/elles fin**issent**

attend**re** (*to wait for*) → **attend-**
j'attend**s**
tu attend**s**
il/elle/on attend (*no added ending*)
nous attend**ons**
vous attend**ez**
ils / elles attend**ent**

For each verb, the underlined forms sound the same.

Écrire 1 **Copy and complete the sentences with the correct form of the regular *-er* verb in brackets.**

Example: 1 *Je parle avec ma famille en France.*

1. Je ___ avec ma famille en France. (*parler*)
2. J'___ des choses sur Vinted. (*acheter*)
3. Est-ce que tu ___ souvent des vidéos? (*regarder*)
4. Elle ___ à des jeux avec sa meilleure amie. (*jouer*)
5. Ils ___ de la musique en streaming. (*écouter*)
6. Vous ___ des idées en ligne. (*chercher*)
7. Nous ___ des photos sur Snapchat. (*partager*)

Watch out for:

- *je* shortens to *j'* in front of a vowel, e.g. *je* + *écoute* = ***j'****écoute*. Pronounce *j'* plus the verb as a single word
- verbs that end in *-ger*, like *manger*, *partager*: the '*nous*' form is *mang**e**ons*
- verbs like *acheter*: the *je/tu/il(s)/elle(s)* forms add a grave accent: *j'ach**è**te / ils ach**è**tent*.

Lire 2 **Translate the sentences into English.**

1. Tu regardes des photos sur ton portable?
2. Il passe trop de temps en ligne.
3. Est-ce que vous parlez avec ma sœur?
4. Nous regardons des vidéos sur TikTok.
5. Elles écoutent souvent de la musique.
6. Je finis les cours à cinq heures.

In French, there is only one present tense. So, *je parle* means 'I speak' and 'I am speaking'. Time phrases often give you a clue about which of the two English meanings applies.

Parler 3 **In pairs, read out the sentences from exercise 2. Pay attention to the pronunciation of the subject pronouns (*je*, *nous*, etc.) and the verb endings (which ones are silent?). Then listen and check.**

Pronouncing subject pronouns

- ***j**e* (or ***j'***): ***j*** is a soft sound. like a fast car whizzing by: 'jjjuuuhhh!'
- *t**u***: ***u*** sounds similar to 'ew' in 'few'.
- *n**ou**s* and *v**ou**s*: ***ou*** sounds like an 'oooh!' of surprise.
- ***i**l* and ***i**ls*: ***i*** sounds like 'e' in 'evil'.
- ***e**lle* and ***e**lles*: ***e*** sounds like 'e' in 'bed'.

Écouter 4 **Listen to the sentences with the subject pronouns missing. (1–6) Can you work out from the sound of each verb what the missing pronoun is? Choose from the pronouns listed. Then listen and check.**

1. je / nous / ils
2. elle / nous / vous
3. je / on / ils
4. tu / vous / elles
5. je / nous / vous
6. tu / elle / nous

Remember, the final **-s** is silent (unless the next word starts with a vowel), so *il* and *ils* are pronounced the same and so are *elle* and *elles*.

Remember that the pronunciation of regular *-er* verbs in the plural of the present tense (ending in ***-ent***) is the same as the singular (ending in ***-e***/***-es***).

The present tense of irregular verbs (Unit 2, page 10)

The following key verbs are irregular in the present tense:

aller (*to go*)	avoir (*to have*)	être (*to be*)	faire (*to do/make*)
je vais tu vas il/elle/on va nous allons vous allez ils/elles vont	j'ai tu as il/elle/on a nous avons vous avez ils/elles ont	je suis tu es il/elle/on est nous sommes vous êtes ils/elles sont	je fais tu fais il/elle/on fait nous faisons vous faites ils/elles font

If there is no subject pronoun, think about which part of the verb to use:
mon équipe et moi = *nous* (we)
mes amis = *ils* (they)

Écrire 5 **Copy and complete the sentence for each day in French, using the correct form of the verb in brackets.**

Example: 1 *Le lundi, on fait du vélo.*

1. Le lundi, on ___ du vélo. (*faire*)
2. Le mardi, j'___ un cours de guitare. (*avoir*)
3. Le mercredi, nous ___ au centre sportif. (*aller*)
4. Le jeudi, tu ___ de la cuisine. (*faire*)
5. Le vendredi, on ___ au théâtre. (*aller*)
6. Le samedi, mon équipe et moi ___ un match de foot. (*avoir*)
7. Le dimanche, mes amis ___ au parc. (*aller*)

Negatives (Unit 2, page 11)

Parler 6 **In pairs, one person asks the questions and the other plays Norman Négatif who always answers in the negative! Try to use all three negatives from the grammar box.**

- *Est-ce que tu es sportif?* ■ *Non, je **ne** suis **pas** sportif.*

1. Est-ce que tu es sportif?
2. Est-ce que tu joues de la guitare?
3. Est-ce que tu fais du vélo?
4. Est-ce que tu vas au cinéma?
5. Qu'est-ce que tu fais, le soir ou le week-end?
6. Est-ce que tu utilises ton portable après vingt heures?

Norman Négatif

Negatives are usually in two parts:
ne … pas (not)
ne … rien (nothing/not anything)
ne … jamais (never)

In the present tense, they make a 'sandwich' around the verb:
*Je **ne** joue **pas** au tennis.*
I don't play tennis.
*Je **ne** fais **rien**.*
I don't do anything./I do nothing.

After a negative, *du*, *de la* and *des* usually change to *de*:
*Je ne fais jamais **de** cuisine.*
I never cook.

Forming questions (Unit 3, page 12)

Lire 7 **Read the answers (1–5). What were the questions (a–e)? Match the answers to the questions.**

1. J'aime regarder des émissions de télé-réalité avec mes amis.
2. Je regarde des vidéos amusantes d'animaux.
3. Je préfère regarder des films en ligne.
4. Je regarde des films avec ma famille.
5. Le film finit à douze heures.

a Le film finit à quelle heure?
b Qu'est-ce que tu aimes regarder avec tes amis?
c Avec qui est-ce que tu regardes des films?
d Comment est-ce que tu préfères regarder des films?
e Quelle sorte de vidéos est-ce que tu regardes?

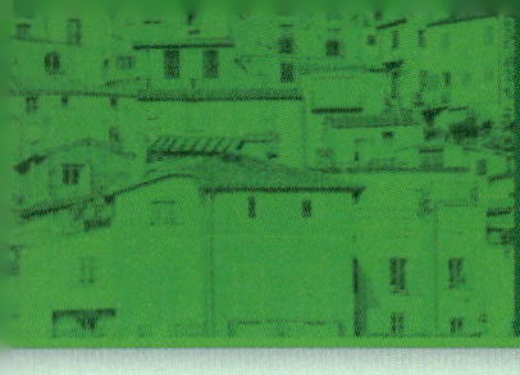

Grammaire 2

The near future tense (Unit 4, page 14)

Parler 1 **Read the grammar box on page 14. Imagine this is your diary for today and tomorrow. In pairs, take turns to describe what you are going to do. Try to use a variety of verb forms (*je*, *on*, *nous*).**

- *Ce matin, je vais aller au centre commercial avec … On va faire …*
- *Cet après-midi, nous allons jouer …*

samedi	
matin	centre commercial avec Clara 
après-midi	

dimanche	
matin	 avec amis
après-midi	(parents)  (moi) 

The perfect tense (Unit 5, page 16)

You use the perfect tense to refer to things that happened in the past. It is formed of two parts:

1 the auxiliary verb (part of ***avoir*** or ***être***)

2 the past participle.

You form the past participle of **regular *-er*** verbs like this:

*dans**er*** (to dance) → *dansé*

j'**ai** dansé	*I danced*
tu **as** dansé	*you* (singular) *danced*
il/elle/on **a** dansé	*he/she/we danced*
nous **avons** dansé	*we danced*
vous **avez** dansé	*you* (plural or polite) *danced*
ils/elles **ont** dansé	*they danced*

The following verbs have an **irregular** past participle:

boire (to drink) → *j'ai bu* (I drank)
lire (to read) → *j'ai lu* (I read)
faire (to do/make) → *j'ai fait* (I did/made)
prendre (to take) → *j'ai pris* (I took)

Some verbs take ***être*** (not *avoir*), e.g.

aller (to go) → *je suis allé* (I went)
rester (to stay) → *je suis resté* (I stayed)

For verbs which take *être*, the past participle must agree with the subject:

il est resté (he stayed *(m)*)
*elle est resté**e*** (she stayed *(f)*)
*ils sont resté**s*** (they stayed *(m pl)*)
*elles sont resté**es*** (they stayed *(f pl)*)

Écrire 2 **Copy out the sentences, putting the verbs in brackets into the perfect tense.**

Example: 1 *Je suis allée au centre commercial et …*

1 Je (f) ___ au centre commercial et j'___ un bracelet. (*aller, acheter*)
2 Est-ce que tu ___ la télé? (*regarder*)
3 Mon frère ___ à la maison. (*rester*)
4 On ___ de la natation. (*faire*)
5 Nous ___ de la musique. (*écouter*)
6 Qu'est-ce que vous ___ au restaurant? (*manger*)
7 Mes amis ___ et ___. (*danser, chanter*)
8 Les filles ___ au centre sportif. (*aller*)

Don't forget, the perfect tense is formed of two parts!

Remember, *je* shortens to *j'* in front of a vowel: *je* + *ai* = *j'ai*.

Écrire 3 **Translate the sentences into French.**

Example: 1 *Samedi dernier, mes amis et moi sommes allés à un concert.*

1. Last Saturday, my friends and I went to a concert.
2. I danced, but I didn't sing.
3. We saw our favourite group.
4. My friend Thomas bought a tee-shirt.
5. We took lots of photos.

In the perfect tense, negatives go around the auxiliary verb (the part of *avoir* or *être*):
Je ***ne*** *suis* ***pas*** *allé(e) au concert.*

Remember that *ne* shortens to ***n'*** in front of a vowel:
Je ***n'****ai* ***pas*** *chanté.*
Nous ***n'****avons* ***rien*** *acheté.*

Questions in the perfect tense (Unit 6, page 18)

Écrire 4 **Complete the questions using the verb in brackets and the pronoun *tu*. Remember to use inversion. Copy out the questions and translate them.**

Example: 1 *À quel âge as-tu commencé à jouer au handball?*

1. À quel âge ___ à jouer au handball? (*commencer*)
2. Quand ___ à la compétition? (*participer*)
3. Quand ___ au tennis de table pour la première fois? (*jouer*)
4. L'année dernière, ___ aux Jeux de la Francophonie? (*gagner*)
5. Quel film ___ hier soir à la télé? (*regarder*)

When you use inversion, put a hyphen between the verb and the subject:
Comment as-tu ...?

Using the present tense and the perfect tense together (Unit 6, page 19)

Parler 5 **In pairs, play 'tenses tennis'. Take turns to change each sentence from the present tense to the perfect tense or vice versa.**

- *Je joue de la guitare.*
- *J'ai joué de la guitare. J'ai fait ...*

1. Je joue de la guitare. → (*perfect*)
2. J'ai fait de la natation. → (*present*)
3. J'écoute de la musique. → (*perfect*)
4. J'ai regardé une émission de télé-réalité. → (*present*)
5. Je vais au cinéma. → (*perfect*)
6. Je suis allé(e) à la piscine. → (*present*)

Listen and repeat the sentences.
*J****e*** *joue de la guitare.*
*J'****ai*** *joué de la guitare.*

Make sure you pronounce ***je*** and j'***ai*** as different sounds. Remember that ***j*** is a soft sound in French.

C'est parti!

Écouter 6 **Listen and note down the missing word or words. Remember, some endings are silent in French!**

J'aime faire du sport. **1** membre d'une équipe de foot et nous **2** un match tous les week-ends. Le dimanche, je **3** fais **4** de sport.

Samedi dernier, je **5** au centre commercial. J'ai acheté un tee-shirt. Ensuite, j'**6** quelque chose au café. Et toi, qu'est-ce que tu **7** samedi dernier? Demain, je **8** le château. Tu viens?

Module 1

Contrôle de lecture et d'écoute

Reading

Lire 1

***TV.* These French students are talking about TV. Which type of programme does each student mention? Write the correct letter for each person.**

1 

Manon
Je regarde souvent des émissions de télé-réalité.

2 

David
Moi, j'adore les comédies françaises!

3 

Pauline
Moi, je préfère regarder des émissions de cuisine.

A	French films
B	cooking programmes
C	reality TV
D	comedies
E	action films

Lire 2

***My hobbies.* You see a French website. Some French teenagers are talking about their hobbies. Match the correct person with each question. Write I for Ismaya, K for Kévin and M for Mohammed.**

Ismaya
Je suis très active et j'aime faire beaucoup de choses: jouer de la musique, regarder la télé, aller sur Internet et faire du sport!

Kévin
J'aime écouter de la musique mais je ne joue pas d'un instrument car, à mon avis, c'est difficile.

Mohammed
J'aime aller sur Internet, regarder des réseaux sociaux et écrire mon blog sur le foot. J'adore regarder le foot mais je ne fais pas de sport!

1 Who has a blog?
2 Who is sporty?
3 Who plays music?
4 Who thinks music is not easy?
5 Who does not do any sport?

Make sure you read the sentences fully. Look out for negatives, like *ne ... pas*.

Lire 3

***Internet.* Read this text on Malik's opinion of the internet. Answer the questions in English.**

Malik Pour nous les jeunes, les réseaux sociaux, c'est génial car on envoie des messages et on parle avec nos amis.

Mais Internet a ses problèmes. Les jeunes passent beaucoup de temps devant leur écran et ce n'est pas bon pour la santé. Il y a aussi des problèmes de sécurité et des problèmes avec les fausses informations.

1 What does Malik think of social media?
2 Why does he think that? Give two details.
3 According to Malik, what is not good for your health?
4 According to Malik, what other problems are there?

Lire 4

Translation. **Translate these sentences into English.**

What do these words mean?

Make sure you revise the more uncommon vocabulary.

1 À mon avis, Internet, c'est bien.
2 Je suis dans l'équipe de foot du collège.
3 De temps en temps, je partage des photos.
4 Je joue de la musique avec mes amis.
5 Le week-end dernier, j'ai acheté des vêtements en ligne.

Plural or singular?

What tense is this?

Listening

Écouter 5

Voice messages. **Your French friend has sent you some voice messages. What is each message about? Write the correct letter. (1–4)**

A	going online
B	singing
C	going out with friends
D	buying clothes
E	gaming
F	playing music

What words might you hear?

- Before listening, read all the options A–F carefully.
- Don't jump to conclusions! Listen to the whole sentence.

Écouter 6

A new series. **You hear this conversation about a new series. Which aspects of the series are mentioned? Write down the <u>two</u> correct letters for each speaker. (1–2)**

A	the number of episodes
B	the actors
C	the country where the series was made
D	the recommended age for the public
E	where you can view it
F	music featuring in the series

You may hear words that are linked to each option, but you should focus on what is actually mentioned.

Écouter 7

Music competition. **You hear this podcast about Francine, a young musician from Senegal. Write down the correct letter (A–C) for questions 1–2. Write down the correct answer in English for question 3.**

1 Francine first took part in the music competition …
A when she was eight. **B** 12 years ago. **C** four years ago.

2 Last year, Francine prepared by …
A playing by herself. **B** playing five times a week. **C** playing in lessons.

3 What was the result of the competition last year?

Écouter 8

Dictation. **You will now hear <u>four</u> short sentences. Listen carefully and, using your knowledge of French sounds, write in French exactly what you hear for each sentence.**

- Be careful when transcribing the sounds ***e*** and ***é/ er***.
- You will hear the sound ***ou***.

Module 1

Contrôle oral

Role-play

Parler 1 **Look at the role-play card and prepare what you are going to say.**

- You are talking to your Canadian friend.
- Your teacher will play the part of your friend and will speak first.
- You should address your friend as *tu*.
- When you see this – **?** – you will have to ask a question.

In order to score full marks, you must include a verb in your response to each task.

1 Say what your favourite hobby is. (Give **one** detail.)
2 Say why it is your favourite hobby. (Give **one** detail.)
3 Say **one** hobby you don't like.
4 Say what you do at the weekend with your friends. (Give **one** detail.)
? 5 Ask your friend a question about sport.

You can say *c'est* and use an adjective.

You can start with *J'aime* or *J'adore.*

You can start with *Je n'aime pas.*

You can ask what they do, or what their favourite sport is, or if they like a particular sport.

Parler 2 **Practise what you have prepared. Then, using your notes, listen and respond to the teacher.**

Écouter 3 **Now listen to Lola doing the role-play task. In English, note down (a) how she answers the questions for tasks 1, 2, 3 and 4, and (b) what question she asks for task 5.**

Reading aloud

Parler 4 **Look at this task. With a partner, take turns to read out the text below, paying attention to the underlined letters.**

Read aloud the following text **in French**.

J'adore la musique.
Le dimanche, je vais au centre sportif.
J'aime regarder des émissions de sport.
Je préfère regarder des films sur mon portable.
Mon frère aime acheter des vêtements en ligne.

Take extra care with how you pronounce the underlined sounds:
- the final ***e*** is silent in these words
- make sure you pronounce ***er*** correctly
- those final consonants are silent.

Make sure you pronounce the highlighted words with a French accent, not an English one.

Écouter 5 **Listen and check your pronunciation.**

Parler 6 **Listen to the teacher asking four questions that relate to the topic of Free-time activities. Translate each question into English and prepare your own answers in French. Then listen again and respond to the teacher.**

Remember to use different opinion phrases.

Photo card task

Écouter 7 **Look at the exam card below and read the first part of the task. Then listen to Lola describing the two photos.**

1 What does Lola say about the people in the first photo?
2 Where are the people in the second photo according to Lola?
3 What does she say the people are doing in each photo?

Photo 1

Photo 2

You will be asked to talk about the content of these photos. You must say at least one thing about each photo.

After you have spoken about the content of the photos, you will be asked questions related to any of the topics within the theme of **Popular culture**.

Your responses should be as **full and detailed** as possible.

To talk about what someone is doing, use the **present tense**. Remember that in French 'they are playing' is the same as 'they play'.

Parler 8 **Prepare your own descriptions of the two photos. You could mention, for example, the people, the location and what they are doing. Then, with a partner, take turns to describe the photos.**

Sur la première photo, il y a ...

Écouter 9 **Read the second part of the task. Then listen to Lola answering the question: *Qu'est-ce que tu aimes faire sur Internet?* Write the letters of the activities in the order you hear them.**

a sending pictures **b** talking to friends **c** watching videos

Écouter 10 **Then the teacher asks: *Qu'est-ce que tu vas faire en ligne le week-end prochain?* Listen to Lola's response and give two things she is going to do.**

Parler 11 **Prepare your own answers to the two questions in exercises 9 and 10. Then, with a partner, take turns to ask and answer the questions.**

Parler 12 **Prepare your own answers to the module 1 questions on page 226. Your responses should be as full and detailed as possible. Then practise with a partner.**

- Remember to express your opinion when you can and give a reason.
- Use time phrases and connectives in your answers.

Module 1

Contrôle écrit

Grammar task

Écrire 1

Write out the sentences, filling the gaps with the correct option in each case. Then translate the sentences into English.

1 Le week-end, j'aime **allez** / **aller** / **vais** au cinéma avec mes copains.
2 Je **regardes** / **regardez** / **regarde** souvent des émissions de sport.
3 Je préfère **regarde** / **regarder** / **regardes** des films d'action.
4 **Je** / **Tu** / **Nous** ne joue pas à des jeux en ligne.
5 Demain, je vais aller en ville avec **mon** / **ma** / **mes** sœur.

Describing a photo

Écrire 2

Look at the photo in the writing exam task. Note down in English what you can say about the following:

1 How many people are there?
2 Who are they?
3 Where are they?
4 What are they doing?
5 What else can you say about the photo?

You and your French friends are sharing photos on Instagram.

What is in this photo?

Write **five** sentences in **French**.

Lire 3

Read Sofiane's answer to the exam task in exercise 2. Answer questions 1–5 in the coloured shapes.

Il y a cinq personnes.
Il y a trois filles et deux garçons.
À mon avis, ils sont dans un groupe au collège.
Ils jouent de la musique.
Au centre, il y a un garçon qui chante.

1 What does this phrase mean?
2 What is this number? Find two other numbers.
3 What does this phrase mean?
4 What do these verbs mean?
5 What does this mean?

Lire 4

Read Sofiane's answer again. Copy and complete the sentences below.

1 Sofiane writes that there are ___ people.
2 There are three ___ and two ___.
3 He thinks that they are in a group at ___.
4 One boy ___.
5 That boy is in the ___.

Écrire 5

Look at the photo in this exam task and write your answer.

- Use ***il y a*** to say what/who is in the photo.
- Use **numbers** and ***garçons / filles***.
- Use verbs like ***ils font*** ('they are doing') and ***ils sont*** ('they are').
- Use verbs for one person, e.g. ***il/elle chante*** ('he/she is singing'), ***il/elle joue*** ('he/she is playing').
- Use ***à mon avis*** ('in my opinion').

You and your Canadian friends are sharing photos on Instagram.

What is in this photo?

Write **five** sentences in **French**.

50-word writing task

Écrire 6

Look at this writing exam task and then, <u>for each bullet point</u>, think about what vocabulary you have learned that you could use in your answer. For example:

- **nouns** and **verbs** to describe a hobby
- **opinion** and **adjectives** to describe likes and dislikes
- **verbs** to talk about activities.

Write a short description of your hobbies.

Write approximately **50** words in **French**.

You must write something about each bullet point.

Mention:
- what hobby you do
- when you do this hobby
- what hobbies you don't like
- what you do at the weekend
- what you do with your friends.

Lire 7

Read Sofiane's answer to the exam task. Then answer the questions.

Je joue à des jeux vidéo. C'est ma passion.

Je joue aux jeux vidéo après le collège.

Je n'aime pas le sport. C'est nul.

Le week-end, je regarde la télé et j'écoute de la musique.

J'aime aller dans les magasins avec mes amis.

1. What verbs does Sofiane use to describe his hobbies?
2. What words does he use to say when he plays video games?
3. What word does he use to link two things that he does at the weekend?
4. How does he express his opinion?
5. Where could he have used *parce que* or *car* ('because')?

Écrire 8

Write your own answer to the 50-word writing task in exercise 6. Try to reuse some of the language from Sofiane's answer in exercise 7.

Module 1

Vocabulaire

Key:
bold = this word will appear in higher exams only
* = this word is not on the vocabulary list, but you may use it in your own sentences

Fêtes et jeux (pages 6–7)

Les opinions	*Opinions*
Les dix jours sans écrans. À ton avis, c'est une bonne idée ou une mauvaise idée?	*Ten days without screens. In your opinion, is it a good idea or a bad idea?*
À mon avis, c'est ...	*In my opinion, it is ...*
une bonne / mauvaise idée.	*a good / bad idea.*
amusant / intéressant.	*fun / interesting.*
ennuyeux / nul.	*boring / rubbish.*
Tu es d'accord?	*Do you agree?*
Oui, je suis d'accord.	*Yes, I agree.*
Non, je ne suis pas d'accord.	*No, I don't agree.*
J'adore / J'aime ...	*I love / I like ...*
Je n'aime pas ...	*I don't like ...*
Je déteste ...	*I hate ...*
Le sport	*Sport*
le *basket / le football	*basketball / football*
la *danse / la natation	*dancing / swimming*
le *tennis de table	*table tennis*
faire de la *danse	*dancing*
faire du sport	*doing sport*
jouer au *basket	*playing basketball*
jouer au *tennis de table	*playing table tennis*

Ma vie en ligne (pages 8–9)

Qu'est-ce que tu fais en ligne?	*What do you do online?*
Je télécharge des applis sur ma *tablette.	*I download apps on my tablet.*
J'écoute des chansons / de la musique.	*I listen to songs / music.*
Je parle avec ma famille au Maroc.	*I speak with my family in Morocco.*
Je partage des photos.	*I share photos.*
Je cherche des idées pour des activités.	*I search for ideas for activities.*
J'achète des vêtements.	*I buy clothes.*
Je joue à des jeux contre ma meilleure amie / mon ami(e).	*I play games against my best friend / my friend.*
Je regarde des vidéos amusantes / *clips sur TikTok.	*I watch funny videos / clips on TikTok.*
J'envoie des messages.	*I send messages.*
sur un portable	*on a mobile phone*
Est-ce que tu fais ça souvent?	*Do you do that often?*
Je fais ça ...	*I do it ...*
souvent.	*often.*
tout le temps.	*all the time.*
tous les jours.	*every day.*
parfois.	*sometimes.*
de temps en temps.	*from time to time.*
À mon avis, Internet est ...	*In my opinion, the internet is ...*
C'est ...	*It is ...*
amusant / essentiel.	*fun / essential.*
dangereux.	*dangerous.*
génial / super.	*great.*
mauvais pour la santé.	*bad for your health.*
mais / par contre	*but / on the other hand*
Il y a ...	*There is/are ...*
des applis pour tout.	*apps for everything.*
des **risques** de sécurité.	*security risks.*
de fausses informations.	*false information.*
des réseaux sociaux géniaux.	*great social media networks.*

Tu as une vie active? (pages 10–11)

Qu'est-ce que tu fais?	*What do you do?*
Qu'est-ce que tu fais comme activités, si tu n'es pas en ligne?	*What activities do you do, if you are not online?*
Je joue ...	*I play ...*
au *basket / au football / au *rugby.	*basketball / football / rugby.*
du *piano / du *violon.	*piano / violin.*
de la *guitare / de la *flûte.	*guitar / flute.*
dans l'équipe du collège.	*in the school team.*
dans un groupe de musique.	*in a music group.*
Je fais ...	*I ...*
du vélo / de la cuisine.	*cycle / cook.*
Je vais ...	*I go ...*
au centre sportif.	*to the sports centre.*
à la piscine.	*to the swimming pool.*
J'écoute de la musique.	*I listen to music.*
avec mon ami(e) / mon copain / ma copine	*with my friend*
avec ma famille	*with my family*
normalement	*normally*
Est-ce que tu as une vie active?	*Do you have an active life?*
Je suis (très) actif/active.	*I am (very) active.*
Je ne suis pas actif/active.	*I am not active.*

Qu'est-ce que tu regardes? (pages 12–13)

Qu'est-ce que tu regardes / aimes regarder?	*What do you watch / like to watch / like watching?*
J'aime regarder ...	*I like to watch ...*
des *comédies.	*comedies.*
des émissions de sport.	*sports programmes.*
des émissions de télé-réalité.	*reality TV shows.*
des **séries**.	*series.*
un peu de tout.	*a bit of everything.*
Quelle sorte de vidéos est-ce que tu regardes / préfères regarder?	*What kind of videos do you watch / prefer watching?*
Je regarde ...	*I watch ...*
des *clips de musique ou de *danse.	*music or dance clips.*
des vidéos amusantes d'animaux.	*funny animal videos.*

Quand est-ce que tu regardes des vidéos / la télé?	*When do you watch videos / TV?*	J'aime regarder des films …	*I like watching films …*
Normalement, je regarde des vidéos / la télé …	*Normally, I watch videos / TV …*	avec les membres de ma famille.	*with members of my family.*
le matin, avant le collège.	*in the morning, before school.*	tout(e) seul(e) dans ma chambre.	*alone in my bedroom.*
le soir, après les cours.	*in the evening, after school.*	Quelle est ton opinion sur …	*What is your opinion of …?*
quand j'ai du temps libre.	*when I have free time.*	Moi, j'adore …	*I love …*
Comment est-ce que tu préfères regarder des films?	*How do you prefer to watch films?*	Tu aimes aller au cinéma?	*Do you like going to the cinema?*
Je préfère regarder des films …	*I prefer watching films …*	Oui, j'aime bien aller au cinéma.	*Yes, I like going to the cinema.*
chez moi, à la télé, ou en streaming.	*at home, on TV, or streaming.*	Non, je n'aime pas (beaucoup) aller au cinéma.	*No, I don't (much) like going to the cinema.*
sur mon portable.	*on my phone/laptop.*	Décris-moi ton film préféré.	*Describe your favourite film.*
Avec qui est-ce que tu aimes regarder des films / aller au cinéma?	*Who do you like to watch films / go to the cinema with?*	Mon film préféré s'appelle …	*My favourite film is called …*

Qu'est-ce qu'on va faire? (pages 14–15)

aujourd'hui	*today*	Je vais …	*I am going …*
demain	*tomorrow*	On va … / Nous allons …	*We are going …*
ce matin / demain matin	*this morning / tomorrow morning*	acheter (un cadeau).	*to buy (a present).*
cet après-midi / demain après-midi	*this afternoon / tomorrow afternoon*	aller au musée.	*to go to the museum.*
ce soir / demain soir	*this evening / tomorrow evening*	faire les magasins.	*to go shopping.*
		jouer au foot / au *tennis.	*to play football / tennis.*
		partir.	*to leave.*
		voir un spectacle.	*to see a show.*
à …	*at …*	Ça t'intéresse?	*Are you interested?*
neuf heures	*nine o'clock*	Tu es libre?	*Are you free?*
neuf heures et demie	*half past nine*	Tu viens?	*Are you coming?*
dix heures moins vingt	*twenty to ten*	Je veux bien, merci.	*I'd like to, thanks.*
dix heures moins le quart	*quarter to ten*	Non, désolé(e), je ne peux pas.	*No, sorry, I can't.*
midi / minuit	*noon / midnight*		

Qu'est-ce que tu as fait? (pages 16–17)

Qu'est-ce que tu as fait, le week-end dernier?	*What did you do last weekend?*	je suis allé(e) au café / au restaurant / à un concert.	*I went to a café / restaurant / concert.*
Samedi matin / après-midi / soir …	*On Saturday morning / afternoon / evening …*	je suis resté(e) à la maison.	*I stayed at home.*
Pour commencer, …	*To start with, …*	on a lu un peu.	*we read a bit.*
Ensuite / Après …	*Next, / After, …*	on a mangé (du *couscous).	*we ate (couscous).*
Finalement, …	*Finally, …*	on a regardé la télé.	*we watched TV.*
j'ai acheté (un *poster).	*I bought (a poster).*	C'était comment?	*How was it?*
j'ai bu (un *coca).	*I drank (a cola).*	C'était …	*It was …*
j'ai fait les magasins.	*I went shopping.*	amusant / nul.	*fun / rubbish.*
j'ai joué au foot sur la plage.	*I played football on the beach.*	(trop) cher / complet.	*(too) expensive / full.*
j'ai marché à la campagne.	*I walked in the countryside.*	passionnant / sympa.	*exciting / nice.*
j'ai pris des photos.	*I took some photos.*	Je n'ai pas regardé la télé.	*I didn't watch TV.*
j'ai vu mon *footballeur préféré.	*I saw my favourite footballer.*	Je n'ai rien fait.	*I didn't do anything.*
		On n'a pas vu le groupe.	*We didn't see the group.*

J'ai participé aux Jeux de la Francophonie! (pages 18–19)

Tu es de quel pays?	*Which country are you from?*	Quand est-ce que tu fais ça?	*When do you do that?*
Je suis du Sénégal / de Belgique.	*I am from Senegal / Belgium.*	Je joue …	*I play …*
Qu'est-ce que tu fais comme activité?	*Which activity do you do?*	tous les jours / le soir.	*every day / in the evenings.*
Je joue au *basket.	*I play basketball.*	À quel âge as-tu commencé à …	*At what age did you start to …*
Où est-ce que tu fais ça?	*Where do you do that?*	**pratiquer** ça?	*practise that?*
Je fais de la *danse …	*I do dancing …*	jouer au *tennis de table?	*play table tennis?*
au centre sportif.	*at the sports centre.*	J'ai commencé à l'âge de (dix) ans.	*I started at (ten) years old.*
à l'école.	*at school.*		

Libre d'être moi

- Talking about your identity
- Using emphatic pronouns

Gaëlle Prudencio

Carrière/Travail: Gaëlle est blogueuse.

Pays d'origine: Elle vient du Sénégal. Maintenant, elle habite en France.

Famille: Elle a un frère. Elle avait une sœur mais sa sœur est morte.

Temps libre: Elle aime la mode.

Langue: Elle parle français et wolof.

elle avait	*she had*
mort(e)	*dead*
la mode	*fashion*
lutter	*to fight*

Many francophone countries are multilingual. While the 'official language' of Senegal is French, Wolof and Pulaar are classed as 'national languages'. There are also many other national languages spoken in Senegal.

Marinette Pichon

Carrière/Travail: Marinette est joueuse de foot international.

Pays d'origine: Elle vient de France et maintenant elle habite au Québec.

Famille: Elle a une sœur.

Temps libre: Elle aime lutter contre la discrimination.

Langue: Elle parle français et anglais.

As in English, French speakers are free to choose their pronouns to talk about themselves. The most commonly used non-binary pronoun is ***iel***, which is a mixture of ***il*** and ***elle***.

Omar Sy

Carrière/Travail: Omar est acteur.

Pays d'origine: Il est né en France. Maintenant, il habite en Amérique.

Famille: Il a sept frères et sœurs. Sa mère vient de Mauritanie et son père vient du Sénégal.

Temps libre: Il aime le football. Il est fan de l'Olympique de Marseille.

Langue: Il parle français, pulaar et anglais.

If you'd like to talk about your gender identity and sexuality, you can say: *je suis* (I am) … / *je me définis comme* (I define myself as) …

masculin	*gay*
féminine	*hétéro*
non-binaire	*lesbienne*
transgenre	*bisexuel(le)*
queer	

Liberté, Égalité, Fraternité

'Liberté, Égalité, Fraternité' est la devise nationale de la France et de la république d'Haïti.

La devise est importante pour beaucoup de personnes.

la devise	*motto*

Liberté • Égalité • Fraternité

RÉPUBLIQUE FRANÇAISE

The values *Liberté* (Freedom), *Égalité* (Equality) and *Fraternité* (Brotherhood) are found on coins, buildings and government documents in both France and Haiti.

Some think that ***Fraternité*** is too masculine. What do you think?

Lire **1** **Read the profiles of Gaëlle Prudencio, Marinette Pichon and Omar Sy. Then, according to their profiles, find …**

one person who:

1 is an international footballer
2 speaks three languages
3 likes fashion

and two people who:

4 come from France
5 live outside France
6 have brothers.

Écouter **2** **Copy the profile card, then listen and complete it in English for each celebrity. (1–2)**

Name:	
Country of origin:	
Family:	
Likes:	

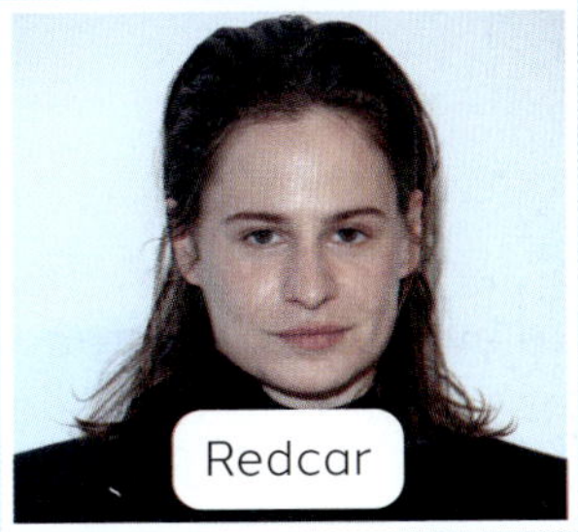
Redcar

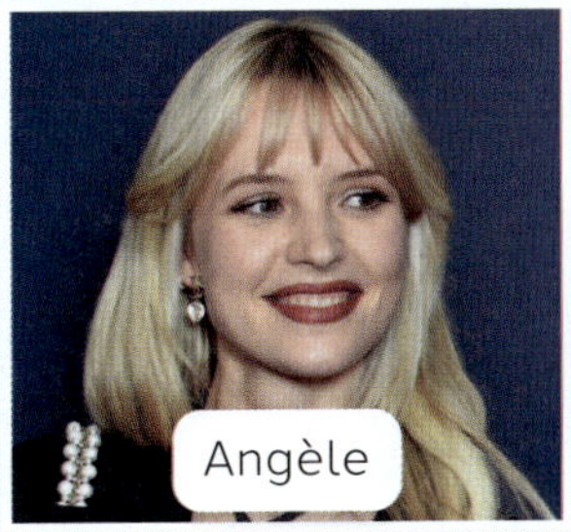
Angèle

Lire **3** **Read the sentences. Write the correct letter to match each heading (a–f) to a sentence.**

1 Je parle français, wolof et anglais.
2 Je suis indépendante et patiente. Ça, c'est moi!
3 J'adore ma sœur! Elle est toujours là pour moi.
4 Je suis religieux. C'est important pour toi aussi?
5 Moi, je suis non-binaire.
6 Je passe beaucoup de temps avec mon groupe d'amis.

toujours	*always*
là	*there*

Ce qui fait mon identité, c'est …

a ma religion
b ma langue
c mes amis
d ma personnalité
e ma famille
f mon genre

G

Emphatic pronouns are used after prepositions such as ***pour*** and ***avec***.

avec moi with me
pour toi for you

G

There are three different ways to say 'my' in French. The word for 'my' has to agree with the gender and number of the noun that follows it.

masculine: ***mon***
feminine: ***ma***
plural: ***mes***

Page 44

Écouter **4** **Listen and write down in English what defines each person. (1–6)**

Qu'est-ce qui fait ton identité?	What defines your identity?
Ce qui fait mon identité, c'est …	What defines my identity is …

Parler **5** **In pairs, talk about what defines your identity.**

- *Qu'est-ce qui fait ton identité?*
- *Ce qui fait mon identité, c'est … et … Tu es d'accord?*
- *Oui, je suis d'accord. / Non, je ne suis pas d'accord. À mon avis, ce qui fait mon identité, c'est … et …*

Lire **6** **Read the text about '*Liberté, Égalité, Fraternité*' on page 32. Copy and complete the English sentences.**

1 *Liberté, Égalité, Fraternité* is the national motto of ___ and ___.
2 It is important for ___.
3 It means Freedom, ___ and Brotherhood.

1 Un week-end en famille

- Talking about your weekend routine
- Using reflexive verbs in the present tense
- Extending sentences using sequencers and connectives

Écouter 1 **Listen and read. Then write down each person's family members in English.**

Il y a combien de personnes dans ta famille?

Qu'est-ce que tu fais le week-end, en famille?

Dans ma famille, il y a trois personnes: ma mère, ma sœur et moi. Le week-end, je me lève tôt, à huit heures. Le soir, on se relaxe devant la télé!

Yanis

J'habite avec ma belle-mère et mon frère. Le samedi matin, je travaille dans un magasin de vêtements, donc le dimanche on se lève tard, à midi. L'après-midi, je mange et le soir, je me couche à 21 heures.

Chloé

J'habite avec mes pères et mes demi-sœurs. Le dimanche, je mets mes vêtements préférés et ensuite, je me prépare pour la semaine. L'après-midi, je fais du vélo. Plus tard, à 22 heures, je vais au lit.

Dorian

tôt	*early*
tard	*late*

Lire 2 **Re-read the texts from exercise 1. Find the French for the verbs below, choosing from the underlined verbs in the text.**

1 I get up
2 I put my clothes on
3 I get ready
4 I go to bed
5 we relax
6 we get up

In French, you don't need a word for 'at', 'in' or 'on' when talking about when you do something.
at the weekend = *le week-end*
in the evening = *le soir*
on Sundays = *le dimanche*

Lire 3 **Re-read the texts from exercise 1. Then answer the questions in English.**

1 Who goes to bed at ten o'clock?
2 Who works on Saturdays?
3 Who gets up at eight o'clock?
4 Who eats in the afternoon?

G

Lots of daily-routine verbs are reflexive. They have a **reflexive pronoun** before the verb.

se lever *(to get up)*	
je **me** lève	*I get up*
tu **te** lèves	*you get up*
il **se** lève	*he gets up*
elle **se** lève	*she gets up*
on **se** lève	*we get up*

Page 44

Parler 4 **In pairs, choose a text from exercise 1 and take turns to read it out.**

Take care with the pronunciation of these two sounds:

1 *è ai ê*
Listen and repeat the words. Open your mouth widely as you say: *p**è**re / j'**ai**me / v**ê**tements*

2 *œu* open *eu*
Listen and repeat the words with your lips in a more rounded shape and your jaw lower: *s**œu**r / h**eu**re*

Écouter 5 **Listen. Then copy and complete the grid in English. (1–2)**

	How many people are in their family?	What do they do on Saturday mornings?	What do they do in the afternoons and evenings?
Fatima			
Lucas			

Parler 6 **In pairs, choose a set of pictures each and take turns to talk about your weekend.**

- *Qu'est-ce que tu fais le week-end, en famille?*
- *Le samedi, je me lève à sept heures. Ensuite, je …*

Use sequencers to link the activities together:

ensuite	next
après	after, afterwards
plus tard	later

A

B

Lire 7 **Read the text. Copy and complete the sentences below in English.**

Clément habite en Guadeloupe avec sa sœur, sa mère, son beau-père et ses grands-parents. Le week-end, Clément se lève tôt car il aide sa mère à la cuisine. Il adore le sport, donc il joue au foot avec ses amis. Le soir, toute la famille mange dans le jardin. Ensuite, la famille se relaxe ensemble.

Use connectives to create extended sentences:

et	and
donc	so, therefore
car	because, for

1 Clément lives in ___ with his ___, his mother, ___ and ___.
2 He gets up ___ because he helps ___ in the kitchen.
3 He loves ___, so he ___.
4 His family ___ in the garden and then they ___.

Écrire 8 **Write a paragraph about your real, or an imagined, family routine at the weekend. Say what you and other people do. Extend your sentences using sequencers and connectives.**

Dans ma famille, il y a (deux / trois / quatre …) personnes.		
Il y a J'habite avec	mon (beau-)père / mon (demi-)frère. ma (belle-)mère / ma (demi-)sœur.	
Le samedi matin, Le dimanche après-midi, Le dimanche soir, Après, Ensuite, Plus tard,	je me lève je me relaxe je me couche mon frère se lève mon grand-père se relaxe ma sœur se prépare je vais au lit	à … heures.

G

Possessive adjectives are words such as 'my', 'your', 'his' and 'her'.

	masculine	feminine	plural
my	***mon***	***ma***	***mes***
your	***ton***	***ta***	***tes***
his/her	***son***	***sa***	***ses***

mon *grand-père*	my grandfather
ta *grand-mère*	your grandmother
son *frère*	his/her brother
sa *demi-sœur*	his/her step(half)-sister

Page 44

2 L'amitié est la clé du bonheur

- Discussing friends and friendship
- Making adjectives agree
- Translating a passage into French

Lire 1 **Read about Nadia's friends. Copy and complete the sentences below by selecting the correct options.**

Tu t'entends bien avec tes amis?

Myriam est ma meilleure amie.
Je m'entends très bien avec elle.
Elle est **calme** et **sympa**.

Je ne m'entends pas bien avec mes **vieux** amis de l'école primaire.
Ils sont **ennuyeux**.
Ils ne sont pas **travailleurs**.

Nadia

Je m'entends bien avec les filles de mon club de natation.
On aime bien passer du temps ensemble.
Elles sont **sportives** et **actives**.

Je m'entends assez bien avec Sofiane.
Il est **travailleur** et **sérieux**.
J'adore son chien. Il est **beau**.

vieux (vieille(s)) *old*

1 Nadia gets on **quite well** / **very well** with Myriam.
2 Nadia **gets on with** / **doesn't get on with** her old friends from primary school.
3 Nadia gets on well with **the girls** / **the boys** at her swimming club.
4 Nadia likes to spend **money** / **time** with her swimming friends.
5 Nadia gets on **quite well** / **very well** with Sofiane.
6 Nadia **loves** / **does not like** Sofiane's dog.

When a reflexive verb is negative, the negative goes around the **reflexive pronoun** and **verb**.
*Je ne **m'entends** pas bien avec ...*
I do not get on well with ...

G

Adjectives must agree with the person or noun they are describing. Most adjectives work like this:

masculine	feminine	masc plural	fem plural
– *intelligent*	add **–e** *intelligent**e***	add **–s** *intelligent**s***	add **–es** *intelligent**es***

Some adjectives follow different patterns:
*sérieu**x**/sérieu**se*** *acti**f**/acti**ve***

Others are irregular:
*vie**ux**/vie**ille*** *be**au**/be**lle***

Adjectives that already end in -e stay the same for describing masculine or feminine nouns, e.g. ***calme**/**calme***.

Some adjectives, such as ***sympa***, never change.

Page 45

Lire 2 **Copy the grid and re-read the texts in exercise 1, paying attention to the adjectives in bold. Write each adjective in the correct column according to who it is describing. Then add the English translations.**

masculine	feminine	masc plural	fem plural
	calme (calm, quiet)		

Écouter 3 **Listen. Write down in English how well each speaker gets on with the person or people they mention. (1–4)**

les amies de ma sœur *my sister's (female) friends*

Écouter 4 **Listen again and write down in English how each person or group of people is described. (1–4)**

Parler 5 **In pairs, take turns to ask and answer the questions below.**

- *Tu t'entends toujours bien avec tes amis? Pourquoi / Pourquoi pas?*

Je m'entends (toujours) Je ne m'entends pas (toujours)	(assez) bien très bien	avec	mon ami(e). mes ami(e)s.

Il est	amusant / travaill**eur** / sporti**f** / sympa / ennuy**eux**.
Elle est	amusant**e** / travaill**euse** / sporti**ve** / sympa / ennuy**euse**.
Ils sont	amusant**s** / travaill**eurs** / sporti**fs** / sympa / ennuy**eux**.
Elles sont	amusant**es** / travaill**euses** / sporti**ves** / sympa / ennuy**euses**.

Écouter 6 **Read the quiz. Listen and note down the answers for Théo.**

Qu'est-ce que c'est, un bon ami, pour toi?

1 Je préfère …
- **a** un ami proche.
- **b** un groupe d'amis sympa.
- **c** beaucoup d'amis amusants.

2 J'aime avoir …
- **a** des amis dans la vraie vie.
- **b** des groupes d'amis différents.
- **c** beaucoup d'amis en ligne.

3 Mes amis sont …
- **a** sérieux.
- **b** intelligents.
- **c** fous.

4 Un bon ami …
- **a** écoute mes problèmes.
- **b** est calme.
- **c** est amusant.

proche	*close*
fou (folle)(s)	*crazy, wild*
l'affaire *(f)*	*matter, business*
la vie	*life*

Résultats
Maximum de a: Les amis sont très importants pour toi – c'est une affaire sérieuse!
Maximum de b: Tu t'entends toujours bien avec tes amis, c'est simple!
Maximum de c: Tu passes de bons moments avec tes amis; la vie, c'est amusant!

Parler 7 **In pairs, do the quiz. Then read the results of the quiz and talk about whether or not you agree with them.**

- *Alors, première question. Je préfère un ami proche. Et toi?*
- ■ *Je préfère beaucoup d'amis amusants.*
- *Ensuite, numéro deux. J'aime avoir …*

- *J'ai un maximum de a. Je suis d'accord. Et toi?*
- ■ *J'ai un maximum de c. Je ne suis pas d'accord!*

Écouter 8 **Listen to Pierre. How well does he get on with each person or group of people? Copy and complete the grid in English.**

Who?	Gets on well? ✓✗	Why?	Extra details?
Ahmed			
basketball friends			
his father			
his friends from primary school			

Écrire 9 **Translate the sentences into French.**

I get on very well with my friend.
She is hard-working and calm.
I like to have lots of friends.
A good friend listens to my problems.

Use a reflexive verb here.

Remember that you need to use *de* or *d'* (not *des*) after *beaucoup*.

Read the next sentence to see if this is masculine or feminine.

Make these adjectives agree.

Use *écoute*: there is no need for a word for 'to' here.

3 Portraits de stars

- Describing your favourite celebrity
- Understanding the position of adjectives
- Describing a photo

Lire 1 **Look at the photos. Write the correct letters (a–f) to match two sentences to each photo. Then listen and check.**

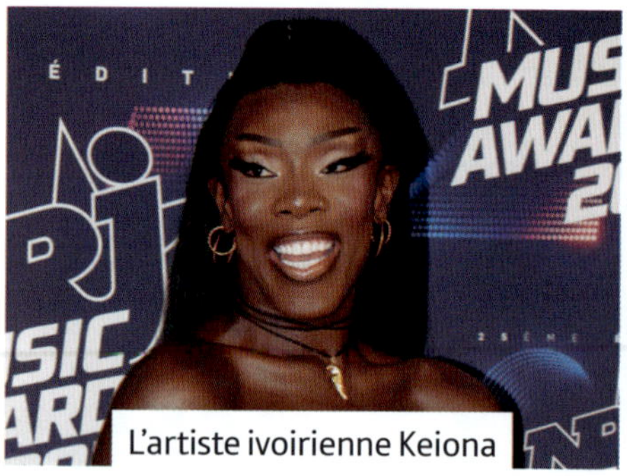
L'artiste ivoirienne Keiona

Le footballeur français Kylian Mbappé

La chanteuse belge Angèle

a Elle a les cheveux longs et noirs.
b Il a les cheveux noirs et courts.
c Elle a les cheveux longs et blonds.
d Elle porte *un* ***collier*** *noir et doré.*
e Elle a les yeux marron.
f Il a les yeux marron.

porter	*to wear*
doré	*golden*

G

Most adjectives come **after** the noun.

Elle a les cheveux ***longs****.*
Il a les yeux ***marron****.*

Page 46

Lire 2 **Read sentence d again. Which is the best translation for the word *collier*?**

a necklace **b** watch **c** sunglasses

Écouter 3 **Listen and fill in the gaps with the correct word from the box. There are more words than gaps.**

1 La femme a les cheveux ___.
2 L'homme a les yeux ___.
3 La personne a les cheveux ___ et noirs.
4 La fille est assez ___.
5 Le garçon a les yeux ___.
6 L'enfant est très ___.

grand marron gris petite longs
bruns roux bleus court blancs

Before you listen, read the sentences and predict which words could make sense in the gaps. When you listen, follow each sentence from the start.

ch is pronounced 'sh'.
Listen and repeat the words:
ch*eveux,* ***ch****anteuse,* ***ch****ose.*

Listen to these tongue-twisters. Then try saying them with a partner:

*Sa****ch****a a****ch****ète une* ***ch****ose pour le* ***ch****ien de Ri****ch****ard.*

Le ***ch****anteur* ***ch****ante* ***ch****aque diman****ch****e.*

Écrire 4 **Write a physical description of your favourite celebrity.**

Mon acteur / chanteur préféré est Mon actrice préférée est Ma chanteuse préférée est	grand(**e**) / petit(**e**). de taille moyenne. chauve.	
Il/Elle a	le visage long.	
	les cheveux	longs / courts. blonds / noirs / bruns / gris / blancs / roux.
	les yeux	bleus / verts / marron.
Il/Elle porte	des lunettes (de soleil). un collier (noir et doré).	

Lire 5 **Look at the photo and read the description. Copy the texts, correcting the six mistakes.**

Décris les personnes *(people)*

Sur la photo, il y a deux jeunes garçons, une femme et un chien.
Les filles ont les cheveux roux.

C'est où? *(location)*

Ils sont dans un restaurant. Il y a une route et une belle cuisine.

Que font-ils? *(activity)*

Ils font du vélo ensemble. L'homme regarde son portable.

la route *road*

Écouter 6 **Listen and write down what is being described: people, location or activity. (1–4)**

à droite *on the right*

G

Some adjectives go **in front of** the noun.

*une **belle** cuisine*
*deux **jeunes** garçons*

Refer to page 46 for a list of other adjectives that come before the noun.

Page 46

When saying what people are doing, you don't need the verb 'to be' in French.

she is cycling = *elle **fait** du vélo*
they are eating = *ils **mangent***

Parler 7 **In pairs, describe the photo below. Remember to describe the people, location and activity.**

Sur la photo, il y a	un (jeune) homme. une (jeune) femme. un garçon.
Il/Elle est	grand(**e**) / petit(**e**).
Ils/Elles sont	grands / petits. grand**s**/grand**es**. petit**s**/petit**es**.
Il/Elle a Ils/Elles ont	les cheveux (noirs). les yeux (marron).
Ils sont	dans un restaurant. en ville.
Il y a	une table. des personnes.
L'homme La femme	regarde ...
Les personnes	mangent / parlent.

4 La place des idoles

- Talking about positive role models
- Using direct object pronouns
- Using the present and perfect tenses

Écouter 1 **Listen and read. Then find the French for the phrases below.**

Qui est ton modèle dans la vie?

Mon modèle s'appelle Aïssa Maïga. Je la suis parce qu'elle est féministe. Elle est connue pour ses films. Elle lutte contre le racisme et le sexisme. Elle encourage l'égalité dans le cinéma et dans la société.

Mon modèle s'appelle Yannis Richardt. Je le suis parce qu'il est actif. Il est connu pour ses messages positifs. Il lutte pour l'environnement. Il partage des informations sur Instagram.

Mon modèle s'appelle Léna Mahfouf. Elle est populaire. Elle est connue pour sa personnalité. Elle partage des vidéos sur la mode, le style de vie et ses expériences personnelles. Elle lutte contre le cyber-harcèlement.

1 I follow her
2 She is known for
3 She fights against
4 She encourages
5 I follow him
6 He fights for
7 He shares information
8 lifestyle
9 cyberbullying

le modèle	*role model*
suivre	*to follow (**je suis** I follow)*
lutter	*to fight*
le harcèlement	*bullying*

Lire 2 **Re-read the texts from exercise 1. Copy and complete the grid in English.**

Name	How are they described?	What are they known for?	What do they fight for/against?	What do they do?

Écouter 3 **Listen. Then copy and complete the grid from exercise 2 in English for Gaëlle Prudencio.**

Écouter 4 **Listen and fill in the gaps.**

Qu'est-ce que c'est, un bon modèle?

1 C'est une célébrité qui ___ les gens.
2 C'est une ___ qui inspire les autres.
3 C'est un ___ qui fait de bonnes ___.
4 C'est une ___ qui change les ___.
5 C'est un influenceur qui améliore ___ conditions de ___.

améliorer *to improve*

G

A **direct object pronoun** replaces a noun that is the object in a sentence. It comes directly before the verb.

masculine ('he'/'it')	**le**
feminine ('she'/'it')	**la**

Je suis Yannis. → *Je **le** suis.*
I follow Yannis. → I follow **him**.
Je suis Aïssa. → *Je **la** suis.*
I follow Aïssa. → I follow **her**.

Page 46

qui means 'who' or 'that' and is useful for creating more complex sentences.

Lire 5

Translate the sentences below about role models into English.

1 Un bon modèle aide les gens.
2 C'est une personne qui change les choses.
3 Un exemple de bon modèle, c'est Arthur Baucheron.
4 Je le suis parce qu'il est intelligent et amusant.
5 Il m'inspire.

Translate as 'role model'.

Add 'a' here.

Think about the English word order.

Who does this refer to?

Do you need a translation for this word here?

Lire 6

Read the text about Diane's role model, Arthur Baucheron. Is each statement below true or false?

Arthur Baucheron est devenu une célébrité sur TikTok à cause de sa personnalité et sa créativité. Il a partagé des photos sur les réseaux sociaux. Ensuite, il a reçu des questions sur son handicap.

Il est né en France avec une maladie génétique. Il a écrit un livre qui s'appelle *Les roues sur terre, la tête dans les étoiles*. Dans le livre, il parle de sa vie.

Maintenant, il est étudiant. Pour changer l'opinion publique, il crée des vidéos amusantes qui expliquent son handicap. Il montre que chaque personne peut faire une différence.

Diane

à cause de	*because of*
la maladie génétique	*genetic condition*
la roue	*wheel*
l'étoile (*f*)	*star*

Arthur Baucheron

1 Arthur became a celebrity because of his music.
2 He shared photos on social media.
3 He was born in France.
4 He wrote a blog about his life.
5 He is still studying at the moment.
6 He makes serious videos to change public opinion.

Lire 7

Re-read the text in exercise 6. Find the French for the verbs below.

1 he became
2 he shared
3 he received
4 he was born
5 he wrote
6 he speaks
7 he makes/creates
8 he shows

G

Use the **present tense** to describe what someone is doing now or usually does.

*Il **lutte** pour l'environnement.* He **fights** for the environment.
*Elle **encourage** l'égalité.* She **encourages** equality.

Use the **perfect tense** to talk about what someone did or has done in the past.

*Il **a partagé** des photos.* He **shared** photos.

For verbs that take *être*, the past participle needs to agree with the subject.

*Elle **est devenue** célèbre.* She **became** famous.

Page 47

Écrire 8

Write a short paragraph about someone you follow. Include the following points:

- what makes a good role model
- who your role model is
- why you follow them
- what they do or have done.

Un bon modèle, c'est une personne qui	inspire les autres / aide les gens.	
Mon modèle s'appelle	Arthur Baucheron / Aïssa Maïga.	
Je le suis parce qu'il est	intelligent / féministe / actif / amusant.	
Je la suis parce qu'elle est	intelligent**e** / féministe / acti**ve** / amusant**e**.	
Il/Elle m'inspire.		
Il/Elle partage Il/Elle a partagé	des photos positives sur les réseaux sociaux. des messages positifs sur les réseaux sociaux.	
Il/Elle lutte Il/Elle a lutté	pour l'environnement. pour l'égalité.	
	contre le racisme. contre le sexisme.	

5 Famille, amour, gâteau

- Talking about celebrations and traditions
- Using the perfect, present and near future tenses
- Recognising adverbs

Lire 1 **Read the captions (1–6). Write the letter of the correct photo for each caption.**

1 Aujourd'hui, **c'est** une occasion spéciale. **Clara a** quinze ans! **On mange** au restaurant.

2 Samedi dernier, **je suis allé** à l'hôpital où **j'ai rencontré** ma nouvelle petite sœur!

3 Cet après-midi, mes mères **vont se pacser**! Le PACS, c'est différent d'un mariage du même sexe. **On va danser** et **on va faire la fête** chez nous.

4 **J'ai fait la fête** avec ma famille et nos voisins après une visite à la mosquée car **nous sommes** musulmans.

5 **Je suis** au mariage de Lucas et d'Éva. En ce moment, **je chante** et **je danse**! Félicitations!

6 Ce soir, **je vais aller** à l'église à la messe de minuit. Après, **je vais manger** de la bûche au chocolat chez moi. **Ça va être** délicieux. Miam-miam!

a

#PACS

b

#AïdMabrouk

c

#Naissance

d

#JoyeuxNoël

e

#BonAnniversaire

f

#Mariage

Chez means 'at' or 'to' someone's home.
chez mes voisins at/to my neighbours' house
chez moi at/to my house

se pacser	*to become civil partners*
la messe de minuit	*Midnight Mass*
la bûche au chocolat	*chocolate Yule log*

Lire 2 **Re-read the photo captions and decide if each event (e.g. the birth, the wedding) is in the present, past or future.**

G Look or listen for different tenses and time phrases to spot if someone is referring to the present, past or future.

	Present	Past	Future
Tense	present e.g. *je mange*	perfect e.g. *j'ai rencontré*	near future e.g. *je vais danser*
Time phrase	e.g. *en ce moment*	e.g. *samedi dernier*	e.g. *demain*

Page 47

Lire 3 **Re-read the photo captions, paying attention to the phrases in bold. Then find at least three verbs in each of the present tense, the perfect tense and the near future tense. Then translate them into English.**

Écouter 4 **Listen. Which question do you hear in each conversation? Write the correct letter. (1–3)**

a Normalement, qu'est-ce que tu fais pour ton anniversaire?

b L'année dernière, qu'est-ce que tu as fait pour ton anniversaire?

c L'année prochaine, qu'est-ce que tu vas faire pour ton anniversaire?

Écouter 5 **Listen again. Copy and complete the grid in English. (1–3)**

	When?	Activities
1		

Present	Perfect	Near future	
Je vais	Je suis allé(e)	Je vais aller	chez (mon voisin) / en ville. au cinéma / au parc.
Je mange	J'ai mangé	Je vais manger	un grand repas / des pizzas / du gâteau.
Je reçois	J'ai reçu	Je vais recevoir	des cartes / des cadeaux.
Je danse / chante	J'ai dansé / chanté	Je vais danser / chanter	avec mes amis.

Parler 6 **In pairs, talk about how you celebrate your birthdays. Use the questions and key language from exercises 4 and 5.**

Lire 7 **Read the article. Answer the questions below in English.**

Traditionnellement, au Maroc, on célèbre l'Aïd avec sa famille et ses amis. Karim explique:

«**Généralement**, j'aide ma mère et ma grand-mère à préparer le repas. Ce matin, on a déjà préparé un couscous parce que c'est **vraiment** délicieux! Je vais **probablement** jouer de la musique avec mon père. On va beaucoup manger et danser. La fête va être **extrêmement** amusante!»

célébrer	*to celebrate*

1 Who do they celebrate Eid with?
2 What food have they already prepared and why?
3 What is Karim going to do? Give three details.
4 What is the party going to be like?

Lire 8 **Translate the adverbs in bold from the exercise 7 text into English.**

G

Adverbs are used to describe a verb, an adjective or a whole sentence.
In English, they often end in '-ly'.
In French, many adverbs are formed from adjectives.
Some are formed by adding ***-ment*** to the feminine form of an adjective, e.g.
traditionnelle → *traditionnelle**ment***
normale → *normale**ment***

The *-ent* at the end of a plural verb is silent. However, you do pronounce the ***-ment*** at the end of an adverb.

Listen to these sentences, then try saying them with a partner:

*Traditionnelle**ment**, les familles célèbrent l'Aïd avec une fête.*
*Générale**ment**, ils organisent un grand repas.*

Écrire 9 **Write a text about a celebration with family or friends. Include:**

- when and what you are going to be celebrating
- what you have already done to prepare
- what usually happens
- what is going to happen at the event.

L'année prochaine, Samedi prochain,	je vais célébrer on va célébrer	l'anniversaire de ma mère. Noël / Pâques / l'Aïd.
J'ai déjà	invité toute la famille / mes amis. préparé un gâteau. acheté des vêtements.	
Normalement,	je vais chez (mon père). je mange (au restaurant / avec ma famille).	
Je vais On va	danser. beaucoup manger. faire la fête.	

Take care with your verbs.
- Is the action in the present, past or future?
- Which tense do you need?
- Have you formed the tense correctly?
- Check your work carefully when you've finished!

Grammaire 1

Possessive adjectives (Culture, page 33)

Parler 1 **In pairs, take turns to throw a dice twice: the first time, choose the possessive adjective; the second time, choose the noun. Say the phrase in French.**

1	my	1	step-mother
2	your (singular)	2	sister
3	his/her/one's	3	half-brother
4	our	4	father
5	your (plural/polite)	5	grandparents
6	their	6	friends

Possessive adjectives are words such as 'our', 'your', 'his' and 'her'.

	masculine	feminine	plural
my	***mon***	***ma***	*mes*
your (singular)	***ton***	***ta***	*tes*
his/her/one's	***son***	***sa***	*ses*
our	*notre*	*notre*	*nos*
your (plural/ polite)	*votre*	*votre*	*vos*
their	*leur*	*leur*	*leurs*

The possessive adjective must agree with the noun that follows it, rather than with the 'possessor':
*Claire et **son** frère* Claire and her brother

With a singular noun that starts with a vowel or *h*, the possessive adjective is always *mon*, *ton* or *son*, even for a feminine noun.
*un**e** amie* → ***ton** ami**e***

When saying 'step' parent, add ***beau*** or ***belle*** before the family member:
beau-père, belle-mère

When saying 'half-brother'/'step-brother' or 'half-sister'/'step-sister', add ***demi***:
demi-frère, demi-sœur

Reflexive verbs in the present tense (Unit 1, page 34)

Écouter 2 **Listen and write the letter of the correct picture for each sentence. Listen again and write the reflexive verb in English. (1–4)**

Example: 1 *d, you …*

a

b

c

d

Reflexive verbs often refer to your body, clothing or relationships. They have a reflexive pronoun before the verb.

se lever (*to get up*)	**s'**entendre (*to get on*)
je **me** lève tu **te** lèves il/elle/on **se** lève	je **m'**entends tu **t'**entends il/elle/on **s'**entend

se lever is a stem-changing verb: the 'e' changes to '**è**' in the *je*, *tu* and *il/elle/on* forms.

me, ***te*** and ***se*** are contracted to ***m'***, ***t'*** and ***s'*** in front of a verb that begins with a vowel or *h*.

Écrire 3 **Copy and complete the sentences with the correct reflexive pronouns.**

Example: 1 *Je m'entends bien avec mon frère.*

1 Je ___ entends bien avec mon frère.
2 Elle ___ relaxe chez sa grand-mère.
3 Je ___ intéresse au sport.
4 Il ___ prépare à huit heures.
5 Le week-end, je ___ lève à midi.
6 On ne ___ entend pas bien.

Adjectival agreement (Unit 2, page 36)

Adjectives are used to describe nouns, including people. They agree with the gender of the noun they are describing and whether it is singular or plural.

Most adjectives follow this pattern.

masculine	feminine	masc plural	fem plural
amusant	*amusant**e***	*amusant**s***	*amusant**es***

Some adjectives follow different patterns. Here are some examples.

ending	masculine	feminine	masc plural	fem plural
-e	*calme*	*calme*	*calme**s***	*calme**s***
-eux/-eur	*sérieu**x***	*sérieu**se***	*sérieu**x***	*sérieu**ses***
-f	*acti**f***	*acti**ve***	*acti**fs***	*acti**ves***
-il/-el	*naturel*	*naturel**le***	*naturel**s***	*naturel**les***
-en/-on	*bon*	*bon**ne***	*bon**s***	*bon**nes***
-al/-ial	*génial*	*génia**le***	*génia**ux***	*génia**les***
-er	*prem**ier***	*prem**ière***	*premi**ers***	*premi**ères***

Some adjectives never change, e.g. ***sympa***, ***marron***.

Some adjectives follow their own special pattern.

masculine	feminine	masc plural	fem plural
*vieux**	*vieille*	*vieux*	*vieille**s***
*beau**	*belle*	*beau**x***	*belle**s***
*nouveau**	*nouvelle*	*nouveau**x***	*nouvelle**s***

* Before a masculine singular noun beginning with a vowel or *h*, the masculine adjective becomes **vieil**, **bel** or **nouvel**:
un vieil homme (an old man); *un bel animal* (a beautiful animal); *un nouvel ami* (a new friend).

Lire 4 **Copy and complete the grid, putting the adjectives under the correct headings. Then underline any plural adjectives.**

masculine	feminine	could be either
Example: *amusant*		

amusant · actifs · sympa · bouddhiste · belle · nouveaux · travailleuse · juive · sportives · calme · grand · religieux

Écouter 5 **Listen to the adjectives. Copy out the one that you hear. (1–6)**

Example: 1 *excellente*

1 excellent / excellente
2 amusant / amusante
3 sportif / sportive
4 sérieux / sérieuse
5 grand / grande
6 actif / active

In the masculine forms of adjectives like *amusant* and *grand*, the final consonant is silent. However, in the feminine forms (*amusante* and *grande*), we pronounce the consonant before the final 'e'.

Lire 6 **Copy out the text, choosing the correct form of each adjective in bold. Then translate the text into English.**

Je m'appelle Norah. Je suis **intelligent** / **intelligente**, mais je ne suis pas **sportif** / **sportive**. Mon frère est très **célèbre** / **célèbres**. Mes sœurs sont toujours **travailleuses** / **travailleurs**. Mes oncles ne sont pas **actifs** / **actives**.

Grammaire 2

The position of adjectives (Unit 3, pages 38 and 39)

Most adjectives come **after** the noun, e.g. *les yeux marron, les cheveux blancs.*

However, these common adjectives go **in front of** the noun: *beau, jeune, vieux, bon, mauvais, grand, petit, haut, nouveau*

Parler 1 **Work in pairs. Partner A chooses one of the people. Partner B asks questions to find out who Partner A chose. Then swap over.**

- *C'est un homme?*
- *Oui.*
- *Est-ce qu'il a les cheveux bruns?*
- *Oui.*
- *Est-ce qu'il porte des lunettes rouges?*
- *Oui.*
- *Est-ce qu'il s'appelle Thomas?*
- *Oui!*

C'est	un homme / une femme?			
Est-ce qu'il Est-ce qu'elle	a	les	cheveux	noirs / bruns / blonds?
				longs / courts?
			yeux	marron / verts?
	porte	des	lunettes	bleues / rouges?

Écrire 2 **Copy and complete the French translations with the missing adjectives. Think carefully about where each adjective should go.**

1 *I have two quiet little brothers.* — J'ai deux ___ frères ___.
2 *Their sister is playing with a big white rabbit.* — Leur sœur joue avec un ___ lapin ___.
3 *Our father loves his old green bike.* — Notre père adore son ___ vélo ___.
4 *My friend is sharing a funny new message.* — Mon ami partage un ___ message ___.

Direct object pronouns (Unit 4, page 40)

A direct object pronoun replaces a noun that is the object in a sentence. It usually goes in front of the verb.
Est-ce que tu partages ***le gâteau****?*
Are you sharing **the cake**?
Oui, je ***le*** *partage.* Yes, I'm sharing **it**.

Here are the direct object pronouns:

me	me
te	you (singular)
le	him/it
la	her/it
vous	you (plural)

In front of a verb that begins with a vowel, ***le*** and ***la*** change to ***l'***, e.g. *Je* ***l'****aime.*

In a negative structure, the direct object pronoun goes between the *ne* and the verb: *Non, je ne* ***le*** *partage pas.* No, I'm not sharing it.

Écrire 3 **Put the words into the correct order to form sentences.**

Example: 1 *Tu me regardes.*

1 me tu regardes
2 il aime t'
3 le suis je
4 elle fait la
5 l' ils encouragent
6 pas invite vous il ne

Écrire 4 **Re-write these sentences, replacing the underlined words with direct object pronouns. Then translate your sentences into English.**

Example: 1 *Elle les partage. She shares them.*

1 Elle partage <u>les vidéos</u>.
2 J'aime <u>l'actrice</u>.
3 Il ne regarde jamais <u>son portable</u>.
4 Ils admirent <u>le chanteur</u>.
5 Elles invitent <u>ton frère et toi</u>.

Using the present and perfect tenses together (Unit 4, page 41)

Écouter 5 **Listen to the sentences and note down whether you hear the present or perfect tense. (1–5)**

1 Je partage des photos. / J'ai partagé des photos.
2 Il écrit un article contre le racisme. / Il a écrit un article contre le racisme.
3 Elle fait des vidéos. / Elle a fait des vidéos.
4 J'encourage l'égalité. / J'ai encouragé l'égalité.
5 On améliore les conditions de vie. / On a amélioré les conditions de vie.

Tense	To talk about ...	Examples
Present tense	• what is happening now • what you usually do • what someone or something is like	*Il fait une vidéo.* *J'encourage tous les jours l'égalité.* *Elle est sympa.*
Perfect tense	completed events or actions in the past	*J'ai partagé des photos.* *Il a reçu des messages.* *On est allé(e)s au cinéma.*

The present, perfect and the near future (Unit 5, page 42)

Lire 6 **Read each sentence and decide on the time frame (past, present or future). Then write out each sentence, putting the verb in brackets into the correct tense.**

Example: 1 *present. Le soir, je* ***mange*** *en ville.*

Look for different tenses and time phrases to spot if someone is referring to the past, present or future.

Time frame:	Present	Past	Future
Tense:	present *je chante*	perfect *j'ai chanté*	near future *je vais chanter*
Time phrase:	*en ce moment*	*lundi dernier*	*demain*

1 Le soir, on ___ en ville. (*manger*)
2 L'année prochaine, elle ___. (*danser*)
3 Hier, il ___ beaucoup de cartes. (*recevoir*)
4 Le mois dernier, j' ___ avec mes amis. (*chanter*)
5 Normalement, tu ___ des gâteaux. (*faire*)
6 Dans huit jours, je ___ un grand repas. (*préparer*)

C'est parti!

Lire 7 **Read the text and answer the questions (1–4) in the coloured lozenges.**

1 These are present tense verbs. Find three more in the text.

2 What kind of verb is this and what does it mean?

3 This is in the perfect tense. Find another verb in the perfect tense.

4 What tense is this?

Aujourd'hui, c'est mon anniversaire. Je suis très content!

Normalement, le week-end, je me lève tôt et je vais au centre sportif. Mes amis jouent au tennis.

J'ai invité toute ma famille chez moi.

Hier, j'ai préparé un excellent gâteau. J'adore ça!

On va manger un grand repas. La fête va être vraiment amusante!

Parler 8 **Listen to the text from exercise 7. In pairs, take turns to read out the text. Listen carefully to each other's pronunciation.**

Remember to:
- pronounce the ***-ment*** at the end of adverbs
- keep ***-ent*** silent at the end of verbs
- watch out for final consonants such as **-s**, **-t**, **-x**, **-p** and **-d** that are usually silent.

Module 2

Contrôle de lecture et d'écoute

Reading

Lire 1

My friends. **What does Nathan's blog say about the events below? Write P for an event that happened in the past, N for something that is happening now, or F for something that will happen in the future.**

Look at the verbs too. What do those verbs mean?

Look out for time phrases that will help you work out the time frame for each event. What do those phrases mean?

Salut!

Je m'appelle Nathan. Au collège, j'ai beaucoup d'amis, filles et garçons. Pour moi, les amis, c'est très important. Je ne me dispute jamais avec mes amis, car c'est stupide! Samedi, nous allons aller au cinéma pour célébrer mon anniversaire. Mon anniversaire, c'était la semaine dernière mais je suis allé au restaurant avec ma famille. Mon meilleur ami s'appelle Rachid; il est amusant, gentil et patient. Hier, je suis allé à un concert avec Rachid et la musique était excellente.

1 Having lots of friends
2 Going to the cinema
3 Nathan's birthday
4 Listening to music

Lire 2

Equality. **Read this entry to a forum about equality. Answer the questions in English.**

#Clara

Salut, c'est Clara!

Récemment, je suis allée à un concert organisé contre les discriminations. La musique est bonne pour aider les personnes à parler de certains problèmes. Dans la société, les gens se disputent trop à cause de la religion et de leurs choix politiques. C'est stupide, à mon avis! C'est à nous, les jeunes d'aujourd'hui, de promouvoir* le respect et l'égalité.

promouvoir *to promote*

1 Why was the concert organised?
2 According to Clara, what is music good for?
3 According to Clara, what is one cause for arguments in our society?
4 Who should promote respect?

In this type of task, sometimes you will be asked to give one or two details. So make sure you do!

In reading tasks, you may come across cognates (words that look like English words). How many can you count in this text?

Lire 3

Translation. **Translate these sentences into English.**

1 J'aime fêter mon anniversaire avec ma famille.
2 Je suis très fière de ma culture.
3 Le week-end, mon frère se lève tôt.
4 Mon chanteur préféré a les cheveux roux.
5 Ma célébrité préférée encourage l'égalité.

Make sure you double-check the meaning of these words.

Listening

Écouter 4

My daily routine. **You hear Raphaël talking about his and his sister's daily routines. Choose the correct answer and write A, B or C for each question.**

1 (I) Every morning, Raphaël gets up at ...
A 6 a.m.
B 6.45 a.m.
C 7.30 a.m.

Focus on the time Raphaël gets up.

(II) Raphaël and his sister ... argue about what to eat in the morning.
A always
B never
C often

Listen out for a time phrase.

2 (I) Raphaël's sister prefers ...
A putting her clothes on before breakfast.
B eating breakfast before putting her clothes on.
C eating breakfast with Raphaël.

Focus on what the sister does, not Raphaël.

(II) Raphaël leaves home at ...
A 8 a.m.
B 8.10 a.m.
C 8.30 a.m.

You will hear three different times, but focus on Raphaël.

Écouter 5

Festivals and celebrations. **You hear some French students talking about festivals and celebrations. What is their opinion on the following? Write P for a positive opinion, N for a negative opinion, or P+N for a positive and negative opinion.**

1 Birthdays **2** Christmas **3** Valentine's Day **4** Civil partnership / marriage

Écouter 6

Celebrating family. **You hear this advert promoting an annual family event in Canada. Complete the sentences in English.**

1 a The event lasts ...
b The event finishes ...
2 a Activities for children under 12 are ...
b Concerts start ...

Listen to the whole sentence before making a decision.

Écouter 7

Dictation. **You will now hear four short sentences. Listen carefully and, using your knowledge of French sounds, write in French exactly what you hear for each sentence.**

Listen out for different tenses.

Module 2 Contrôle oral

Role-play

Parler 1 **Look at the role-play card and prepare what you are going to say.**

- You are talking to your French friend.
- Your teacher will play the part of your friend and will speak first.
- You should address your friend as *tu*.
- When you see this – **?** – you will have to ask a question.

In order to score full marks, you must include a verb in your response to each task.

1 Say which personality you like. (Give **one** detail.)
2 Say why you like them. (Give **one** detail.)
3 Describe the personality you like. (Give **one** detail.)
4 Say where you can see them. (Give **one** detail.)
? 5 Ask your friend a question about their role model.

You can use an adjective (e.g. 'great', 'kind', 'funny') or say what they do (e.g. 'he/she encourages ...').

You can describe their physical appearance or their personality.

You could start with *Qui* ...?

Parler 2 **Practise what you have prepared. Then, using your notes, listen and respond to the teacher.**

Écouter 3 **Now listen to Emma doing the role-play task. In English, note down (a) how she answers the questions for tasks 1, 2, 3 and 4, and (b) what question she asks for task 5.**

Reading aloud

Parler 4 **Look at this task. With a partner, take turns to read out the text below, paying attention to the underlined letters.**

Read aloud the following text **in French**.

Dans ma famille, nous sommes quatre.
Il y a mes sœurs, mon père et moi.
Je m'entends très bien avec mon père.
J'aime regarder des films à la maison.
Dimanche, pour mon anniversaire, on a fait la fête.

Take extra care with how you pronounce the underlined sounds:
- ***è*** and ***ê*** are pronounced the same
- ***qu*** sounds the same as 'k'.

All the examples of a final **s** in this text are silent!

Écouter 5 **Listen and check your pronunciation.**

Parler 6 **Listen to the teacher asking four questions that relate to the topic of Identity and relationships with others. Translate each question into English and prepare your own answers in French. Then listen again and respond to the teacher.**

Use different opinion phrases and adjectives.

Photo card task

Écouter 7 **Look at the exam card below and read the first part of the task. Then listen to Emma describing the photos.**

1 What does Emma say about the person in the centre of the first photo?
2 What else does she mention in the first photo?
3 What does she say about the second photo?

Photo 1

Photo 2

You will be asked to talk about the content of these photos. You must say at least one thing about each photo.

After you have spoken about the content of the photos, you will be asked questions related to any of the topics within the theme of **People and lifestyle**.

Your responses should be as **full and detailed** as possible.

Parler 8 **Prepare your own descriptions of the two photos. You could mention, for example, the people, the location and what they are doing. Then, with a partner, take turns to describe the photos.**

Sur la première photo, il y a ...

To describe someone's hair and eyes, use *il/elle a* or *ils/elles ont* + *les cheveux* / *les yeux* + colour.

Remember that you will need to talk about both photos.

Écouter 9 **Read the second part of the task. Then listen to Emma answering the question: *Est-ce que tu t'entends bien avec ta famille?* Write down the words to complete the sentences.**

Normalement, je m'entends ____ avec ma ____.

Mon ____ est très ____ avec moi, mais ____, on se dispute.

J'____ bien mon frère.

Écouter 10 **Now listen to Emma answering the question: *Qu'est-ce que tu penses des fêtes de famille?* Note in English (a) one reason why she likes family celebrations, and (b) one reason why she doesn't.**

Parler 11 **Prepare your own answers to the two questions in exercises 9 and 10. Then, with a partner, take turns to ask and answer the questions.**

Parler 12 **Prepare your own answers to the module 2 questions on page 226. Your responses should be as full and detailed as possible. Then practise with a partner.**

Remember to use opinion phrases and adjectives.

Module 2

Contrôle écrit

Grammar task

Écrire 1

Write out the sentences, filling the gaps with the correct option in each case. Then translate the sentences into English.

1 Je **me** / **te** / **se** relaxe après les cours.
2 Elle n'est pas très **sérieux** / **sérieuses** / **sérieuse**.
3 Le week-end dernier, je **vais** / **vais aller** / **suis allé** au mariage de ma cousine.
4 J'écris des chansons toutes les semaines. Je **le** / **la** / **les** partage sur mon blog.
5 Pour son anniversaire, il a **invite** / **invité** / **inviter** ses copains.

Translation

Écrire 2

Write down the words for the gaps, keeping the meaning of each phrase or sentence.

1 my favourite singer: *mon chanteur* ___
2 he sings in French: *il* ___ *en* ___
3 my best friend: *ma* ___ *amie*
4 my brother has short hair: *mon frère a les* ___ ___

Remember to change the endings of your adjectives.

Écrire 3

Translate the following sentences into French.

1 I like a lot of singers.
2 I get up early.
3 My friend Emma is kind.
4 There are five people in my family.
5 Yesterday, I ate with my grandparents.

Remember to start with *Je me*.

What phrase is this?

Make sure everything is feminine ('my friend' and the adjective agreement on 'kind').

This is the perfect tense; you need to say 'I have eaten'.

90-word writing task

Écrire 4

Look at this writing exam task and then, <u>for each bullet point</u>, think about what vocabulary you have learned that you could use in your answer. For example:

- **nouns** and **verbs** to describe someone (physique and personality)
- **opinion** and **adjectives** to describe likes and dislikes
- **verbs** to talk about activities.

You don't have to tell the truth! Stick to what you've learned to say in French, and don't worry if it doesn't accurately describe your friend and your activities together in real life.

You are emailing your French friend about friendship.

Write approximately **90** words in **French**.

You must write something about each bullet point.

Describe:
- a friend who is important to you
- something you have done recently with them
- what you would like to do to celebrate their next birthday.

Lire 5 **Read Mehdi's answer to the exam task. Answer questions 1–5 in the coloured shapes.**

1 This is an **adjective**. What does it mean? What other adjectives are there?

4 What does this verb mean? What **tense** is it in?

Ma meilleure copine s'appelle Diane et elle est très gentille. Diane est géniale car je parle beaucoup avec Diane et Diane est très patiente avec moi.

Récemment, avec Diane, je suis allé au concert de mon chanteur préféré. Le concert était super et après nous avons mangé dans un restaurant fast-food. Diane a payé car c'était mon anniversaire!

Pour l'anniversaire de Diane, je voudrais aller à un match de foot car elle aime beaucoup le foot. Je voudrais aussi aller au cinéma. Elle adore regarder des films.

Mehdi

2 What does this **verb** mean?

3 How could Mehdi **avoid repetition** here?

5 What **connective** could Mehdi use here to join up these two sentences?

Lire 6 **Read Mehdi's answer again. Note down in English:**

1 two adjectives about Diane
2 two things Mehdi and Diane did recently together and why
3 two things Medhi would like to do with Diane for her birthday and why.

Écrire 7 **Prepare your own answer to the 90-word writing task in exercise 4.**

- Think about how you can develop your answer for each bullet point.
- Look back at your notes from exercises 4 and 5.
- Look at the 'Challenge checklist' and consider how you can show off your French!
- Write a **brief** plan and organise your answer into paragraphs.
- Write your answer and then carefully check the accuracy of what you have written.

Challenge checklist	
	✓ Use connectives (*car, et, mais*) ✓ Use opinion phrases (*j'aime / je n'aime pas*) ✓ Use verbs in the present tense in the 'I' form (*je parle, j'aime*) ✓ Use *je voudrais* ('I would like')
	✓ Use other little words like *aussi* ('also') and *après* ('after') ✓ Use good adjectives (e.g. *patient, génial, préféré*) ✓ Avoid repetition of verbs and adjectives ✓ Write mostly in extended sentences with connectives
	✓ Use other forms of the verb (e.g. *elle* and *nous*) ✓ Use the present and the perfect tense ✓ Use *c'était* to describe something in the past ✓ Use three time frames (past, present, future)

Vocabulaire

Key:
bold = this word will appear in higher exams only
* = this word is not on the vocabulary list, but you may use it in your own sentences

Libre d'être moi (pages 32–33)

Mon identité	*My identity*
Qu'est-ce qui fait ton identité?	*What defines your identity?*
Ce qui fait mon identité, c'est ...	*What defines my identity is ...*
mon *genre.	*my gender.*
mes amis.	*my friends.*
ma famille.	*my family.*
ma langue.	*my language.*
ma personnalité.	*my personality.*
ma religion.	*my religion.*
Il/Elle est né(e) ...	*He/She was born ...*
au Québec.	*in Quebec.*
en France.	*in France.*
Il/Elle vient ...	*He/She comes ...*
du Sénégal.	*from Senegal.*
de *Mauritanie.	*from Mauritania.*
Il/Elle est *fan de ...	*He/She's a fan of ...*
Il/Elle parle (anglais et *wolof).	*He/She speaks (English and Wolof).*
Tu es d'accord?	*Do you agree?*
Oui, je suis d'accord.	*Yes, I agree.*
Non, je ne suis pas d'accord.	*No, I do not agree.*
À mon avis, ...	*In my opinion, ...*
*masculin(e)	*masculine*
*féminin(e)	*feminine*
non-binaire	*non-binary*
transgenre	*transgender*
gay	*gay*
hétéro(sexuel(le))	*straight*
*lesbien(ne)	*lesbian*
bisexuel(le)	*bisexual*
queer	*queer*
avec moi	*with me*
pour toi	*for you*

Un week-end en famille (pages 34–35)

Il y a combien de personnes dans ta famille?	*How many people are there in your family?*
Dans ma famille, il y a (deux / trois / quatre) personnes.	*In my family, there are (two / three / four) people.*
Il y a ...	*There is/are ...*
J'habite avec ...	*I live with ...*
ma mère / belle-mère.	*my mother / step-mother.*
ma sœur / demi-sœur.	*my sister / step (half)-sister.*
mon père / beau-père.	*my father / step-father.*
mon frère / demi-frère.	*my brother / step (half)-brother.*
Qu'est-ce que tu fais le week-end, en famille?	*What do you do at the weekend with your family?*
Le samedi / Le dimanche ...	*On Saturday / Sunday ...*
matin	*morning*
après-midi	*afternoon*
soir	*evening*
à ... heures.	*at ... o'clock.*
Après, ...	*After, ...*
Ensuite, ...	*Next, ...*
Plus tard, ...	*Later, ...*
Je joue ...	*I play ...*
Je me couche.	*I go to bed.*
Je me lève.	*I get up.*
Je me prépare.	*I get ready.*
Je me relaxe.	*I relax.*
Je mets mes vêtements.	*I put my clothes on.*
Je vais au lit.	*I go to bed.*
et	*and*
donc	*therefore, so*
car	*because*

L'amitié est la clé du bonheur (pages 36–37)

Tu t'entends (toujours) bien avec tes amis?	*Do you (always) get on well with your friends?*
Pourquoi? / Pourquoi pas?	*Why? / Why not?*
Je m'entends (toujours) (assez / très) bien avec ...	*I (always) get on (quite / very) well with ...*
Je ne m'entends pas (toujours) (très) bien avec ...	*I don't (always) get on (very) well with ...*
mon ami(e).	*my friend.*
mon/ma meilleur(e) ami(e).	*my best friend.*
mes ami(e)s.	*my friends.*
Il/Elle est (assez) ...	*He/She is (quite) ...*
Ils/Elles sont (très) ...	*They are (very) ...*
amusant(e)(s).	*fun.*
ennuyeux/ennuyeuse(s).	*boring.*
calme.	*calm / quiet.*
sérieux/sérieuse(s).	*serious.*
sportif(s)/sportive(s).	*sporty.*
sympa.	*nice.*
travailleur(s)/travailleuse(s).	*hard-working.*
Qu'est-ce que c'est un bon ami, pour toi?	*What is a good friend, for you?*
Je préfère ...	*I prefer ...*
un ami proche.	*a close friend.*
un groupe d'amis sympa.	*a group of nice friends.*
beaucoup d'amis amusants.	*lots of fun friends.*
J'aime avoir ...	*I like to have ...*
des amis dans la vraie vie.	*friends in real life.*
des groupes d'amis différents.	*different groups of friends.*
beaucoup d'amis (en ligne).	*lots of friends (online).*
Mes amis sont ...	*My friends are ...*
fous.	*crazy.*
intelligents.	*intelligent.*
Un bon ami écoute mes problèmes.	*A good friend listens to my problems.*

Portraits de stars (pages 38–39)

### Décris les personnes	*Describe the people*
Mon acteur / Mon actrice préféré(e) est ...	*My favourite actor is ...*
Mon chanteur / Ma chanteuse préféré(e) est ...	*My favourite singer is ...*
grand(e) / petit(e).	*tall / short.*
de taille moyenne.	*medium height.*
*chauve.	*bald.*
Il/Elle a ...	*He/She has ...*
le visage long.	*a long face.*
les cheveux longs / courts.	*short / long hair.*
les cheveux blancs / *blonds / bruns.	*white / blond / brown hair.*
les cheveux **gris** / noirs / *roux.	*grey / black / red hair.*
les yeux bleus / verts / *marron.	*blue / green / brown eyes.*
Il/Elle porte un *collier (noir et *doré).	*He/She wears a (black and gold) necklace.*
Sur la photo, il y a (cinq) personnes.	*In the photo, there are (five) people.*
### C'est où?	*Where is it?*
Ils/Elles sont ...	*They are ...*
dans un restaurant.	*in a restaurant.*
en ville.	*in town.*
Il y a ...	*There is/are ...*
une route.	*a road.*
une table.	*a table.*
des personnes.	*some people.*
### Que font-ils?	*What are they doing?*
L'homme / La femme ...	*The man / The woman ...*
regarde ...	*is looking at ...*
Les personnes / Les amis ...	*The people / The friends ...*
font du vélo.	*are cycling.*
mangent.	*are eating.*
parlent.	*are talking.*

La place des idoles (pages 40–41)

Qui est ton *modèle dans la vie?	*Who is your role model in life?*
Mon *modèle s'appelle ...	*My role model is called ...*
Je le suis parce qu'il est ...	*I follow him because he is ...*
Je la suis parce qu'elle est ...	*I follow her because she is ...*
actif/active.	*active.*
*féministe.	*a feminist.*
intelligent(e).	*intelligent.*
Il/Elle **m'inspire**.	*He/She inspires me.*
Il/Elle partage ... sur les réseaux sociaux.	*He/She shares ... on social media.*
Il/Elle a partagé ... sur les réseaux sociaux.	*He/She shared ... on social media.*
des messages positifs	*positive messages*
des photos amusantes	*funny photos*
Il/Elle **lutte** ...	*He/She fights ...*
Il/Elle a **lutté** ...	*He/She fought ...*
pour l'égalité.	*for equality.*
pour l'environnement.	*for the environment.*
contre le *racisme.	*against racism.*
contre le *sexisme.	*against sexism.*
Il/Elle est devenu(e) célèbre.	*He/She became famous.*
Qu'est-ce que c'est, un bon *modèle?	*What is a good role model?*
Un bon *modèle, c'est une personne qui ...	*A good role model is someone who ...*
aide les gens.	*helps people.*
inspire les autres.	*inspires others.*
encourage l'égalité.	*encourages equality.*

Famille, amour, gâteau (pages 42–43)

Normalement, qu'est-ce que tu fais pour ton anniversaire?	*What do you normally do for your birthday?*
L'année dernière, qu'est-ce que tu as fait pour ton anniversaire?	*Last year, what did you do for your birthday?*
L'année prochaine, qu'est-ce que tu vas faire pour ton anniversaire?	*Next year, what are you going to do for your birthday?*
Je vais / Je suis allé(e) / Je vais aller ...	*I go / I went / I am going to go ...*
chez mon voisin.	*to my neighbour's house.*
chez moi.	*home.*
au cinéma / au parc.	*to the cinema / to the park.*
en ville.	*into town.*
Je mange / J'ai mangé / Je vais manger ...	*I eat / I ate / I am going to eat ...*
un grand repas.	*a big meal.*
des *pizzas.	*pizza.*
du gâteau.	*cake.*
Je reçois / J'ai reçu / Je vais recevoir ...	*I receive / I received / I am going to receive ...*
des cadeaux / des cartes.	*presents / cards.*
Je danse / J'ai dansé / Je vais danser ...	*I dance / I danced / I am going to dance ...*
Je chante / J'ai chanté / Je vais chanter ...	*I sing / I sang / I am going to sing ...*
avec mes amis.	*with my friends.*
L'année prochaine, / Samedi prochain, on va célébrer ...	*Next year, / Next Saturday, we are going to celebrate ...*
l'anniversaire de ma mère.	*my mother's birthday.*
Noël / Pâques / L'Aïd.	*Christmas / Easter / Eid.*
J'ai déjà ...	*I have already ...*
acheté des vêtements.	*bought some clothes.*
invité toute la famille.	*invited the whole family.*
préparé un gâteau.	*made a cake.*
Normalement, ...	*Normally, ...*
je vais chez mon père.	*I go to my father's house.*
je mange (au restaurant / avec ma famille).	*I eat (at a restaurant / with my family).*
On va ...	*We are going to ...*
beaucoup manger.	*eat a lot.*
faire la fête.	*party.*

Révisions de grammaire

Plurals (Pages 10, 20 and 22)

Écrire 1 **Copy and complete the plural forms of the nouns.**

Example: 1 *une émission* → *dix émissions*

1. une émission → dix ___
2. un gâteau → trois ___
3. le journal → les ___
4. l'animal → les ___
5. une table noire → cinq ___ ___
6. un bateau bleu → trois ___ ___
7. une grande pizza → des ___ ___
8. un jeu intéressant → des ___ ___

To make a noun plural, you normally add *-s*.
Some nouns have a plural form which ends in *-x*.

- *-al* to *-aux* → *animal* to *animaux*
- *-eau* to *-eaux* → *château* to *châteaux*
- *-eu* to *-eux* → *jeu* to *jeux*

Nouns which already end in *-x*, *-z* or *-s* don't change in the plural form.
Remember that if you are changing a noun into the plural form, the adjective agreement will also need to change.

Écrire 2 **Re-write the singular verb forms, changing them into the plural form.**

Example: 1 *il déteste* → *ils détestent*

1. il déteste – ils ___
2. tu vas – vous ___
3. elle est – elles ___
4. j'ai – nous ___
5. il a célébré – ils ___
6. elle sort – elles ___
7. tu viens – vous ___
8. on a fait – nous ___

Écrire 3 **Re-write these sentences, changing the underlined subject and verb into the plural form.**

Example: 1 *Les profs jouent au tennis de table.*

1. Le prof joue au tennis de table.
2. Ma tante va au centre sportif.
3. L'élève est toujours travailleur.
4. Ton frère se lève à onze heures.
5. Sa sœur a couru un kilomètre.

Watch out for any other words (articles, adjectives, etc.) which you also need to change to the plural form, as well as the plural nouns and verb forms.

Perfect tense verbs (Pages 16, 22 and 47)

Lire 4 **Read the sentences. Write whether each sentence uses *avoir* or *être* as the auxiliary verb in the perfect tense. Then translate the sentences into English.**

Example: 1 *être – I went to the Taylor Swift concert with my dad and my sister.*

1. Je suis allée au concert de Taylor Swift avec mon père et ma sœur.
2. C'est la première fois que Taylor Swift est venue à Londres.
3. Le concert a commencé à huit heures et demie.
4. Nous avons dansé et chanté.
5. Nous sommes sortis du stade à onze heures.

The vast majority of verbs use *avoir* as the auxiliary verb in the perfect tense. However, there are a group of very useful verbs that use *être* as the auxiliary verb.

Verb		Perfect tense	
aller (to go)	→	*je suis allé(e)*	I went
arriver (to arrive)	→	*je suis arrivé(e)*	I arrived
rester (to stay)	→	*je suis resté(e)*	I stayed
sortir (to go out)	→	*je suis sorti(e)*	I went out
venir (to come)	→	*je suis venu(e)*	I came

Some other verbs which also use *être* as the auxiliary verb are: *descendre* (to go down), *entrer* (to enter), *monter* (to go up), *partir* (to leave), *retourner* (to return), *revenir* (to come back) and *tomber* (to fall).

Remember that the past participle needs to agree with the subject of verbs that take *être*, e.g. *elle est resté**e***, *ils sont sorti**s***.

Écrire 5

Copy and complete the sentences with the correct form of the auxiliary verb.

1 Elle ___ allée chez son grand-père. (*être*)
2 Il ___ compris les règles scolaires. (*avoir*)
3 On ___ célébré l'anniversaire de mon frère. (*avoir*)
4 Nous ___ arrivés très tôt. (*être*)
5 Pourquoi ___ -vous invité toute la famille? (*avoir*)
6 J' ___ lu un magazine et j' ___ surfé sur Internet. (*avoir*)
7 Ils ___ restés à la maison hier soir. (*être*)
8 Est-ce que tu ___ sorti à neuf heures et demie? (*être*)

Negatives (Pages 11, 13, 17 and 21)

Lire 6

Read the sentences. Make each one negative by adding the phrase given in brackets to the underlined verb. Then translate the negative sentences into English.

Example: 1 *Mon père n'aime pas regarder la télé.* → *My dad doesn't like watching TV.*

1 Mon père aime regarder la télé. (*ne … pas*)
2 Nous allons au théâtre avec mes parents. (*ne … jamais*)
3 Je discute souvent avec mes copains. (*ne … pas*)
4 Elle est allée chez sa grand-mère. (*ne … pas*)
5 J'ai mangé au restaurant samedi dernier. (*ne … rien*)

Asking questions (Pages 12, 18 and 21)

You have seen lots of ways of forming questions in Modules 1 and 2.

- Intonation (making your voice go up at the end) — Tu es sportif?
- Using *est-ce que* for a yes/no question — **Est-ce que** tu partages des photos sur Instagram?
- Using *est-ce que* after a question word — Quand **est-ce que** tu regardes des vidéos?
- Using *quel, quelle, quels, quelles* (what/which) — **Quel** est ton film préféré?
- Inverting the subject and verb, after a question word — Que **fais-tu** le week-end, en famille?
- Using *qu'est-ce que* — **Qu'est-ce que** tu as fait le week-end dernier?

Écrire 7

Copy the questions. Then re-write them using the question style below.

Example: 1 *Tu as une vie active? Est-ce que tu as une vie active?*

1 Tu as une vie active? (*Est-ce que tu …*)
2 Que fais-tu en ligne? (*Qu'est-ce que …*)
3 Tu suis qui? (*Qui est-ce …*)
4 Tu es allé(e) où le week-end dernier? (*Où …*)
5 Tu fais quoi cet après-midi? (*Que …*)
6 Tu as un film préféré? (*Quel est …*)

Using a range of tenses (Pages 23 and 47)

Écrire 8

Translate the conversation into French.

I often watch TV with my parents at the weekend, but last Saturday, they went to the cinema. Do you like going to the cinema?

No, I never go to the cinema because it's very expensive. Next weekend, I'm going to watch a film online.

This will go after the verb.

Use *aimer* + infinitive.

Remember, the negative parts go around the verb or the auxiliary.

This is an adjective and needs to go after the noun.

Use the perfect tense; remember, the verb *aller* uses the auxiliary *être*.

Use the near future tense.

Module 3

Ma vie scolaire

Au collège chez nous

- Learning about school life in francophone countries
- Describing photos

La vie au collège dans le monde francophone

C'est comment, la vie au collège? Voici les réponses de deux jeunes de pays différents.

Emma, en France

Salut! Je suis en quatrième au collège Jacques Brel à Toulouse en France.

J'adore le collège et j'aime bien voir mes amis tous les jours.

Le collège est très grand et il y a une bibliothèque moderne.

En France, on n'a pas d'uniforme au collège: c'est excellent! En plus, on n'a pas de cours de religion.

Matthieu, au Sénégal

Salut! J'ai treize ans et je suis en cinquième au collège Saint François à Dakar au Sénégal.

Le collège est bilingue et on étudie toutes les matières en français et en anglais. Ma matière préférée, c'est la musique.

Au collège, on a une académie de foot, et le week-end, on joue avec des footballeurs professionnels. Voici une photo de mon équipe.

en plus	*in addition*
bilingue	*bilingual*

Écouter **1** **Listen and read. Then answer the questions.**

1 Who has practice at the weekends?
2 Who says they like seeing their friends every day?
3 Who is musical?
4 Who is in the equivalent of Year 9?
5 Whose school is big?

Year groups in *collège*:

sixième	Year 7
cinquième	Year 8
quatrième	Year 9
troisième	Year 10

Whereas in the UK school year groups count upwards, in most of the Francophone world, they count downwards.

After *collège*, students go to *lycée* for three years to prepare for their final exams, the *baccalauréat* (*bac*).

Lire **2** **Re-read the texts in exercise 1. Match the underlined phrases with the English translations below.**

1 I love school
2 I am in Year 9
3 My favourite subject is music.
4 Here is a photo of my team.
5 I am 13 years old
6 we don't have a uniform

G

The definite article 'the' changes according to the noun:

masculine singular	*le*
feminine singular	*la*
before a vowel or a silent h (masc/fem singular)	*l'*
plural	*les*

You often need the definite article in French even where we wouldn't use it in English, e.g. *Ma matière préférée, c'est* ***le*** *théâtre.* My favourite subject is drama.

Look for examples of this in exercise 2.

Page 70

Écouter 3 **Look at the photo and listen. Put the words in the statements in the correct order. Is each statement true or false? (1–4)**

1 jeunes | sur | il y a | trois | la photo

2 un uniforme | portent | scolaire | ils

3 une salle de classe | sont | dans | ils

4 des arbres | il y a | derrière

Écrire 4 **Write <u>three</u> sentences to describe this photo, including the people, location and activity.**

Les personnes *(people)*

Sur la photo, il y a	un prof / deux personnes / trois jeunes.
Il y a	un garçon / deux garçons et une fille / deux filles.
Ils portent	un uniforme scolaire.
Ils ne portent pas	d'uniforme scolaire.

C'est où? *(location)*

Ils/Elles sont	au collège / au stade.
← À gauche, il y a	un professeur / des arbres.
→ À droite, il y a	des élèves / des tables / de la nourriture.

Que font-ils? *(activity)*

Les élèves / Les enfants	discutent / mangent / jouent …
Le/La prof Un garçon / Une fille	discute / mange / joue …

Parler 5 **In pairs, describe one of the photos below, including the people, location and activities.**

Use or adapt phrases from the boxes above.

1 Quelle est ta matière préférée?

- Talking about school subjects and school life
- Using comparative adjectives
- Giving opinions with reasons

Parler 1 **In pairs, take turns to read out the subjects for each day in the timetable. Then listen and check.**

Take care with the words that look very similar to the English – the pronunciation may be very different!

Lire 2 **Read what these students say about their subjects. Translate the phrases in blue into English.**

Quelle est ta matière préférée et pourquoi?

	lundi	mardi
8h00	les maths	l'informatique
9h00	l'anglais	la biologie
10h00	récréation	
10h15	la physique	les maths
11h15	le français	l'EPS
12h15	déjeuner	
13h30	la musique	
14h30		le français
15h30	le théâtre	l'histoire-géo

Ma matière préférée est le théâtre, car je suis très créative.

J'aime aussi les maths parce que la prof est sympa.

Alice

Ma matière préférée est la musique parce que c'est passionnant.

J'adore chanter et jouer du piano.

Toni

Ma matière préférée est la physique parce que je suis forte en sciences.

Je déteste l'anglais parce que **le prof est très strict**.

Zélie

Ma matière préférée, c'est l'EPS parce que je suis sportif.

Je n'aime pas l'informatique car **on a trop de devoirs**.

Arthur

l'informatique *(f)*	*ICT, computing*
l'EPS *(f)*	*PE*

Lire 3 **Re-read the texts. Copy and complete the sentences below in English.**

1 Drama is Alice's ___.
2 She likes maths because ___.
3 Toni's favourite subject is ___.
4 He loves ___ and ___ the piano.
5 Zélie is ___ at science.
6 She does not like ___.
7 Arthur is ___.
8 He ___ computer science.

Écouter 4 **Listen to the teenagers talking about their favourite subjects. Then copy and complete the grid in English. (1–4)**

	Favourite subject	Reason
1		

Parler 5 **In pairs, take turns to ask and answer the following questions.**

- *Quelle est ta matière préférée? Pourquoi?*
- *Ma matière préférée est (l'anglais) parce que (la prof est sympa).*
- *Tu n'aimes pas quelle matière? Pourquoi?*
- *Je déteste (les sciences) parce que (je suis faible en biologie).*

Ma matière préférée est J'aime J'adore Je n'aime pas Je déteste	le français la physique l'anglais les maths	parce que	c'est facile / utile / amusant / intéressant / passionnant. c'est difficile / inutile / ennuyeux. je suis créati**f**/créati**ve**. je suis sporti**f**/sporti**ve**. le/la prof est sympa / strict(**e**).
		parce qu'	on a trop de devoirs.
Je suis fort(**e**) en Je suis faible en	anglais / informatique / maths.		

Écouter 6 **Listen and read sentences 1–4. Then translate them into English. Finally, listen and note down details for sentences 5–8.**

1 La musique est moins utile que l'anglais.
2 Le théâtre est plus amusant que les maths.
3 Les sciences sont plus difficiles que l'histoire-géo.
4 L'informatique est moins intéressante que le français.

G

You use comparative adjectives to compare things.

plus *+ adjective +* ***que***	more + adjective + than
moins *+ adjective +* ***que***	less + adjective + than

The adjective must agree (in gender and number) with the first noun:

Le *français est* ***plus*** *intéressant* ***que*** *l'histoire-géo.*
French is more interesting than history and geography.

La *technologie est* ***moins*** *important****e*** ***que*** *les maths.*
Technology is less important than maths.

Page 70

Écouter 7 **Listen to Jasmine talking about her school subjects. Is each statement below true or false? (1–5)**

1 Jasmine's favourite subject is English.
2 She likes her favourite subject because the teacher is nice.
3 She thinks biology is more interesting than English.
4 She loves maths.
5 She thinks they don't have enough maths homework.

Parler 8 **Choose a pair of subjects. In pairs, take turns to give your opinions and make a comparison.**

À mon avis,	c'est plus amusant que …
Je pense que	**le** français est plus (facile) que (la physique). **la** physique est moins (intéressant**e**) que (les maths). **les** maths sont plus (difficile**s**) que (l'anglais).

a

b

c

d

Lire 9 **Listen and read the text. Answer the questions in English.**

Moi, je suis élève au collège du Vieux Port à la Martinique. En ce moment, je suis en quatrième.

Le premier cours commence à 7h15, mais le collège finit à 14h, car l'après-midi, il fait très chaud. La pause de midi dure cinquante minutes.

Je n'ai pas de matière préférée, mais je déteste l'informatique car c'est ennuyeux. Je pense que la musique est plus intéressante que l'informatique. Je n'aime pas les sciences parce que les sciences sont difficiles.

durer *to last*

1 Which year is Luis in?
2 Why do lessons at Luis's school finish at 14:00?
3 How long is Luis's lunch break?
4 Why does Luis hate computer science?
5 Which subject does Luis think is more interesting than technology?
6 Does Luis like science? Why / Why not?

Écrire 10 **Write a text about your school subjects and life at school. Include the following points:**

- your favourite subject and why
- which subjects you don't like, with reasons
- comparisons of some of your subjects
- information about your school day

Use some connectives to extend your sentences: *et, mais, car, parce que.*

Ma matière préférée, c'est les sciences car c'est intéressant …

Je n'aime pas la musique parce que le prof est strict …

L'EPS est plus amusante que l'informatique …

Le premier cours commence à … et le collège finit …

2 C'est injuste!

- Discussing school rules
- Using *il faut* + infinitive
- Expressing opinions, agreeing and disagreeing

Lire 1 **Read the school rules. Write the letter of the correct picture for each school rule.**

Règlement intérieur

✓

1. Il faut porter l'uniforme scolaire.
2. Il faut faire ses devoirs.
3. Il faut respecter les profs.

✗

4. Il ne faut pas arriver en retard.
5. Il ne faut pas manger en classe.
6. Il ne faut pas utiliser son portable en classe.

le règlement intérieur *set of rules*

a 

b 

c 

d 

e 

f 

G

To talk about rules, use:
il faut + **infinitive**
Il faut ***porter*** *l'uniforme scolaire.*
You have to wear school uniform.

il ne faut pas + **infinitive**
Il ne faut pas ***arriver*** *en retard.*
You must not arrive late.

Page 71

Écouter 2 **Listen to Enzo and Nadia talking about the school rules. Note down the number of the rule they mention from exercise 1, and if they agree (✓) or disagree (✗) with the rule. (1–6)**

Example: 1 6, ✗

Qu'est-ce que tu penses des règles?					
À mon avis, Je pense que	c'est	un peu assez très trop	important juste	parce que parce qu' car	c'est essentiel pour les examens. c'est utile pour le travail scolaire.
					il faut respecter les autres.
			injuste nul stupide strict		l'uniforme scolaire est pratique. l'uniforme scolaire n'est pas confortable.
					j'ai des problèmes avec le bus.

la règle *rule*

Parler 3 **In pairs, talk about the school rules from exercise 1 and give your opinions.**

- *Il faut / Il ne faut pas ...*
  À mon avis, c'est ...
  Tu es d'accord?
- *Oui, je suis d'accord parce que ... /*
  Non, je ne suis pas d'accord parce que ....
  Je pense que ...

je suis d'accord *I agree*

Try to extend your answers by giving reasons for your opinions. You can use these connectives to do this (both mean 'because'):
car
parce que

Écrire 4 **Write at least <u>three</u> ridiculous school rules in French.**

Il faut manger de la pizza en classe.

Il ne faut pas faire ses devoirs.

Écouter 5 **Listen and read. Then find the French for the phrases below.**

Les règles scolaires et TikTok

Au collège Saint Paul à la Martinique, on a organisé des manifestations. Les élèves ont demandé à avoir le droit de porter un short ou une jupe en été. Ils pensent qu'il fait trop chaud pour un pantalon. Les élèves ont aussi demandé à avoir le droit de quitter le collège pendant la pause de midi.

Les élèves ont filmé les manifestations et utilisé TikTok pour partager des vidéos. La directrice du collège a refusé de changer toutes les règles. Madame Quirin dit, «Il faut écouter les élèves et respecter leurs opinions, mais il faut aussi préparer les jeunes pour la vie et le travail.» Mais les élèves peuvent maintenant porter un short ou une jupe en été.

la manifestation	*demonstration*
la jupe	*skirt*
la directrice du collège	*headteacher*

1 the students can now wear
2 in summer
3 to have the right to
4 share videos
5 you have to listen to the students

Start with any words that you already know. For example, you might not know the French for 'share', but you should be able to spot 'videos'.

Lire 6 **Read the article again, and copy and complete the sentences below in English.**

1 They protested because they think it is too hot to wear ___ in summer.
2 They also wanted the right to ___ during the lunch hour.
3 They used TikTok to ___.
4 The headteacher refused to ___.
5 She thinks that you have to prepare young people for ___.

Parler 7 **In pairs, take turns to read out the first paragraph of the article, paying careful attention to your pronunciation.**

Écrire 8 **Translate the sentences into French.**

1 You have to respect the rules.
2 It's fair because it's essential for exams.
3 I think that school uniform isn't practical.
4 I can wear trousers.
5 I shared videos of my school online.

Use *Il faut* + infinitive.

Use *Je peux* + infinitive.

Which words could you use to say 'because'?

Negatives go around the verb.

Remember that the perfect tense is made of the part of *avoir* or *être*, and the past participle.

3 As-tu fait des progrès?

- Talking about what has happened at school
- Using irregular verbs in the perfect tense
- Pronouncing ***oi*** and ***oy***

Écouter 1 **Listen to the teachers giving feedback to Lucas and Manon at parents' evening. For each student, write the letters of the four statements the teacher makes, in the order in which you hear them. (1–2)**

Une soirée parents-profs

a Tu as appris beaucoup de choses.

b Tu as écrit une histoire extraordinaire.

c Tu as fait beaucoup de progrès.

d Tu as lu beaucoup de livres.

e Tu as bu du coca en classe.

f Tu as pris des selfies en classe.

g Tu as reçu de mauvaises notes.

h Tu as ri pendant un examen.

mauvais(e)(s) *bad*

Lire 2 **Look at the infinitives of these irregular verbs. What is the past participle for each one (underlined in exercise 1)? Copy out the correct sentence from exercise 1 next to each infinitive.**

Example: 1 *prendre: Tu as pris des selfies en classe.*

1 prendre (*to take*)
2 lire (*to read*)
3 faire (*to do/make*)
4 apprendre (*to learn*)
5 rire (*to laugh*)
6 boire (*to drink*)
7 recevoir (*to receive*)
8 écrire (*to write*)

G

Lots of verbs are irregular and have **irregular past participles**, e.g.

avoir (to have) → *j'ai* ***eu*** (I had)
lire (to read) → *j'ai* ***lu*** (I read)
faire (to do/make) → *tu as* ***fait*** (you did/made)

Page 71

Lire 3 **Translate the sentences from exercise 1 into English.**

Écouter 4 **Listen to the teenagers talking about the positive and negative things that happened in their lessons. Then copy and complete the grid in English. (1–3)**

	School subject	Positive	Negative
1			

Parler 5 **Listen to the tongue-twister. Then read it aloud, paying attention to your pronunciation.**

C'est incr**oy**able, mais j'ai oublié mes dev**oi**rs d'hist**oi**re tr**oi**s f**oi**s.

incroyable *incredible, unbelievable*

If you know how to say *tr**oi**s*, this can help you pronounce the sound ***oi*** in other words.

Écouter 6 **Listen to and read Gabriel's school report. Is each statement below true or false?**

En maths et en sciences, Gabriel a reçu de bonnes notes et il n'a jamais oublié ses devoirs. En histoire-géo, il a fait beaucoup de progrès. Il est très créatif, et en musique, il a écrit une chanson géniale.

Par contre, Gabriel n'a pas fait beaucoup d'efforts en anglais et en français. Malheureusement, son professeur de français dit qu'il n'a pas lu son livre. Donc, il n'a rien appris et il a reçu de mauvaises notes.

oublier *to forget*

G

In the perfect tense, **negatives** go around the part of *avoir* or *être*.

*Je **n'**ai **pas** lu le livre.*
I haven't read the book.

*Tu **n'**as **jamais** fait tes devoirs.*
You have never done your homework.

*Il **n'**a **rien** appris.*
He didn't learn anything. / He learned nothing.

Page 73

1. Gabriel received good grades in maths and science.
2. He forgot his homework.
3. He hasn't made progress in history and geography.
4. In music, he wrote a great song.
5. He hasn't made an effort in English and French.
6. He didn't read his English book.

Parler 7 **In pairs, choose to be either Ana or Thomas and tell your partner what you have done or not done at school.**

Ana
- learned a lot in French
- never forgot her homework
- took selfies in class

Thomas
- made lots of progress in music
- made no effort in English
- received bad grades

En ... , j'ai ...
En plus, j'ai ...
Par contre, je n'ai pas ...

To say 'in' a subject (e.g. 'in music'), use ***en*** + the subject.
You don't need *le*/*la*/*l'*/*les* as well.

***en** musique*

Écrire 8 **Write a paragraph about your own progress at school this year, using the key language from the grid. Include:**

- details about your progress in different subjects
- things that you have and haven't done
- opinions.

En anglais, En français, En histoire-géo, En musique,	j'ai reçu de bonnes notes / de mauvaises notes. j'ai appris beaucoup de choses. j'ai bu du coca en classe.		
	j'ai fait	des efforts / beaucoup de progrès / mes devoirs.	
Je n'ai jamais oublié mes devoirs.			
Je n'ai pas fait d'efforts.			
Je n'ai rien appris.			
J'aime J'adore	l'anglais les sciences les maths le théâtre	parce que car	c'est génial. c'est intéressant.
Je n'aime pas Je déteste			c'est nul. c'est ennuyeux.

4 Souvenirs d'école

- Talking about what school used to be like when you were younger
- Using verbs in the imperfect tense
- Translating into French

Écouter **1** **Listen and read. Put the headings in the order in which the information appears in the text.**

Salut, je m'appelle Théo et j'habite à Antsiranana dans le nord de Madagascar.

Quand j'étais petit, j'allais à l'école à pied. Mon école primaire s'appelait ECAR Sainte Thérèse et il y avait une énorme cour. Le foot, c'était mon sport préféré. Tous les jours pendant la pause de midi, je jouais au foot avec mes copains.

À l'école, j'aimais beaucoup l'anglais et aussi la musique. Parfois, je lisais des magazines en anglais!

Après l'école, j'aidais mon frère sur son bateau. Il était pêcheur. C'était assez difficile pour un enfant! Puis, le soir, je retournais à la maison et je mangeais avec toute la famille. Après, je faisais mes devoirs ou je regardais un peu la télévision.

l'école** (f) **primaire	*primary school*
le pêcheur	*fisherman*

a what he used to do straight after school

b information about his school subjects

c what he used to do at lunchtime

d how he used to get to school

e what he used to do when he got home

Lire **2** **Find the French for the verbs below, choosing from the underlined words in the text.**

1 I used to be / I was
2 I used to like
3 I used to go
4 I used to read
5 I used to do
6 it used to be / it was
7 there used to be / there was

G

The **imperfect tense** is used to talk about what things were like in the past / what used to happen.
To form the imperfect tense, remove the *-ons* from the *nous* form of the verb in the present tense:
regarder (to watch) → *nous regardons* (we watch) → ***regard-***

Then add these endings:

je regard**ais**	*I used to watch*
tu regard**ais**	*you* (singular) *used to watch*
il/elle/on regard**ait**	*he/she/we used to watch*

The verb *être* has the stem ***ét-***, e.g. *c'**ét**ait* (it used to be / it was).

Page 72

Écouter **3** **Listen to Nadia talking about what life was like at primary school. Choose the correct answer for each question and write 'a' or 'b'.**

1 What did you use to be like?
  a very hard-working **b** not very hard-working
2 How did you use to get to school?
  a by bus **b** by bike
3 What subjects did you use to like?
  a maths and music **b** maths and drama
4 What did you use to do at lunchtime?
  a eat with my friends **b** play football outside
5 What did you use to do after school?
  a watch TV with brother **b** read music magazines

J'allais à l'école …

 à pied

 en bus

 à vélo

 en voiture

Parler 4 **In pairs, take turns to ask and answer the questions.**

- *Quand tu étais petit(e), tu étais comment?*
- *J'étais … / Je n'étais pas …*
- *Tu allais à l'école comment?*
- *J'allais à l'école …*
- *Qu'est-ce que tu aimais, comme matières?*
- *J'aimais le/la/l'/les …*
- *Qu'est-ce que tu faisais pendant la pause de midi?*
- *Je faisais / Je jouais / Je mangeais …*
- *Qu'est-ce que tu faisais après l'école?*
- *Je regardais / Je lisais / J'allais …*

When there is an **-s-** in the middle of a word, **between two vowels**, it is pronounced as a 'z' sound.
Listen and repeat these phrases.
je fai<u>s</u>ais
une mai<u>s</u>on
la télévi<u>s</u>ion
Take care to pronounce them correctly if you use them in exercise 4.

Lire 5 **Read the sentences. Write the letters of the <u>three</u> correct sentences for each picture. Then listen and check.**

a Elle m'envoyait des cartes d'anniversaire.
b Elle me disait que je n'étais pas travailleur.
c Elle n'était jamais contente.
d Elle me parlait avec respect.
e Elle me donnait de bonnes notes.
f Elle me donnait trop de devoirs.

1 La prof géniale

2 La prof nulle

G

The **indirect object pronoun** *me* (or *m'*) means 'to me'.
It replaces *à* + noun, e.g. after the verbs *donner à* (to give to) and *parler à* (to speak to).
The word 'to' is not always used in English.

Indirect object pronouns go before the verb.

*Il **me** parlait.*	He used to talk **to me**.
*Tu **m'**envoyais des cadeaux.*	You used to send **me** presents. You used to send presents **to me**.

Page 72

Lire 6 **Which <u>one</u> of the six phrases in exercise 5 does not include an indirect object pronoun? From the five that do, choose any <u>three</u> to translate into English.**

Example: *Elle me donnait de bonnes notes. She used to give me good grades.*

Écouter 7 **Listen to Xavier talking about school. Is each statement below true or false? (1–5)**

1 Xavier's favourite subject was physics.
2 His physics teacher didn't respect him.
3 He received bad grades in French.
4 The music teacher was always happy.
5 He had too much maths homework.

Écrire 8 **Write out the jumbled words and phrases to make sentences.**

1 parlais | avec patience | Tu | me
2 envoyait | m' | des lettres | Il
3 me | des cartes d'anniversaire | donnait | Elle
4 Tu | disais | travailleur | que j'étais | me

Écrire 9 **Copy out the parallel translations and complete them with the missing words.**

1	When I was ____, I used to like ____.	____ j'étais petit(e), j' ____ l'école.
2	I used to play tennis ____ the lunch break.	Je ____ au tennis pendant la pause de midi.
3	____ favourite teacher was called Mr Gasson.	Mon ____ préféré ____ Monsieur Gasson.
4	He used to give me birthday ____.	Il ____ donnait des cartes ____.

5 Les langues et l'avenir

- Talking about learning languages
- Using the imperfect, present and near future tenses
- Using negatives in different time frames

Lire 1 **Read the text. Find the French for the phrases below.**

Laurent

Quand j'étais plus jeune, j'habitais à Paris. Au collège, j'apprenais l'anglais.

Maintenant, j'habite à Nice et je suis élève au lycée hôtelier. Je travaille dans de grands hôtels et j'ai l'occasion de parler anglais et italien avec mes collègues.

L'année prochaine, je vais travailler dans un hôtel traditionnel à Turin, en Italie. Je vais utiliser une appli de langues sur mon portable pour améliorer mon italien.

Zahra

Avant, j'habitais à Arolla, un petit village à la montagne en Suisse. Au collège et au lycée, j'apprenais l'allemand.

En ce moment, je suis étudiante à l'université de Genève. J'étudie le commerce. J'ai dix heures de cours par semaine, donc je continue à apprendre l'allemand.

L'année prochaine, je vais continuer à améliorer mon allemand. Je vais regarder des films allemands et je vais écouter des podcasts en allemand.

le lycée hôtelier	*hospitality school*
l'allemand *(m)*	*German*
le commerce	*business*

1 when I was younger
2 now
3 next year
4 before
5 at the moment

Lire 2 **Re-read the texts in exercise 1. Find three different verbs in the imperfect tense, six verbs in the present tense and five verbs in the near future tense.**

G

Tense:	**Imperfect**	**Present**	**Near future**
To talk about …	what **used to** happen	what **is** happening **now**	what is **going to** happen
être (to be)	*j'étais*	*je suis*	*je vais être*
aller (to go)	*j'allais*	*je vais*	*je vais aller*
faire (to do/make)	*je faisais*	*je fais*	*je vais faire*
apprendre (to learn)	*j'apprenais*	*j'apprends*	*je vais apprendre*

Lire 3 **Re-read the texts in exercise 1. Answer the questions in English.**

1 Where did Laurent use to live?
2 Where is he doing work placements now?
3 Where is he going to work next year?
4 What language did Zahra use to learn at school?
5 How many hours of lessons does Zahra have each week?
6 How is she going to improve her German skills?

Pay attention to the tense used in each question. This will help you locate the answer in the text more confidently.

Écouter 4 **Listen to Kader and Agathe talking about languages. Then copy and complete the grid in English.**

	Before (used to speak / learn)	**Now (speaks / uses now)**	**Future (going to speak / learn)**
Kader			
Agathe			

Écouter 5 **Listen. Write the correct verb phrase from the box to fill each gap. Then write what tense each verb is in (imperfect, present or near future).**

Example: 1 *j'écoutais*, imperfect

Avant, **1** des podcasts en anglais, mais maintenant **2** des films américains ou canadiens.

En ce moment, **3** l'espagnol et je le trouve passionnant. Bientôt, **4** des cours d'allemand aussi parce que c'est une langue très utile.

L'année prochaine, **5** dans une entreprise de marketing à Paris. En ce moment, **6** des cours de français.

À l'école primaire, **7** les langues assez difficiles. À l'avenir, je **8** une appli pour améliorer mon italien.

- je prends
- j'apprends
- je vais utiliser
- je regarde
- je vais prendre
- j'écoutais
- je vais travailler
- je trouvais

l'espagnol *(m)* *Spanish*

Parler 6 **Listen and repeat the words on the right. Then, in pairs, take turns to read out sentences 1 and 2, paying attention to your pronunciation of the sound *ien*.**

1 J'aime b**ien** l'ital**ien**, mais je ne comprends r**ien**.

2 Comb**ien** de langues parle-t-il, Jul**ien**, ton ami canad**ien**?

b**ien**	ital**ien**
r**ien**	canad**ien**
comb**ien**	Jul**ien**

Écouter 7 **Listen and write down the negative you hear in each sentence (1–5). Listen again and note in English what the people don't do.**

Lire 8 **Translate the sentences below into English. Each pair of sentences is in a different tense.**

1 Je n'écoute rien en classe.
2 Je ne déteste personne.
3 Je ne trouvais pas les langues intéressantes.
4 Je n'allais jamais à l'étranger.
5 Je ne vais pas regarder de films allemands.
6 Je ne vais jamais faire mes devoirs.

G

ne … pas	not
ne … jamais	never
ne … personne	not anyone/no one
ne … rien	nothing

Most **negatives** are in two parts and go around the verb:

Je ***ne*** *regarde* ***jamais*** *de films français.*
I never watch French films.

Je ***ne*** *connais* ***personne*** *qui travaille à l'étranger.*
I don't know anyone who works abroad.

Je ***ne*** *faisais* ***rien*** *en classe.*
I didn't use to do anything in class.

Remember that in the near future, the negative goes around the part of the verb *aller*.

Je ***ne*** *vais* ***pas*** *écouter de podcasts en allemand.*

Page 73

Parler 9 **In pairs, take turns to ask and answer the following questions.**

1 Est-ce que tu apprenais une langue à l'école primaire? *(imperfect tense)*

Oui, j'apprenais (le français) et (l'espagnol).
Non, je n'apprenais pas de langue.

2 Tu apprends quelles langues au collège? *(present tense)*

Au collège, j'apprends (l'allemand) et (l'italien).
En ce moment, j'apprends (le français), mais je n'apprends pas (l'espagnol).

3 À l'avenir, comment est-ce que tu vas améliorer ton français? *(near future tense)*

À l'avenir, je vais	regarder des films (allemands). écouter des podcasts en (français). utiliser une appli sur mon portable. lire des magazines en (français).

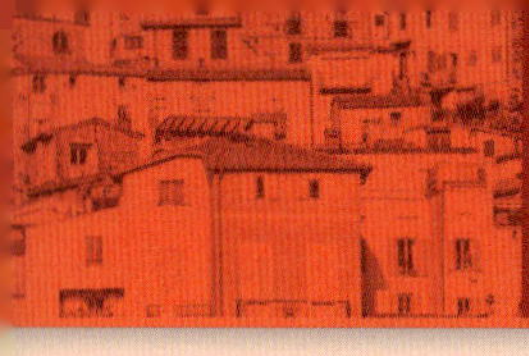

Grammaire 1

The definite article (Culture, page 58)

Lire 1 **Copy and complete the sentences with the correct definite article (*le*, *la*, *l'* or *les*). Then translate the sentences into English.**

1 Je n'aime pas ___ histoire car c'est ennuyeux.
2 ___ musique est ma matière préférée.
3 Je pense que ___ professeur est assez amusant.
4 ___ cours commencent à neuf heures du matin.
5 Au collège, ___ uniforme est très strict.
6 Ma sœur aime ___ anglais, mais moi, je préfère ___ maths.

Comparative adjectives (Unit 1, page 61)

Use comparative adjectives to compare things:

plus + adjective + ***que***	more + adjective + than
moins + adjective + ***que***	less + adjective + than
aussi + adjective + ***que***	as + adjective + as

The adjective must agree (in gender and number) with the first noun:
***La** musique est aussi amusant**e** que l'anglais.*
Music is as fun as English.

Écouter 2 **Listen and complete the dictation task.**

1 La géographie est ___ amusante que l'histoire.
2 La ___ est moins ennuyeuse que la ___.
3 Thomas est ___ ___ que Maxime.
4 Le théâtre est ___ intéressant que les ___.
5 La bibliothèque est ___ grande que la ___ de classe.

Écrire 3 **Write out the words in the correct order to form sentences using the comparative. Then listen and check.**

Example: 1 *L'informatique est plus intéressante que le français.*

The first school subject in each sentence has a capital letter.

1 plus | le français | intéressante | que | est | L'informatique
2 important | est | plus | la technologie | que | Le sport
3 amusante | La musique | l'anglais | est | moins | que
4 les maths | est | La biologie | aussi | ennuyeuse | que

Parler 4 **In pairs, play 'comparatives tennis'. Partner A 'serves' by saying a sentence according to the prompts. Partner B 'returns' by disagreeing and swapping the order of the two school subjects. Make sure that you make the adjective agree with the first noun! Swap who 'serves' each time.**

- *Le français est plus amusant que la géographie.*
- *Non, la géographie est plus amusante que le français.*

1  more fun 

2  more interesting 

3  less boring 

4  more important 

Using *il faut* + infinitive (Unit 2, page 62)

Écrire 5

Copy and complete the French translations with the missing words.

1. *You have to wear school uniform.* ___ ___ porter l'uniforme scolaire.
2. *You have to respect the teachers.* ___ ___ ___ les profs.
3. *You must not arrive late.* ___ ___ ___ ___ arriver en retard.
4. *You must do your homework.* ___ ___ ___ ses devoirs.
5. *You must not eat in class.* ___ ___ ___ ___ ___ en classe.

The perfect tense (Unit 3, page 64)

Lire 6

Copy and complete the sentences, choosing the correct irregular past participle from the box for each gap.

1. Qu'est-ce que tu as ___ au collège hier?
2. Olivier a ___ beaucoup de progrès.
3. J'ai ___ un magazine de musique.
4. Nous avons ___ du café ce matin.
5. Ils ont ___ des cadeaux.

lu appris reçu fait bu

Remember, the perfect tense includes an **auxiliary verb** (part of *avoir* or *être*) and a **past participle**, e.g.
j'ai mangé (I ate)

Verbs that take ***être*** must agree with the subject (the person who is doing the action):
*elle est allé**e*** (she went)

You form the past participle of regular *-er* verbs like this:
*étudi**er*** (to study) → *étudi**é***

However, many verbs are irregular and have irregular past participles, e.g.
faire (to do/make) → *fait*
mettre (to put) → *mis*
apprendre (to learn) → *appris*

Écrire 7

Copy out the sentences, putting the verbs in brackets into the perfect tense.

Example: 1 *J'ai travaillé dur pour l'examen.*

1. J'___ dur pour l'examen. (*travailler*)
2. À midi, nous ___ avec la prof. (*manger*)
3. Elle ___ ses devoirs de maths. (*faire*)
4. En classe d'histoire-géo, elles ___ un film. (*regarder*)
5. Tu ___ combien de temps pour le déjeuner? (*prendre*)
6. Nous ___ un magazine de sport. (*lire*)

Think carefully about whether the verb is a regular *-er* verb or if you need to use an irregular past participle.

Lire 8

Translate the sentences from exercise 7 into English.

Lire 9

Find the <u>two</u> mistakes in each sentence and write out the corrected sentence in French.

1. En anglais, je reçu de mauvaises notes et je n'ai rien apprendu.
2. Il n'as jamais fait ses devoirs et il as ri pendant un examen.
3. Elle a allé au café avec ses copines.
4. Nous avoir écouté un podcast mais nous n'avons pas lire de magazines en français.

Grammaire 2

The imperfect tense (Unit 4, page 66)

The imperfect tense is used to talk about what things were like in the past / what used to happen.
To form the imperfect tense, remove the *-ons* from the *nous* form of the verb in the present tense, e.g.
jouer (to play) → *nous jouons* → ***jou-***

Then add these endings:

je jou**ais**	*I used to play*
tu jou**ais**	*you* (singular) *used to play*
il/elle/on jou**ait**	*he/she/we used to play*

The verb être has the stem ***ét-***:
*j'**ét**ais* (I used to be / I was)

Take care with verbs ending in ***-ger***: the *nous* form in the present tense has an extra *e*, so 'I used to eat' is *je mang**e**ais*.

Lire 1 **Translate the sentences into English.**

1 Quand j'étais à l'école primaire, j'aimais bien mon professeur.
2 Mon frère allait au collège à vélo.
3 J'allais à l'école à pied avec mon père.
4 Pendant la pause de midi, je lisais beaucoup de livres.
5 Après l'école, je jouais souvent au tennis.

Parler 2 **In pairs, take turns to read out the sentences from exercise 1. Pay particular attention to the pronunciation of the imperfect tense verbs. Then listen and check.**

Écrire 3 **Copy out the sentences, putting the verbs in brackets into the imperfect tense.**

1 J'___ plus sportif. (*être*)
2 J'___ à la bibliothèque. (*aller*)
3 Tu n'___ pas ton collège. (*aimer*)
4 Elle ___ un énorme sandwich. (*manger*)
5 Je ___ au rugby pour l'école. (*jouer*)
6 Il ___ assez intelligent. (*être*)

Indirect object pronouns (Unit 4, page 67)

Indirect object pronouns mean 'to me', 'to him', etc. They are used to replace *à* + noun, e.g. after the verbs *donner à* (to give to), *parler à* (to speak to) and *envoyer à* (to send to). The word 'to' is not always used in English.

(to) me	***me*** or ***m'***	(to) him/her	***lui***
(to) you (singular)	***te*** or ***t'***	(to) you (plural or polite)	***vous***

Indirect object pronouns go before the verb.
*Il **me** parle en français.* He speaks **to me** in French.

Lire 4 **Copy out the parallel translations and complete them with the missing words.**
Example: 1 *I used to talk to him every day. Je lui parlais tous les jours.*

1	I ___ to him every day.	Je ___ parlais tous les jours.
2	___ used to send me birthday cards.	Le prof ___ envoyait des cartes d'anniversaire.
3	Did ___ use to give you too much homework?	Est-ce qu'il ___ donnait trop de devoirs?
4	He used to ___ to me a lot.	Il ___ parlait beaucoup.
5	I used to give her ___ every year.	Je ___ donnais un cadeau chaque année.

The near future tense (Unit 5, page 68)

Remember that the near future tense is formed by using the present tense of the verb *aller* + an **infinitive**, e.g.
*Je vais **faire** des progrès.* I am going to make progress.
*Elle va **utiliser** une appli.* She is going to use an app.

Écouter 5 **Listen. Write the words from the boxes in the correct order to complete these questions.**

Example: 1 *Est-ce que demain tu vas …?*

1 Est-ce que …? — vas / à la bibliothèque / aller / tu / demain
2 Comment est-ce que …? — nous / le français / allons / apprendre
3 À quelle heure est-ce que …? — commencer / le premier cours / va
4 Pourquoi est-ce que …? — tu / aller / ne vas pas / au collège

Using negatives in different time frames (Unit 5, page 69)

Écrire 6 **Read the grammar box on page 69. Make these sentences negative by putting the negative expression in brackets in the correct place. Then translate the sentences into English.**

Example: 1 *Les règles ne sont pas justes. The rules …*

1 Les règles sont justes. (*ne … pas*)
2 Elle jouait au foot pendant la récréation. (*ne … jamais*)
3 Je vais apprendre en classe. (*ne … rien*)
4 La prof était amusante. (*ne … jamais*)

Lire 7 **Complete the English translation of these negative sentences and questions.**

1 Je ne comprends rien en classe de maths. — I don't …
2 Tu n'as rien fait pendant la pause-déjeuner? — Didn't you do …
3 Ce matin, au collège, je n'ai vu personne. — This morning, I didn't …
4 Est-ce que tu ne vas jamais faire tes devoirs? — Are you never …

C'est parti!

Écrire 8 **Translate the sentences into French.**

1 I used to love music.
2 My teacher was very happy.
3 I did not use to learn a language.

Use the imperfect tense in each sentence.

4 I like school.
5 Lessons are hard because the teachers are strict.
6 I don't learn anything in German but the teacher is nice.

Think about where you need to include the definite article (the word for 'the').

7 I am going to go abroad.
8 She is going to listen to podcasts.
9 We are going to read a lot of books in French.

You need to use the near future tense in these sentences.

Module 3

Contrôle de lecture et d'écoute

Reading

Lire 1

My school. **You read Alex's blog about his school. Answer the questions in English.**

Bonjour les amis!

À mon avis, mon collège n'est pas trop strict et les profs sont très gentils mais je n'aime pas l'uniforme parce que je pense qu'il n'est pas confortable.

Au collège, il ne faut pas utiliser son portable en classe et je trouve ça juste car les téléphones peuvent être un problème. En plus, on a le droit de manger dans une salle de classe car la cantine n'est pas assez grande pour tous les élèves et ça, c'est vraiment bien!

Alex

1 What does Alex say about his school?
2 How does he describe his uniform?
3 What is the rule about mobile phones at his school?
4 Why are they allowed to eat in the classroom?

Questions follow the order of the text.

Watch out for negatives.

Lire 2

Rules at school. **You read a school internet forum. What do these students think about their school rules? For each person, write P for a positive opinion, N for a negative opinion, or P+N for a positive and negative opinion.**

Gabriel
Dans mon collège, il faut respecter un règlement* très strict. Je pense qu'il n'est pas juste mais qu'il est nécessaire.

Samantha
Selon mes copains, le règlement n'est pas nécessaire, mais moi, je pense que les règles du collège sont importantes pour bien apprendre.

Momo
Dans mon collège, il y a des règles qui sont nulles mais il y a des règles qui sont nécessaires. Par exemple, on n'a pas le droit de parler en classe et ça, c'est nul!

Arturo
Il faut respecter tout le monde. Mon collège est très strict sur le respect et ça, c'est bien!

Charline
Quand tu n'écoutes pas ou quand tu parles en classe, tu as une ***colle*** de 30 minutes après le collège. Je trouve ça vraiment injuste!

le règlement *set of rules*

Read Charline's opinion again. What do you do if you have *une colle*? Write the correct letter.

A	Go to a club.
B	Stay at school.
C	Do your homework.

Lire 3

A new school. **Read Charlie's blog. Answer the questions in English.**

Je suis en troisième et bientôt je vais être en seconde au lycée. La rentrée est en septembre et j'ai déjà acheté mon sac et mes stylos, mais je cherche encore un ordinateur portable.

Le bâtiment principal du lycée est très beau et il y a un terrain de foot, mais je pense que le règlement* est trop strict. Si tu arrives en retard, tu as une colle de 30 minutes après le lycée!

Je vais aller au lycée en bus parce que je n'ai pas de vélo et parce que j'habite loin du lycée.

1 Which year will Charlie soon be in?
2 What has he not yet bought?
3 At the sixth-form college, what does he not like?
4 How is he going to go to sixth-form college?

Lire 4

Translation. **Translate these sentences into English.**

Don't forget to translate these words.

Take care when translating the different verbs.

1 J'étudie beaucoup de matières.
2 Je suis assez forte en français.
3 J'ai commencé le collège l'année dernière.
4 Je voudrais apprendre une nouvelle langue.
5 Les professeurs ne sont pas stricts et ils sont très gentils.

Be aware of false friends! They look like English words but don't have the same meaning. Think carefully about what they mean before translating them.

Listening

Écouter 5

My school. **You hear some students talking about their school. What is each person talking about? Write the correct letter (A–F) for each speaker. (1–4)**

A	homework
B	favourite subject
C	clubs
D	subject they don't like
E	teachers
F	rules

Think of the key vocabulary you may hear for each option.

Écouter 6

School rules. **You hear Lucas and Lola talking about school rules. Complete the sentences in English.**

1 Lucas thinks that the rules are important for ...
2 He does not like the rule on ...
3 Lola thinks that wearing a uniform is ...
4 She says that a lot of pupils don't want ...

Écouter 7

Dictation. **You will now hear four short sentences. Listen carefully and, using your knowledge of French sounds, write down in French exactly what you hear for each sentence.**

Listen carefully to the endings of the words.

Read your answers carefully to check they make sense. Your knowledge of grammar and vocabulary will help you in the dictation task.

Module 3

Contrôle oral

Role-play

Parler 1 **Look at the role-play card and prepare what you are going to say.**

- You are talking to your French friend.
- Your teacher will play the part of your friend and will speak first.
- You should address your friend as *tu*.
- When you see this – **?** – you will have to ask a question.

In order to score full marks, you must include a verb in your response to each task.

1 Describe your school. (Give **one** detail.)
2 Give **one** opinion of your uniform.
3 Say what you wear to school. (Give **one** detail.)
4 Say which school subject you like. (Give **one** detail.)
? 5 Ask your friend something about their school.

You can use an adjective such as 'big', 'small', 'strict'.

Use the verb *porter*.

You can say if you like it or not, or if it is too expensive, or not good/nice.

Remember to use *le/la/l'/les* in front of the school subject.

You can start with *Tu aimes ...?* ('Do you like ...?') or *Qu'est-ce que tu penses de ...?* ('What do you think of ...?').

Parler 2 **Practise what you have prepared. Then, using your notes, listen and respond to the teacher.**

Écouter 3 **Now listen to Maxime doing the role-play task. In English, note down (a) how he answers the questions for tasks 1, 2, 3 and 4, and (b) what question he asks for task 5.**

Reading aloud

Parler 4 **Look at this task. With a partner, take turns to read out the text below, paying attention to the underlined letters.**

Read aloud the following text **in French**.

Mon coll<u>è</u>ge e<u>st</u> gran<u>d</u>.
Les r<u>è</u>gle<u>s</u> du coll<u>è</u>ge sont tr<u>ès</u> stricte<u>s</u>.
Je pense que l'anglai<u>s</u> e<u>st</u> tr<u>ès</u> difficile.
Ma mati<u>è</u>re pr<u>é</u>f<u>é</u>r<u>é</u>e, c'e<u>st</u> la musique car c'e<u>st</u> facile.
Tou<u>s</u> le<u>s</u> jour<u>s</u>, j'ai beaucou<u>p</u> de devoir<u>s</u> e<u>t</u> c'e<u>st</u> nul!

Take extra care with how you pronounce the underlined sounds:
- silent final consonants
- ***é*** and ***è***.

Remember that these examples of a final ***e*** are silent.

Écouter 5 **Listen and check your pronunciation.**

Parler 6 **Listen to the teacher asking <u>four</u> questions that relate to the topic of Education and work. Translate each question into English and prepare your own answers in French. Then listen again and respond to the teacher.**

Make sure you use a range of adjectives to justify your opinion, and use connectives such as *car* and *parce que*.

Photo card task

Écouter **7** **Look at the exam card below and read the first part of the task. Then listen to Maxime describing the two photos. Answer the questions in English.**

1 What does Maxime say about the locations in the two photos?
2 What does Maxime say about what people are wearing?
3 What else does Maxime mention?

Photo 1

Photo 2

You will be asked to talk about the content of these photos. You must say at least one thing about each photo.

After you have spoken about the content of the photos, you will be asked questions related to any of the topics within the theme of **People and lifestyle**.

Your responses should be as **full and detailed** as possible.

Parler **8** **Prepare your own descriptions of the photos. You could mention, for example, the people, the location and what they are doing. Improve your initial version by using some of the details and vocabulary that Maxime uses in his descriptions. Then, with a partner, take turns to describe the photos.**

Sur la première photo, il y a ...

If you are saying what people are doing, use the 'they' form of the verb, e.g. *ils travaillent, ils parlent*. Remember that *-ent* is silent.

Écouter **9** **Read the second part of the task. Then listen to Maxime answering the question: *Tu aimes ton uniforme? Pourquoi?* Write down in English three things he says about his uniform.**

Écouter **10** **Now listen to Maxime answering the question: *Qu'est-ce que tu penses des règles du collège?* Write down in English two rules he mentions.**

Parler **11** **Prepare your own answers to the module 3 questions on page 226. Your responses should be as full and detailed as possible. Then practise with a partner.**

Module 3

Contrôle écrit

Grammar task

Écrire 1

Using your knowledge of grammar, copy and complete the following sentences in French. Choose the correct word from the three options.

1 Mon collège est ___.	**grande / grand / grands**
2 Nous ___ tous les jours des devoirs.	**a / ai / avons**
3 Mon uniforme est ___.	**belle / beau / beaux**
4 Les professeurs ___ gentils.	**sont / es / est**
5 Hier, j'ai ___ dans la bibliothèque.	**travailler / travaillé / travaille**

Translation

Écrire 2

Rearrange the French words to translate the English sentences.

1 My school is quite big.
collège / grand / assez / Mon / est

2 We have a lot of clubs.
clubs / Nous / avons / de / beaucoup

3 We must wear a black uniform.
porter / Il / un / noir / uniforme / faut

4 Yesterday I received a good mark in English.
note / une / anglais / reçu / en / j'ai / bonne / Hier,

Look for the capital letter to find the first word in the sentence.

Écrire 3

Translate the following sentences into French.

1 I have a blue uniform.
2 Every day, there are a lot of clubs.
3 Last week, French was very interesting.
4 Yesterday, I read a book in English.
5 At my school, we must learn music.

Think of word order.

Don't forget *le*/*la*/*l'*/*les* in front of school subjects.

Use *il faut* + infinitive.

Use *il y a*.

What tense is needed here?

Describing a photo

Écrire 4

Look at the photo in the writing exam task. Note down in English what you can say about the following:

1 How many people are there?
2 Who are they?
3 Where are they?
4 What are they doing?
5 What else can you say about the photo?

You and your French friends are looking at this photo found on your school website.

What is in this photo?

Write **five** sentences in **French**.

Lire 5 **Read Farida's answer to the exam task in exercise 4. Answer questions 1–5 in the coloured shapes.**

1 What does this phrase mean?

2 What is this number? Find two other numbers.

3 What do these verbs mean?

4 What do these verbs mean?

5 What does this phrase mean?

Sur la photo, je vois cinq personnes.

Je pense qu'il y a cinq élèves: trois filles et deux garçons.

Ils sont au collège, dans une salle de classe ou à la bibliothèque.

Ils travaillent et les trois élèves du milieu parlent.

Les élèves ne portent pas d'uniforme.

Lire 6 **Read Farida's answer again. Copy and complete the sentences below.**

1 Farida writes that there are ___ people in the photo.
2 She thinks that there are ___ boys and ___ girls.
3 She thinks that they are in ___ or in ___.
4 Three students are ___.
5 All the students are ___. They are not ___.

Écrire 7 **Look at the photo in this exam task and write your answer.**

You and your Swiss friends are sharing photos on WhatsApp.

What is in this photo?

Write **five** sentences in **French**.

- Use ***il y a*** or ***je vois*** to say what/who is in the photo.
- Use **numbers** and ***garçons*** / ***filles*** or specific words like ***élèves*** to refer to the people.
- Use ***il est*** / ***ils sont*** and ***dans*** or ***à*** to say what location they are in.
- Remember to use the present tense to say what people are doing, e.g. ***ils travaillent*** ('they are working'), ***ils parlent*** ('they are talking').
- Use ***je pense que ...*** ('I think that ...').

Vocabulaire

Key:
bold = this word will appear in higher exams only
* = this word is not on the vocabulary list, but you may use it in your own sentences

Au collège chez nous (pages 58–59)

C'est comment, la vie au collège?	*What is life at school like?*
Je suis en quatrième / troisième.	*I am in Year 9 / 10.*

Les personnes — *People*

Sur la photo, il y a ...	*In the photo, there is/are ...*
un(e) prof.	*a teacher.*
deux personnes.	*two people.*
trois jeunes.	*three young people.*
Il y a ...	*There is/are ...*
un garçon.	*a boy.*
deux garçons et une fille.	*two boys and a girl.*
deux filles.	*two girls.*
Ils portent un uniforme scolaire.	*They are wearing school uniform.*
Ils ne portent pas d'uniforme scolaire.	*They aren't wearing school uniform.*

C'est où? — *Where is it?*

Ils/Elles sont ...	*They are ...*
au collège.	*at school.*
dans une salle de classe.	*in a classroom.*
au stade.	*at the stadium.*
À gauche / droite, il y a ...	*On the left / right, there is/are ...*
un professeur.	*a teacher.*
des élèves.	*some pupils.*
des tables.	*some tables.*

Que font-ils? — *What are they doing?*

Les élèves / enfants ...	*The pupils / children ...*
discutent.	*are talking.*
mangent.	*are eating.*
jouent.	*are playing.*
Le/La prof ...	*The teacher ...*
Un garçon / Une fille ...	*A boy / A girl ...*
discute / mange / joue.	*is talking / eating / playing.*

Quelle est ta matière préférée? (pages 60–61)

Quelle est ta matière préférée et pourquoi? — *What is your favourite subject and why?*

Ma matière préférée est ...	*My favourite subject is ...*
l'anglais.	*English.*
le français.	*French.*
le théâtre.	*drama.*
la *biologie.	*biology.*
l'*EPS.	*PE.*
l'*histoire-géo.	*history and geography.*
l'informatique.	*computing/ICT.*
la musique.	*music.*
les maths.	*maths.*
la physique.	*physics.*
la technologie.	*technology.*
les sciences.	*science.*
J'aime (l'anglais) parce que c'est ...	*I like (English) because it's ...*
amusant / facile.	*fun / easy.*
génial / utile.	*great / useful.*
J'adore (*l'EPS) parce que ...	*I love (PE) because ...*
je suis *créatif/*créative.	*I'm creative.*
je suis sportif/sportive.	*I'm sporty.*
le/la prof est sympa.	*the teacher is nice.*
Je n'aime pas (les sciences) parce que c'est ...	*I don't like (science) because it's ...*
difficile.	*difficult.*
ennuyeux.	*boring.*
inutile.	*useless.*
Je déteste (*l'histoire-géo) parce que/qu' ...	*I hate (history and geography) because ...*
le/la prof est strict(e).	*the teacher is strict.*
on a trop de devoirs.	*we have too much homework.*
Je suis fort(e) / faible en ...	*I'm good / bad at ...*
anglais / informatique.	*English / ICT.*
À mon avis, c'est plus amusant que ...	*In my opinion, it's more fun than ...*
Je pense que ...	*I think that ...*
le français est plus/moins passionnant que ...	*French is more/less exciting than ...*
la musique est plus/moins intéressante que ...	*music is more/less interesting than ...*
les maths sont plus/moins utiles que ...	*maths is more/less useful than ...*

C'est injuste! (pages 62–63)

Il faut ...	*You have to ...*
porter l'uniforme scolaire.	*wear the school uniform.*
faire ses devoirs.	*do your homework.*
respecter les profs.	*respect the teachers.*
Il ne faut pas ...	*You must not ...*
arriver en retard.	*arrive late.*
manger en classe.	*eat in class.*
utiliser son portable en classe.	*use your phone in class.*

Qu'est-ce que tu penses des règles? — *What do you think of the rules?*

À mon avis, c'est ...	*In my opinion, it's ...*
Je pense que c'est ...	*I think that it's ...*
un peu / assez ...	*a bit / quite ...*
très / trop ...	*very / too ...*
important.	*important.*
juste / injuste.	*fair / unfair.*
nul.	*rubbish.*
strict.	*strict.*
*stupide.	*stupid.*
parce que/qu' / car ...	*because / as ...*
c'est essentiel pour les examens.	*it's essential for exams.*
c'est utile pour le travail scolaire.	*it's useful for schoolwork.*
il faut **respecter** les autres.	*you must respect others.*
l'uniforme scolaire (n')est (pas) *confortable / pratique.	*the school uniform is (not) comfortable / practical.*

j'ai des problèmes avec le bus.	*I have problems with the bus.*
Tu es d'accord?	*Do you agree?*
Oui, je suis d'accord.	*Yes, I agree.*
Non, je ne suis pas d'accord.	*No, I do not agree.*
Je peux porter …	*I can wear …*
J'ai partagé des vidéos de mon collège en ligne.	*I shared videos of my school online.*

As-tu fait des progrès? (pages 64–65)

J'ai / Tu as …	*I have / You have …*
Il/Elle a …	*He/She has …*
Je n'ai pas / Tu n'as pas …	*I haven't / You haven't …*
Il/Elle n'a pas …	*He/She hasn't …*
appris beaucoup de choses (en anglais).	*learned lots of things (in English).*
bu du *coca en classe.	*drunk cola in class.*
écrit une histoire extraordinaire.	*written an extraordinary story.*
fait beaucoup de progrès (en français).	*made lots of progress (in French).*
fait des efforts (en …).	*made an effort (in …).*
fait mes devoirs.	*done my homework.*
lu beaucoup de livres.	*read lots of books.*
pris des selfies en classe.	*took selfies in a lesson.*
reçu de bonnes / mauvaises notes (en musique).	*got good / bad marks (in music).*
ri pendant un examen.	*laughed during an exam.*
Je n'ai jamais oublié mes devoirs.	*I have never forgotten my homework.*
Je n'ai rien appris.	*I have learned nothing.*
Il/Elle n'a rien appris.	*He/She has learned nothing.*
En (théâtre), j'ai …	*In (drama), I have …*
Par contre, je n'ai pas …	*On the other hand, I haven't …*
En plus, j'ai …	*Also, I have …*

Souvenirs d'école (pages 66–67)

Quand tu étais petit(e), tu étais comment?	*When you were little, what were you like?*
J'étais / Je n'étais pas …	*I was / I wasn't …*
(très) travailleur/ travailleuse.	*(very) hard-working.*
Tu allais à l'école comment?	*How did you go to school?*
J'allais à l'école …	*I went to school …*
à pied / à vélo.	*on foot / by bike.*
en bus / en voiture.	*by bus / by car.*
Qu'est-ce que tu aimais, comme matières?	*Which subjects did you like?*
J'aimais le/la/l'/les …	*I liked …*
Qu'est-ce que tu faisais pendant la *pause de midi?	*What did you do during the lunch break?*
Qu'est-ce que tu faisais après l'école?	*What did you do after school?*
Je faisais / Je jouais …	*I did / I played …*
Je mangeais / Je regardais …	*I ate / I watched …*
Je lisais / J'allais …	*I read / I went …*
Il y avait un(e) prof génial(e) / nul(le). Il/Elle …	*There was a great / rubbish teacher. He/She …*
m'envoyait des cartes d'anniversaire.	*sent me birthday cards.*
n'était jamais content(e).	*was never happy.*
me parlait avec **respect** / *patience.	*spoke to me with respect / patience.*
me donnait de bonnes notes / trop de devoirs.	*gave me good grades / too much homework.*
Quand j'étais petit(e), …	*When I was little, …*
j'aimais l'école.	*I liked school.*
je jouais au *tennis pendant la *pause de midi.	*I played tennis during the lunch break.*
mon/ma prof préféré(e) s'appelait …	*my favourite teacher was called …*
C'était …	*It was …*

Les langues et l'avenir (pages 68–69)

Est-ce que tu apprenais une langue à l'école *primaire?	*Did you learn a language at primary school?*
Oui, j'apprenais …	*Yes, I learned …*
l'allemand.	*German.*
l'espagnol.	*Spanish.*
le français.	*French.*
l'*italien.	*Italian.*
Non, je n'apprenais pas de langue.	*No, I didn't learn a language.*
Tu apprends quelles langues au collège?	*Which languages are you learning at school?*
Au collège, j'apprends …	*At school, I am learning …*
En ce moment, j'apprends …, mais je n'apprends pas …	*At the moment, I am learning …, but I am not learning …*
Comment est-ce que tu vas améliorer ton (français) à l'avenir?	*How are you going to improve your (French) in the future?*
À l'avenir, je vais …	*In the future, I'm going to …*
regarder des films.	*watch films.*
écouter des *podcasts.	*listen to podcasts.*
utiliser une appli sur mon portable.	*use an app on my phone.*
lire des *magazines.	*read magazines.*
Je ne vais pas écouter de *podcasts en *italien.	*I am not going to listen to podcasts in Italian.*
Je ne regarde jamais de films français.	*I never watch French films.*
Je ne connais personne qui travaille à l'étranger.	*I don't know anyone who works abroad.*
Je ne faisais rien en classe.	*I didn't use to do anything in class.*

Module **4** **En pleine forme**

C'est bon pour la santé?

- Describing and giving opinions about dishes
- Understanding advice in the *vous*-form imperative

Des plats du monde francophone

A

la France: les religieuses
#PâtisseriesFrançaises

B

le Québec: la poutine
#PlatQuébécois

C

le Maroc: le couscous
#CouscousTraditionnel

D

la Belgique: les gaufres
#GoûtDeBelgique

E

le Sénégal: le thiéboudienne
#PlatTraditionnelSénégalais

le plat	*dish*
le riz	*rice*
le sucre	*sugar*

Il y a	**du**	chocolat. fromage / poisson. riz / sucre.
	de la	glace / sauce. viande.
	des	frites / fruits. légumes.

Écouter **1** **Look at the photos and captions, then listen. Write the letter of the correct dish. (1–5)**

Parler **2** **How do you pronounce these words? Read them out, then listen and check.**

1 le goût (*the taste*)
2 délicieux (*delicious*)
3 sain (*healthy*)
4 malsain (*unhealthy*)
5 les légumes (*vegetables*)
6 les végans (*vegans*)
7 les végétariens (*vegetarians*)

Écouter **3** **Listen and note down in English (a) if they think each dish is healthy or unhealthy, and (b) which foods are mentioned. (1–2)**

Parler **4** **In pairs, discuss the dishes in the photos above.**

- *À ton avis, le plat A, c'est sain?*
- *À mon avis, il a bon goût, mais c'est malsain.*
- *Pourquoi?*
- *Parce que dans ce plat, il y a …*

👍	👎
C'est sain.	C'est malsain.
C'est bon pour la santé.	C'est mauvais pour la santé.
Le plat a bon goût.	Je n'aime pas le goût.
C'est parfait pour les végétariens.	Ce n'est pas bon pour les végans.

MANGERBOUGER.FR

RÉPUBLIQUE FRANÇAISE
Liberté Égalité Fraternité

Santé publique France

Mangez mieux!

- Mangez au moins cinq fruits et légumes tous les jours.
- Buvez plus d'eau.

Bougez plus!

- Faites au moins une heure d'activité intense tous les jours.
- Pour les distances de moins de cinq kilomètres, allez au collège ou au travail à vélo ou à pied.
- Essayez un nouveau sport.

au moins	*at least*
Bougez plus!	*Move more!*

Dormez bien!

- Allez au lit tôt.
- Arrêtez d'utiliser votre portable au moins une heure avant de dormir.

***l'astuce** (f)* *tip*

Manger Bouger is a campaign by the French government to help people of all ages with their health and fitness. The website *mangerbouger.fr* has lots of hints and tips about healthy eating and exercise.

Note these two meanings of the word *moins*:

moins de (+ noun)	less, fewer
au moins	at least

Écouter 5 **Listen to and read the text above. Then copy and complete the translation of each piece of advice.**

1. Eat at least ___ fruits and vegetables every day.
2. Drink more ___.
3. Do at least ___ every day.
4. For distances of less than five kilometres, go to school or work ___ or ___.
5. Try a ___.
6. Go to bed ___.
7. Stop using your mobile phone at least ___ before sleeping.

G

The *vous*-form imperative is often used to give instructions or advice.
It is the present tense of the verb without the word '*vous*':

vous allez (you go) → *Allez!* (Go!)
vous buvez (you drink) → *Buvez!* (Drink!)
vous dormez (you sleep) → *Dormez!* (Sleep!)
vous faites (you make/do) → *Faites …!* (Do …!)
vous choisissez (you choose) → *Choisissez!* (Choose!)
vous mangez (you eat) → *Mangez!* (Eat!)

Page 94

Écrire 6 **Choose options from the box to write as many pieces of good and bad advice as possible. Write your sentences in both French and English.**

Example: Allez moins souvent au centre sportif. – Go to the sports centre less often.

Buvez	moins de	coca.
Mangez	plus de	frites / chocolat.
Faites	moins d' plus d'	exercice.
	de la natation plus souvent.	
Allez	moins souvent au centre sportif. au collège à pied ou à vélo. au lit plus tard / plus tôt.	
Dormez	au moins huit heures toutes les nuits.	
Essayez	un nouveau sport.	

1 Bon appétit!

- Talking about meals and mealtimes
- Using the partitive article (*du, de la, de l', des*)
- Using present and perfect tenses in translations

Écouter 1 **Listen and read. Then copy and complete the grid in English.**

	Breakfast	Lunchtime	Snack	Dinner
Drinks ...	coffee			
Eats ...				

Qu'est-ce que tu manges (normalement)?

Mes repas

Qu'est-ce que tu manges pour le petit-déjeuner?
Pour le petit-déjeuner, je bois du café et si j'ai le temps, je mange du pain.

Qu'est-ce que tu manges et bois à midi?
À midi, je mange au collège. Normalement, je choisis de la viande avec des légumes. Ensuite, je mange des fruits parce que c'est sain! Je bois du lait.

Est-ce que tu manges quelque chose après les cours?
Après les cours, si j'ai faim, je mange un sandwich. Quand j'ai soif, je bois seulement de l'eau. C'est bon pour la santé.

Normalement, qu'est-ce que tu manges le soir?
Le soir, on mange en famille. Normalement, on mange quelque chose de simple, comme du poisson. On boit du lait.

le repas	*meal*
j'ai faim	*I'm hungry*
j'ai soif	*I'm thirsty*
quelque chose de simple	*something simple*

Lire 2 **Re-read the text in exercise 1. Then find the French for the phrases below.**

1 I eat at school
2 if I have time
3 because it's healthy
4 I drink only
5 normally, I choose

G

In French, the partitive article ('some') agrees with the noun it refers to:

masculine singular	feminine singular	before a vowel sound	plural
du poisson	***de la*** viande	***de l'***eau	***des*** légumes

After a negative or a quantity, just use **de** (**d'** before a vowel):
*Je ne mange pas **de** viande.* *Je bois beaucoup **d'**eau.*

Page 94

Parler 3 **Listen and repeat the following words, paying attention to your pronunciation.**

en, souv**en**t, comm**en**t
d**an**s, m**an**ge, qu**an**d
t**em**ps, ch**am**bre
p**ain**, s**ain**, mat**in**
important, f**aim**

Take care with the pronunciation of the letter combinations **in bold** in exercise 3. They are nasal sounds. Say them at the back of your throat, as if you have a cold!

There are four different ways of spelling each sound:

- *en, an, em, am*
- *ain, in, im, aim*

Listen and repeat the tongue-twister:
*Qu**an**d j'ai f**aim**, je m**an**ge souv**en**t du p**ain**.*
*C'est **im**port**an**t de m**an**ger s**ain**.*

Écouter 4 **Listen to Raphaël talking about what he eats and drinks in a day. Copy the grid from exercise 1 and complete it in English.**

Parler 5 **Prepare your answers to the questions in exercise 1. Then, in pairs, take turns to interview your partner.**

- *Qu'est-ce que tu prends pour le petit-déjeuner?*
- *Pour le petit-déjeuner, je bois du thé et ...*

Écouter **6** **Look at the sentences and predict the missing words. Then listen and fill in the gaps.**

1 Le ___ est bon pour la santé.
2 Pour le ___, je bois du ___.
3 À midi, je mange de la ___ avec des ___.
4 C'est un ___ délicieux et ___.
5 Quand j'ai ___, je mange des ___.

- Look at the words before and after each gap.
- Spot grammar clues (e.g. *du* is followed by a masculine noun).
- Check your spelling and accents!

Lire **7** **Read the text. Is each statement below true or false?**

Bienvenue à Chef de Cuisine Junior!

Yasmina, qu'est-ce que tu as fait?

J'ai préparé un tagine car ma famille vient d'Algérie.
Ce matin, je suis allée au marché et j'ai acheté beaucoup de légumes.
Traditionnellement, dans ce plat, il y a de la viande, mais moi, j'ai mis des olives.

Le résultat de la compétition
Yasmina a gagné quatre étoiles. ★★★★☆

Jules, qu'est-ce que tu as fait?

J'ai préparé une recette malgache car ma famille vient de Madagascar.
J'ai fait ça avec du poisson, des légumes et du lait de coco.
J'ai essayé la recette chez moi et toute ma famille a adoré ça!

Le résultat de la compétition
Jules a gagné cinq étoiles. ★★★★★

l'étoile *(f)*	*star*
la recette malgache	*Madagascan recipe*
le lait de coco	*coconut milk*

1 Yasmina's family is from Algeria.
2 Yasmina went to the market yesterday.
3 Her dish contained meat.
4 Jules's meal included fish and vegetables.
5 He tried making the meal at home.
6 His family didn't like it.

G

Use the perfect tense to say what you did.
There are three parts:

subject	auxiliary verb	past participle	
Je	*suis*	*allé(e)*	I went
J'	*ai*	*fait*	I did/made
Elle	*a*	*adoré*	She loved

How many perfect tense verbs can you find in the text in exercise 7?

Page 96

Écrire **8** **Translate these sentences into French.**

1 For breakfast, I often eat bread.
2 When I am thirsty, I drink water.

- These are both in the present tense.
- Both need a partitive article (*du/ de la/ de l'/ des*).
- Take care with where you place the word for 'often'.

3 This morning, I made a French dish.
4 I bought lots of fish at the market.

- These are both in the perfect tense.
- Take care with where you place the word for 'French'.
- Use *de* after *beaucoup*.

2 Bien dans ma peau

- Talking about good mental health
- Using modal verbs (*devoir*, *vouloir*, *pouvoir*)
- Giving advice

Écouter 1 **Listen to the teenagers talking about how they feel and why. Note down (a) the letter of the correct emoji, and (b) the reason in English. (1–4)**

Comment ça va aujourd'hui?

Je suis …

a  heureux/heureuse

b  triste

c  fatigué(e)

d  calme

Écouter 2 **Listen again. Match the advice given below to the speakers. (1–4) Some of the advice may be used more than once.**

a Fais de la cuisine. (*Do some cooking.*)

b Parle avec moi. (*Speak to me.*)

c Va au lit. (*Go to bed.*)

d Reste calme. (*Stay calm.*)

e Écoute de la musique. (*Listen to music.*)

G

You use the *tu*-form imperative to give advice or instructions to someone you know well.

The *tu*-form of the imperative works like this:
tu écoute<u>s</u> (you listen) → *Écoute!* (Listen!)
tu va<u>s</u> (you go) → *Va!* (Go!)
tu reste<u>s</u> (you stay) → *Reste!* (Stay!)
Note that you drop the final 's' from the verb.

In the negative, *ne/n'* … *pas* goes around the verb:
<u>*Ne*</u> *parle* <u>*pas*</u>. (Don't speak.)

Page 94

Parler 3 **In pairs, put yourselves in the place of the teenagers in these two photos. Ask and answer questions about how you are doing.**

- *Comment ça va aujourd'hui?*
- *Je suis triste.*
- *Pourquoi es-tu triste?*
- *Je suis triste parce que j'ai perdu mon chien.*
- *Reste calme et parle avec moi!*

Comment ça va aujourd'hui? Ça ne va pas?	Ça va très bien. Ça ne va pas bien.
Pourquoi es-tu …?	Je suis (un peu / assez / très / vraiment) triste, car … Je suis heureux/heureuse parce que …

Lire **4** **Read the forum posts. Write the letter of the correct piece of advice below for each problem. Then listen and check. (1–4)**

D'ados à ados

Ne continue pas en silence – partage ton problème ici! D'autres ados donnent des conseils.

1 
Le soir, j'adore jouer à des jeux vidéo contre mes amis. Mais je dors mal.
@megajeuxfan

2 
J'ai beaucoup de travail scolaire en ce moment. Je suis tout le temps inquiète avec les examens.
@mimilou5

3 
En ce moment, je suis triste car je ne m'entends pas bien avec mon père. À mon avis, il est trop strict.
@anon2012

4 
Mon meilleur ami a changé de collège et maintenant je suis tout seul – je dois trouver de nouveaux amis, mais comment?
@basketsrouges

a Tu dois parler avec tes profs. Ils peuvent t'aider. Bouge un peu aussi – fais une activité.

b Je suis sûr qu'il t'aime. Parle avec lui. Tu peux être heureuse.

c Tu dois arrêter de passer du temps devant l'ordinateur avant d'aller au lit. C'est difficile de dormir après les jeux vidéo; les écrans sont mauvais.

d Si tu veux trouver de nouveaux amis, tu peux devenir membre d'un club sportif. Cherche en ligne ou sur les réseaux sociaux.

l'ado (m/f)	*adolescent, teenager*
donner des conseils	*to give advice*

G

These are key modal verbs in the present tense:

devoir *(to have to/must)*	**pouvoir** *(to be able to/can)*	**vouloir** *(to want (to))*
je dois	je peux	je veux
tu dois	tu peux	tu veux
il/elle/on doit	il/elle peut	il/elle veut
nous devons	nous pouvons	nous voulons
vous devez	vous pouvez	vous voulez
ils/elles doivent	ils/elles peuvent	ils/elles veulent

Modal verbs are usually followed by another verb in its <u>infinitive</u> form:

*Tu **dois** <u>rester</u> calme.*
You must stay calm.

*Je **veux** <u>dormir</u> mieux.*
I want to sleep better.

Negatives go around the modal verb:
*Il <u>ne</u> **peut** <u>pas</u> parler avec son prof.*
He can't talk to his teacher.

Page 95

Écrire **5** **Copy out the parallel translations, completing them with the missing words.**

1	I want to change ___.	Je ___ changer de collège.
2	She must ___ ___ ___.	___ doit trouver son chien.
3	He wants to go to a ___ ___.	Il ___ ___ à un cours de yoga.
4	___ ___ stay calm!	On ne peut pas rester ___!
5	You must work this weekend.	___ ___ ___ ce week-end.
6	You can be ___!	___ ___ être heureux!

The closed sound -**eu** rhymes with '*d**eu**x*'.

Listen and repeat the sentences.
*Je p**eu**x être h**eu**r**eu**x.*
*Il v**eu**t montrer qu'il p**eu**t être séri**eu**x.*
*Je ne v**eu**x pas faire mes devoirs.*

Écrire **6** **Write a reply to this post on the *D'ados à ados* forum.**

Je suis souvent très inquiète et, au collège, je n'ai pas d'énergie. Pendant les cours, je ne peux pas écouter et je ne veux pas parler avec mes profs. Donnez-moi des conseils, s'il vous plaît!

Tu peux …	Parle …
Tu dois …	Fais …
Si tu veux …	

3 Bien choisir pour ta santé

- Describing unhealthy lifestyle choices
- Using the perfect tense (with both *être* and *avoir*)
- Taking part in a role-play about lifestyle

Lire 1 **Read the texts. Find the French in bold for the phrases below.**

Comprendre les risques

On peut dire que les cigarettes, c'est une drogue. **Fumer** reste un problème grave chez les jeunes. C'est **une habitude qui est dangereuse** pour la santé. Par exemple, si on fume une cigarette ou si **on vapote** quand on a faim, on peut avoir mal au cœur ou mal à la tête.

Le tabac et le vapotage créent aussi des risques plus importants, comme par exemple le cancer.

Un mode de vie sédentaire peut avoir des effets dangereux sur **votre corps**. Si on passe de longues heures sur une chaise, on peut avoir des problèmes au cœur ou mal au dos, aux bras et aux jambes.

En plus, si on passe tout son temps devant son écran, on peut avoir mal aux yeux. Et si on écoute de la musique trop fort, on peut avoir des problèmes aux oreilles. Il est important de faire des pauses fréquentes pour protéger **votre santé physique et mentale**.

le risque	*risk*
la drogue	*drug*
le tabac	*tobacco*
sédentaire	*sedentary, inactive*
l'effet (m)	*effect*

1 a habit that is dangerous
2 a sedentary lifestyle
3 to smoke / smoking
4 we vape
5 your body
6 your physical and mental health

G

To say that something hurts, aches or is sore, use *avoir mal à* + a noun.

à + ***le*** = ***au*** *à* + ***les*** = ***aux***

masculine noun	**feminine** noun	**plural** noun
J'ai mal ***au*** *dos.* I have a sore back.	*J'ai mal* ***à la*** *tête.* I have a headache.	*J'ai mal* ***aux*** *yeux.* I have sore eyes.

Note: *le cœur* means 'heart', but *avoir mal au cœur* means 'to feel sick'.

Lire 2 **Re-read the texts in exercise 1. Select the three correct statements.**

A Smoking remains a serious problem amongst young people.
B Smoking or vaping when you are hungry can give you an earache.
C Smoking can lead to cancer.
D Sitting down for too long can hurt your eyes.
E Taking frequent breaks from your screen can help your mental and physical health.

Parler 3 **In pairs, take turns to read out the texts from exercise 1. Give feedback on each other's pronunciation.**

Écouter 4 **Listen to the podcast about alcohol. Fill in the gaps. (1–4)**

1 C'est un problème très grave chez les ______.
2 Même si cela vous donne confiance, boire de l'alcool quand on est jeune peut avoir des conséquences très ______.
3 Si vous avez ______ ou si vous avez ______, buvez de l'eau ou un jus de fruit.
4 C'est moins ______ pour votre ______.

These expressions in French use *avoir* (to have) rather than *être* (to be).

avoir chaud	to be hot
avoir froid	to be cold
avoir faim	to be hungry
avoir soif	to be thirsty
avoir peur	to be afraid

Écouter 5 **Listen to people talking to the doctors. Then copy and complete the grid in English. (1–3)**

	What is the issue?	What happened?	What advice is given?
1			

24 heures aux urgences

malade	*ill*
la gorge	*throat*
tousser	*to cough*

G

Remind yourself how to form the **imperative** using the grammar boxes on pages 83 and 86, then read the examples below.

***tu*-form**	***vous*-form**	
Reste *au lit.*	***Restez*** *au lit.*	Stay in bed.
Va *à l'hôpital.*	***Allez*** *à l'hôpital.*	Go to the hospital.
Ne ***bouge*** *pas.*	*Ne* ***bougez*** *pas.*	Don't move.

Page 94

Lire 6 **Read the A&E doctor's diary entry for a day at the hospital. Answer the questions in English.**

Journal de Samir, médecin aux urgences

09h00: *On peut déjà entendre les sirènes de l'ambulance dans la rue. Une nouvelle journée aux urgences commence.*

09h30: *Une ambulance arrive à l'hôpital. Un patient a eu un accident. Il a perdu beaucoup de sang.*

10h00: *Je pose des questions au patient. Il explique qu'il est tombé dans la cuisine chez lui. Apparemment, il dansait. Il est clair qu'il a bu de l'alcool au petit-déjeuner.*

14h15: *Le patient retourne dans sa chambre d'hôpital, fatigué après l'opération. Il doit rester au lit.*

17h20: ***Les heures passent lentement même si j'ai beaucoup à faire. Le patient dort un peu, mais c'est difficile car il y a toujours beaucoup de bruit à l'hôpital. Il demande s'il peut fumer dans la chambre, mais c'est interdit.***

21h30: *Le patient peut quitter l'hôpital. Je recommande au patient de ne pas boire d'alcool. Le patient doit prendre rendez-vous chez son propre médecin dans une semaine.*

22h00: *Je peux rentrer chez moi. Ma journée aux urgences est enfin finie.*

le sang *blood*

1 What can you hear on the street?
2 What happened to the patient?
3 What does the patient ask?
4 What does Samir recommend to the patient?

G

You use the **perfect tense** to say what happened in the past.

Most verbs use *avoir* as the auxiliary verb:
J'ai eu un accident. I had an accident

But some verbs use *être* as the auxiliary verb:
Je suis tombé(e) de vélo. I fell off my bike.
For verbs that use *être*, the past participle must agree with the subject:
Elle est allée à l'hôpital. She went to the hospital.

Lire 7 **Translate the paragraph in blue in exercise 6 into English.**

Parler 8 **Prepare answers to this role-play. Then, in pairs, take turns to play each part.**

1 • *Qu'est-ce qui ne va pas?*
■ *[Say what's wrong.]*

2 • *Qu'est-ce que tu as fait?*
■ *[Say what happened. (Give* ***two*** *details.)]*

3 • *Que penses-tu des cigarettes?*
■ *[Give* ***one*** *opinion about smoking.]*

4 ■ **?** *[Ask your friend a question about alcohol.]*
• *Give* ***one*** *opinion about alcohol.*

5 • *Quels sont les dangers d'un style de vie sédentaire?*
■ *[Explain the dangers of a sedentary lifestyle. (Give* ***two*** *details.)]*

4 Je change ma vie

- Saying what you are going to do to improve your life
- Using the near future tense
- Using *plus* and *moins*

Écouter **1** **Listen and read. Then write the letter of the correct photo for each speaker. (1–6)**

Qu'est-ce que tu vas faire pour améliorer ta vie?

1 Je vais manger plus de légumes.

2 Je vais prendre des cours de danse.

3 Je vais moins penser à moi et je vais aider les autres.

4 Je vais être plus patient(e) avec ma petite sœur.

5 Je vais aller à la piscine chaque week-end.

6 Je ne vais pas faire mes devoirs à la dernière minute.

les autres *other people*

a

b

c

d

e

f

Lire **2** **Translate the sentences in exercise 1 into English.**

G

Use the near future tense to say 'going to' (or will) do something.
Put the infinitive of the verb you want to use after the present tense of the verb ***aller***.

je ***vais*** *manger*	I am going to eat
tu ***vas*** *aider*	you are going to help
il/elle/on ***va*** *travailler*	he/she is / we are going to work

Negatives in the near future tense go around the part of *aller*.
Je ne vais pas manger de frites. I am not going to eat chips.

Page 96

Écrire **3** **In pairs, look at the verbs in the box and decide if they are an infinitive or a part of *aller*. Copy and complete the text, using the verbs. Then listen and check.**

Example: 1 *Je vais faire plus de vélo.*

va travailler être faire vais parler va boire avoir

Les bonnes résolutions

Moi – Alessandro

Santé

1 Je vais ____ plus de vélo.

2 Mon ami Louis ____ jouer au tennis tous les jours.

3 Ma mère Sylvie va ____ plus d'eau.

Famille

4 Je ____ aider ma mère et mes grands-parents.

5 Mon ami Louis ne va pas ____ impatient avec son frère.

6 Ma mère Sylvie va ____ une meilleure attitude avec ses sœurs.

Collège

7 Je ne vais pas ____ en même temps que la prof.

8 Mon ami Louis va ____ plus dur en cours de maths.

9 Ma mère Sylvie ____ arriver avant ses élèves.

Parler 4 **In pairs, take turns to answer each of the criticisms by saying what you are going to do differently in the future.**

- *Tu ne manges pas assez de légumes.*
- *À l'avenir, je vais manger plus de légumes.*

1 Tu ne manges pas assez de légumes.
2 Tu ne fais pas assez de sport.
3 Tu ne travailles pas sérieusement au collège.
4 Tu n'aides pas à la maison.
5 Tu n'es pas très patient(e).
6 Tu ne vas pas souvent au centre sportif.

- Use *plus* to say 'more' (or 'more' + adjective/adverb):

Je vais aider plus.	I am going to help more.
Je vais être plus calme.	I am going to be calmer.

- Use *plus* **de/d'** to say 'more' + noun:

Tu vas manger plus ***de*** *fruits.*	You are going to eat more fruit.
Je vais faire plus ***d'****exercice.*	I am going to do more exercise.

Lire 5 **Look at the *Mission Bien-Être* calendar and read the two blogs. For each blogger, write down in French the three days on the calendar that have inspired them to change their lifestyle.**

Mission Bien-Être Plus heureux – Plus sympa – Tous les jours

le rêve *dream*

lundi	mardi	mercredi	jeudi	vendredi	samedi	dimanche
Aujourd'hui, mange bien. Choisis des repas sains.	Bouge. Fais quelque chose d'actif.	Ne va pas au lit tard. Reste calme.	Apprends quelque chose de nouveau.	Écris tes rêves et tes projets pour l'avenir.	Dis bonjour à tes voisins/voisines.	N'utilise pas ta tablette une heure avant de dormir.

The calendar suggestions use the *tu*-form imperative of the verb:
mange *bien* (**eat** well)
ne ***va*** *pas au lit tard* (don't **go** to bed late)

1

Je veux être plus actif. Je vais faire du vélo tous les jours. Je vais aussi commencer une nouvelle activité – demain, je vais prendre un cours de guitare! Je veux manger moins de choses sucrées. Je vais aller au marché pour acheter des légumes. Je vais préparer des repas végétariens sains.
Clément

sucré(e) *sweet*

2

Je veux mieux dormir, alors je vais aller au lit plus tôt. Je veux avoir plus d'amis, donc je vais parler avec la nouvelle famille qui habite dans l'appartement numéro dix. Je veux beaucoup voyager. Je vais écrire mes projets de vacances.
Nadia

Écouter 6 **Listen to each person and note down (a) what they want to do, and (b) what they are going to do in the future. (1–3)**

Both *je vais* and *je veux* are followed by an infinitive:

je vais + infinitive	I am going to …
je veux + infinitive	I want to …

Écrire 7 **Write a list of five resolutions for yourself.**

Je veux Je vais	faire	plus de vélo. une nouvelle activité. quelque chose d'actif.
	être	plus actif/active. en forme.
	manger plus de / moins de	fruits / légumes. chocolat / fromage.
	jouer	au tennis. au rugby.
	aller	au lit plus tôt.

5 Mieux vivre

- Talking about lifestyle changes
- Using the imperfect, present and near future tenses
- Distinguishing between tenses when listening

Écouter 1 **Listen to the podcast and read the texts. Copy and complete the sentences in English.**

Quand tu étais plus jeune, ta vie était comment?

En ce moment, comment est ta vie?

À l'avenir, qu'est-ce que tu vas faire?

- Quand j'étais ado, j'habitais dans un quartier difficile à Paris. J'étais membre d'un gang et je n'étais pas heureuse.
- Maintenant, j'étudie la musique et j'écris des chansons. Je vais dans des collèges et je parle de ma vie aux élèves.
- À l'avenir, je vais aider d'autres jeunes comme moi. Je vais changer des vies, avec la musique et la danse.

- Quand j'étais plus jeune, je ne faisais rien le soir, car je n'avais pas beaucoup d'amis. J'étais timide et j'étais victime de racisme. C'était très difficile.
- Maintenant, j'ai une chaîne sur YouTube et je lutte contre le racisme. Je suis plus fort et plus heureux.
- À l'avenir, je vais être homme politique et je vais travailler pour l'égalité. Je ne vais jamais accepter l'inégalité.

1 Sarah used to live ___. She was a member of ___.
2 Now she studies ___ and she ___. She talks to students about ___.
3 In the future, she is going to help ___. She is going to change ___ with ___.
4 Malik didn't use to have ___. He was ___ and he was a victim of racism.
5 Now, he ___ a YouTube channel and he fights against racism. He is ___ and ___.
6 In the future, he is going ___ a politician. He is going to work for ___.

la chaîne	*channel*
lutter pour/contre	*to fight for/against*
l'inégalité *(f)*	*inequality*

G

There are two parts to most **negatives** in French:

ne ... pas not
ne ... rien nothing
ne ... jamais never

Remember that the two parts of the negative go around the verb:

*Je **n'**étais **pas** fort(e).* I wasn't strong.
*Je **ne** vais **jamais** être homme politique.*
I am never going to be a politician.

Lire 2 **Re-read the texts in exercise 1. Then find four phrases in the negative and translate them into English.**

Lire 3 **In exercise 1, find at least four verbs in the imperfect tense, four in the present tense and four in the near future tense. Translate them into English.**

G

You use:

- the imperfect tense to say what you used to do
  *je travaill**ais*** (I used to work)
- the present tense to say what you do now
  *je travaill**e*** (I work)
- the near future tense to say what you are going to do
  *je **vais** travaill**er*** (I am going to work)

Watch out for these irregular verbs:

	imperfect	present	near future
avoir (to have)	*j'avais* (I used to have)	*j'ai* (I have)	*je vais avoir* (I am going to have)
être (to be)	*j'étais* (I used to be)	*je suis* (I am)	*je vais être* (I am going to be)
faire (to do/make)	*je faisais* (I used to do/make)	*je fais* (I do/make)	*je vais faire* (I am going to do/make)

Page 97

Écouter 4 **Listen and read. Then fill in the gaps with the verb(s) that you hear. Then note what tense the sentence is in (imperfect, present or near future). (1–4)**

Example: 1 *je vais être, ...*

1 À l'avenir, ___ professeure de danse. ___ avec des jeunes handicapés.
2 Quand ___ jeune, ___ beaucoup d'amis. ___ heureux.
3 Maintenant, ___ triste. ___ beaucoup d'espoir pour l'avenir.
4 ___ les victimes de racisme en ligne. ___ pour l'égalité.

Lire
5 **Read the text and choose the correct word to complete each sentence.**

Sadio Mané est joueur de foot. Il est né au Sénégal et quand il était petit, il habitait dans un petit village. «La vie était dure», dit Sadio.

À dix-neuf ans, il a commencé sa carrière professionnelle avec l'équipe française de Metz. Il a ensuite joué pour les équipes de Southampton, Liverpool et Bayern Munich.

Maintenant, Sadio gagne des milliers d'euros! Pourtant, il reste modeste et il est très généreux: il a déjà payé pour la construction d'un lycée et d'un hôpital dans son village au Sénégal.

À l'avenir, Sadio va continuer à aider les Sénégalais. Il va travailler pour l'association *Right to Play*, qui lutte pour les droits des enfants. «Je crois que la base du succès, c'est le travail, de croire en ses rêves et le respect de soi-même», dit-il.

il est né	*he was born*
des milliers	*thousands*
***l'association** (f)*	*charity*
croire en ses rêves	*to believe in one's (your) dreams*
soi-même	*oneself (yourself)*

1 Sadio Mané grew up in **France** / **Senegal** / **Canada**.
2 His early life was **happy** / **easy** / **hard**.
3 He started his professional career when he was **seventeen** / **eighteen** / **nineteen**.
4 Sadio earns thousands of **pounds** / **euros** / **dollars**.
5 In the future, he is going to **work for** / **help** / **give money to** *Right to Play*.

Écouter
6 **Listen to Sacha. Copy and complete the table in English.**

When he was young	At the moment	In the future

Parler
7 **Read the notes on the two celebrities with your partner, then create a podcast interview with one of them. Use the questions from exercise 1.**

Grew up in Ivory Coast (*en Côte d'Ivoire*)
Used to work in a hotel
Now a politician (*femme politique*) in France
Works for the rights of workers (*les travailleurs*)
Is going to work for equality

Grew up in France
Used to play tennis and basketball
Now writes songs and poems (*des poèmes*)
Is also an actor (*acteur*)
Is going to sing and act (*jouer*) in films

Écrire
8 **Imagine you are the other famous person from exercise 7. Write a short article about your life.**

Example:
Je m'appelle …
J'habitais …

Quand j'étais jeune, j'habitais …
Je travaillais dans …
Je jouais …

Maintenant, je travaille pour …
Je suis …
J'écris …

À l'avenir, je vais continuer à …
Je vais chanter …
Je vais jouer …

Rachel Keke used to clean hotel rooms. In 2019, she organised a successful strike for better pay and working conditions for hotel cleaners. She became an MP in 2022.

Grand Corps Malade (real name Fabien Marsaud) is a slam poet, actor and musician. He changed his name after a diving accident which damaged his spine and affected his legs. Can you work out what his new name means?

Grammaire 1

The partitive article (Unit 1, page 84)

Écrire 1

Axel's parents want him to eat properly while they are out for the day. Look at their message. Imagine you are Axel and write out your meal plan in full.

Example: Pour le petit-déjeuner, je mange du pain et je bois ...

Axel, voici ton plan repas:

Le petit-déjeuner – le pain, le café

Le déjeuner – le riz, l'eau

Après l'école – les fruits, le thé

Le dîner – la viande, les légumes, le lait

Pas de chocolat, pas de frites

You use the partitive article to say 'some'. It must agree with the noun it refers to.

masculine singular	feminine singular	before a vowel sound	plural
du *poisson*	**de la** *viande*	**de l'***eau*	**des** *légumes*

After a **negative** or a **quantity**, these shorten to de (d' before a vowel):

Je ne mange pas de poisson. I don't eat fish.

Je bois beaucoup d'eau. I drink a lot of water.

In French, you use the partitive article even when we would not use 'some' in English:

*Je mange **du** poisson avec **des** légumes.*
I eat fish with vegetables.

Je ne mange pas de viande ou de fromage.
I don't eat meat or cheese.

Parler 2

Your French exchange partner has never been to the UK before. They ask you about some typical dishes. In pairs, take turns to be the exchange partner. Create three conversations, using the ideas below.

- *Qu'est-ce que c'est, le Lancashire hotpot?*
- *Dans ce repas, il y a du/de la/des ...*

Lancashire hotpot – meat, vegetables

Trifle – cake, fruit

Welsh rarebit – bread, cheese

The imperative (Culture, page 83, Unit 2, page 86 and Unit 3, page 89)

Écrire 3

Read the grammar boxes about the imperative on pages 83, 86 and 89. Then put the French words into the correct order to translate these sentences into French.

1 Eat lots of fruit and vegetables. — de fruits / Mangez / et / de légumes / beaucoup

2 Talk to your family or to your friends. — Parle / tes amis / ou / ta famille / avec / avec

3 Do some sport – play football. — au football / Faites / du sport – / jouez

4 Don't watch TV – go to bed. — au lit / Ne / pas / regarde / la télé – / va

Lire 4

Note down if each sentence in exercise 3 is in the *tu*- or *vous*-form of the imperative.

Écouter 5 **Listen. Which form of the imperative do you hear? Write *tu* or *vous* and choose the correct English translation from the box. (1–5)**

Example: 1 *tu – Listen to some music.*

Go to school on foot.
Listen to some music.
Stay in bed.
Do some exercise.
Go to the sports centre.

With -***er*** verbs in the imperative:
- the *tu*-form ending is silent: *Écout**e**!*
- the *vous*-form ending is pronounced: *Écout**ez**!*

Irregular verbs are different in spelling and sound:

	tu-form	***vous-form***
aller (*to go*)	Va	Allez
faire (*to do/make*)	Fais	Faites

The present tense of modal verbs (Unit 2, page 87)

The modal verbs *pouvoir*, *vouloir* and *devoir* are usually followed by an infinitive.

pouvoir (*to be able to, can*)	**vouloir** (*to want (to)*)	**devoir** (*to have to, must*)
je peux	je veux	je dois
tu peux	tu veux	tu dois
il/elle/on peut	il/elle/on veut	il/elle/on doit
nous pouvons	nous voulons	nous devons
vous pouvez	vous voulez	vous devez
ils/elles peuvent	ils/elles veulent	ils/elles doivent

The underlined parts of each modal verb are pronounced the same. Think carefully about which spelling of the verb you need in exercise 6.

Écouter 6 **Look at the sentences and predict what modal verb goes in each gap. There is often more than one possibility. Then listen and fill in the gaps.**

1 Je ___ trouver de nouveaux amis. Qu'est-ce que je ___ faire?
2 Il ___ essayer de parler avec lui s'il ___ être plus heureux.
3 Si tu ___ mieux dormir, tu ___ arrêter de regarder ton portable au lit.
4 Mon meilleur ami ne ___ pas parler avec ses parents. Vous ___ l'aider?
5 Mon frère et moi ___ être en forme, donc nous ___ faire plus de sport.

Parler 7 **In pairs, take turns to read out the advice poster. Give feedback on each other's pronunciation. Then listen and check.**

Pay special attention to the pronunciation of these sounds:

eu – count to two in French. These words rhyme with '*d**eu**x*' or '*délici**eu**x*'.
ou – make a small 'o' with your lips to form this sound (*n**ou**s*, *t**ou**j**ou**rs*).
oi – count to three in French. This sound is in '*tr**oi**s*' or '*m**oi***'.

Si tu veux être heureux ou heureuse ...

- Tu dois avoir une vie active. Tu peux faire du sport ou essayer une nouvelle activité.

- Tu dois bien dormir. Tu peux lire un bon livre avant de dormir.

- Tu dois parler avec quelqu'un quand tu as des problèmes. Tu peux toujours parler avec nous.

si *if*

Lire 8 **Find the French for the following modal verb expressions in the poster in exercise 7. Write them out in English and French.**

1 You must have
2 You can read
3 You must speak
4 If you want to be
5 You can do
6 You must sleep well

Grammaire 2

The perfect tense (Unit 1, page 85 and Unit 3, page 89)

Lire 1 **Copy out the sentences, filling in the gaps with the correct auxiliary verb and past participle from the box. Then listen and check.**

ai fait   ai pris   ai fini   ai commencé
avons mangé   ai trouvé   ai servi   suis allé

1 Le week-end dernier, j'___ un gâteau d'anniversaire pour ma mère.

2 D'abord, je ___ au supermarché pour acheter tous les ingrédients.

3 J'ai cherché des recettes en ligne et j'___ une recette pour un gâteau au chocolat.

4 J'___ à préparer le gâteau le matin, et j'___ le gâteau à 14h30.

5 Le soir, ma famille et moi ___ ensemble et en dessert, j'___ mon gâteau.

6 Le gâteau était vraiment délicieux! J'___ une photo pour Instagram.

Zachary

You use the perfect tense to say what you did or have done.
Remember, there are two parts to the perfect tense:

1 the auxiliary verb (part of *avoir* or *être*)
2 the past participle.

Different groups of verbs work in different ways:

- Regular -**er** verbs, e.g. *regard**er*** (to watch)
  *j'**ai** regardé* (I watched)
- Regular -**ir** verbs, e.g. *chois**ir*** (to choose)
  *elle **a** choisi* (she chose)
- Regular -**re** verbs, e.g. *attend**re*** (to wait)
  *nous **avons** attendu* (we waited)
- Some verbs are irregular, e.g. *prendre* (to take)
  *j'**ai** pris* (I took)
- Some verbs use *être*, e.g. *aller* (to go)
  *elle **est** allée* (she went)

You may not know every word in the sentences, or every verb in the box, but can you guess what any new words might be according to the context and the other words in the sentence?

The near future tense (Unit 4, page 90)

Lire 2 **Separate out these words to make accurate near future tense sentences.**

Example: 1 *Je vais manger des frites.*

1 jevaismangerdesfrites
2 ellevaboireducoca
3 onvaprendredescoursdefoot
4 nousallonsfairedelanatation
5 ilsvontaiderlesautres

For the near future tense, use the correct part of ***aller*** followed by the infinitive:

*je **vais** manger*	I am going to eat
*tu **vas** parler*	you are going to speak
*il/elle/on **va** être*	he/she is / we are going to be
*nous **allons** avoir*	we are going to have
*vous **allez** faire*	you are going to do/make
*ils/elles **vont** aller*	they are going to go

Negatives go around the part of ***aller***.

*Je ne **vais** pas faire mes devoirs.*
I am not going to do my homework.

Lire 3 **Translate the sentences in exercise 2 into English.**

Example: 1 *I am going to eat chips.*

Écrire 4

Copy and complete each sentence in the near future tense with the correct part of *aller* and the correct infinitive from the box. Then make up <u>three</u> sentences in the near future tense using the remaining three infinitives.

Example: 1 *Elle **va aller** à la piscine tous les week-ends.*

acheter	être
aller	faire
avoir	jouer
écouter	manger

1 Elle ___ ___ à la piscine tous les week-ends.
2 Il ___ ___ plus gentil avec sa petite sœur.
3 Tu ___ ___ plus d'efforts au collège, surtout en maths.
4 Nous ___ ___ au handball chaque semaine.
5 Ils ___ ___ cinq fruits ou légumes tous les jours.

Using three tenses (imperfect, present and near future) (Unit 5, page 92)

Parler 5

Read the grammar box on page 92. Then, in pairs, play 'tenses tennis'. Take turns to change each present tense sentence into both the imperfect and the near future tenses.

- *J'habite à Toulouse.*
- *J'habitais à Toulouse.*
- *Je vais habiter à Toulouse.*

1 J'habite à Toulouse. → *(imperfect)* → *(near future)*
2 J'ai une chaîne sur YouTube. → *(imperfect)* → *(near future)*
3 Je travaille dans un magasin. → *(imperfect)* → *(near future)*
4 Je suis célèbre. → *(imperfect)* → *(near future)*
5 J'ai beaucoup d'amis. → *(imperfect)* → *(near future)*
6 J'aide mes grands-parents. → *(imperfect)* → *(near future)*

Écrire 6

Translate the passage fully into French by changing the English words and phrases in bold.

When j'étais **young**, je **used to go swimming** tous les week-ends.
Maintenant, **I don't do** de sport. **I go to school** en bus.
À **the future**, je vais **take dance lessons**.

C'est parti!

Écouter 7

Listen and complete the sentences with the missing word or words. Remember, some verb forms sound the same (e.g. *je <u>veux</u>, il/elle <u>veut</u>*), so think carefully about which spelling you need.

Write something down for every gap, even if you're not 100% sure.

1 D'habitude, le midi au collège, je ___ du poisson avec des frites.
2 Ma sœur ___ être végane.
3 Pour être en forme, on ___ avoir une vie active.
4 En ce moment, je ne ___ pas beaucoup de sport.
5 J'ai mal à la jambe parce que je ___ tombé de vélo.
6 À l'avenir, je ___ aller au collège en bus.
7 Quand j'étais plus jeune, j'___ souvent triste.
8 Un jour, je ___ être professeur de sport dans un collège.

Module 4

Contrôle de lecture et d'écoute

Reading

Lire 1

Staying healthy. **What does Nadia's blog say about these events? Write P for something that happened in the past, N for something that is happening now or F for something that will happen in the future.**

Avant, je n'étais pas très active, mais maintenant je pense que faire une activité sportive est important pour être en bonne santé. Maintenant, je fais du yoga trois fois par semaine avec mon amie. Je mange moins de choses grasses* et au moins cinq fruits et légumes chaque jour.

La semaine prochaine, je vais commencer à aller au lit moins tard tous les soirs. Le ***sommeil*** est important. Il faut dormir au moins huit heures par nuit.

gras/grasse(s) *fatty, oily, greasy*

1 not being very active
2 being active with a friend
3 eating fruit and vegetables
4 going to bed early

Read Nadia's blog again. What is *le sommeil*? Write the correct letter.

A	eating
B	sleeping
C	watching TV

Look for time phrases to help you work out whether something is in the past, present or future.

Look at the sentences before and after the one containing the word *sommeil*. Make a list of the words there that could help you decide between the three options: 'eating', 'sleeping' and 'watching TV'.

Lire 2

Eat well. **You read a guide about healthy eating.**

Tout le monde doit penser à sa santé, pas seulement les enfants ou les ados. Voici des recommandations pour être en bonne santé.

- Marche et cours! Ces activités ne sont pas chères et ne prennent pas beaucoup de temps. Tu peux aller à l'école à pied, tu peux descendre du bus cinq minutes avant ton arrêt ou aller au parc et courir 30 minutes.
- Mange de la nourriture saine! Maintenant, dans notre société, il est facile d'acheter de la nourriture qui n'est pas saine, comme du fast-food, des biscuits et des chips*. En plus, on mange trop vite et toute la journée. Le ***grignotage***, ce n'est pas sain. Il faut arrêter de manger tout le temps!

les chips *(f) crisps*

1 Answer the following questions in **English**.
a According to the guide, what are two advantages of walking and running?
b According to the guide, what are two disadvantages of the way we eat in our society?

2 Read the last three sentences again. What is *le* ***grignotage***? Write the correct letter: **A**, **B** or **C**.

A	sleeping
B	buying
C	snacking

This question is testing your ability to work out the meaning of a word that you haven't seen before (e.g. by looking at the **context** in which it is used).

Lire 3

Translation. **Translate these sentences into English.**

Take care to get your tenses right.

Don't forget to translate these words.

1 Je mange beaucoup de légumes.
2 Il faut boire de l'eau tous les jours.
3 Je vais commencer une nouvelle activité.
4 On ne doit pas manger tout le temps. Ce n'est pas sain.
5 Hier, j'ai marché avec mes amis pour aller au collège.

Listening

Écouter 4

Fast food. **You hear Fathia and Arthur talking about fast food.**

1 What do Fathia's parents think of fast food? Give two details in **English**.

Listen out for 'distractors' (words or phrases that are mentioned but not needed for any of your answers). These test your ability to listen for **detail**, not simply gist. You need to listen out for Fathia's parents' opinion, not Fathia's.

2 What does Arthur like about fast food? Write the two correct letters.

A	the ability to eat any time
B	the rapidity of the service
C	the price
D	the choice

Think of words that can be associated with each of the four options.

Écouter 5

A bad day! **You hear some people talking about their problems. What is the problem in each case? Write the correct letter. (1–4)**

A	technology
B	an accident
C	homework
D	sleeping
E	illness
F	weather

Écouter 6

Dictation. **You will now hear four short sentences. Listen carefully and, using your knowledge of French sounds, write in French exactly what you hear for each sentence.**

Listen out for:
- nasal sounds like ***in***, ***an***, ***ain*** and ***en***
- ***é*** and ***ai***
- ***oi***.

Module 4

Contrôle oral

Role-play

Parler 1 **Look at the role-play card and prepare what you are going to say.**

- You are talking to your French friend.
- Your teacher will play the part of your friend and will speak first.
- You should address your friend as *tu*.
- When you see this – **?** – you will have to ask a question.

In order to score full marks, you must include a verb in your response to each task.

1 Say what you have for breakfast. (Give **one** detail.)
2 Describe your favourite meal. (Give **one** detail.)
? 3 Ask your friend a question about food.
4 Say what activity you do to stay healthy. (Give **one** detail.)
5 Give **one** opinion about this activity.

Start with *Je mange* or *Je bois*.

You could start with *Je préfère …* or *Mon repas préféré …*

You could ask what they eat or what they like to eat, or if they like a particular food: *Qu'est-ce que tu manges? Tu aimes …?*

Parler 2 **Practise what you have prepared. Then, using your notes, listen and respond to the teacher.**

Écouter 3 **Now listen to Nicolas doing the role-play task. In English, note down (a) how he answers the questions for tasks 1, 2, 4 and 5, and (b) what question he asks for task 3.**

Reading aloud

Parler 4 **Look at this task. With a partner, take turns to read out the text below, paying attention to the underlined letters.**

Read aloud the following text **in French**.

Je dors bien.
Je fais du sport avec ma mère.
Tous les matins, je prends des fruits.
Il est important de manger des légumes.
Quand j'ai faim, je choisis de la nourriture saine.

Take extra care with how you pronounce the underlined sounds:
- ***an*** and ***en***
- ***ain***, ***im***, ***in***, ***aim*** and ***ien***
- ***u***.

All the examples of a final **s** in this text are silent!

Écouter 5 **Listen and check your pronunciation.**

Parler 6 **Listen to the teacher asking four questions that relate to the topic of Healthy living and lifestyle. Translate each question into English and prepare your own answers in French. Then listen again and respond to the teacher.**

Remember to use different opinion phrases and to justify your opinion.

Photo card task

Écouter 7 **Look at the exam card below and read the first part of the task. Then listen to Nicolas describing the two photos.**

1 How does Nicolas describe the people in the first photo?
2 Where are the people in the second photo, according to Nicolas?
3 What does he say the people are doing in each photo?

Photo 1

Photo 2

You will be asked to talk about the content of these photos. You must say at least one thing about each photo.

After you have spoken about the content of the photos, you will be asked questions related to any of the topics within the theme of **People and lifestyle**.

Your responses should be as **full and detailed** as possible.

Parler 8 **Prepare your own descriptions of the two photos. You could mention, for example, the people, the location and what they are doing. Then, with a partner, take turns to describe the photos.**

Sur la première photo, il y a …

To talk about where people are, you can use *à gauche, à droite, au centre, ici.*

Écouter 9 **Read the second part of the task. Listen to Nicolas answering the question: *Quelle nourriture est-ce que tu aimes?* Write down the missing word or words for each gap.**

J'aime manger des **1** car je suis **2**. Je mange aussi beaucoup de **3**. Je n'aime pas la **4**. Je pense que ce n'est pas **5**.

Écouter 10 **Now listen to Nicolas answering the question: *Qu'est-ce que tu voudrais manger demain?* Write down the food he would like to eat for each meal of the day.**

1 breakfast **2** lunch **3** dinner

Parler 11 **Prepare your own answers to the module 4 questions on page 226. Your responses should be as full and detailed as possible. Then practise with a partner.**

Contrôle écrit

Grammar task

Écrire 1

Using your knowledge of grammar, copy and complete the following sentences in French. Choose the correct French word from the three options.

1 Tu ___ parler avec tes parents.	**dois / doit / devez**
2 J'ai mal ___ oreilles.	**à la / à l' / aux**
3 On ___ être plus fatigués.	**vais / vas / va**
4 Normalement, ___ assez sportif.	**j'étais / je suis / je vais être**
5 Je ne mange jamais ___ viande.	**de / du / de la**

Translation

Écrire 2

Match up the beginnings (1–5) and endings (a–e) of the sentences.

1 Je suis ...	**a** ... plus de sport.
2 Je dois boire ...	**b** ... manger plus de légumes.
3 Je veux faire ...	**c** ... mange un fruit.
4 Si j'ai faim, je ...	**d** ... plus d'eau.
5 Il faut ...	**e** ... végétarienne.

Écrire 3

Translate the following sentences into French.

1 I do a lot of sport.
2 I want to be in good health.
3 I am not vegetarian.
4 I have to eat vegetables every day.
5 When I am thirsty, I drink water.

What verb is this?

Use *je dois*.

What verb do you use in French to say 'to be thirsty'?

Remember where to put *ne ... pas*.

Remember to say 'some water'.

90-word writing task

Écrire 4

Look at this writing exam task and then, for each bullet point:

1 think about what vocabulary you have learned that you could use in your answer. For example:
- **nouns** and **verbs** to talk about what you do to stay healthy
- **verbs of opinion** and **adjectives** to explain your point of view
- how to explain what you **will do**.

2 write down three or four ideas for what you could write about.
3 write down which tense(s) you will need to use in your answer.

Make sure you vary your vocabulary and avoid repetition.

You are writing a post for a French forum on healthy living.

Write approximately **90** words in **French**.

You must write something about each bullet point.

Describe:
- what you do to be healthy
- a recent meal
- what you will do to be healthier in future.

Lire **5** **Read Charlie's answer to the exam task. Answer questions 1–5 in the coloured shapes.**

1 Which **connective** could you use here to form an **extended sentence**? What other connectives does Charlie use?

2 This is an example of **complex language**. What does it mean? Find three more examples from the text.

Bonjour

Dans ma ville, il y a un centre sportif. Au centre sportif, mon activité préférée est la natation. Je fais du sport pour être en bonne santé. J'aime le sport parce que c'est génial. Généralement, je mange bien aussi et j'essaye de dormir beaucoup.

Hier, j'ai mangé au restaurant fast-food avec mes amis. J'ai choisi des frites et un hamburger et j'ai bu du coca. C'était bon. Malheureusement, à mon avis, le fast-food est mauvais pour la santé.

Je pense que je suis en bonne santé mais je voudrais aller au lit plus tôt et manger moins de nourriture qui est mauvaise pour ma santé.

3 How could he **avoid repetition** by using a synonym here?

4 Which **tense** is this? What other examples can you find? Does he use any other tenses?

5 This phrase shows a **variety of vocabulary**. What does it mean? Find two more examples.

Lire **6** **Read Charlie's answer again. Answer the questions in English.**

1 Where does Charlie swim?
2 What is his opinion of sport?
3 What other things does he do to be healthy?
4 What did he do recently with his friends?
5 What two things would he like to change?

Écrire **7** **Prepare your own answer to the 90-word writing task in exercise 3.**

- Think about how you can develop your answer for each bullet point.
- Look back at your notes from exercises 4 and 5.
- Look at the 'Challenge checklist' and think about how you can show off your French!
- Write a **brief** plan and organise your answer into paragraphs.
- Write your answer and then carefully check the accuracy of what you have written.

Challenge checklist	
	✓ Past, present and future time frames ✓ Connectives, time phrases, sequencers ✓ Some extended sentences (*parce que …*) ✓ Different opinion phrases ✓ A range of opinions (e.g. *j'aime, je n'aime pas*) ✓ Negatives (*ne … pas*) ✓ *C'est* + adjective
	✓ A variety of opinion structures (e.g. *je pense que c'est …*) ✓ Opinion verbs with infinitives (*j'aime jouer*) ✓ A range of connectives (*et, mais, ou*) ✓ A wide range of interesting vocabulary
	✓ Complex language (e.g. *pour* + infinitive, reflexive verbs) ✓ Direct object pronouns

Module **4**

Vocabulaire

Key:
bold = this word will appear in higher exams only
* = this word is not on the vocabulary list, but you may use it in your own sentences

C'est bon pour la santé? (pages 82–83)

Dans ce **plat**, il y a ...	*In this dish, there is/are ...*
du *chocolat / fromage	*chocolate / cheese*
du poisson / *riz / *sucre	*fish / rice / sugar*
de la glace / *sauce	*ice cream / sauce*
de la viande	*meat*
des frites / fruits / légumes	*chips / fruit / vegetables*
À ton avis, le **plat**, c'est sain?	*In your opinion, is the dish healthy?*
C'est sain / *malsain.	*It is healthy / unhealthy.*
C'est bon / mauvais pour la santé.	*It is good / bad for your health.*
Le **plat** a bon goût.	*The dish tastes good.*
Je n'aime pas le goût.	*I don't like the taste.*
C'est parfait pour les végétariens.	*It's perfect for vegetarians.*
Ce n'est pas bon pour les végans.	*It's not good for vegans.*
À mon avis, il a bon goût, mais c'est *malsain.	*In my opinion, it tastes good, but it's unhealthy.*
délicieux/délicieuse	*delicious*
Buvez plus/moins de *coca!	*Drink more/less cola!*
Mangez plus/moins de frites et de *chocolat!	*Eat more/less chips and chocolate!*
Faites plus/moins d'exercice!	*Do more/less exercise!*
Faites de la natation plus/moins souvent!	*Go swimming more/less often!*
Allez plus/moins souvent au centre sportif!	*Go to the sports centre more/less often!*
Allez au collège à pied ou à vélo!	*Go to school on foot or by bike!*
Allez au lit plus tôt / tard!	*Go to bed earlier / later!*
Dormez au moins huit heures toutes les nuits!	*Sleep at least eight hours every night!*
Essayez un nouveau sport!	*Try a new sport!*

Bon appétit! (pages 84–85)

Qu'est-ce que tu manges (normalement)?	*What do you (usually) eat?*
Qu'est-ce que tu manges pour le petit-déjeuner?	*What do you eat for breakfast?*
Qu'est-ce que tu manges et bois à midi?	*What do you eat and drink at lunchtime?*
Est-ce que tu manges quelque chose après les cours?	*Do you eat something after school?*
Normalement, qu'est-ce que tu manges le soir?	*What do you usually eat in the evening?*
Pour le petit-déjeuner, ...	*For breakfast, ...*
À midi, ...	*At lunchtime, ...*
Après les cours, ...	*After school, ...*
Le soir, ...	*In the evening, ...*
je bois / on boit ...	*I / we drink ...*
je mange / on mange ...	*I / we eat ...*
je choisis ...	*I choose ...*
du café / lait / thé.	*coffee / milk / tea.*
du pain / poisson / **poulet**.	*bread / fish / chicken.*
de la glace / viande.	*ice cream / meat.*
des fruits / légumes / *olives.	*fruit / vegetables / olives.*
de l'eau.	*water.*
un *sandwich.	*a sandwich.*
beaucoup de (légumes).	*lots of (vegetables).*
Je mange souvent du pain.	*I often eat bread.*
Quand j'ai soif, ...	*When I'm thirsty, ...*
Si j'ai faim, ...	*If I'm hungry, ...*
Si j'ai le temps, ...	*If I have time ...*

Bien dans ma peau (pages 86–87)

Comment ça va aujourd'hui?	*How are you today?*
Ça ne va pas?	*Are you OK?*
Ça va très bien.	*I am very well.*
Ça ne va pas bien.	*I am not well / not good.*
Je suis ...	*I am ...*
un peu / assez	*a little / quite*
très / vraiment	*very / really*
heureux/heureuse.	*happy.*
triste.	*sad.*
fatigué(e).	*tired.*
calme.	*calm.*
Pourquoi es-tu ...?	*Why are you ...?*
Je suis ... parce que / car ...	*I am ... because / as ...*
j'adore jouer à des jeux vidéo contre mes amis.	*I love playing video games against my friends.*
je ne travaille pas ce week-end.	*I am not working this weekend.*
je ne m'entends pas bien avec (mon père).	*I don't get on with (my father).*
j'ai beaucoup de travail scolaire.	*I have lots of schoolwork.*
je suis tout le temps / souvent inquiet/inquiète avec les examens.	*I am always / often worried about exams.*
je dors mal.	*I am sleeping badly.*
j'ai perdu mon *chat / chien.	*I have lost my cat / dog.*
je dois trouver de nouveaux amis.	*I must find new friends.*
je n'ai pas d'énergie.	*I don't have any energy.*
mon meilleur ami a changé de collège.	*my best friend has changed school.*
mon équipe a gagné.	*my team won.*
Je ne sais pas pourquoi.	*I don't know why.*
Écoute de la musique.	*Listen to music.*
Fais de la cuisine.	*Do some cooking.*
Parle avec moi.	*Speak to me.*
Reste calme.	*Stay calm.*
Va au lit.	*Go to bed.*
Tu dois rester calme.	*You must stay calm.*
Je veux dormir mieux.	*I want to sleep better.*

Bien choisir pour ta santé (pages 88–89)

Reste/Restez au lit.	*Stay in bed.*
Va/Allez à l'hôpital.	*Go to hospital.*
Ne **bouge**/**bougez** pas.	*Don't move.*
avoir chaud / froid	*to be hot / cold*
avoir faim / soif / peur	*to be hungry / thirsty / afraid*
Qu'est-ce qui ne va pas?	*What's wrong?*
Qu'est-ce que tu as fait?	*What have you done?*
Je suis malade.	*I'm ill.*
J'ai mal au dos.	*I've got backache.*
J'ai mal à la tête.	*I have a headache.*
J'ai mal aux jambes / oreilles / yeux.	*My legs / ears / eyes hurt.*
J'ai mal au cœur.	*I feel sick.*
Qu'est-ce qui s'est passé?	What happened?
Je suis tombé(e) de vélo.	I fell off my bike.
J'ai bu de l'alcool.	I drank some alcohol.
fumer / vapoter	*to smoke / to vape*
Que penses-tu des cigarettes?	*What do you think of cigarettes?*
C'est mauvais pour la santé.	*It's / They're bad for your health.*
Fumer est une habitude terrible.	*Smoking is a terrible habit.*
Il y a un **risque** de *cancer.	*There is a risk of cancer.*
À l'avenir, les jeunes ne vont pas fumer.	*In the future, young people won't smoke.*
un mode/style de vie *sédentaire	*a sedentary lifestyle*
On peut avoir mal au dos.	*You can get backache.*
Si on passe trop de temps devant un écran, on peut avoir mal aux yeux.	*If you spend too much time in front of a screen, you can get sore eyes.*
Il faut **bouger** souvent pour protéger votre santé.	*You have to move often to protect your health.*
Les ados passent trop de temps devant un écran.	*Teenagers spend too much time in front of screens.*

Je change ma vie (pages 90–91)

Qu'est-ce que tu vas faire pour améliorer ta vie?	*What are you going to do to improve your life?*
Je vais manger plus de légumes / fruits.	*I am going to eat more vegetables / fruit.*
Je vais prendre des cours de *danse.	*I am going to take dance classes.*
Je vais moins penser à moi et je vais aider les autres.	*I am going to think less about myself and I am going to help others.*
Je vais être plus **patient**(e).	*I am going to be more patient.*
Je vais aller à la piscine chaque week-end.	*I am going to go to the swimming pool every weekend.*
Je ne vais pas faire mes devoirs à la dernière minute.	*I am not going to do my homework at the last minute.*
À l'avenir, je vais / je veux ...	*In the future, I am going to / I want to ...*
aider ma mère et mes *grands-parents.	*help my mother and my grandparents.*
aider plus à la maison.	*help around the house more.*
aller plus souvent au centre sportif.	*go to the sports centre more often.*
aller au lit plus tôt.	*go to bed earlier.*
être plus actif/active / en forme.	*be more active / in better shape.*
faire une nouvelle activité.	*do a new activity.*
faire plus de sport / de vélo.	*do more sport / cycling.*
jouer au *tennis / *rugby.	*play tennis / rugby.*
manger moins de fromage.	*eat less cheese.*
travailler plus dur / *sérieusement au collège.	*work harder at school.*
Je ne vais pas ...	*I am not going to ...*
Il/Elle va arriver / jouer ...	*He/She is going to arrive / play ...*
Il/Elle ne va pas être ...	*He/She is not going to be ...*

Mieux vivre (pages 92–93)

Quand tu étais plus jeune, ta vie était comment?	*When you were younger, how was your life?*
Quand j'étais ado / jeune / petit(e) ...	*When I was a teenager / young / little ...*
j'habitais en *Côte d'Ivoire / France.	*I lived in Côte d'Ivoire / France.*
je jouais au *tennis / *basket.	*I played tennis / basketball.*
je travaillais dans un hôtel.	*I worked in a hotel.*
En ce moment, comment est ta vie?	*At the moment, how is your life?*
Maintenant, ...	*Now, ...*
je suis acteur/actrice.	*I am an actor.*
je suis homme/femme politique.	*I am a politician.*
j'écris des chansons.	*I write songs.*
je travaille pour les droits des travailleurs.	*I work for the rights of workers.*
À l'avenir, qu'est-ce que tu vas faire?	*In the future, what are you going to do?*
À l'avenir, ...	*In the future, ...*
je vais continuer à ...	*I am going to continue to ...*
je vais chanter / écrire ...	*I am going to sing / write ...*
J'avais / J'ai / Je vais avoir ...	*I used to have / I have / I'm going to have ...*
J'étais / Je suis / Je vais être ...	*I used to be / I am / I'm going to be ...*
Je faisais / Je fais / Je vais faire ...	*I used to do / I do / I'm going to do ...*

Module 5

Numéro vacances

Voudrais-tu voyager?

- Talking about holidays and accommodation
- Using *pour* + infinitive

Pourquoi voudrais-tu voyager?

Selon les jeunes Français, il y a beaucoup de raisons!

Je voudrais voyager …

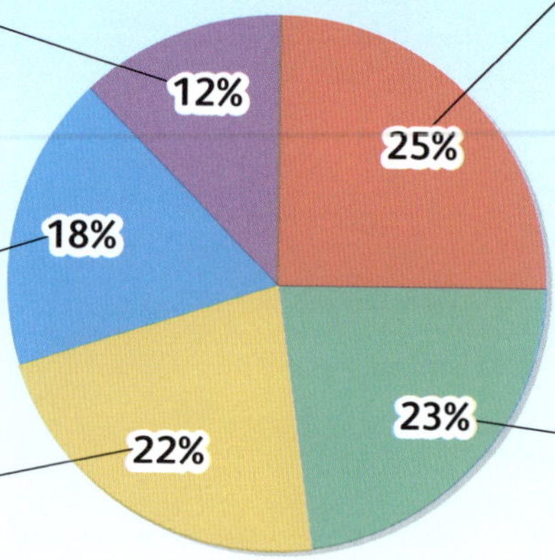

selon *according to*

Logements extraordinaires

Le Village Flottant de Pressac

Où: dans la Vienne
Description: un village calme sur l'eau
Équipement: une piscine, un grand choix de restaurants
Parfait pour: être près de la nature

La Troglo à Plumes

Où: dans le Maine-et-Loire
Description: une maison historique et confortable
Équipement: trois chambres, une belle vue sur la campagne
Parfait pour: se couper du monde

Le camping Le Haut-Village

Où: en Loire-Atlantique
Description: un camping avec des logements extraordinaires – avion, voitures de train et de métro
Équipement: des aires de jeux pour enfants, des terrains de sport
Parfait pour: faire une expérience unique en famille sur la côte

L'Hôtel de la Cité à Carcassonne

Où: dans l'Aude
Description: un hôtel-château au cœur d'une vieille ville
Équipement: des chambres confortables, un grand jardin
Parfait pour: se relaxer

flottant(e)	*floating*
se couper du monde	*to switch off from the world*
l'aire (f) de jeux	*playground*
le terrain de sport	*sports ground*

L'Aude, la Loire-Atlantique, le Maine-et-Loire and la Vienne are all French *départements*. These are similar to counties in the UK.

Lire 1 **Read the results of the survey at the top of page 106 and answer the questions.**

What percentage of young people would like to travel so they can …

1 relax?
2 learn a new language or sport?
3 change their routine?
4 get to know a different culture?
5 make new friends?

Écouter 2 **Listen to the interviews and note in English two reasons why each person would like to travel. (1–3)**

G *Je voudrais* means 'I would like' and is in the conditional. Follow it with an infinitive such as *voyager* to say what you would like to do:
Je voudrais voyager. I would like to travel.

Pages 108 and 118

G Use *pour* + infinitive to say 'in order to':
pour sortir de la routine
in order to change (my) routine

Parler 3 **In pairs, talk about why you would like to travel.**

- *Pourquoi voudrais-tu voyager?*
- *Je voudrais voyager pour … et pour …*
  Et toi, pourquoi voudrais-tu voyager?
- *Je voudrais voyager pour … et …*

Je voudrais voyager pour	me relaxer. me faire de nouveaux amis. connaître une culture différente. sortir de la routine. apprendre une nouvelle langue. apprendre un nouveau sport.

Écouter 4 **Read the article called *Logements extraordinaires* on page 106. Then listen. For each conversation, write 'Le Village', 'La Troglo', 'Le camping' or 'L'Hôtel'. (1–8)**

Parler 5 **In pairs, choose one of the places to stay, then make up your own version of the dialogue below, changing the underlined phrases.**

- *Où voudrais-tu passer tes vacances?*
- *Je voudrais passer mes vacances dans le Village Flottant.*
- *C'est où?*
- *C'est dans la Vienne.*
- *Qu'est-ce que c'est?*
- *C'est un village calme sur l'eau.*
- *Qu'est-ce qu'il y a là-bas?*
- *Il y a une piscine et un grand choix de restaurants.*
- *Qu'est-ce qu'on peut faire là-bas?*
- *On peut être près de la nature.*

là-bas *over there, out there*

Château, *haut*, *nos* and *côte* all contain the same sound.
Say this sound with rounded lips and your tongue back.

In French, *h* is always silent.

Listen and repeat these sentences:
Huit hommes heureux habitent dans l'hôtel historique.
Vos châteaux sur l'eau sont près de la côte.

Écrire 6 **Write a description of one of the places in the *Logements extraordinaires* texts on page 106. Include:**

- where it is
  La Troglo à Plumes est dans le Maine-et-Loire.
- what it is
  C'est une maison …
- what there is
  Il y a …
- what you can do there.
  On peut …

1 Des vacances de rêve

- Talking about your ideal holiday
- Using the conditional of *vouloir*
- Giving reasons for your preferences

Écouter 1 **Listen and write the <u>four</u> correct letters for each speaker. (1–4)**

Quel type de vacances voudrais-tu?

Je voudrais …

a

des vacances calmes.

b

des vacances éco-responsables.

c

des vacances culturelles.

d

des vacances actives.

Où voudrais-tu passer tes vacances idéales?

Je voudrais passer mes vacances …

e

à la campagne.

f

à la montagne.

g

sur une île ou sur la côte.

h

en ville.

Comment voudrais-tu voyager?

Je voudrais voyager …

i

en avion privé.

j

en bateau.

k

en train.

l

à dos de chameau.

Où voudrais-tu loger?

Je voudrais loger …

m

sous une tente.

n

dans un hôtel de luxe.

o

dans une ferme.

p

dans un château.

loger	*to stay*

G

The conditional of *vouloir* is used to say what you would like:

*je voudr**ais***	I would like
*tu voudr**ais***	you would like
*il/elle/on voudr**ait***	he/she/we would like

You can use it with an <u>infinitive</u> to say what you would like to do:
Je voudrais <u>voyager</u>. I would like to travel.

You can also use it with **a noun**:
*Je voudrais **des vacances calmes**.* I would like a quiet holiday.

Page 118

Parler 2 **In pairs, take turns to ask and answer the <u>four</u> questions from exercise 1.**

- *Quel type de vacances voudrais-tu?*
- *Je voudrais <u>des vacances calmes</u>. Et toi, quel type de vacances voudrais-tu?*
- *Je voudrais <u>des vacances éco-responsables</u>. Où voudrais-tu passer tes vacances idéales?*
- *Je voudrais passer mes vacances <u>à la campagne</u>. Et toi, …*

The ***gn*** in *monta**gn**e* and *campa**gn**e* is pronounced a bit like the middle of 'onion' in English. It is made up of two sounds: 'n' and 'yuh'.

Listen to the sound and the words. In pairs, try saying '*monta**gn**e, campa**gn**e*' repeatedly, getting faster each time. How many sets can you say correctly?

Lire 3 **Read the texts. Match each picture (a–f) to one of the phrases in bold.**

Example: a – visiter de beaux sites, b …

Spécial vacances: des vacances idéales!

Je voudrais aller au Maroc avec ma famille parce que je préfère des vacances culturelles.

Je voudrais aller en ville parce que je voudrais **acheter des vêtements**.

Et pour me relaxer, je voudrais **passer du temps à la piscine**.

Mehdi

Je voudrais aller à l'île de Vanuatu pour passer des vacances éco-responsables avec mon ami Alex.

Il voudrait **faire de la natation avec des poissons** dans l'eau claire parce qu'il aime les poissons. Moi aussi! Après, on voudrait **faire la fête sur la plage**!

Chloé

Je voudrais aller à la campagne avec mon amie Zoé car j'aime les vacances actives.

Zoé voudrait **faire des activités passionnantes** car elle adore le danger!

On aime aussi le tourisme, donc on voudrait **visiter de beaux sites**.

Jade

a 

b 

c 

d 

e 

f 

Lire 4 **Re-read the texts in exercise 3. Choose the correct option to complete each sentence.**

1 Mehdi would like to go into town because he would like to **buy clothes** / **visit tourist sites**.
2 He would like to go to the swimming pool in order to **get some exercise** / **relax**.
3 Chloé would like to go to Vanuatu in order to have **an environmentally responsible holiday** / **a calm holiday**.
4 Her friend Alex would like to go swimming because he likes **fish** / **the sea**.
5 Jade would like to go to the countryside because she likes **walking** / **active holidays**.
6 Jade's friend Zoé would like to do exciting activities because she loves **a challenge** / **danger**.

Écouter 5 **Listen to the podcast about ideal holidays. Look at pictures a–f in exercise 3. For each speaker, write down (a) the letter of the activity they would like to do, and (b) their reason, in English. (1–4)**

There are different ways to explain why you would like to do something.
- because you like, love or prefer something:
  … ***parce que je préfère*** *des vacances culturelles.*
  … ***car elle adore*** *le danger.*
- because you would like to do something:
  … ***parce que je voudrais*** *acheter des vêtements.*
- in order to do something:
  … ***pour*** *me relaxer.*

Écrire 6 **Write a presentation about your dream holiday. Include:**
- what type of holiday you would like to have
- where you would like to go
- what you would like to do.

Give reasons for your preferences.

Je voudrais des vacances … car …
Je voudrais passer mes vacances … parce que …
Je voudrais aller … / faire … / visiter … parce que … / pour …

Parler 7 **In groups, take turns to read out your presentations.**

2 On part pour la Corse

- Discussing what you can see and do on holiday
- Forming different types of questions
- Giving advice with *il faut*, *on doit* and *on peut*

Écouter 1 **Listen and write down the letter of each holiday top tip. (1–5)**

Qu'est-ce qu'il faut faire en Corse?

Il faut ...

a 
essayer les desserts locaux.

b 
connaître la culture corse.

c 
faire une visite en bateau.

d 
pratiquer un sport extrême.

e 
aller à la plage.

Écouter 2 **Listen again and note down in English the extra advice given. (1–5)**

Il faut ... On doit ... On peut ...

aller au marché.

faire du vélo.

monter une montagne.

réserver toutes les activités.

visiter le musée de Bastia.

tout/toute/tous/toutes	*all*

G

To give advice you can use *il faut* (you must), *on doit* (you must) or *on peut* (you can) followed by an infinitive:

*il faut **faire*** you must do *on doit **réserver*** you must book
*on peut **aller*** you can go

Page 118

Lire 3 **Translate these sentences into English.**

Corte

1 Il faut visiter cette ville pour comprendre l'histoire de la Corse.
2 On peut monter des montagnes.
3 On doit aller au marché pour acheter des cadeaux.
4 Et après, on peut réserver une table dans un restaurant pour essayer les desserts traditionnels.

cette *(f)*	*this*
comprendre	*to understand*

Parler 4 **In pairs, take turns to read out the sentences from exercise 3, paying particular attention to your pronunciation of the sound *on/om*. Then listen and check.**

Listen and repeat this nasal sound and the words. To make this sound, put your mouth into a round shape and push your lips forward.

on, om

b**on** m**on**ter c**om**prendre

Écouter 5

Listen to the conversation. Fill in each gap with the correct word from the box.

- *Qu'est-ce qu'il faut visiter dans la région?*
- *Il faut visiter un des* **1** *touristiques.*
- *Qu'est-ce que tu as fait pour te relaxer en vacances?*
- *Je suis allé à la* **2** *et j'ai aussi lu un livre.*
- *Quels plats est-ce qu'il faut essayer dans la région? Pourquoi?*
- *Il faut essayer les fromages corses car ils sont* **3** .
- *Qu'est-ce que tu veux faire comme visite?*
- *Je veux visiter la vieille* **4** .
- *Comment trouves-tu la région?*
- *Je trouve que la Corse est très* **5** .

belle bon délicieux intéressante jolie lieux
musée piscine plage traditionnel ville

G

There are different ways to form questions in French.

		with a question word	without a question word
1	*est-ce que*	*Comment* ***est-ce que*** *tu te relaxes en vacances?*	***Est-ce que*** *tu te relaxes en vacances?*
2	inversion of subject and verb	*Où* ***peut-on*** *prendre un taxi?*	***Peut-on*** *prendre un taxi?*

Page 118

Lire 6

Read the conversation you completed in exercise 5. Find the French for the phrases below.

1 You must visit …
2 What did you do to relax …?
3 Which dishes …?
4 I want (to) …
5 I find that …

Écrire 7

You are planning a holiday with your Belgian friend. Write answers to this role-play.

1 • *Qu'est-ce qu'on peut faire dans la région?*
▪ *[Say what you can do. (Give* ***one*** *detail.)]*

2 • *Qu'est-ce que tu as fait récemment en vacances?*
▪ *[Say what you did recently on holiday. (Give* ***two*** *details.)]*

3 • *Que fais-tu pour te relaxer?*
▪ *[Say how you relax. (Give* ***two*** *details.)]*

4 • *Qu'est-ce qu'il faut visiter? Pourquoi?*
▪ *[Say what you should visit and why. (Give* ***one*** *detail and* ***one*** *reason.)]*

5 • **?** *[Ask your friend what food you should try from the region.]*
▪ *[Give an appropriate response.]*

Parler 8

In pairs, take turns to play each part of the role-play you prepared in exercise 7.

3 Le monde en fête

- Talking about festivals
- Using the perfect and imperfect tenses together
- Understanding more complex sentences using *qui*

Les fêtes du monde francophone

Écouter 1 **Listen and read. Then answer the questions by writing the letter of the correct festival.**

a

Le carnaval à la Martinique

C'est un festival qui se passe en février. Le carnaval dure plusieurs jours et nuits! Il y a des défilés avec des danseurs et il y a beaucoup de touristes dans les rues. C'est une fête amusante.

b

La fête des goyaviers à la Réunion

C'est un événement qui se passe en juin. Les chefs préparent des desserts avec des goyaves, qui sont de petits fruits rouges. Il y a des marchés, des jeux pour les enfants et des concerts. C'est une fête populaire.

c

Le festival international des Masques et des Arts au Burkina Faso

C'est un événement qui se passe en février et en mars. On écoute de la musique traditionnelle. Il y a des masques qui viennent de divers pays d'Afrique et des spectacles extraordinaires. C'est un festival culturel.

le défilé	*parade, procession*
le goyavier	*guava tree*
la goyave	*guava (fruit)*
divers(e)	*various*

Which festival …

1 has chefs preparing fruit desserts?
2 has traditional music?
3 lasts several days and nights?
4 features masks from various African countries?
5 has lots of tourists in the streets?
6 is described as a fun festival?
7 has extraordinary shows?
8 takes place in June?

Écouter 2 **Listen to the description of the festival. Choose the correct option to complete each sentence.**

1 *La Fête du Citron®* takes place in **February** / **April**.
2 Chefs prepare **desserts** / **cakes**.
3 There are sculptures with yellow and orange **objects** / **fruits**.
4 Tourists love the **markets** / **parades**.
5 It's a **popular** / **fun** festival.

G

Qui is a relative pronoun that helps you extend your sentences.
It can be translated as 'who', 'which' or 'that':
*C'est un festival **qui** se passe en février.*
It's a festival that takes place in February.

Page 119

Écrire 3 **Write about *Le Festival d'Avignon* using the notes below.**

Le Festival d'Avignon
July
• shows • concerts
• parade • games for children
Popular and cultural

C'est un festival / une fête qui se passe en		janvier / février / mars.	
Il y a		des	danseurs / concerts. groupes de musique. marchés / masques. jeux pour les enfants. défilés / spectacles.
		beaucoup de touristes.	
C'est	un festival	amusant / culturel / populaire.	
	une fête	amusante / culturelle / populaire.	

Lire 4 **Read the text. Correct the mistake in each of the sentences below. (1–6)**

Camille

En février dernier, je suis allée chez mon oncle qui habite à la Martinique.

J'étais très contente car c'était le carnaval!

Pendant plusieurs jours, il y avait beaucoup de gens dans les rues.

J'ai vu des danseurs et j'ai entendu de la musique. J'ai aussi dansé, c'était amusant!

Un autre jour, je suis allée au marché. Il y avait beaucoup d'activités.

J'ai mangé du sorbet coco qui est comme une glace. C'était délicieux!

J'ai adoré ma première expérience du carnaval. C'était extraordinaire!

entendre *to hear*

1. Last February, Camille went to her friend's house in Martinique.
2. For several days, there were lots of people on the beaches.
3. Camille heard music and played as well.
4. Another day, she went to the park.
5. She didn't enjoy the coconut sorbet.
6. She loved her second visit to the carnaval.

Use words like ***plusieurs*** (several) and ***beaucoup de*** (lots of) for variety.
Beaucoup is usually followed by ***de*** unless the noun begins with a vowel or h.

beaucoup ***de g****ens*   *beaucoup* ***d'a****ctivités*

G

The **perfect tense** is used to talk about single actions that happened in the past:
Je suis allé(e) *chez mon oncle.* I went to my uncle's house.

One of the uses of the imperfect tense is to describe what something was like:
J'étais contente. I was happy.
C'était extraordinaire. It was extraordinary.
Il y avait beaucoup de gens. There were lots of people.

Can you find more examples of each tense in the exercise 4 text?

Page 119

Écouter 5 **Listen. Then copy and complete the grid in English. (1–2)**

	Name of festival	What was there?	What did they do?	What was it like?
1	Dunkirk Carnival …			
2	Winter Festival …			

Parler 6 **In pairs, take turns to talk about the two festivals below.**

- *Est-ce que tu es allé(e) à une fête?*
- *Oui, je suis allé(e) au … / à la …*
- *Qu'est-ce qu'il y avait?*
- *Il y avait …*
- *Qu'est-ce que tu as fait?*
- *J'ai mangé … / dansé / vu … / entendu …*
- *C'était comment?*
- *C'était …*

Le carnaval de Binche
Shows and concerts
Ate local desserts
Delicious

Le carnaval de Nice
Dancers and music
Danced
Extraordinary

Écrire 7 **Translate these sentences into French.**

Use the imperfect tense.

1. Last April, I went to my aunt's house.
2. It was the Festival of Rice.
3. There was a market and I heard music in the street.
4. Another evening, I ate a lot of rice. It was fun!

Use *la fête du riz.*

Use the perfect tense. Think about whether you need to use *avoir* or *être* for each verb.

4 Guide de voyage

- Reviewing and booking holiday accommodation
- Using negatives in the imperfect and perfect tenses
- Identifying positive and negative opinions

Lire 1 **Read the reviews of the hotel. Write the letter of the correct picture for each of the phrases in bold in the texts.**

Example: J'ai bien dormi – b; ma chambre n'était pas …

Comment était l'hôtel?

Vacances à la cool

Hôtel Bonne Nuit à Cabourg – vos avis

1
En décembre, j'ai passé une nuit dans cet hôtel avec mes enfants. **J'ai bien dormi** car il n'y avait pas de bruit le soir. Il y avait une grande piscine, mais **ma chambre n'était pas très propre**. En plus, la fenêtre de ma chambre était trop petite. **Louis**

2
J'ai passé une semaine dans cet hôtel. Je n'ai pas joué au tennis de table. **Il n'y avait pas d'équipement dans la salle de jeux. J'ai perdu la clé de ma chambre.** Je n'ai trouvé personne à la réception. Par contre, le lit était très confortable et j'ai lu beaucoup de livres. **Yasmina**

3
J'ai choisi cet hôtel parce qu'il est sur la côte. **La vue sur la mer était très belle! L'hôtel n'était pas cher** et c'était pratique. Par contre, Internet ne marchait pas. En plus, je n'ai rien mangé au petit-déjeuner. Malheureusement, il n'y avait jamais de place dans le restaurant! **Théo**

a

b

c

d

e

f
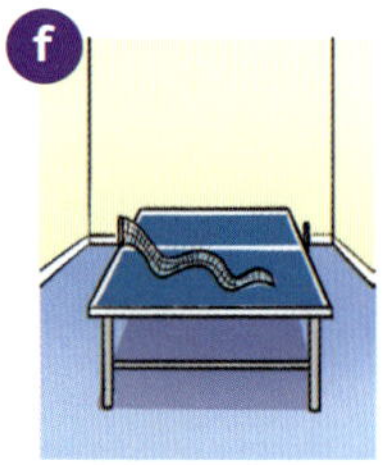

Lire 2 **Re-read the reviews in exercise 1. Then answer the questions below.**

Who …

1 spent one week at the hotel?
2 had a window that was too small?
3 found no one at reception?
4 ate nothing for breakfast?
5 thought there was no noise at night?
6 says there was never space in the restaurant?

G

In the imperfect tense, negatives go around the verb:
*L'hôtel **n'**était **pas** cher.*
The hotel was **not** expensive.
*Il **n'**y avait **jamais** de place dans le restaurant.*
There was **never** space in the restaurant.

In the perfect tense, most negatives go around the part of *avoir* or *être*:

*je **n'**ai **pas** joué*	I did **not** play
*je **n'**ai **rien** mangé*	I ate **nothing**
*je **ne** suis **jamais** allé*	I have **never** been

Personne goes after the past participle:
*Je **n'**ai trouvé **personne**.* I found **no one**.

Page 119

Écouter 3 **Listen to people talking about their stay in a hotel. Are they positive (P) or negative (N) about the following things? (1–3)**

1 **a** the breakfast **b** the pool
2 **a** the room **b** the restaurant
3 **a** the bed **b** the price

When you hear a negative, don't assume it means a negative opinion. For example, *il n'y avait pas de bruit* means 'there wasn't any noise', which is a positive opinion in this context.

Parler 4 **Listen to these sentences. Then practise saying them with a partner.**

En déc**em**bre, j'ai trouvé **un** excell**en**t c**am**ping.
Les **enfan**ts m**an**gent d**an**s **un** restaur**an**t.

Listen and repeat these <u>two</u> nasal sounds.
Try to say them from the back of your throat.
un
en ***an*** ***em*** ***am***

Écrire 5 **Imagine that you have stayed at this hotel. Write a review.**

- Say how long you spent in this hotel.
- Say what the hotel and room were like.
- Describe a problem in the hotel.

J'ai passé une nuit / deux nuits / une semaine dans cet hôtel.		
L'hôtel	était n'était pas	pratique / cher.
Le lit		confortable.
La vue		belle.
La chambre		propre.
La fenêtre		(trop) petit(e).
Internet ne marchait pas.		
Il n'y avait pas	de	place dans le restaurant. bruit.
	d'équipement.	
J'ai perdu la clé. Je n'ai trouvé personne à la réception.		
Je n'ai rien mangé. Je n'ai pas joué.		

Écouter 6 **Listen and read. Copy and complete the grid in English. Then listen and complete the grid for the next two conversations. (1–3)**

	Number of rooms booked	Number of people	Number of nights	Question asked about hotel – Is there …?
1				

- *Demain, je vais en vacances. Ça va être super!*
- *Fantastique! Tu loges dans un hôtel?*
- *Oui. J'ai réservé <u>une chambre pour deux personnes car ma mère vient avec moi</u>.*
- *Pour combien de nuits?*
- *C'est pour <u>cinq nuits</u>.*
- *Est-ce qu'il y a <u>un restaurant</u> dans l'hôtel?*
- *Oui, bien sûr.*

G
The French word for 'in' depends on the context.
- inside something: ***dans** <u>ma</u> chambre, **dans** <u>l'</u>hôtel*
- in a named town: ***à** Cabourg*
- in the town centre: ***au** centre-ville*
- in town: ***en** ville*

Page 120

Parler 7 **In pairs, create <u>two</u> new versions of the dialogue in exercise 6, using the pictures in the boxes.**

Écrire 8 **Write an email to book holiday accommodation using the prompts from the box.**

You could use *Bonjour* to start your email and end with *Merci* and *Au revoir*. You could use expressions like *Je voudrais* + an infinitive verb like *réserver*.

5 Vive les vacances!

- Talking about staycation activities
- Using a range of tenses
- Using *si* + the present tense + the near future tense

Écouter 1 **Listen to the conversations about today's weather. Write the letters of the two correct pictures for each one. (1–4)**

Quel temps fait-il aujourd'hui?

a Il fait chaud. 

b Il fait froid. 

c Il fait beau. 

d Il fait mauvais. 

e Il y a du soleil. 

f Il y a du vent. 

g Il pleut. 

Lire 2 **Read and listen. Then copy and complete the sentences in English.**

Ça va bientôt être les vacances! Qu'est-ce qu'on va faire?

J'ai beaucoup d'idées pour les vacances!

- S'il fait beau, je vais faire du vélo à la campagne.
- S'il y a du soleil, je vais organiser un concert au parc avec mes amis. Ça va être super amusant!
- S'il fait chaud, je vais faire du camping car j'adore dormir sous une tente.
- S'il fait mauvais, je vais faire un repas. J'adore le poisson!
- S'il y a du vent, je vais prendre le train pour aller à la plage avec ma famille.
- S'il fait froid, je vais aller au musée avec mon frère parce qu'on aime l'histoire.
- S'il pleut, je vais rester à la maison et je vais faire une appli! Ça va être cool!

1 If the weather is nice, Clément is going to ___ in the ___.
2 If it's sunny, he's going to ___ with his friends.
3 If it's hot, he's going to ___.
4 If the weather is bad, he's going to ___.
5 If it's windy, he's going to ___ to go to ___.
6 If it's cold, he's going to ___ with ___.
7 If it rains, he's going to ___ and he's going to ___.

G

To say **what you are going to do** if something happens or is a particular way (for example, the weather), use: *Si* + present tense + **near future tense**

*S'il fait froid, je **vais rester** chez moi.*
If it's cold, I am going to stay at home.

Remember that the near future is formed by using the correct part of *aller* + an infinitive.

Page 120

Parler 3 **In pairs, adapt the dialogue below to talk about your weekend plans.**

- *Qu'est-ce que tu vas faire ce week-end?*
- *S'il fait beau, je vais aller à la plage.*
- *Bonne idée! Et s'il pleut?*
- *Je vais aller au musée.*
- *S'il fait chaud? Qu'est-ce que tu vas faire?*
- ...

S'il fait beau / chaud / mauvais / froid,	je vais	aller ... faire ... prendre ... organiser ... rester ...
S'il y a du vent / du soleil,		
S'il pleut,		

Lire 4 **Read the texts. Find the French for the phrases below.**

Normalement, pendant les grandes vacances, je suis avec ma grand-mère.
L'année dernière, j'ai passé trop de temps sur les réseaux sociaux car il faisait froid. Ce n'était pas bon pour ma santé.
Cette année, je vais apprendre une nouvelle langue. Ça va être génial!

L'été dernier, j'ai passé des vacances extraordinaires! Il faisait mauvais et je ne suis pas partie en vacances. J'ai passé beaucoup de temps en ville avec mes amis et j'ai adoré ça.
Mais cet été, je vais aller à Paris en train avec ma mère et on va monter à la tour Eiffel. Ça va être super!

Normalement, je joue au tennis avec mes amies pendant les grandes vacances. C'est amusant.
Un jour, l'été dernier, je suis allée au parc à vélo. Il y avait du vent et je suis tombée de vélo. Aïe!
Cette année, je vais faire quelque chose de moins actif!

1 I spent too much time
2 it was cold
3 the weather was bad
4 it was windy
5 I'm going to do something less active

Use the imperfect tense to describe what the weather was like in the past:
Il faisait chaud. It was hot.
Il y avait du soleil. It was sunny.

Lire 5 **Re-read the texts in exercise 4. Write down the letters for the <u>two</u> correct pictures for each text. Then decide if each picture refers to an event in the present, in the past or in the future.**

Example: Dorian: a – present, …

G When referring to the present, past and future, you need to use several tenses. For the past, use the imperfect tense for descriptions and the perfect tense for single, completed actions.

Page 120

a 

b 

c 

d 

e 

f 

Écouter 6 **Listen to Lola and Rachid talking about their holidays. Which time frame do they use to talk about each of the categories below? Write 'past', 'present' or 'future' for each one. (1–6)**

Lola **1** accommodation **2** activities **3** transport
Rachid **4** food **5** a problem **6** weather

le Royaume-Uni *United Kingdom*

Écrire 7 **Write a text about your holidays in the past, present and future.**

As in the texts in exercise 4, try to extend your answer by recycling structures and vocabulary that you have met in different contexts.

Normalement,	pendant les grandes vacances,	je reste … / je vais … je joue … / je dors …	C'est amusant. C'est génial.
L'été dernier, L'année dernière,	j'ai passé	du temps … mes vacances …	C'était super. C'était nul.
	j'ai fait … je suis allé(e) … je (ne) suis (pas) parti(e) en vacances.		
	il faisait froid / il y avait du vent.		
Cet été, Cette année,	je vais aller … / je vais faire … je vais apprendre …		Ça va être cool / extraordinaire.

Grammaire 1

The conditional of *vouloir* (Unit 1, pages 108 and 109)

Lire 1

Read the grammar box on the conditional of *vouloir* on page 108. Then copy out the sentences below, choosing the correct form of the conditional each time.

1 Je **voudrait** / **voudrais** passer des vacances avec mes amis Luc et Lucie.
2 On **voudrais** / **voudrait** passer nos vacances à la campagne.
3 Moi, je **voudrait** / **voudrais** aller en vacances à vélo.
4 Lucie, elle **voudrait** / **voudrais** voyager en train.
5 Luc, il **voudrais** / **voudrait** aller en vacances en bateau.
6 Et toi, où **voudrait** / **voudrais**-tu passer tes vacances idéales?

Giving advice using *il faut*, *on doit* and *on peut* followed by an infinitive (Unit 2, page 110)

Parler 2

Read the grammar box about giving advice with *il faut* (you must), *on doit* (you must) and *on peut* (you can) followed by an infinitive on page 110. Then, in pairs, take turns to be the holidaymaker and the person who works in a tourist information office in Corsica. The holidaymaker says one thing that they like. Their partner then suggests something they *must* or *can* do.

- *J'aime l'histoire.*
- *On peut visiter des musées. J'aime la natation …*
- …

J'aime J'adore	l'histoire. la natation. le danger. le shopping. les desserts.

Il faut visiter la Corse!

- aller à la plage
- faire un sport extrême
- visiter des musées
- aller au marché
- réserver une table dans un restaurant

Forming questions (Unit 2, page 111)

Lire 3

Read the grammar box on the different ways of forming questions on page 111. Match the question beginnings and endings below, and write the questions out in full. Then translate the questions into English.

1	Comment	peux acheter un poster au musée?
2	Quel plat	peut faire ici?
3	Où est-ce qu'	est-ce qu'on réserve une visite en bateau?
4	Est-ce que je	faut-il essayer?
5	Qu'est-ce qu'on	on peut faire du vélo?

Écouter 4

Listen to the six questions. The answers below are in the wrong order. Write the letter of the correct answer for each question you hear. (1–6)

a Il faut visiter le musée.
b Je suis allé à la plage.
c On peut acheter des posters au château.
d Oui, je peux te recommander le restaurant 'Bon Appétit!'
e Je trouve la vieille ville vraiment intéressante.
f Oui, on peut réserver la visite ici.

The relative pronoun *qui* (Unit 3, page 112)

Écrire 5 **Re-write each pair of sentences as one sentence. For 1–3, replace the underlined words with *qui*. For 4–6, work out which word or words you should replace.**

Example: 1 *J'ai un oncle qui habite en Asie.*

1 J'ai un oncle. Mon oncle habite en Asie.
2 Il y a des chefs. Les chefs préparent des desserts.
3 C'est une fête. La fête dure trois jours.
4 J'ai un ami. Mon ami aime les défilés.
5 Il y a des danseurs. Les danseurs viennent d'Afrique.
6 C'est un festival. Le festival se passe en novembre.

Relative pronouns such as *qui* refer to a noun that has just been mentioned.
Qui can be translated as 'who', 'which' or 'that'. You can use it to join two sentences together:

Il y a un restaurant. Le restaurant s'appelle Bon Appétit.
Il y a un restaurant ***qui*** *s'appelle Bon Appétit.*

Using the perfect and imperfect tenses together (Unit 3, page 113)

Lire 6 **Read the grammar box about using the perfect and imperfect tenses together on page 113. Then copy out the sentences. Circle each imperfect tense verb and underline each perfect tense verb.**

1 Je suis allé chez mon oncle. Il y avait beaucoup de gens.
2 J'ai écouté de la musique; c'était extraordinaire.
3 J'étais content car il a vu ma famille.
4 Mon amie est allée au marché mais elle était fatiguée.

To form the imperfect tense, remove the *-ons* from the *nous* form of the verb in the present tense, e.g.
regarder (to watch) → *nous regardons* → *regard-*
Then add these endings:
*je regard****ais*** *tu regard****ais*** *il/elle/on regard****ait***
The verb *être* has the stem ***ét-***
*c'****ét****ait* (it used to be/it was).

The imperfect tense is used to talk about what you were doing during a certain period of time:
Hier matin, entre 7 heures et 9 heures, je travaillais.
Yesterday morning, between 7 and 9 a.m., I was working.

Lire 7 **Sabrina the detective wants to know what these people were doing last night between 8 and 10 p.m. Read their alibis and translate them into English.**

Qu'est-ce que tu faisais hier soir entre 20 heures et 22 heures?

1 Je jouais au football au parc avec Sadio Mané.
2 Je chantais en concert avec Angèle.
3 Je regardais un film au cinéma avec Aïssa Maïga.
4 J'organisais un concert avec le groupe Teriya.
5 J'écrivais des chansons avec Grand Corps Malade.
6 Je travaillais pour l'égalité avec Rachel Keke.

Negatives in the imperfect and perfect tenses (Unit 4, page 114)

Écouter 8 **Read the grammar box about negatives in the imperfect and perfect tenses on page 114. Listen, then copy and complete the sentences with the missing negatives. Translate the sentences into English. (1–8)**

Remember that ***ne*** shortens to ***n'*** in front of a vowel.

1 Ce ___ était ___ amusant.
2 Il ___ y avait ___ à l'hôtel.
3 Je ___ étais ___ patient.
4 Il ___ y avait ___ dans la chambre.
5 Elle ___ a trouvé ___.
6 Il ___ a ___ fait.
7 Je ___ ai ___ bien dormi.
8 Il ___ est ___ allé au marché.

Grammaire 2

Saying 'in' (Unit 4, page 115)

Lire 1 **Copy out each sentence and complete it with the correct word for 'in'.**

1 Il y a des défilés ___ la rue.
2 Il a fait du vélo ___ campagne.
3 Ma mère habite ___ montagne.
4 Il y a un musée ___ centre-ville.
5 J'achète des cadeaux ___ ville.
6 Il passe une semaine ___ Paris.

The word for 'in' depends on where you are talking about:

- inside something: ***dans*** *une chambre*
- in the countryside or mountains: ***à la*** *campagne*, ***à la*** *montagne*
- in the town centre: ***au*** *centre-ville*
- in town: ***en*** *ville*
- in a named town: ***à*** *Paris*

Using *si* + the present tense + the near future tense (Unit 5, page 116)

Écrire 2 **Put the words in the correct order to make sentences. Then write the letter of the correct weather condition for each sentence.**

Example: 1 *S'il fait beau, je vais jouer au basket.* b

1 beau fait s'il jouer je au vais basket
2 fait s'il froid visiter vas le tu musée
3 s'il chaud fait faire elle du va vélo
4 s'il du y a soleil se relaxer au va on parc
5 fait acheter vais des mauvais cadeaux s'il je
6 on faire du pleut pas va camping ne s'il
7 du aller s'il au va vent y concert on a

Si + weather phrase in the present tense, + near future tense

When using a reflexive verb, remember to make the reflexive pronoun agree with the person doing the action:
je *vais* ***me*** *lever*   ***on*** *va* ***se*** *coucher*

Talking about the present, past and future (Unit 5, page 117)

le cheval	*horse*

Écouter 3 **Listen and write down which of the verbs in bold you hear each time. Then identify the name of the tense. (1–8)**

Example: 1 *Il faisait* – imperfect

1 **Il faisait** / **Il fait** tout le temps froid.
2 **Je vais jouer** / **Je joue** en ligne chez moi.
3 **Je voyage** / **J'ai voyagé** à vélo ou en bus.
4 **Je vais manger** / **J'ai mangé** du fromage.
5 **On chante** / **On va chanter** ensemble.
6 **Je suis tombé** / **Je vais tomber** de cheval.
7 **C'était** / **C'est** très amusant.
8 **On se relaxe** / **On va se relaxer** en famille.

When referring to the present, you usually use the **present tense**.
When referring to the future, you usually use the **near future tense** (*aller* + an infinitive).
When referring to the past, you need to choose between the **perfect tense** and the **imperfect tense**.

- Use the **perfect tense** for completed actions.
- Use the **imperfect tense** for descriptions and to say what was happening or what used to happen.

Écrire 4 **Copy out the sentences, filling in the gaps by translating the verbs in brackets into French.**

1 Normalement, pendant les grandes vacances, ___ chez moi. (*I stay*)
2 ___ au parc avec mes amis. (*I go*)
3 ___ au football. (*We play*)
4 L'année dernière, ___ du temps avec ma famille à la campagne. (*I spent*)
5 ___ à la plage. (*I went*)
6 Cependant ___ très froid. (*it was*)
7 Cet été, ___ deux semaines chez mon ami. (*I'm going to spend*)
8 ___! (*We are going to relax*)

C'est parti!

Parler 5 **In pairs, play 'trapdoor'.**

- Partner A: in secret, select one of the three options for each of numbers 1 to 7 in the sentences below.
- Partner B: your goal is to read out the sentences from start to finish, filling in gaps 1 to 7 with the options that your partner chose. Start to read out the story. Each time you get to a number, make a choice. If you read out what your partner selected, you can continue reading. If you don't, Partner A shouts 'trapdoor!' and you have to go back to the beginning.
- Then swap roles!

Je voudrais passer mes vacances idéales **(1)** en ville / à la campagne / à la montagne avec mes amis et on voudrait **(2)** aller à la plage. / faire du sport. / visiter de beaux sites.

En vacances, **(3)** on peut / on doit / il faut connaître une culture différente.

L'année dernière, je suis allé(e) à un festival. C'est un festival qui **(4)** se passe en mars. / dure une semaine. / est célèbre.

Je n'ai **(5)** rien mangé / pas dansé / trouvé personne **(6)** parce qu'il y avait du vent. / parce qu'il faisait froid. / parce que c'était ennuyeux.

Cet été, s'il fait chaud, je vais **(7)** retourner / me relaxer / danser à la fête.

Lire 6 **Translate the sentences from exercise 5, with your own options for each of gaps 1 to 7, into English.**

Module 5

Contrôle de lecture et d'écoute

Reading

Lire 1

A disastrous holiday. **You read this review that Rachid's parents have written on a website. Write the correct letter, A, B or C, to complete each sentence.**

Une catastrophe! Nous sommes partis le dix août et nous sommes restés quinze jours en Martinique. Le vol n'était pas long mais on est partis avec deux heures de retard!

Quand nous sommes arrivés, le taxi attendait mais il était trop petit pour tous nos sacs! On a attendu 30 minutes pour prendre un autre taxi.

À l'hôtel, encore un problème! Notre chambre était trop petite. On voulait une chambre pour trois personnes avec un grand lit et un petit lit. La chambre réservée pour notre famille était une chambre pour une personne!

1 The family spent ... days on holiday.
- **A** 5
- **B** 10
- **C** 15

2 The flight was ...
- **A** late.
- **B** too long.
- **C** cancelled.

3 The taxi didn't ...
- **A** arrive.
- **B** have enough space.
- **C** wait for them.

4 The room was ...
- **A** the wrong size.
- **B** dirty.
- **C** not available.

First, locate where the answers may be. Then read the sentences carefully and fully.

Lire 2

Newspaper headlines. **You see some headlines in a French newspaper. Which headline matches each event? Write the correct letter (A–E) for each event.**

A	L'hôtel «La belle saison» va fermer la semaine prochaine
B	Concerts et spectacles ce week-end!
C	Trop de touristes dans notre ville?
D	Beaucoup de vent demain!
E	Notre ville: la plus visitée de la région!

1 a weather alert **2** a closure **3** a festival

Lire 3

Translation. **Translate these sentences into English.**

What tenses are they?

1 J'aime voyager en avion.
2 Les vacances actives, ce n'est pas pour moi.
3 L'année dernière, je suis allé à un festival de nourriture.
4 Je vais passer une semaine au bord de la mer.
5 Un jour, j'aimerais aller en Suisse.

Listening

Écouter 4

Transport. **You hear some French students talking about transport. What is their opinion on the following? Write P for a positive opinion, N for a negative opinion, or P+N for a positive and negative opinion.**

1 planes **2** trains **3** boats **4** public transport

Écouter 5

Les Francofolies. **You hear Mariam talking about a music festival in La Rochelle, in France. Complete the sentences in English.**

1 a The festival takes place every …
  b Mariam says that all the good hotels are …
2 a During the festival, the weather is usually …
  b More tourists come from …

Écouter 6

Weather. **You hear this weather report for the area where you are staying on holiday. Choose the correct letter and write A, B or C for each question.**

1 Today, in the north, it is going to be …
  A hotter.
  B less hot.
  C rainy.

2 Tomorrow, in the south, it is going to be …
  A as hot as today.
  B hotter than today.
  C less hot than today.

Écouter 7

An interesting trip. **You hear Sarah talking about a recent holiday.**

1 What type of holidays does Sarah like and why? Give two details in **English**.
2 What did she do during her holiday? Write the two correct letters.

A	She went to a food festival.
B	She ate in her hotel room.
C	She discovered a new kind of food.
D	She visited a museum.

Écouter 8

Dictation. **You will now hear four short sentences. Listen carefully and, using your knowledge of French sounds, write in French exactly what you hear for each sentence.**

Beware of liaisons.

Contrôle oral

Role-play

Parler 1 **Look at the role-play card and prepare what you are going to say.**

- You are talking to your Canadian friend.
- Your teacher will play the part of your friend and will speak first.
- You should address your friend as *tu*.
- When you see this – **?** – you will have to ask a question.

In order to score full marks, you must include a verb in your response to each task.

1 Say where you like to spend your holiday. (Give **one** detail.)
2 Say what your favourite type of holiday is. (Give **one** detail.)
3 Describe a place you would like to visit. (Give **one** detail.)
4 Give **one** opinion about that place.
? 5 Ask your friend a question about a means of transport.

You could talk about a seaside holiday, or an active or cultural holiday.

You could ask what they like or prefer, or what they think.

Use the verb *passer*.

Use *je voudrais* followed by an infinitive.

Parler 2 **Practise what you have prepared. Then, using your notes, listen and respond to the teacher.**

Écouter 3 **Now listen to Lola doing the role-play task. In English, note down (a) how she answers the questions for tasks 1, 2, 3 and 4, and (b) what question she asks for task 5.**

Reading aloud

Parler 4 **Look at this task. With a partner, take turns to read out the text below, paying attention to the underlined letters.**

Read aloud the following text **in French**.

J'aime fair<u>e</u> du camping.
Je d<u>é</u>test<u>e</u> v<u>oy</u>ag<u>er</u> en v<u>oi</u>tur<u>e</u>.
Pendant les vacance<u>s</u>, je pr<u>é</u>fèr<u>e</u> all<u>er</u> dans le<u>s</u> magasin<u>s</u>.
L'ann<u>ée</u> derniè<u>re</u>, j'ai mang<u>é</u> de la n<u>ou</u>rritur<u>e</u> local<u>e</u>.
Un j<u>ou</u>r, je v<u>ou</u>drai<u>s</u> visit<u>er</u> un endr<u>oi</u>t trè<u>s</u> chaud.

Take extra care with how you pronounce the underlined sounds:
- ***oi***, ***oy*** and ***ou***
- ***er*** and ***é***
- final silent ***e***.

Don't say the ***s***.

Écouter 5 **Listen and check your pronunciation.**

Parler 6 **Listen to the teacher asking <u>four</u> questions that relate to the topic of Travel and tourism. Translate each question into English and prepare your own answers in French. Then listen again and respond to the teacher.**

Listen carefully to the question words.

Photo card task

Écouter 7 **Look at the exam card below and read the first part of the task. Then listen to Lola describing the two photos.**

1 In Lola's opinion, where are the four people in the first photo?
2 Where are the people in the second photo, according to Lola?
3 What does she say the people are doing in the first photo?

Photo 1

Photo 2

You will be asked to talk about the content of these photos. You must say at least one thing about each photo.

After you have spoken about the content of the photos, you will be asked questions related to any of the topics within the theme of **Communication and the world around us**.

Your responses should be as **full and detailed** as possible.

Parler 8 **Prepare your own descriptions of the two photos. You could mention, for example, the people, the location and what they are doing. Then, with a partner, take turns to describe the photos.**

Sur la première photo, il y a …

To talk about a group of similar people, you can use prompts to set them apart, e.g. *la première fille* ('the first girl'), *l'autre fille* ('the other girl'), *la dernière fille* ('the last girl').

Écouter 9 **Read the second part of the task. Listen to Lola answering the question: *Qu'est-ce que tu penses des vacances avec des amis?* Write down in English <u>two</u> advantages and <u>two</u> disadvantages.**

Écouter 10 **Now listen to Lola answering the question: *Comment est-ce que tu voudrais passer tes vacances idéales?* Write down in English the following details of her ideal holiday.**

1 Where? **2** Why? **3** With whom? **4** How long?

Parler 11 **Prepare your own answers to the module 5 questions on page 227. Your responses should be as full and detailed as possible. Then practise with a partner.**

Contrôle écrit

Grammar task

Écrire 1

Using your knowledge of grammar, copy and complete the following sentences in French. Choose the correct French word from the three options.

1 Je ___ le camping.	**préfère / préférer / préférée**
2 La chambre est trop ___.	**petit / petite / petites**
3 Le voyage ___ très bien.	**était / étais / été**
4 ___ sommes restés en France.	**Nous / On / Je**
5 Je ___ aller en vacances avec mes amis.	**peux / peut / pouvons**

Translation

Écrire 2

Translate the following sentences into French.

You need the infinitive, e.g. 'to travel'.

Check how to describe the weather.

Which prepositions are you going to use?

1 I like travelling by train.
2 It is too hot today.
3 At the hotel, there is a swimming pool.
4 Yesterday, it was very windy at the beach.
5 One day, I would like to go on holiday with my friends.

90-word writing task

Écrire 3

Look at this writing exam task and then, for each bullet point:

1 think about what vocabulary you have learned that you could use in your answer. For example:
- **nouns** and **verbs** to talk about holiday activities and problems
- **verbs of opinion** and **adjectives** to explain your point of view
- language for **narrating a story** about what went wrong
- *vouloir* in the **conditional** (*je voudrais*) **+ infinitive** to express how you **would like** to spend your holiday.

2 write down three or four ideas for what you could write about.
3 write down which tense(s) you will need to use in your answer.

Make sure your ideas are linked to produce a coherent piece of writing that makes sense as a whole.

You are emailing your Belgian friend about your holiday.

Write approximately **90** words in **French**.

You must write something about each bullet point.

Describe:
- how you usually spend your summer holiday
- a disaster that happened during your last holiday
- your ideal way to spend your summer holiday.

Lire 4 **Read Sarah's answer to the exam task. Answer questions 1–5 in the coloured shapes.**

Salut

Normalement, l'été, j'aime rester en Angleterre. Mes parents pensent que les vacances à l'étranger, c'est cher. J'adore être active et visiter beaucoup d'endroits.

L'été dernier, nous avons eu un problème. Nous sommes arrivés à la maison de vacances, mais il y avait une autre famille! Mon père a téléphoné à l'entreprise de vacances car il n'était pas content. L'autre famille avait la mauvaise adresse!

Pour mes vacances idéales, je voudrais aller dans un endroit où il fait chaud. Je voudrais aller dans un pays où les gens parlent espagnol. Je voudrais apprendre cette langue.

1 This is an example of **complex language**. What does it mean? Find three more examples from the text.

2 This phrase shows a **variety of vocabulary**. What does it mean? Find two more examples.

3 Which **tense** is this? What other examples can you find? Does Sarah use any other tenses?

4 How could she **avoid repetition** by using an alternative phrase here?

5 Which **connective** could you use here to form an **extended sentence**? What other connectives does she use?

Lire 5 **Read Sarah's answer again. Answer the questions in English.**

1 Why does Sarah's family normally like to stay in England in the summer?
2 What problem did her family experience on their last holiday?
3 What was the reason?
4 Where would she like to spend her ideal holiday and why?

Écrire 6 **Write your own answer to the 90-word writing task in exercise 3.**

- Think about how you can develop your answer for each bullet point.
- Look back at your notes from exercises 3 and 4.
- Look at the 'Challenge checklist' and think about how you can show off your French!
- Write a **brief** plan and organise your answer into paragraphs.
- Write your answer and then carefully check the accuracy of what you have written.

Challenge checklist	
	✓ Past, present and future time frames ✓ Connectives, time phrases, sequencers ✓ Some extended sentences ✓ Different opinion phrases
	✓ A wider range of structures (e.g. conditional of *vouloir*) ✓ Different persons of the verb (e.g. 'he/she') ✓ Weather phrases (e.g. *il fait* ...) ✓ A wide range of interesting vocabulary (e.g. *à l'étranger*)
	✓ The perfect tense and imperfect tense together ✓ Complex language (e.g. *sans*, reflexive verbs) ✓ Using *nous* and *on* ✓ More varied connectives (*donc*)

Module 5

Vocabulaire

Key:
bold = this word will appear in higher exams only
* = this word is not on the vocabulary list, but you may use it in your own sentences

Voudrais-tu voyager? (pages 106–107)

Pourquoi voudrais-tu voyager?	*Why would you like to travel?*
Je voudrais voyager pour ...	*I would like to travel to ...*
apprendre une nouvelle langue / un nouveau sport.	*learn a new language / sport.*
connaître une culture différente.	*get to know a different culture.*
me faire de nouveaux amis.	*make new friends.*
me relaxer.	*relax.*
sortir de la *routine.	*escape the routine.*
Où voudrais-tu passer tes vacances?	*Where would you like to spend your holiday?*
Je voudrais passer mes vacances ...	*I would like to spend my holiday ...*
au camping.	*at a campsite.*
à l'hôtel.	*at a hotel.*
à la maison.	*at home.*
dans le village.	*in the village.*
C'est où?	*Where is it?*
Qu'est-ce que c'est?	*What is it?*
C'est ...	*It is ...*
un camping avec des logements extraordinaires.	*a campsite with extraordinary accommodation.*
un hôtel-château au cœur d'une vieille ville.	*a castle hotel in the heart of an old town.*
une maison historique et *confortable.	*a historic and comfortable house.*
un village calme sur l'eau.	*a quiet village on the water.*
Qu'est-ce qu'il y a là-bas?	*What is there?*
Il y a ...	*There is/are ...*
un grand choix de restaurants.	*a large choice of restaurants.*
un grand jardin.	*a big garden.*
une belle vue sur la campagne.	*a beautiful view of the countryside.*
une piscine.	*a swimming pool.*
des *aires de jeux pour enfants.	*play areas for children.*
des chambres *confortables.	*comfortable bedrooms.*
des **terrains** de sport.	*sports grounds.*
Qu'est-ce qu'on peut faire là-bas?	*What can you do there?*
On peut ...	*You can ...*
être près de la nature.	*be close to nature.*
faire une expérience **unique** en famille sur la côte.	*have a unique experience as a family on the coast.*
se couper du monde.	*switch off from the world.*

Des vacances de rêve (pages 108–109)

Quel type de vacances voudrais-tu?	*What type of holiday would you like?*
Je voudrais ...	*I would like ...*
des vacances calmes.	*a quiet holiday.*
des vacances *éco-responsables.	*an eco-friendly holiday.*
des vacances culturelles.	*a cultural holiday.*
des vacances actives.	*an active holiday.*
Où voudrais-tu passer tes vacances idéales?	*Where would you like to spend your ideal holiday?*
Je voudrais passer mes vacances ...	*I would like to spend my holiday ...*
à la campagne.	*in the countryside.*
à la montagne.	*in the mountains.*
sur une île ou sur la côte.	*on an island or on the coast.*
en ville.	*in a town.*
Comment voudrais-tu voyager?	*How would you like to travel?*
Je voudrais voyager ...	*I would like to travel ...*
en avion *privé.	*in a private plane.*
en bateau / en train.	*by boat / by train.*
Où voudrais-tu *loger?	*Where would you like to stay?*
Je voudrais *loger ...	*I would like to stay ...*
sous une *tente.	*in a tent.*
dans un hôtel de *luxe / un château / une ferme.	*in a luxury hotel / a castle / a farm.*
Je voudrais ...	*I would like ...*
parce que je préfère ...	*because I prefer ...*
car j'adore ...	*because I love ...*
acheter des vêtements.	*to buy clothes.*
faire des activités passionnantes.	*to do exciting activities.*
faire de la natation.	*to swim.*
passer du temps à la piscine.	*to spend time at the swimming pool.*
visiter de beaux sites.	*to visit beautiful sites.*
Je voudrais ... pour me relaxer.	*I would like to ... (in order) to relax.*

On part pour la Corse (pages 110–111)

Qu'est-ce qu'il faut faire en *Corse?	*What must you do in Corsica?*
Qu'est-ce qu'on peut faire dans la région?	*What can you do in the area?*
Il faut ... / On doit ...	*You must ...*
On peut ...	*You can ...*
essayer les *desserts locaux.	*try the local desserts.*
connaître la culture *corse.	*get to know Corsican culture.*
faire une visite en bateau.	*go on a boat trip.*
pratiquer un sport *extrême.	*practise an extreme sport.*
aller à la plage.	*go to the beach.*
aller au marché.	*go to the market.*
faire du vélo.	*go cycling.*
monter une montagne.	*climb a mountain.*
réserver toutes les activités.	*book all the activities.*
visiter le musée de *Bastia.	*visit the Bastia museum.*
Qu'est-ce que tu as fait récemment en vacances?	*What did you do recently on holiday?*
Je suis allé(e) à la piscine / la plage.	*I went to the swimming pool / the beach.*
J'ai lu un livre.	*I read a book.*

Que fais-tu pour te relaxer?	*What do you do to relax?*
Je vais à la plage ou je lis un livre.	*I go to the beach or I read a book.*
Qu'est-ce qu'il faut visiter?	*What should you visit?*
Il faut visiter le musée / la vieille ville.	*You should visit the museum / the old town.*

Quels **plats** est-ce qu'il faut essayer?	*What food / dishes should you try?*
Il faut essayer les fromages / les glaces car ils/elles sont *délicieux/*délicieuses.	*You should try the cheeses / the ice creams because they're delicious.*

Le monde en fête (pages 112–113)

C'est un festival / une fête qui se passe en (janvier).	*It is a festival that happens in (January).*
Il y a des ...	*There are ...*
*danseurs / concerts.	*dancers / concerts.*
groupes de musique.	*music groups.*
jeux pour les enfants.	*games for children.*
marchés / *masques.	*markets / masks.*
défilés / spectacles.	*parades / shows.*
Il y a beaucoup de touristes.	*There are lots of tourists.*
C'est un festival / une fête ...	*It is a ... festival.*
amusant(e) / culturel(le).	*fun / cultural*
En (avril) dernier, je suis allé(e) chez ma tante / mon oncle.	*Last (April), I went to my aunt / uncle's house.*
C'était (la fête du *riz).	*It was (the Festival of Rice).*

Qu'est-ce qu'il y avait?	*What was there?*
Pendant plusieurs jours, ... il y avait ...	*For several days, ... there was/were ...*
Qu'est-ce que tu as fait?	*What did you do?*
J'ai dansé / mangé ...	*I danced / ate ...*
Un autre jour / soir, j'ai entendu ... / vu ...	*Another day / evening, I heard ... / saw ...*
C'était comment?	*How was it?*
C'était ...	*It was ...*
amusant / *délicieux.	*fun / delicious.*
extraordinaire.	*extraordinary.*
J'ai adoré ma première expérience (du festival).	*I loved my first experience (of the festival).*

Guide de voyage (pages 114–115)

Comment était l'hôtel? — *What was the hotel like?*

J'ai passé une nuit / deux nuits / une semaine dans cet hôtel.	*I spent a night / two nights / a week in this hotel.*
L'hôtel ...	*The hotel ...*
Le lit ...	*The bed ...*
La chambre / fenêtre / vue (sur la mer) ...	*The bedroom / window / (sea) view ...*
était / n'était pas ...	*was / was not ...*
beaux/belle.	*beautiful.*
cher/chère.	*expensive.*
*confortable.	*comfortable.*
(trop) petit(e).	*(too) small.*
pratique / propre.	*practical / clean.*
Internet ne marchait pas.	*The internet wasn't working.*
Il n'y avait pas de bruit le soir.	*There was no noise in the evening.*

Il n'y avait pas d'équipement (dans la salle de jeux).	*There was no equipment (in the games room).*
Il n'y avait pas de place dans le restaurant.	*There was no space in the restaurant.*
J'ai perdu la clé.	*I lost my key.*
Je n'ai trouvé personne à la **réception**.	*I didn't find anyone at reception.*
Je n'ai rien mangé.	*I ate nothing.*
Demain, je vais en vacances.	*I'm going on holiday tomorrow.*
Tu *loges dans un hôtel?	*Are you staying in a hotel?*
Oui. J'ai réservé une chambre pour (trois) personnes.	*Yes. I've booked a room for (three) people.*
Pour combien de nuits?	*For how many nights?*
C'est pour une nuit.	*It's for one night.*
Est-ce qu'il y a une piscine?	*Is there a swimming pool?*
Je voudrais une chambre avec une vue sur la mer / la plage.	*I would like a room with a view of the sea / the beach.*

Vive les vacances! (pages 116–117)

Quel temps fait-il aujourd'hui? — *What is the weather like today?*

Il fait / faisait ...	*It is / was ...*
chaud / froid.	*hot / cold.*
beau / mauvais.	*nice / bad weather.*
Il y a / avait du soleil / du vent.	*It is / was sunny / windy.*
Il pleut / *pleuvait.	*It is / was raining.*

Qu'est-ce qu'on va faire? — *What are we going to do?*

Qu'est-ce que tu vas faire ce week-end?	*What are you going to do this weekend?*
S'il fait beau / chaud / froid / mauvais ...	*If it's nice / hot / cold / bad weather ...*
je vais ...	*I am going to ...*
aller au musée.	*go to the museum.*
faire du vélo.	*go cycling.*
prendre un train ...	*take a train ...*
organiser un concert.	*organise a concert.*
rester chez moi.	*stay at home.*

Normalement, pendant les grandes vacances, ...	*Normally, during the summer holidays, ...*
je vais à la campagne.	*I go to the countryside.*
je dors dans un hôtel.	*I sleep in a hotel.*
L'été dernier, / L'année dernière, ...	*Last summer, / Last year, ...*
j'ai passé du temps / mes vacances ...	*I spent time / my holidays ...*
j'ai fait ...	*I did ...*
je suis allé(e) ...	*I went ...*
je suis parti(e) / je ne suis pas parti(e) en vacances.	*I went / I didn't go on holiday.*
Cet été, / Cette année, ...	*This summer, / This year, ...*
je vais ...	*I am going to ...*
aller à Paris.	*go to Paris.*
faire quelque chose de plus/moins actif.	*do something more/less active.*
apprendre une nouvelle langue.	*learn a new language.*

Révisions de grammaire 1

Using different articles (Pages 58, 84 and 94)

Lire 1 **Copy and complete these sentences with the correct definite article (*le/la/l'/les*) or indefinite article (*un/une/des*).**

Example: 1 *Ma matière préférée, c'est l'histoire.*

1 Ma matière préférée, c'est ___ histoire.
2 Sur la photo, il y a ___ maison.
3 Quand j'étais jeune, ma matière préférée était ___ musique.
4 ___ parc est ouvert tous les jours.
5 Il n'y avait pas beaucoup d'activités pour ___ jeunes.
6 ___ rendez-vous est à dix heures.

Écrire 2 **Copy and complete the sentences, choosing the correct partitive article to complete each one.**

1 À l'avenir, je vais faire **du / de la / des** sport chaque jour.
2 Le vendredi, je mange **du / de l' / des** poisson.
3 Tu as acheté **du / de la / de** viande au marché?
4 Il y a beaucoup **du / de / des** plages au Portugal.
5 Je ne bois jamais **du / de l' / d'** eau.

After a negative or a quantity, just use *de* (*d'* before a vowel).

Choosing the correct word for 'in' (Pages 112, 115 and 119)

Écrire 3 **Copy out the parallel translations, completing the missing words.**

1	Je voudrais dormir ___ une ferme.	I ___ ___ to stay in a ___.
2	Elle a trouvé un portable ___ la salle de classe?	Did she ___ a ___ ___ in the classroom?
3	Tu achetais des fruits au marché ___ ville?	Did you used to ___ fruit at the ___ in ___?
4	Est-ce qu'il a passé ses vacances ___ Espagne?	Did he ___ his ___ in ___?
5	As-tu visité un musée ___ Maroc?	___ you ___ a ___ in Morocco?

There are several words for 'in'.

- *au* + masculine country, or in the town centre
- *en* + feminine country, or in town
- *à* + village/town/city
- *dans* – inside something

Comparative adjectives (Pages 60 and 70)

Écrire 4 **Copy and complete the comparative sentences with the correct adjective from the box.**

1 La musique est plus ___ que l'anglais.
2 À mon avis, TikTok est moins ___ que Facebook.
3 Mon père trouve les émissions de sport plus ___ que les informations.
4 Je pense que les voyages en bateau sont aussi ___ que les voyages en train.

agréables
passionnantes
amusante
ennuyeux

The comparative adjective needs to agree with the first noun mentioned.

Lire 5 **Translate the sentences into English.**

1 Ma sœur est plus intelligente que mes frères.
2 Le lit à l'hôtel était moins grand que mon lit.
3 Le déjeuner est aussi important que le petit-déjeuner.
4 Tu trouves Netflix moins cher qu'un film au cinéma?

Indefinite adjectives

Écrire 6 **Copy and complete the sentences with the French translation of the indefinite adjectives in brackets.**

1 J'ai une heure de devoirs pour ___ matière. (*each, every*)
2 Le couscous est bon, mais j'aime ___ les repas. (*all*)
3 ___ les fêtes sont très amusantes pour ma famille. (*all*)
4 Est-ce que tu regardes des vidéos sur TikTok ___ soir? (*each, every*)
5 Elle va ___ le temps à la plage avec son chien. (*all*)
6 Pendant les vacances, tu vas à la piscine ___ jour? (*each, every*)

Indefinite adjectives talk about people or things in a general way, without being specific.

chaque	each, every
tout/toute/tous/toutes	all, the whole

A definite article isn't needed with *chaque* but is needed with *tout*.
chaque jour
*tous **les** jours*

Direct object pronouns and indirect object pronouns (Pages 67 and 73)

Lire 7 **Copy out the sentences. Circle the object pronoun and write if it is a direct (D) or indirect (I) object pronoun.**

Example: 1 *Je (la) regarde tous les soirs.* → *D*

1 Je la regarde tous les soirs.
2 Nous l'avons chanté quatre fois.
3 Il ne lui envoie pas de carte d'anniversaire.
4 Il va la voir en concert demain soir.
5 Je vous ai vu au centre commercial.
6 Ma tante m'a demandé de rester chez elle.

Object pronouns go before the verb. In the perfect tense, they go **before** the auxiliary verb (*avoir* or *être*).

In the near future tense, they go **before** the infinitive.

Écrire 8 **Re-write the sentences, replacing the underlined noun with the direct object pronoun in brackets. Make sure you put the pronoun in the correct place in the sentence.**

1 Vous cherchez la salle de classe? (*la*)
2 Je vais acheter la voiture. (*l'*)
3 Elle a attendu moi. (*m'*)
4 Je lis le journal tous les jours. (*le*)

Écrire 9 **Replace the underlined noun with the indirect object pronoun in brackets. Make sure you put the pronoun in the correct place in the sentence.**

1 Il donne un gâteau à moi. (*me*)
2 Tu envoyais des cartes d'anniversaire à ta sœur? (*lui*)
3 Elle parlait à toi avec respect. (*te*)
4 Le prof donne trop de devoirs à vous. (*vous*)

Expressions with *avoir* (Page 88)

Lire 10 **Match up the sentence halves and then translate them into English.**

Example: 1c *I'm cold and I don't want to go outside.*

1 J'ai froid et je ...
2 Elle avait faim ...
3 Tu n'as pas chaud ...
4 Ils vont avoir ...

a donc elle a mangé un sandwich.
b très soif après le match.
c ne veux pas aller dehors.
d à la plage?

There are lots of useful expressions using *avoir* in French, some of which are the equivalent of 'to be' expressions in English.

avoir chaud	to be hot
avoir froid	to be cold
avoir faim	to be hungry
avoir soif	to be thirsty

Révisions de grammaire 2

Modal verbs (Pages 87 and 95)

Modal verbs include *pouvoir*, *vouloir* and *devoir*.
They are all followed by an infinitive.

Je veux acheter un gâteau.	I want to buy a cake.
Je peux sortir ce samedi.	I can go out this Saturday.
Je dois faire mes devoirs.	I have to do my homework.

Savoir is also a modal verb.

savoir (*to know (how to)*)	
je sais	nous savons
tu sais	vous savez
il/elle/on sait	ils/elles savent

Lire 1 **Separate out the words to make accurate sentences. Then match the English translations.**

1 tupeuxfairetesdevoirsplustard
2 ellenesaitpasdanser
3 jeneveuxpasallerauconcert
4 nousdevonssortircesoir
5 ildoitparleràsongrandpère

a She doesn't know how to dance.
b He has to speak to his grandfather.
c You can do your homework later.
d I don't want to go to the concert.
e We have to go out tonight.

Écrire 2 **Copy and complete the sentences with the correct form of the verb in brackets.**

1 Tu ___ écrire un article. (*devoir*)
2 Il ___ voyager en avion. (*vouloir*)
3 Vous ___ faire vos devoirs de maths? (*pouvoir*)
4 Un bon ami ___ être sympa. (*devoir*)
5 Est-ce que tu ___ faire du judo? (*savoir*)
6 Nous ne ___ pas acheter la maison. (*pouvoir*)

Infinitive expressions (Pages 62, 70 and 91)

Écrire 3 **Choose one option from each column to make at least four logical sentences. Write out your sentences in French. Then translate them into English.**

Example: *Il faut aller au collège. – You have to go to school.*

	aller	les profs.
	arriver	ses devoirs.
Il faut	boire	au collège.
Il ne faut pas	écouter	de l'eau.
Il est interdit de/d'	faire	du piano.
Il est essentiel de/d'	jouer	en classe.
	manger	en retard.
	voyager	en train.

il faut (+ infinitive)	you have to ...
il ne faut pas (+ infinitive)	you must not ...
il est interdit de (+ infinitive)	it is forbidden to ...
Il est essentiel de (+ infinitive)	it is essential to ...
pour (+ infinitive)	in order to ...

Écrire 4 **Copy out the parallel translations, completing the missing words.**

1	Le ___, je me lève tôt ___ aller chez ma grand-mère.	On weekends, I ___ early to go to my ___ house.
2	Pour ___ en forme, il faut faire du ___.	___ to be healthy, you must ___ sport.
3	Tu ___ les réseaux sociaux pour ___ des photos?	Do you use ___ media to share ___?
4	On va à l'___ pour se ___.	We ___ to the hotel ___ rest.
5	Pour avoir de bonnes ___, il ne faut ___ manger en classe.	In order to ___ good grades, you ___ not eat in class.

Talking about the past (Pages 71, 72 and 96)

Écrire 5 **Copy and complete the perfect tense sentences with the correct auxiliary verb from the box.**

as ai avons est suis

1 J'___ fait beaucoup de progrès cette année.
2 Nous ___ passé une nuit dans cet hôtel en décembre.
3 Elle ___ allée au marché pour acheter des pommes.
4 Je ne ___ pas resté chez moi le week-end dernier.
5 Tu n'___ pas très bien dormi?

Écrire 6 **Write the French words in the correct order to translate the English sentences.**

1 I used to watch music clips. — des clips / regardais / Je / de musique
2 There were lots of people. — beaucoup de / avait / Il / monde / y
3 She used to find English boring. — trouvait / Elle / ennuyeux / l'anglais
4 It was hard for me. — pour / C'était / moi / dur
5 It was sunny. — soleil / y / Il / du / avait

Lire 7 **For each of these past tense sentences, write whether the underlined verb is in the perfect tense or imperfect tense. Then translate the sentences into English.**

Example: 1 *Perfect tense – I read a very good book.*

1 J'ai lu un très bon livre.
2 Elle a acheté un pantalon pour la fête.
3 Tu allais à l'école primaire à pied?
4 J'étais très triste à cause des examens.
5 Elles ont dormi dans une tente dans la forêt.
6 Je gagnais souvent les matchs de tennis.

Using verbs in a range of tenses (Pages 71, 97, 120 and 121)

Lire 8 **In each set of verbs, one is in a different tense from the other three. Write down which is the odd one out, and the tense of the other three: perfect, imperfect, present or near future tense.**

Example: 1 *j'ai acheté is the odd one out. The other three are in the present tense.*

1 nous mangeons / il y a / j'ai acheté / ils travaillent
2 je jouais / tu as étudié / c'était / on regardait
3 nous allons rester / je vais voyager / il va aller / vous avez
4 je n'ai pas vu / il est allé / vous chantez / ils sont restés
5 elle va danser / elle aimait / je partais / tu faisais
6 c'est / on boit / vous allez / tu vas ouvrir

Écrire 9 **Translate the sentences into French.**

1 I like seeing my friends every day.
2 She doesn't want to eat lots of vegetables.
3 Last weekend, we went to my aunt's house.
4 The hotel wasn't expensive.
5 If it's hot, I am going to go to the beach.

For 'seeing', use the infinitive *voir*.

Take care with where you place the negative.

Just use *de* for the partitive article after a quantity.

Use *chez ma tante* for 'to my aunt's house'.

The first part of the sentence needs a present tense verb and the second part a near future tense verb.

Module 6

Notre planète

Madagascar: miroir du monde?

- Understanding infographics about the environment
- Practising numbers and percentages

Madagascar is a large island located to the south-east of Africa.

The main languages spoken there are Malagasy and French.

There are more unique species of plants and animals living in Madagascar than on the entire African continent. More than 80 per cent of its species can be found nowhere else on Earth.

Source: https://www.usaid.gov/madagascar/environment-and-climate-change

a silky sifaka lemur, one of the many endangered species of Madagascar

Lire 1 **Read the infographic. Then answer each question (1–6) with the correct number from the box. Write your answer in French.**

L'écologie à Madagascar

concerné(e)	*concerned*
rarement	*rarely*

À ton avis, est-ce que l'écologie est importante?

Oui, très importante	Oui, assez importante	Pas très importante	Pas du tout importante
87%	**11%**	**1%**	**1%**

Es-tu concerné(e) par la planète?

Très concerné(e)	Assez concerné(e)	Un peu concerné(e)	Pas du tout concerné(e)
61%	**34%**	**3%**	**2%**

Est-ce que tu aides à protéger l'environnement?

Oui, chaque jour	Oui, souvent	Parfois	Non, rarement	Non
40%	**26%**	**26%**	**7%**	**1%**

onze   soixante-et-un   trente-quatre   vingt-six   quatre-vingt-sept   quarante

What percentage of respondents ...

1 think that ecology is very important?
2 think that ecology is quite important?
3 are very concerned about the planet?
4 are quite concerned about the planet?
5 help to protect the environment every day?
6 help to protect the environment sometimes?

20	vingt	**61**	soixante-et-un
30	trente	**64**	soixante-quatre
40	quarante	**71**	soixante-et-onze
50	cinquante	**86**	quatre-vingt-six
60	soixante	**98**	quatre-vingt-dix-huit
70	soixante-dix		
80	quatre-vingts		
90	quatre-vingt-dix		
100	cent		
200	deux-cents		
1000	mille		

pour cent	*per cent*
vingt-deux pour cent	*twenty-two per cent*

Écouter 2 **Listen and write down the number that you hear. Check your answers and then write each number as a word in French. (1–8)**

1 26 / 28   **4** 52 / 56   **7** 81 / 83
2 31 / 41   **5** 65 / 75   **8** 93 / 97
3 45 / 49   **6** 66 / 76

Écouter **3** **Listen and write down the correct percentage for each environmental problem. There are two options too many. (1–5)**

Les problèmes environnementaux à Madagascar

Quel est le plus grand problème à Madagascar, à ton avis?

1 
la **déforestation**
%

2 
la **pollution**
%

3 
l'**extinction** des espèces
%

4 
l'**utilisation** des ressources naturelles
%

5 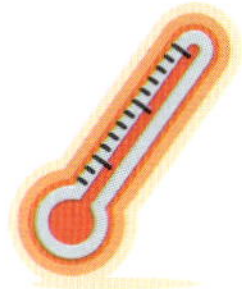
les effets du changement climatique
%

32% 23% 18% 14% 10% 9% 8%

le plus grand problème	*the biggest problem*
l'espèce *(f)*	*species*
le changement climatique	*climate change*

The sound ***-tion*** is pronounced a bit like 'ss-ee-on'.
As you do exercise 3, listen carefully to how the words in bold are pronounced.
Note that all nouns ending in ***-tion*** are feminine!

Parler **4** **In pairs, take turns to read out the following words, paying attention to the -*tion* sound. Then listen and check.**

la pollution | l'extinction
la protection | l'organisation
la solution | la population

All of the words in exercise 4 are cognates. This means that they look the same as, or are similar to, English words, and mean the same things. Other examples of cognates in this unit include *l'environnement* and *la planète*. Which other cognates can you spot in the unit?

Parler **5** **Conduct a survey. Copy out the grid, then ask the question below to at least eight people in your class. Keep a tally of your results.**

Quel est le plus grand problème dans ta région, à ton avis?

À mon avis, c'est ...

la déforestation	
la pollution	
l'extinction des espèces	
l'utilisation des ressources naturelles	
les effets du changement climatique	

Écrire **6** **Write some sentences in French to summarise the findings from your survey.**

Une personne pense que ...,	c'est le plus grand problème.
Deux / Trois / Quatre personnes pensent que ...,	

1 Notre monde est beau

- Talking about geography and the climate
- Using comparative adjectives
- Learning about francophone countries

Lire 1 **Read the cards. Is each statement below true (write *vrai*) or false (write *faux*)? Then listen and check. (1–5)**

La France

Population	68 000 000
Rivière	la Loire, 1 012 km
Montagne	le mont Blanc, 4 808 m
Forêt	la forêt d'Orléans, 350 km²

La République démocratique du Congo (RDC)

Population	103 000 000
Rivière	le Congo, 4 700 km
Montagne	le pic Marguerite, 5 109 m
Forêt	la forêt tropicale congolaise, 154 135 km²

1. Le mont Blanc est plus haut que le pic Marguerite.
2. Le Congo est plus long que la Loire.
3. La forêt d'Orléans est plus grande que la forêt tropicale congolaise.
4. La population de la France est moins grande que la population de la République démocratique du Congo.
5. La Loire est moins longue que le Congo.

G

Remember, you use comparative adjectives to compare things:

plus + adjective + ***que*** more + adjective + than

moins + adjective + ***que*** less + adjective + than

The adjective must agree (in gender and number) with the first noun:

***Le** Congo est plus long que la Loire.* The Congo is longer than the Loire.

***La** forêt d'Orléans est moins grand**e** que la forêt tropicale congolaise.* The forest of Orléans is less big/smaller than the Congo rainforest.

	big	high	long
masculine	*grand*	*haut*	*long*
feminine	*grand**e***	*haut**e***	*long**ue***

Page 146

Écrire 2 **Using information from the cards, copy and complete the sentences to compare geographical features in Canada with those in France and/or the Democratic Republic of the Congo.**

1. La population du Canada est moins grande que ___.
2. Le Mackenzie est plus long que ___.
3. Le mont Logan est ___.
4. La forêt boréale canadienne est ___.

Compare some of the geographical features to those in France and some to those in Democratic Republic of the Congo.

Le Canada

Population	38 250 000
Rivière	le Mackenzie, 1 738 km
Montagne	le mont Logan, 5 950 m
Forêt	la forêt boréale canadienne, 3 000 000 km²

Lire 3 **Read the texts. Find the French for the phrases below.**

Notre monde est *beau*

***l'ours** (m)*	*bear*
la baleine	*whale*
le paysage	*landscape*

Le Canada est bien connu pour ses hautes montagnes et ses grandes forêts.

La forêt boréale canadienne est plus grande que les forêts de France.

Au Canada, il y a beaucoup d'animaux, comme par exemple des ours noirs et des baleines.

En hiver et au printemps, il fait très froid et il neige beaucoup. Il fait plus froid qu'en France, par exemple!

La République démocratique du Congo (RDC) est en Afrique.

Le paysage est divers. Il y a de grandes villes et de petits villages.

La RDC est bien connue pour ses montagnes et son volcan, le Nyiragongo.

Dans le nord, il pleut beaucoup en automne. Le soir, il y a du brouillard.

En été et au printemps, il fait très chaud. Il fait plus chaud qu'en Europe!

1. is well known for
2. there are lots of animals
3. it snows a lot
4. in the north, it rains a lot in autumn
5. in the evening, there is fog

au printemps	*in spring*
en été	*in summer*
en automne	*in autumn*
en hiver	*in winter*

Lire 4 **Re-read the texts in exercise 3. Are the statements below true of Canada (write 'C') or Democratic Republic of the Congo (write 'DRC')?**

1. This country is well known for its forests.
2. This country's mountains are described as high.
3. This country has a varied landscape.
4. This country is very hot in summer.
5. The text about this country mentions lots of animals.
6. This country has large cities and small towns.

Écouter 5 **Listen and write down the missing words in French. Then translate the sentences into English. (1–5)**

1. ___ en Suisse.
2. La Suisse est connue pour ses ___ et ses lacs.
3. En ___, dans les Alpes, il ___ beaucoup.
4. Dans ma région, en ___, il fait ___.
5. Il ne fait ___ très ___.

le lac	*lake*

Parler 6 **In pairs, play 'trapdoor'.**

- Partner A: in secret, select one of the options for each of numbers 1 to 5 in the sentences below.
- Partner B: start to read out the sentences. When you get to a number, if you read out what your partner selected, you can continue. If you don't, Partner A shouts 'trapdoor' and you have to go back to the beginning!
- Then swap roles.

Ma région est connue pour ses **1** **forêts** / **montagnes** / **lacs**.

2 **En été** / **Au printemps**, ici, **3** **il fait beau** / **il fait chaud** / **il pleut**

et **4** **en hiver** / **en automne**, **5** **il fait mauvais** / **il fait froid** / **il neige**.

2 Planète en danger

- Talking about environmental problems
- Talking about future weather
- Pronouncing the 'open *o*'

Lire 1 **Look at the photos and read the captions. Copy and complete the grid in French. Listen and check.**

Grands problèmes	Solutions possibles

a 
la destruction des forêts

b 
le recyclage

c 
la pollution de l'air

d 
la faim

e 
le changement climatique

f 
la pollution de la mer

g 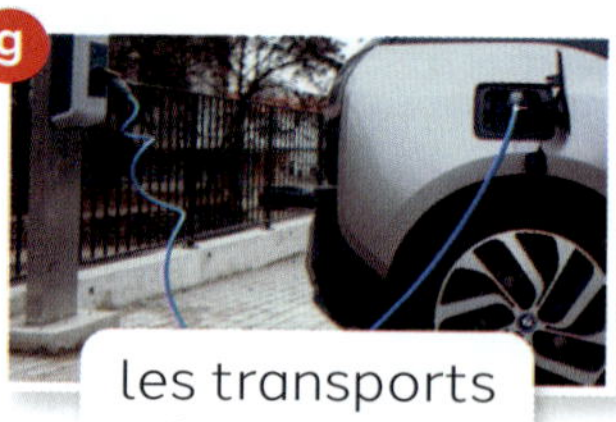
les transports électriques

h 
planter plus d'arbres et de fleurs

Écouter 2 **Listen. What are these students talking about? Write the letter of the correct photo from exercise 1. (1–8)**

Lire 3 **Read the texts. Then answer the questions below by writing the correct name.**

Zachary
La pollution de l'air est un problème énorme. Les transports électriques améliorent la situation. Le recyclage aussi!

Lucas
La pollution de la mer tue les poissons. Je trouve que la protection de la mer sauve les animaux et améliore l'environnement.

Khalida
À mon avis, le changement climatique cause la faim dans le monde. C'est un grand problème pour la population humaine.

sauver *to save*

Who …

1 wants to protect the sea? **2** is concerned by hunger? **3** is concerned by air pollution?

Parler 4 **Listen and repeat the following words.**

protéger notre pollution forêt améliorer catastrophe

The French ***o*** is an open sound in these words.

Écrire 5 **Write four sentences using the grid. Then swap sentences with a partner and translate your partner's sentences into English.**

À mon avis, Je pense que Je trouve que	la pollution le changement climatique la destruction des forêts	est	un problème énorme. une catastrophe.
	le recyclage la protection de la mer planter plus de fleurs et d'arbres	est	une solution possible.
		améliore	la situation.
	les transports électriques	sont	une solution possible.
		améliorent	la situation.

Écouter 6 **Look at the map. Listen and read. Then write down the letter of the correct city for each weather forecast. (1–4)**

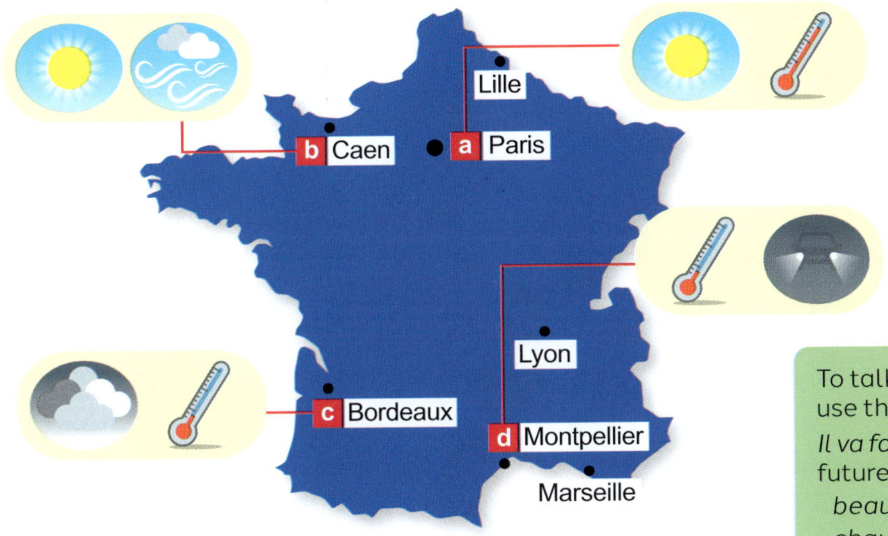

1 Il y aura du soleil, mais il y aura aussi du vent.
2 Il va faire très froid et il y aura du brouillard.
3 Ce week-end, il va faire chaud et il y aura du soleil.
4 Il va faire mauvais et il va faire froid.

G

To talk about the weather in the future, use the following structures:

Il va faire ... (the near future tense)	*Il y aura* ... (this is '*il y a*' in the future)
beau	*du soleil*
chaud	*du vent*
froid	*du brouillard*
mauvais	

Page 147

Écouter 7 **Listen to the forecasts. Write <u>two</u> details in English about the weather in each of Marseille, Lille and Lyon. (1–3)**

Parler 8 **In pairs, talk about what the weather will be like, using the prompts below.**

- *Quel temps va-t-il faire?*
- *Il va faire ... Il y aura ...*

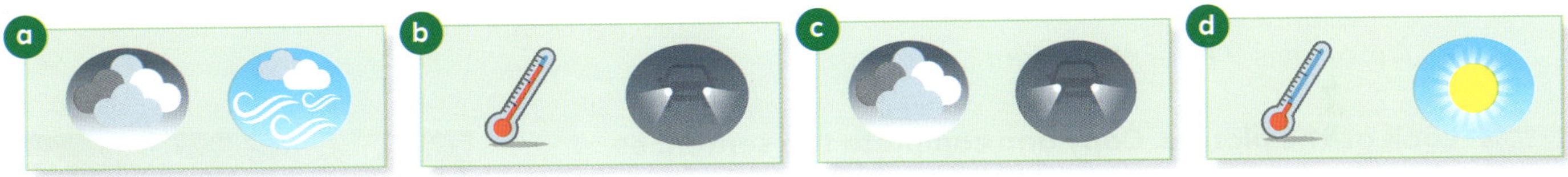

Lire 9 **Read the text. Match each <u>underlined</u> phrase to one of the pictures (a–d) below.**

Le climat en 2050? Le choix est à nous!

On lutte pour limiter le réchauffement de la planète à 1,5°C. Voici deux scénarios possibles ...

Scénario A ✓

1 <u>Les nouvelles technologies, comme les voitures électriques par exemple, vont limiter le danger</u>.

2 <u>On va sauver les habitats des animaux et limiter la pollution de la mer</u>.

3 <u>On va limiter le changement climatique</u>. Les pays vont être plus froids ou plus chauds, mais les effets vont être moins extrêmes.

Scénario B ✗

4 <u>Il va faire beaucoup plus chaud</u>. Le changement climatique va continuer à cause de la pollution.

Le climat va être plus extrême.

Les effets du changement climatique vont avoir un impact terrible sur les animaux.

3 Des grands gestes

- Discussing what we can do together to protect the environment
- Using the present and perfect tenses
- Describing a photo taken outside in nature

Écouter 1 **Listen, then write down (a) the phrase used to introduce the opinion, and (b) the letter of the correct picture. (1–6)**

Qu'est-ce qu'il faut faire pour protéger l'environnement?

pour moi, | à mon avis, | je pense que | je trouve que | je crois que

a  Il faut travailler ensemble pour arrêter le changement climatique.

b  Il faut respecter la nature.

c  Il faut arrêter la pollution et la destruction des forêts.

d  Il faut être bénévole pour des projets verts.

e  Il faut arrêter de fabriquer des produits en plastique.

f  Il faut organiser des manifestations pour la protection des animaux.

le/la bénévole volunteer

Parler 2 **Conduct a survey. Ask the question below to six people in the class.**

- *Qu'est-ce qu'il faut faire pour protéger l'environnement?*
- *À mon avis, / Pour moi, il faut ...*

Make your own speaking and writing more interesting by varying how you introduce your opinions.
Remember that *que* changes to *qu'* in front of a vowel:
Je pense qu'il faut ...

Lire 3 **Look at the picture. Copy and complete the sentences, choosing from the correct option each time. Then listen and check.**

1 Sur la photo, il y a **cinq personnes** / **des amis** / **une famille**.
2 La femme a les cheveux **courts** / **longs et noirs** / **blonds**.
3 Ils sont dehors, **sur la côte** / **à la montagne** / **à la campagne**.
4 Il fait **beau** / **mauvais** / **froid**.
5 Les gens **marchent** / **font du vélo** / **jouent**.
6 Je pense qu'ils **sont heureux** / **ne sont pas heureux**.

Écrire 4 **Write <u>four</u> sentences about this photo. Adapt some of the sentences from exercise 3.**

Lire **5** **Read the texts. Then answer the questions by writing 'Michel' or 'Charlotte'.**

J'adore la nature et je crois qu'il faut travailler avec les autres pour arrêter le changement climatique.
J'admire beaucoup Youna Marette. Elle est connue pour ses actions pour protéger l'environnement. Moi aussi, je fais un effort pour arrêter la pollution. J'écris un blog sur mon travail comme bénévole pour des projets verts.
Le mois dernier, je suis allé à une manifestation à Paris contre la destruction des forêts. J'ai pris le bus. J'ai rencontré des personnes sympa et j'ai appris beaucoup de choses.

Michel

Je pense qu'il faut arrêter la pollution.
Je vais souvent à des manifestations pour la protection de la planète. Je rencontre toujours des personnes intéressantes.
Au mois d'août, j'ai participé à une manifestation contre la pollution de l'air. Il y avait beaucoup de gens dans les rues et j'ai écouté Victor Noël, un jeune activiste. J'ai passé du temps avec de nouveaux amis.
Après la manifestation, j'ai écrit un article sur mon expérience pour le collège.

Charlotte

1 Who writes about giving time for green projects?
2 Who took public transport to a demonstration?
3 Who went to a demonstration about air pollution?
4 Who listened to a speaker?
5 Who learned lots of things?
6 Who has written about a recent demonstration for school?

Youna Marette

Victor Noël

Écrire **6** **Copy out each of the underlined phrases from the texts in exercise 5. Note down if each one is in the present tense or the perfect tense. Then translate the phrases into English.**

G

Remember that the perfect tense is formed of two parts: the auxiliary verb (part of *avoir* or *être*) and a past participle. Some past participles are irregular. The past participle of verbs that take *être* must agree with the subject.

	present	**perfect**
regular -*er* verbs, e.g. rencontrer (to meet)	je rencontre	j'**ai** rencontr**é**
écrire (to write)	j'écris	j'**ai écrit**
aller (to go)	je vais	je **suis allé**(**e**)

Page 147

Écouter **7** **Listen, then write down (a) the letter of the correct activity, and (b) the tense (present or perfect) used. (1–4)**

a participating in protests
b giving time for green projects
c listening to activists
d writing blog posts

Écrire **8** **Translate these sentences into French.**

Which structure could you use here?

The present tense is needed in both parts of this sentence.

1 In my opinion, we have to protect animals.
2 My brother works as a volunteer for green projects.
3 I admire Greta Thunberg because she works hard to stop pollution.
4 Last week, I went to a demonstration against deforestation.
5 Afterwards, I wrote an article on my blog about my experience.

Use *travaille comme* here.

The perfect tense is needed for these sentences.

4 Des petits gestes

- Talking about day-to-day actions to protect the environment
- Using the imperfect tense to describe what you used to do
- Extending spoken and written answers

Écouter 1 **Listen and write down the <u>two</u> correct letters for each speaker. (1–3)**

a

Je prends les transports publics.

b

Je ne mange pas de viande.

c

Je recycle les déchets.

d

Je n'utilise pas de produits en plastique.

e

Je vais en ville à vélo et non pas en voiture.

f

J'achète du papier recyclé.

Parler 2 **Play a memory game. Work in groups of four. Each person has to repeat what the previous person said, and add something new!**

Qu'est-ce que tu fais pour protéger l'environnement?

- ● *J'achète du papier recyclé.*
- ■ *J'achète du papier recyclé et je prends les transports publics.*
- ▲ *J'achète du papier recyclé, je prends les transports publics et je ne mange pas de viande.*
- ◆ *J'achète du papier recyclé, je prends les transports publics, je ne mange pas de viande et …*

Lire 3 **Read Tom's text. Copy and complete the sentences in English.**

Sept jours pour sauver la planète!

Le lundi, je vais en ville à vélo. Je ne prends jamais la voiture.
Le mardi, je fais les courses. J'utilise toujours les mêmes sacs en plastique.
Le mercredi, je recycle les déchets: le papier et le plastique.
Le jeudi, j'achète des fruits et des légumes au marché.
Le vendredi, je travaille comme bénévole pour un projet qui protège les hérissons.
Le samedi, je prends toujours le bus pour aller chez ma grand-mère.
Le dimanche, je ne mange pas de viande. C'est mieux pour l'environnement.

le hérisson *hedgehog*

You sometimes need the definite article in French even where we wouldn't use it in English.
***le** lundi* on Mondays
*Je recycle **les** déchets.*
I recycle rubbish.

1 On Mondays, he goes into town ___. He never ___.
2 On Tuesdays, he goes ___. He always uses the same ___.
3 On Wednesdays, he ___.
4 On Thursdays, he buys ___.
5 On Fridays, he works as a volunteer for ___.
6 On Saturdays, he always ___ in order to go ___.
7 On Sundays, he doesn't ___. It's better ___.

Écrire 4 **Write your own diary of a week to save the planet.**

Expand on your answers by adding extra details where possible (e.g. where, when, who, what, how).

Lire 5 **Read the text. Copy and complete the grid with the letters of the correct pictures.**

What she used to do (imperfect)	What she does now (present)

Ma visite au Québec

L'année dernière, je suis allée au Québec. Ma visite a changé ma vie parce que là-bas, j'ai vu les effets du changement climatique!

Avant, je ne m'intéressais pas beaucoup à l'environnement, mais maintenant, après ma visite au Québec, je fais beaucoup d'efforts pour protéger l'environnement.

Par exemple, avant, je mangeais de la viande tous les jours. Maintenant, je ne mange pas de viande. Je suis végétarienne. En plus, dans ma famille, on achète nos légumes au marché.

Ensuite, je recycle les déchets et j'utilise du papier recyclé. Avant, je ne recyclais rien!

Enfin, j'allais au collège en voiture, mais maintenant, je vais tous les jours au collège à pied – quand il fait beau mais aussi quand il pleut! **Rosalie**

a

b

c

d

e

f

Lire 6 **Re-read the text in exercise 5. Find the French for the phrases below.**

1 my visit changed my life
2 I saw the effects of climate change
3 I wasn't very interested in the environment
4 I make a lot of effort to protect the environment
5 I didn't use to recycle anything

G

Use the **perfect tense** to talk about **single, completed events or actions in the past,** e.g. *ma visite a changé ma vie* (my visit changed my life – one action, completed).
Look at page 141 to see how the perfect tense is formed.

Use the **imperfect tense** to talk about **what happened in the past over a period of time** (what used to happen), e.g. *j'allais au collège en voiture* (I used to go to school by car – repeatedly).
Look at page 148 to see how the imperfect tense is formed.

Page 148

Écouter 7 **Listen. Then copy and complete the grid in English. (1–3)**

	What did they use to do?	What do they do now?
1		

imperfect	present
j'utilisais	j'utilise / je n'utilise pas
je (ne) mangeais (pas)	je (ne) mange (pas)
je recyclais	je recycle
j'allais	je vais

Parler 8 **In pairs, take turns to ask and answer the two questions.**

- *Quand tu étais plus jeune, qu'est-ce que tu faisais pour protéger l'environnement?*
- *Quand j'étais plus jeune, <u>je m'intéressais beaucoup à l'environnement</u> / <u>je ne m'intéressais pas beaucoup à l'environnement</u>. Je ...*
- *Qu'est-ce que tu fais pour protéger l'environnement maintenant?*
- *Maintenant, je <u>fais beaucoup d'efforts</u>. Je ...*

Can you extend your answer by also saying what you **didn't** use to do in the past? For example:
*Je **ne** recyclais **pas** ...*
I did not use to recycle ...
*Je **ne** recyclais **jamais** ...*
I never used to recycle ...

5 Innovation verte

- Discussing school environmental projects
- Using the present, perfect, imperfect and near future tenses
- Answering questions using a variety of tenses

Lire 1 **Read the questions below. Which tense is each one in? Write 'present', 'perfect', 'imperfect', or 'near future'.**

Innovation verte au collège

1 Quelle est votre innovation?
2 Quel était le problème, avant?
3 Et qu'est-ce que vous avez fait?
4 Et c'est comment, maintenant?
5 Et à l'avenir, qu'est-ce que vous allez faire?

Lire 2 **Match each question (1–5) from exercise 1 to an answer (a–e) below. Then listen and check.**

a On a parlé avec le directeur et **on a décidé d'organiser un jardin** et le recyclage de la nourriture en compost. On a arrêté le gaspillage.

b Il y avait beaucoup de gaspillage et **on jetait de la nourriture à la poubelle avec les autres déchets**. **On ne faisait pas beaucoup pour protéger l'environnement**.

c **On va parler à une conférence** et participer à un concours interscolaire. On va aussi interdire les sacs en plastique au collège.

d Dans notre collège, on évite le gaspillage de nourriture. On fait pousser nos propres légumes dans le jardin de l'école. **On fait aussi du compost**.

e C'est beaucoup mieux! On protège l'environnement – **il n'y a pas de gaspillage de nourriture**. Ça fait une énorme différence.

le gaspillage	*waste*
la poubelle	*bin*
interdire	*to ban*
éviter	*to avoid*
faire pousser	*to grow*

Lire 3 **Re-read the answers in exercise 2 and find the French for the phrases below, choosing from the phrases in bold.**

1 there is no food waste
2 we also make compost
3 we decided to organise a garden
4 we did not (use to) do much to protect the environment
5 we are going to speak at a conference
6 we threw / used to throw food in the bin with the other rubbish

G

Tense	Used to talk about	Examples
present	what is happening now what you usually do what someone or something is like	*Il travaille dans le jardin.* *On lutte pour l'environnement.* *C'est mieux!*
perfect	single, completed actions in the past	*J'ai écrit un blog.* *Elle est allée à une manifestation.*
imperfect	what something or someone was like what used to happen in the past, over a period of time	*C'était bien.* *On allait toujours au collège à pied.*
near future	what is going to happen in the future	*On va parler avec les profs.*

Page 148

Écouter 4 **Listen to the conversation. Choose the correct option to complete each sentence. (1–5)**

1 At our school **cars have been banned** / **new buses are in operation**.
2 Before, there **were too many cars on site** / **was too much air pollution**.
3 We encouraged pupils to go to school by **bike** / **bus**.
4 Now, although the journey is **slower** / **less practical**, it is better for the environment.
5 In the future, we will **encourage more people to walk** / **have free bikes at school**.

G

Comparative adverbs work in a similar way to adjectives, but they are invariable (i.e. there are not different masculine, feminine or plural forms). They are placed after the verb:
On arrive ***plus vite*** *en avion.*
You arrive more quickly by plane.
On voyage ***moins vite*** *à vélo.*
You travel less quickly by bike.

Note these irregular forms:
bien (well) *mieux* (better)

Parler 5 **In pairs, take turns to read out the matched answers and questions from exercises 1 and 2 to recreate the interview. Focus on good pronunciation.**

Before reading aloud, look at the interview and talk with your partner about how to pronounce:
- the question words
- the verbs in different tenses
- the French words that look similar to English words. How many of these can you find?

Lire 6 **Read the article. Answer the questions below in English.**

Sac à dos électrique: le transport vert du futur?

Amir habite en France. Il est ingénieur.

Quand il était plus jeune, il voyageait toujours en voiture et il prenait l'avion pour partir en vacances.

Maintenant, Amir pense qu'il faut protéger l'environnement et réduire la pollution. On voyage plus vite en avion, mais c'est pire pour la planète.

Amir a fait des recherches sur les transports verts. Récemment, il a fini un projet très important, un nouveau moyen de transport: le sac à dos électrique. C'est mieux pour l'environnement que les moyens de transport traditionnels.

À l'avenir, Amir va rechercher d'autres possibilités. Un sac à dos solaire, peut-être?

le sac à dos	*backpack*
l'ingénieur(e)	*engineer*
solaire	*solar*

1 What two things did Amir do when he was younger?
2 What two things does he think we should do now?
3 What has Amir researched?
4 What project has he recently finished?
5 What may he research in the future?

Écouter 7 **Listen to the conversation. Copy and complete the grid in English.**

la bouteille d'eau	*water bottle*
remplir	*to fill (up)*

Innovation	
Problem before	
What they did	
What it's like now	
What they are going to do in the future	

Écrire 8 **Translate these sentences into French.**

1 At school, we did not use to recycle rubbish.
2 Now we go to school by bike.
3 In the future, I am going to work in the garden.
4 Last month, I finished an important project.
5 Recently, I took the train in order to go on holiday.

- Remember that you can use ***on*** to mean 'we'.
- Take care with the tenses. You need the imperfect tense for one sentence, and the perfect for two of the sentences. Which ones?

Grammaire 1

Numbers (Culture, page 134)

Lire **1** **Read the language box on numbers on page 134. Then rewrite these calculations as figures. Put a tick next to the ones that have correct answers, and a cross next to the incorrect ones.**

Example: 1 *34 + 18 = 54* ✗

1 trente-quatre + dix-huit = cinquante-quatre
2 vingt-sept + quarante-et-un = soixante-huit
3 quatre-vingt-trois – vingt-deux = soixante-et-onze
4 soixante-cinq – onze = cinquante-deux
5 soixante-quinze – quatorze = soixante-et-un
6 treize × quatre = quarante-deux
7 seize × trois = quarante-huit
8 quatre-vingt-dix-neuf ÷ trois = trente-trois

Parler **2** **In pairs, take turns to read out a number from one of the four cards. Your partner says the letter of the card that features the number.**

- *soixante-sept*
- *C*

A

16	35
42	63

B

18	26
57	71

C

14	37
41	67

D

12	28
59	74

Comparative adjectives (Unit 1, page 136)

Lire **3** **Copy and complete the sentences, choosing the correct form of the adjective each time.**

1 Le pic Marguerite est plus **haut** / **haute** que le mont Blanc.
2 Le mois de juillet est aussi **chaud** / **chaude** que le mois de septembre.
3 La forêt d'Orléans est moins **grand** / **grande** que la forêt tropicale congolaise.
4 Le mois de janvier est plus **froid** / **froide** que le mois de juin.
5 La Loire est moins **long** / **longue** que le Congo.
6 Le mois de novembre est aussi **long** / **longue** que le mois d'avril.

You use **comparative** adjectives to compare things:

- *plus* + adjective + *que*
  more + adjective + than
- *moins* + adjective + *que*
  less + adjective + than
- *aussi* + adjective + *que*
  as + adjective + as

The adjective must agree (in gender and number) with the first noun:

***La** Loire est moins long**ue** que le Congo.*

The Loire is less long than the Congo. / The Loire is shorter than the Congo.

Just like in English, 'good' and 'bad' are irregular in French:

*bon(**ne**)(**s**)* (good) *meilleur(**e**)(**s**)* (better)
*mauvais(**e**)(**s**)* (bad) *pire(**s**)* (worse)

Écouter 4 **Listen to these people comparing modes of transport. For each person, write the letters of the <u>two</u> modes of transport and the comparison made in English. (1–6)**

Example: 1 *e, a – e less fast than a*

a 
b 
c 
d 
e 
f 

rapide(s)	*fast*
facile(s)	*easy*
propre(s)	*clean*
pratique(s)	*practical*
bon(ne)(s) pour l'environnement	*good for the environment*
mauvais(e)(s) pour l'environnement	*bad for the environment*

Talking about future weather (Unit 2, page 139)

Écrire 5 **What is the weather going to be like in Belgium? Write a weather forecast for each of the cities on the map. Then listen and check.**

Example: À Bruxelles, il y aura du soleil.

present	future
Il fait ...	Il va faire ...
Il y a ...	Il y aura ...

1 Bruxelles 
2 Liège 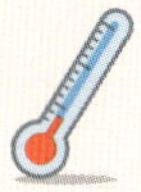
3 Namur 
4 Bruges 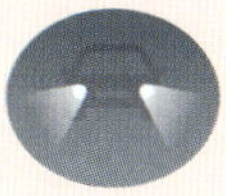
5 Charleroi 
6 Anvers 

Using the present and perfect tenses (Unit 3, page 141)

Écrire 6 **Read the grammar box on page 141. Change the tense of the sentences below.**

- Change 1–4 from the present to the perfect.
- Change 5–8 from the perfect to the present.

Example: 1 *<u>J'ai participé</u> à des manifestations.*

Remember that some verbs are irregular. This could be either present tense forms, the past participle or both. If you are unsure, check the verb tables on pages 235–239.

1 Je participe à des manifestations.
2 J'écris des articles pour le magazine du collège.
3 J'écoute des activistes.
4 Je prends le bus.
5 J'ai fait un effort contre la pollution.
6 Je ne suis pas allée à la manifestation.
7 J'ai rencontré des personnes intéressantes.
8 J'ai passé du temps avec de nouveaux amis.

Grammaire 2

Using the imperfect tense (Unit 4, page 143)

Écrire **1** **Copy and complete the sentences, putting each verb in brackets into the imperfect tense.**

Example: 1 *Quand j'étais plus jeune, je faisais beaucoup d'efforts pour l'environnement.*

1 Quand j' ___ plus jeune, je ___ beaucoup d'efforts pour l'environnement. (*être, faire*)
2 J' ___ au collège à vélo. (*aller*)
3 J' ___ souvent les transports publics. (*utiliser*)
4 Je ___ le plastique. (*recycler*)
5 Ma sœur ne ___ pas beaucoup de viande. (*manger*)
6 Qu'est-ce que tu ___ pour protéger l'environnement, avant? (*faire*)
7 Zoé, quand elle ___ au collège, elle ne ___ rien! (*être, recycler*)
8 Marc ___ du papier recyclé. (*acheter*)

Remember, to form the imperfect tense, remove the -*ons* from the *nous* form of the verb in the present tense:
regarder (to watch) → *nous regardons* → *regard-*
Then add these endings:
*je regard**ais***
*tu regard**ais***
*il/elle/on regard**ait***

The verb *être* has the stem ***ét***-: *c'**ét**ait* (it used to be/it was)

Understanding when to use the perfect tense and when to use the imperfect tense (Unit 4, page 143)

Lire **2** **Read the grammar box on page 143. Copy and complete the sentences, choosing the correct form of the verb from the options in bold. Then translate the sentences into English.**

1 Quand j'étais petit, **je suis allée / j'allais** tous les jours à l'école à pied.
2 Le week-end dernier, **j'ai pris / je prenais** le bus.
3 Hier, **j'ai recyclé / je recyclais** des déchets et du papier.
4 Quand j'étais au collège, **j'ai participé / je participais** souvent aux manifestations.
5 Samedi dernier, au restaurant, **j'ai mangé / je mangeais** un plat végétarien.

Using the present, perfect, imperfect and near future tenses (Unit 5, page 144)

- Use the **present tense** for things that usually happen or are happening now.
- Use the **perfect tense** for single, completed actions in the past.
- Use the **imperfect tense** to say what used to happen in the past, over a period of time.
- Use the **near future tense** to refer to the future.

Écrire **3** **Copy and complete the table. Choose from the verb forms in the box for the first three rows. Then complete the final three rows on your own.**

present	perfect	imperfect	near future
je vais			*je vais aller*
je mange		*je mangeais*	
	j'ai acheté		*je vais acheter*
je participe			*je vais participer*
	j'ai recyclé		
		j'utilisais	

je vais manger
je suis allé(e)
j'achète
j'ai mangé
j'allais
j'achetais

Écouter 4 **Listen. Which tense is each sentence in? Choose from the options. (1–6)**

1 present / near future
2 present / perfect
3 present / imperfect
4 perfect / near future
5 imperfect / perfect
6 present / near future

Parler 5 **Tense challenge! Ask your partner one of the four questions and say the letter of one of the pictures. Your partner must answer in the correct tense.**

- *Quand tu étais jeune, qu'est-ce que tu faisais pour protéger l'environnement? b*
- *Je recyclais les déchets. Qu'est-ce que tu as fait récemment pour protéger l'environnement? a*
- *J'ai acheté du papier recyclé. À l'avenir, ...*

Qu'est-ce que tu fais d'habitude pour protéger l'environnement?

Quand tu étais jeune, qu'est-ce que tu faisais pour protéger l'environnement?

Qu'est-ce que tu as fait récemment pour protéger l'environnement?

À l'avenir, qu'est-ce que tu vas faire pour protéger l'environnement?

a

acheter du papier recyclé

b

recycler les déchets

c

aller au collège à vélo

d

participer à une manifestation

e

utiliser les transports publics

f

manger des plats végétariens

C'est parti!

Lire 6 **Translate these sentences into English.**

1 À mon avis, il faut travailler pour arrêter la pollution.
2 Quand j'étais jeune, je ne recyclais rien.
3 Maintenant, je vais en ville à pied et je prends souvent les transports publics.
4 Samedi dernier, j'ai participé à une manifestation pour la protection des animaux.
5 Ce week-end, je vais acheter des fruits au marché.
6 À l'avenir, il va faire beaucoup plus chaud en été.
7 En hiver, il fait plus froid au Canada qu'en France.
8 Ma mère, qui a trente-neuf ans, ne mange pas de viande.

Parler 7 **In pairs, take turns to read out the sentences from exercise 6.**

Contrôle de lecture et d'écoute

Reading

Lire 1

Newspaper headlines. **You see some headlines in a French newspaper. Which headline matches each event? Write the correct letter (A–E) for each event.**

A	Un nouveau magasin dans notre centre commercial!
B	Trop de déchets dans nos espaces naturels
C	Une vue extraordinaire!
D	Un temps très froid demain!
E	Une manifestation pour les droits des animaux

1 a weather warning
2 a demonstration
3 an environmental issue

Lire 2

Where I live. **You read this blog that Clément has written about his town. Write the correct letter, A, B or C, to complete each sentence.**

Salut!

Où j'habite, nous avons des problèmes. Le bruit causé par les voitures n'est pas agréable. Avant, c'était plus calme ici! Le problème le plus grave, c'est que les rues sont moins propres qu'avant. Il y a vraiment trop de déchets.

Récemment, un groupe d'élèves de mon lycée a commencé un projet pour améliorer les conditions de vie dans notre ville. Ces élèves vont tous les jours au parc pour mettre les déchets dans des poubelles et ils parlent aux gens. Vivre dans une ville propre est important.

1 There was … noise in his town before.
- **A** as much
- **B** more
- **C** less

2 Now, the streets are …
- **A** clean.
- **B** less clean.
- **C** cleaner.

3 To improve living conditions in Clément's town, a group of students …
- **A** started to act last year.
- **B** has already started to act.
- **C** will launch a project soon.

4 Every day, they …
- **A** clean the park.
- **B** watch people in the park.
- **C** empty the bins.

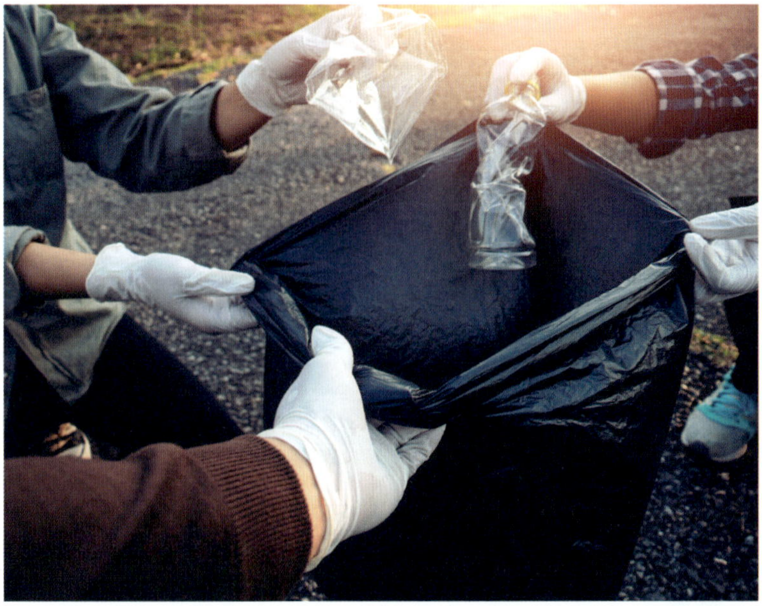

Lire 3

Let's act together! **You read an article about a local environmental group. What does the article say about these events? Write P for something that happened in the past, N for something that is happening now or F for something that will happen in the future.**

To identify the time frames, look out for time markers and use your knowledge of tenses.

Selon le groupe «vert» de notre ville, la pollution est très inquiétante. Récemment, certains membres ont trouvé plus de trente sacs en plastique dans le parc, alors maintenant ils y vont tous les soirs pour contrôler*.

Le groupe va contacter le collège local pour demander à des élèves de venir les aider. Le mois dernier, quelques membres du groupe sont allés au lycée pour parler des problèmes de notre ville et pour essayer de trouver des solutions.

contrôler *to check, inspect, control*

1 finding bags in the park
2 checking the park in the evenings
3 contacting the local school
4 talking to sixth formers

Lire 4

Translation. **Translate these sentences into English.**

Think about how you are going to translate these structures.

What tenses are these?

1 Il y a trop de déchets.
2 Je fais beaucoup pour protéger la planète.
3 Je veux améliorer la situation.
4 Mes parents vont utiliser la voiture moins souvent.
5 Tout le monde peut changer.

Think about how you are going to translate these words.

Listening

Écouter 5

Weather. **You hear a weather forecast. Which types of weather are mentioned? Write down the two correct letters for each region.**

A	getting colder	D	rain at night
B	fog at night	E	warm weather
C	rain today	F	rainy morning

1 the south
2 the north

Écouter 6

Town life. **You hear some French teenagers talking about where they live. What is their opinion on the following? Write P for a positive opinion, N for a negative opinion or P+N for a positive and negative opinion.**

1 transport 2 recycling bins 3 the park 4 the people

Listen out for adjectives and quantifiers such as *trop* and *très* to work out the answers.

Écouter 7

Dictation. **You will now hear four short sentences. Listen carefully and, using your knowledge of French sounds, write in French exactly what you hear for each sentence.**

Contrôle oral

Role-play

Parler 1 **Look at the role-play card and prepare what you are going to say.**

- You are talking to your French friend.
- Your teacher will play the part of your friend and will speak first.
- You should address your friend as *tu*.
- When you see this – **?** – you will have to ask a question.

In order to score full marks, you must include a verb in your response to each task.

1 Say what you do to help the environment. (Give **one** detail.)

2 Describe an environmental problem in your town. (Give **one** detail.)

3 Say **one** thing you would like to do to change your town.

4 Say what you think is a big problem about the environment. (Give **one** detail.)

? 5 Ask your friend a question about the environment.

You could say that you recycle, buy, use …

Use the conditional: you could say *je voudrais plus/moins de …*

You could start with *Il y a …*

You could ask what they do or what they think of something.

Parler 2 **Practise what you have prepared. Then, using your notes, listen and respond to the teacher.**

Écouter 3 **Now listen to Mohammed doing the role-play task. In English, note down (a) how he answers the questions for tasks 1, 2, 3 and 4, and (b) what question he asks for task 5.**

Reading aloud

Parler 4 **Look at this task. With a partner, take turns to read out the text below, paying attention to the underlined letters.**

Read aloud the following text **in French**.

Je fais beauc<u>ou</u>p p<u>ou</u>r l'envi<u>r</u>onnement.
Chez moi, je rec<u>y</u>cle toujours le plastique.
La pollu<u>tion</u> est inquiétante.
Les voit<u>u</u>res sont un <u>pro</u>blème p<u>ou</u>r notre planète.
À mon av<u>i</u>s, il faut réd<u>uire</u> le nombre de voit<u>u</u>res dans t<u>ou</u>tes les v<u>i</u>lles.

Take extra care with how you pronounce the underlined sounds:
- ***-tion*** sounds like 'ss-ee-on'
- ***u*** and ***ou*** will sound different
- ***i*** and ***y*** sound like 'ee'.

All the examples of a final **s** in this text are silent!

Take extra care with how you pronounce cognates, and spellings that are used in English words. The underlined letters will be pronounced very differently.

Écouter 5 **Listen and check your pronunciation.**

Parler 6 **Listen to the teacher asking <u>four</u> questions that relate to the topic of The environment and where people live. Translate each question into English and prepare your own answers in French. Then listen again and respond to the teacher.**

Use the specific environmental vocabulary you have learned in module 6 in your answers.

Photo card task

Écouter 7 **Look at the exam card below and read the first part of the task. Then listen to Mohammed describing the two photos.**

1 Who does Mohammed mention in the first photo?
2 Where are they, according to Mohammed?
3 What are the children in the second photo doing?

Photo 1

Photo 2

You will be asked to talk about the content of these photos. You must say at least one thing about each photo.

After you have spoken about the content of the photos, you will be asked questions related to any of the topics within the theme of **Communication and the world around us**.

Your responses should be as **full and detailed** as possible.

Parler 8 **Prepare your own descriptions of the two photos. You could mention, for example, the people, the location and what they are doing. Then, with a partner, take turns to describe the photos.**

Sur la première photo, il y a ...

To say where a person is, you can use a preposition, e.g. *derrière* ('behind'), *devant* ('in front of') or *entre* ('between').

Écouter 9 **Read the second part of the task. Listen to Mohammed answering the question: *Qu'est-ce que tu fais pour protéger la planète?* Write down in French all the verbs that you hear.**

Écouter 10 **Now listen to Mohammed answering the question: *Qu'est-ce que tu penses des voitures?* Give (a) <u>one</u> advantage and (b) <u>one</u> disadvantage that he mentions.**

Parler 11 **Prepare your own answers to the module 6 questions on page 227. Your responses should be as full and detailed as possible. Then practise with a partner.**

Remember to use opinion phrases, time phrases and connectives.

Contrôle écrit

Translation

Écrire 1

Match the French phrases (1–6) to the English (a–f).

1 il faut
2 on doit changer
3 il ne faut pas
4 on peut
5 il est important
6 pour réduire

a we/one must not
b in order to reduce
c it is important
d we/one must
e we have to / one has to change
f we/one can

Écrire 2

Translate the following sentences into French.

Look at exercise 1.

1 I recycle a lot.
2 We must change.
3 We can make a difference.
4 I can improve the situation.
5 It is important to encourage everybody.

You need the infinitive form of these verbs.

Use *tout le monde.*

Look out for two verbs together and the use of the infinitive form of a verb.

90-word writing task

Écrire 3

Look at this writing exam task and then, <u>for each bullet point</u>:

1 think about what vocabulary you have learned that you could use in your answer. For example:
- **nouns** and **verbs** to talk about the environment and problems
- **verbs of opinion** and **adjectives** to explain your point of view
- how to explain **what you have done** to help protect the environment.

2 write down <u>three or four</u> ideas for what you could write about.
3 write down which tense(s) you will need to use in your answer.

You are writing a post for a French environmental forum.

Write approximately **90** words in **French**.

You must write something about each bullet point.

Describe:
- what you do to protect the environment
- something you have done recently to help the planet
- something you would like to do to improve the situation where you live.

Look at the vocabulary you have noted to give you ideas for what to write.

Lire 4 **Read Chloé's answer to the exam task. Answer questions 1–5 in the coloured shapes.**

1 This is an example of **complex language**. What does it mean? Find three more examples from the text.

4 Which **connective** could you use here to form an **extended sentence**? What other connectives does she use?

Salut!

Je suis très active pour protéger l'environnement. Je fais beaucoup de choses au collège, chez moi et dans ma ville. Je mets mes déchets dans les poubelles, j'utilise les transports publics et j'apporte mon déjeuner dans une boîte.

Récemment, au collège, avec mes amis, j'ai créé un club. Le club s'appelle «Les verts!». Nous avons discuté avec les élèves pour trouver des solutions.

Dans ma ville, il y a trop de déchets et de voitures et c'est un grand problème. Je voudrais organiser une petite manifestation avec mes amis car il faut montrer les problèmes aux gens!

Chloé

2 This word shows a **variety of vocabulary**. What does it mean? Find two more examples.

3 Which **tense** is this? What other examples can you find? Does Chloé use any other tenses?

Lire 5 **Read Chloé's answer again. Answer the questions in English.**

1 Where does Chloé do things to protect the environment?
2 What does she do to help the environment?
3 What has she done at school with her friends to help the environment?
4 What would she like to do and why?

Écrire 6 **Prepare your own answer to the 90-word writing task in exercise 3.**

- Think about how you can develop your answer for each bullet point.
- Look back at your notes from exercises 3 and 4.
- Look at the 'Challenge checklist' and think about how you can show off your French!
- Write a **brief** plan and organise your answer into paragraphs.
- Write your answer and then carefully check the accuracy of what you have written.

Challenge checklist	
	✓ Connectives, time phrases, sequencers ✓ Opinion phrases ✓ Past, present and future time frames
	✓ Different persons of the verb ✓ A variety of opinions ✓ Interesting vocabulary
	✓ Infinitive phrases (e.g. *on doit, on peut, il faut*) ✓ Complex language (e.g. *pour* + infinitive) ✓ A variety of connectives ✓ Other forms of the verb (e.g. *nous*)

Vocabulaire

Key:
bold = this word will appear in higher exams only
* = this word is not on the vocabulary list, but you may use it in your own sentences

Madagascar: miroir du monde? (pages 134–135)

Les nombres	***Numbers***
vingt, vingt-six	*twenty, twenty-six*
trente, trente-quatre	*thirty, thirty-four*
quarante	*forty*
cinquante	*fifty*
soixante	*sixty*
soixante-dix	*seventy*
quatre-vingts	*eighty*
quatre-vingt-dix	*ninety*
cent	*one hundred*
deux-cents	*two hundred*
mille	*one thousand*
pour cent	*per cent*
vingt-deux pour cent	*twenty-two per cent*
À ton avis, est-ce que l'*écologie est importante?	*In your opinion, is ecology important?*
Oui, l'*écologie est très / assez importante.	*Yes, ecology is very / quite important.*
Non, l'*écologie n'est pas très / n'est pas du tout importante.	*No, ecology is not very / not at all important.*
Es-tu **concerné(e) par** la planète?	*Are you concerned about the planet?*
Oui, je suis très / assez / un peu **concerné(e) par** la planète.	*Yes, I am very / quite / a bit concerned about the planet.*
Non, je ne suis pas du tout **concerné(e) par** la planète.	*No, I am not at all concerned about the planet.*
Est-ce que tu aides à protéger l'environnement?	*Do you help to protect the environment?*
Oui, chaque jour / souvent.	*Yes, every day / often.*
Parfois.	*Sometimes.*
Non, **rarement**.	*No, rarely.*
Quel est le plus grand problème à Madagascar, à ton avis?	***Which is the biggest problem in Madagascar, in your opinion?***
À mon avis, c'est …	*In my opinion, it is …*
la *déforestation.	*deforestation.*
les **effets** du **changement** *climatique.	*the effects of climate change.*
l'*extinction des **espèces**.	*the extinction of species.*
l'utilisation des ressources naturelles.	*the use of natural resources.*
Une personne pense que …	*One person thinks that …*
Deux / Trois personnes pensent que …, c'est le plus grand problème.	*Two / Three people think that … is the biggest problem.*
l'organisation	*the organisation*
la population	*the population*
la **protection**	*the protection*
la solution	*the solution*

Notre monde est beau (pages 136–137)

plus/moins grand(e) que …	*bigger / less big than …*
plus/moins long(ue) que …	*longer / less long than …*
plus/moins haut(e) que …	*higher / less high than …*
La Suisse est bien connue pour ses forêts / montagnes.	*Switzerland is well known for its forests / mountains.*
Au Canada, il y a beaucoup d'animaux, comme par exemple …	*In Canada, there are lots of animals, like for example …*
En **République démocratique** du *Congo, il y a de grandes villes et de petits villages.	*In the Democratic Republic of the Congo, there are large towns and small villages.*
Le **paysage** est **divers**.	*The landscape is varied.*
Dans ma région, …	*In my region, …*
Dans le nord, …	*In the north, …*
Au printemps, …	*In spring, …*
En été, …	*In summer, …*
En automne, …	*In autumn, …*
En hiver, …	*In winter, …*
il fait plus chaud / froid … qu'en France / Europe.	*it is hotter / colder … than in France / Europe.*
il neige / pleut beaucoup.	*it snows / rains a lot.*
il y a du brouillard.	*it is foggy.*

Planète en danger (pages 138–139)

Quel est le problème le plus important pour la planète?	***Which is the most important problem for the planet?***
À mon avis, …	*In my opinion, …*
le **changement** *climatique …	*climate change …*
la **destruction** des forêts …	*destruction of the forests …*
la faim …	*hunger …*
la pollution de l'air / la mer …	*air / sea pollution …*
est un problème énorme.	*is an enormous problem.*
est une catastrophe.	*is a catastrophe.*
Je pense que …	*I think that …*
*planter plus d'arbres et de fleurs …	*planting more trees and flowers …*
la **protection** de la mer …	*protecting the sea …*
le recyclage …	*recycling …*
améliore la situation.	*is improving the situation.*
est une solution possible.	*is a possible solution.*
va sauver les *habitats des animaux.	*is going to save animal habitats.*
Je trouve que …	*I find that …*
les transports électriques …	*electric transport …*
les nouvelles technologies …	*new technologies …*
améliorent la situation.	*are improving the situation.*
sont une solution possible.	*are a possible solution.*
vont *limiter le danger.	*are going to limit the danger.*
Quel temps va-t-il faire?	***What is the weather going to be like?***
Il va faire beau / chaud / froid / mauvais.	*It is going to be nice / hot / cold / bad weather.*
Il y aura du soleil / du vent / du brouillard.	*It will be sunny / windy / foggy.*

Des grands gestes (pages 140–141)

Qu'est-ce qu'il faut faire pour protéger l'environnement?	***What must we do to protect the environment?***
À mon avis, / Pour moi, il faut …	*In my opinion, / For me, we must …*
Je pense / crois qu'il faut …	*I think / believe that we must …*
arrêter de fabriquer des produits en plastique.	*stop making plastic products.*
être bénévole pour des projets verts.	*volunteer for green projects.*
arrêter la pollution et la **destruction** des forêts.	*stop pollution and the destruction of forests.*
organiser des manifestations pour la **protection** des animaux.	*organise demonstrations for the protection of animals.*
respecter la nature.	*respect nature.*
travailler ensemble pour arrêter le **changement** *climatique.	*work together to stop climate change.*
Sur la photo, il y a quatre personnes / des amis.	*In the photo, there are four people / some friends.*
La femme a les cheveux longs et noirs.	*The woman has long, black hair.*
Ils sont dehors, à la campagne / montagne.	*They are outside, in the countryside / mountains.*
Les gens marchent.	*The people are walking.*
Je pense qu'ils (ne) sont (pas) heureux.	*I think they are (not) happy.*
J'*admire beaucoup …	*I admire … a lot.*
La semaine dernière, j'ai participé à une manifestation pour/contre …	*Last week, I took part in a demonstration for/against …*
J'ai rencontré des personnes intéressantes / sympa.	*I met some interesting / nice people.*
Après, j'ai écrit un blog sur mon expérience.	*Afterwards, I wrote a blog about my experience.*

Des petits gestes (pages 142–143)

Qu'est-ce que tu fais pour protéger l'environnement?	***What do you do to protect the environment?***
J'achète du **papier** recyclé.	*I buy recycled paper.*
Je ne mange pas de viande.	*I do not eat meat.*
Je prends (toujours) les transports publics.	*I (always) take public transport.*
Je recycle les déchets.	*I recycle rubbish.*
Je n'utilise pas de produits en plastique.	*I do not use plastic products.*
Je vais en ville à vélo et non pas en voiture.	*I go to town by bike and not by car.*
Quand tu étais plus jeune, qu'est-ce que tu faisais pour protéger l'environnement?	*When you were younger, what did you do to protect the environment?*
Quand j'étais plus jeune, …	*When I was younger, …*
je (ne) m'intéressait (pas) beaucoup à l'environnement.	*I was (not) very interested in the environment.*
Avant, …	*Before, …*
j'utilisais / je (ne) mangeais (pas) / je recyclais / j'allais	*I used / I ate (did not eat) / I recycled / I went*
Maintenant, …	*Now, …*
je fais beaucoup d'efforts.	*I make a big effort.*
j'utilise / je ne mange pas …	*I use / I do not eat …*
je recycle / je vais …	*I recycle / I go …*
je suis végétarien(ne).	*I am vegetarian.*
C'est mieux pour l'environnement.	*It is better for the environment.*

Innovation verte (pages 144–145)

Quelle est votre *innovation?	*What is your innovation?*
À notre collège, …	*At our school, …*
on évite le *gaspillage de nourriture.	*we avoid food waste.*
on fait *pousser nos propres légumes dans le jardin de l'école.	*we grow our own vegetables in the school garden.*
on fait (aussi) du *compost.	*we (also) make compost.*
Quel était le problème, avant?	*What was the problem before?*
On ne faisait pas beaucoup pour protéger l'environnement.	*We did not do a lot to protect the environment.*
Il y avait beaucoup de *gaspillage.	*There was a lot of waste.*
On jetait de la nourriture à la poubelle avec les autres déchets.	*We threw food in the bin with the other rubbish.*
On ne recyclait pas.	*We did not recycle.*
Qu'est-ce que vous avez fait?	*What did you do?*
On a parlé avec le directeur.	*We spoke to the head teacher.*
On a décidé d'organiser …	*We decided to organise …*
un jardin.	*a garden.*
le recyclage de la nourriture en *compost.	*recycling of food into compost.*
On a arrêté le *gaspillage.	*We stopped waste.*
Et c'est comment, maintenant?	*And how are things now?*
Il n'y a pas de *gaspillage de nourriture.	*There is no food waste.*
C'est beaucoup mieux!	*It is a lot better!*
Ça fait une énorme différence.	*It makes an enormous difference.*
Et à l'avenir, qu'est-ce que vous allez faire?	*And in the future, what are you going to do?*
On va parler à une *conférence.	*We are going to speak at a conference.*
On va participer à un concours *interscolaire.	*We are going to participate in an inter-school competition.*
On va interdire les sacs en plastique au collège.	*We are going to ban plastic bags at school.*
On arrive plus/moins vite en avion / à vélo.	*You arrive more/less quickly by plane / by bike.*
C'est mieux / pire pour la planète que les moyens de transport traditionnels.	*It is better / worse for the planet than traditional means of transport.*

Module 7

Mon petit monde à moi

C'est combien?

- Understanding adverts
- Using demonstrative adjectives (*ce*, *cet*, *cette*, *ces*)

Appartements à louer

A

Appartement 650€ / mois
ROUEN 1 chambre
1

B

Appartement 1 030€ / mois
DIEPPE 2 chambres
2

C

Appartement 800€ / mois
DEAUVILLE 3 chambres
3

Clé des symboles

chambre(s)
cuisine
avec accès pour les personnes handicapées
salle de bains
entrée
jardin

louer	*to rent*
le coin	*corner*
le fauteuil roulant	*wheelchair*

1 Près du centre-ville
Grand appartement avec trois chambres
Cuisine moderne, jardin, salle de bains
Accès pour les personnes handicapées avec fauteuil roulant

2 Dans le centre-ville
Agréable appartement pour une personne
Une salle de bains
Jardin

3 À vingt minutes du centre-ville
Deux chambres
Une cuisine
Une salle de bains
Très moderne

Lire 1 **Match each text (1–3) with an advert (A–C).**

Écouter 2 **Look at the adverts and listen. Write the letter of the flat these people are talking about. (1–2)**

Parler 3 **How do you pronounce these words? Read them out, then listen and check.**

accès pour les personnes handic**a**pées
adresse
appartement
s**a**lle de bains
entrée
chambre
cuisine

Notice the difference between the bold ***a*** sound and the underlined nasal sounds.

Parler 4 **In pairs, talk about the third advert above. Describe the flat and give your opinion.**

- *Cet appartement est grand?*
- *Il y a …*
- *Est-ce qu'il y a un/une …?*
- *Oui, il y a un/une … / Non, il n'y a pas de/d' …*
- *Qu'est-ce que tu penses de cet appartement?*
- *À mon avis, c'est assez / très / trop / un peu …*

Not sure whether to use *un* or *une* in exercise 4?
Many (but not all) nouns that end in a consonant are masculine (e.g. ***un*** *appartement*).
Many (but not all) nouns that end in *-e* are feminine (e.g. ***une*** *cuisine*).

Remember, *un* and *une* are not needed after a negative. Use **de**/**d'** instead:
Il n'y a pas ***de*** *jardin.*
Il n'y a pas ***d'****accès pour les personnes handicapées.*

Section mode

A

Chemise bleue
Maintenant 13,00€

B

Tee-shirt gris
22,99€

C

Robe
Maintenant 14,50€

D

Pantalon noir
39,99€

E

Chaussures noires
34,99€

assez	*enough*
trop	*too (much)*
seulement	*only*

Écouter 5 **Look at the adverts and listen. Write down (a) the letter of the item of clothing the speakers are talking about, and (b) if they are going to buy it. (1–3)**

Parler 6 **In pairs, make up a dialogue using one of the other adverts above.**

- *Qu'est-ce que tu vas porter pour aller … ?*
- *Je vais acheter ce (pantalon) / cette (robe) / ces (chaussures) …*

G

The demonstrative adjective 'this' varies in French according to gender.

masculine singular	feminine singular	plural
ce *tee-shirt* (this tee-shirt)	***cette*** *robe* (this dress)	***ces*** *chaussures* (these shoes)

Note: Before a masculine noun that starts with a vowel, you use ***cet***. This creates a liaison to make the pronunciation easier: *cet appartement* (this flat).

Page 170

Qu'est-ce que tu vas	porter acheter	pour aller	à la fête / au mariage de …?
Je vais Je voudrais		ce tee-shirt / ce pantalon, … cette chemise / cette robe, … ces baskets / ces chaussures, …	
… mais	c'est trop cher pour moi. je n'ai pas assez d'argent.		

Écrire 7 **Write a message to a French friend about what you are thinking of wearing or buying for a birthday party this weekend. Ask their opinion.**

> Pour aller à la fête d'anniversaire ce week-end, je pense que je vais acheter / porter (ce pantalon bleu) avec (ces chaussures noires). Qu'est-ce que tu penses de (ce pantalon)?

Remember, adjectives of colour go after the noun in French and must agree with the noun:

ce *pantalon vert* ***cette*** *chemise vert****e***
ces *baskets vert****es***

Blanc (white) is irregular in the feminine forms: *blan****che(s)***.

1 Là où j'habite

- Describing your town or village
- Using indefinite adjectives *chaque, tous, tout(e)(s)*
- Using the correct preposition for 'in'

Écouter 1 **In pairs, take turns to read out the compass points. Then listen and check.**

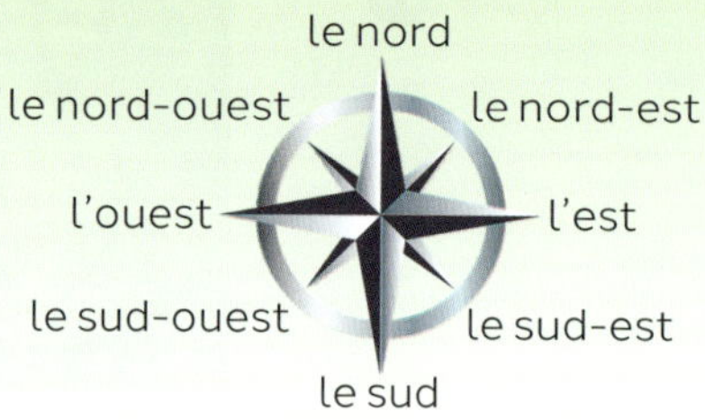

Écouter 2 **Listen and read. Then copy and complete the sentences in English.**

J'habite en Algérie dans un petit village près de la capitale, Alger. Alger se trouve sur la côte, dans le nord du pays. La partie ancienne de la ville s'appelle la médina. Chaque jour, beaucoup de touristes viennent visiter ce quartier. Dans la médina, il y a des petites rues avec beaucoup de beaux bâtiments blancs, et la Grande Mosquée. Vivre à la campagne est ennuyeux, car il n'y a rien à faire. Je voudrais habiter en ville.

Ma famille et moi habitons à Rouen. C'est une grande ville dans le nord-ouest de la France. Il y a une partie historique, avec beaucoup de vieux bâtiments et de musées. Il y a aussi une partie moderne, avec beaucoup d'entreprises. Vivre ici est parfait pour moi parce que je peux faire les magasins ou sortir avec tous mes amis.

la médina	*medina (usually the historical district / old town in North African cities; the word comes from Arabic and means 'city')*
le quartier	*district, quarter*
la mosquée	*mosque*

1. Fathia lives in a ___, near ___.
2. Algiers is in the ___ of Algeria. The medina has streets with lots of ___ buildings, and the Great Mosque.
3. Fathia thinks living in the ___ is ___. She would like to live ___.
4. Sofiane lives in Rouen, which is a ___ in the ___ of France.
5. There is a ___ part with ___ businesses.
6. He thinks it's the perfect place to live, because he can ___ or ___ with all his friends.

The verbs *habiter* and *vivre* both mean 'to live (in a place)'. *Habiter* is a regular verb but *vivre* is an irregular verb.

habiter	vivre
j'habite	je vis
tu habites	tu vis
il/elle/on habite	il/elle/on vit
nous habitons	nous vivons
vous habitez	vous vivez
ils/elles habitent	ils/elles vivent

Lire 3 **Translate the sentences into English.**

1. Tous mes amis habitent à la campagne.
2. Toutes les rues sont petites.
3. Je fais tout le temps les magasins.
4. Chaque année, je pars en vacances dans le nord de la France.
5. Toute ma famille aime habiter en ville.

G

Indefinite adjectives talk about people or things in a general way, without being specific:

chaque	each, every
tout/toute/tous/toutes	all, the whole, every

They need to agree with the noun in number and gender, just like all adjectives.

masculine singular	*tout le temps* (all the time)	*chaque jour* (every day)
feminine singular	*tout**e** ma famille* (my whole family)	*chaque année* (each year)
masculine plural	*tous mes amis* (all my friends)	
feminine plural	*tout**es** les filles* (all the girls)	

Page 170

Écouter 4

Listen to the interviews. Then copy and complete the grid in English. (1–2)

Est-ce que tu habites dans une ville ou un village?

Où se trouve ta ville / ton village?

Comment est ta ville / ton village?

Est-ce que tu aimes habiter dans cette ville / ce village? Pourquoi (pas)?

	Town / Village	Country	Location details	Size and description	Opinion and reason
1	Town (Dakar)				

Parler 5

In pairs, take turns to ask and answer the questions from exercise 4.

- *Est-ce que tu habites dans une ville ou un village?*
- *J'habite dans une petite ville.*
- *Où se trouve ta ville?*
- *Elle se trouve dans le nord-est de l'Angleterre.*

Lire 6

Read the text. Then answer the questions in English.

J'habite à Montréal, qui est une des plus grandes villes du Québec, au Canada. J'adore habiter dans cette ville parce qu'il y a toujours quelque chose à faire.

L'année dernière, je suis allé en vacances à Lyon. Lyon se situe dans le sud-est de la France. J'ai trouvé que certaines parties de Lyon étaient comme certains quartiers de Montréal, avec beaucoup de bâtiments modernes. Mais la ville de Lyon est plus vieille que Montréal.

Je suis très content d'habiter à Montréal mais un jour, je voudrais passer plus de temps à Lyon.

Hugo

1. Why does Hugo love living in Montreal?
2. Where is Lyon?
3. According to Hugo, in what way is Lyon similar to Montreal?
4. In what way does he say Lyon is different from Montreal?
5. What would he like to do one day?

Écrire 7

Translate the sentences into French.

1. I live in Dinan, in the west of France.
2. I love living in Dinan.
3. Every year, I visit England with my parents.
4. Last year, I visited York.
5. There are lots of beautiful buildings in York.

There are different words for 'in' depending on the context. Make sure you use the correct one.

dans + point of compass	***dans*** *le sud-ouest*
à + name of town/village	***à*** *Londres*
en + feminine country	***en*** *France*
au + masculine country	***au*** *Canada*

2 Sur la bonne route

- Asking for and understanding directions
- Using *à* and *de* with the definite article
- Using negatives to talk about your town

Écouter 1 **Listen to the people talking about where they want to go, and the directions. Write the letters of the correct place and the correct map. (1–3)**

a 

b 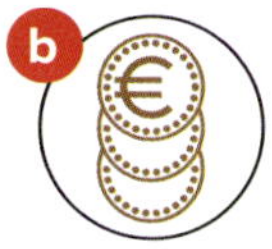

c 

d 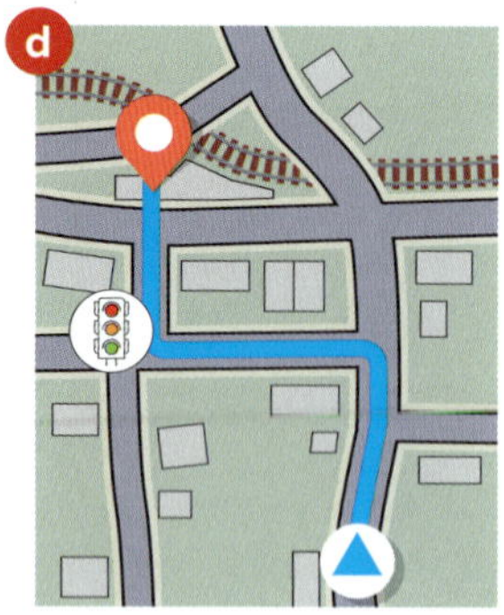

e 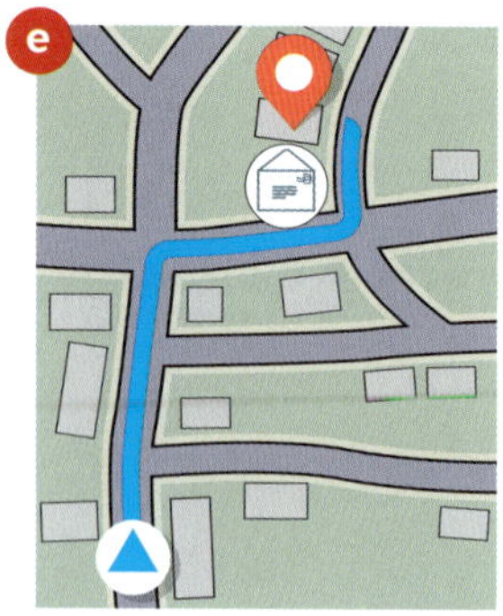

f 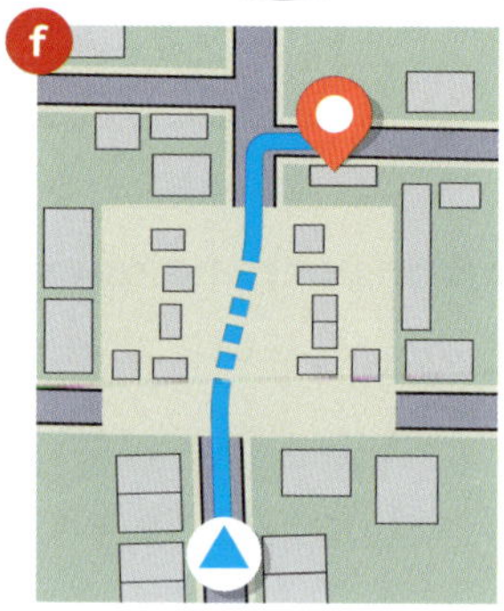

la gare	*station*
les feux *(m)*	*traffic lights*
la place	*square*

Allez / Continuez	tout droit.
Tournez	à gauche / à droite.
Traversez	le pont.
Prenez	la première / la troisième rue (à gauche / à droite).
C'est loin / près d'ici?	

Pronounce the letter ***r*** as a raspy sound in the back of your throat.
The letters ***th*** are always pronounced 't' in French.

Listen and repeat the sentence.
*Tou**r**nez à d**r**oite à côté du **th**éât**r**e.*

Lire 2 **Copy and complete the text with the correct word or phrase from the boxes below. There are <u>three</u> words or phrases you don't need. Then listen and check.**

G The prepositions *à* and *de* merge with ***le*** and ***les*** to form new words.

		le	*la*	*l'*	*les*
à	*pour aller …*	***au** parc?*	***à la** gare?*	*à l'hôpital?*	***aux** magasins?*
de	*à côté …*	***du** musée*	***de la** poste*	*de l'hôtel*	***des** toilettes*

Page 171

Pour aller **1** musée, allez tout droit et tournez à gauche **2** feux. Traversez le pont, puis tournez à droite au coin **3** rue. Le musée est sur la place, près **4** jardin public, à côté **5** Hôtel Bellevue et du théâtre.

de la | aux | à la | du
des | à l' | au | de l'

le pont	*bridge*

Parler 3 **In pairs, make up two dialogues using the maps below.**

A 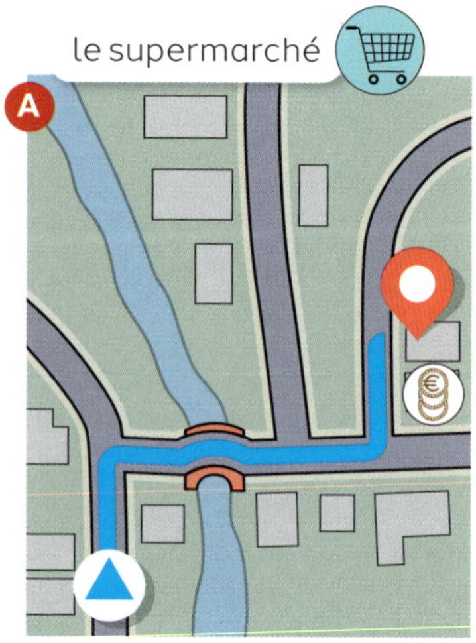

B 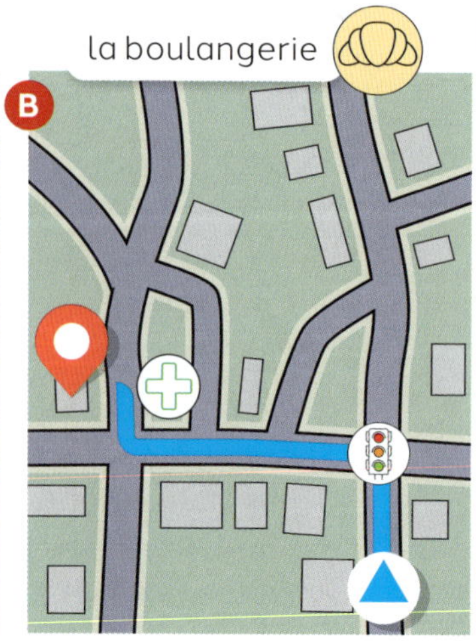

Pour aller	au supermarché, à la boulangerie,	s'il vous plaît?
Prenez	la première / la troisième rue à gauche / à droite.	
Traversez	la place. le pont.	
Tournez	à gauche / à droite aux feux.	
C'est à côté	de la banque. de la pharmacie. du jardin public.	
C'est loin? C'est près d'ici?	Oui, … Non, …	
Et voilà, vous êtes arrivé(e)(s)!		

Écouter 4

Read the sentences. Then listen and fill in the gaps.

1 On peut acheter du pain au ___.
2 À Paris, il faut visiter les ___.
3 Il n'y a pas de ___ dans ma ville.
4 Au centre-ville, il y a une ___.

Look at the words before each gap for clues, e.g. is the word going to be masculine or feminine? Singular or plural?

Écouter 5

Listen and read. Then note down if each statement is true or false.

Où habites-tu? Qu'est-ce que tu aimes? Qu'est-ce que tu n'aimes pas?

La parole aux jeunes Belges!

Enzo
Dans mon village, il n'y a rien et il n'y a personne de mon âge. Mais je suis content d'habiter ici car c'est un endroit calme.

Nadia
J'habite au centre-ville et il y a une boulangerie et beaucoup de cafés dans ma rue. Il y a même un hôpital en face de notre maison. Malheureusement, il n'y a pas de cinéma.

Zoé
Il y a beaucoup de trafic devant notre appartement et ce n'est jamais calme. Il y a du bruit et la pollution est terrible.

Maxime
Dans mon quartier, il y a quelques petits magasins. C'est pratique pour faire les courses. Il y a aussi une pharmacie derrière la maison.

G
The following prepositions are followed by *de*:

près de	near to
loin de	far from
à côté de	next to
en face de	opposite

The following are used on their own:

devant	in front of
derrière	behind
entre	between

Page 171

malheureusement	*unfortunately*
quelques	*some*
faire les courses	*to go food shopping*

1 Enzo enjoys living in his village.
2 Nadia lives next to a hospital.
3 It's very quiet where Zoé lives.
4 Maxime can go shopping where he lives.

G
Like most negatives, the following go around the verb:

ne ... pas	not
ne ... jamais	never, not ever
ne ... rien	not anything, nothing
ne ... personne	nobody, no one

For a reminder about other negative expressions, see page 69.

Page 171

Lire 6

Translate the negative phrases that are underlined from exercise 5 into English.

Écrire 7

Write a paragraph about the place where you live. Include:

- where exactly your town or village is
- what it is like (e.g. big, small, old, modern, pretty)
- what there is and is not in your town/village
- whether you like living there and why / why not.

Include at least two negative expressions in your writing.

J'habite	dans	un village près de Manchester. une ville dans le nord-est de l'Angleterre.
Ma ville est	grande / petite / vieille / belle.	
Mon village est	grand / petit / vieux / beau.	
Il y a	un	supermarché / musée. hôtel / hôpital.
	une	banque / poste / gare.
	beaucoup de quelques	cafés / magasins.
Malheureusement, Mais	il n'y a personne de mon âge. il n'y a rien à faire. il n'y a pas de cinéma. ce n'est jamais calme.	

3 Mode et shopping

- Talking about shopping for clothes
- Using *de* to indicate possession
- Practising shopping role-plays

Écouter 1 **Listen and read. Then translate the sentences in bold into English.**

@Mohammed

J'ai acheté **ce beau tee-shirt blanc** et je l'ai mis pour aller à la fête de mon meilleur copain. Je l'ai porté avec **mon pantalon noir et mes chaussures noires**. Il n'a pas coûté cher et les couleurs sont cool! 😎

#teeshirtcool

@Jade

J'ai vu **cette belle jupe verte et grise** dans un magasin de mode, mais elle n'était pas à ma taille! J'ai cherché dans les autres magasins du centre commercial sans succès. Puis j'ai trouvé la jupe en ligne! C'est une bonne marque et elle va super bien avec **ma chemise blanche et jaune** et le sac à main vert de ma sœur.

#manouvellejupe

@Gabriel

Ouais! J'ai vendu mes vieilles baskets sur Vinted pour un très bon prix! Avec l'argent, j'ai acheté **ce manteau marron** et **ce sac blanc, bleu, orange et rose** comme cadeau pour l'anniversaire de mon père. Papa a dit qu'il va prendre le manteau et le sac pour aller au bureau la semaine prochaine! 🎁

#cadeaudanniversaire

mettre	*to put on* (***j'ai mis*** *I put on (past)*)
sans succès	*without success*
la bonne marque	*good brand*

Lire 2 **Re-read the posts in exercise 1. Who …**

1 bought something online?
2 sold something online to buy a birthday present?
3 wore what they bought to their best friend's party?
4 bought a bag?

Lire 3 **Find, copy out and translate <u>three</u> phrases in exercise 1 which use *de* to indicate possession.**

G

In English, an apostrophe is used to indicate possession:
my best friend**'**s birthday; my brother**'**s shoes

In French, you use *de* (of):
l'anniversaire ***de*** *ma meilleure amie*
('the birthday of my best friend')
les chaussures ***de*** *mon frère*
('the shoes of my brother')

Page 172

Écouter 4 **Listen to the teenagers talking about their clothes shopping. Copy and complete the grid in English. (1–2)**

	What did they buy? (item(s) and colour)?	Where did they buy it/them?	How much did it/they cost?	When will they wear it/them?
1				

en vente	*for sale*

Parler 5 **In pairs, take turns to read out Jade's text from exercise 1. Give feedback on each other's pronunciation.**

If you add **-e** or **-es** to *vert* or *gris*, you pronounce the final consonant of the original word.
Listen and repeat the words.
vert *ver**t**e*
gris *gri**s**es*

Écouter 6 **Listen and read. Then find the French for the English phrases.**

A

B

1 It's for me.
2 How much does it cost?
3 Can I exchange it if there is a problem?
4 You have to bring it back to the checkout.
5 I'd like to exchange …
6 Unfortunately, it's too small.
7 Do you have the same thing in …?
8 Can I try it on, please?

Parler 7 **In pairs, create <u>two</u> new shopping dialogues using the ones above as a model. Change as many details as possible, e.g. clothing, colours, prices, sizes.**

- *Qu'est-ce que vous cherchez?*
- *Je cherche un pantalon noir ou gris.*

Écrire 8 **Write a social media post about an item of clothing you bought online which wasn't quite right.**

- Describe what item you bought …
- … and for what special occasion you bought it.
- Mention where you found/saw it/them …
- … and how much it/they cost.
- Mention a problem (too small, too big).

J'ai acheté	ce pantalon noir cette jupe bleue ces chaussures blanches	pour l'anniversaire de ma sœur.
J'ai trouvé ça	dans un magasin de mode.	
Il/Elle a coûté Ils/Elles ont coûté	quarante euros. peu / beaucoup d'argent.	
Il/Elle (n')a (pas) coûté	cher.	
Malheureusement, Mais	il/elle est trop petit(e). ils/elles sont trop grand(e)s.	

4 La maison de mes rêves

- Describing your ideal home
- Working out if adjectives go before or after the noun
- Using *si* clauses

Écouter 1 **Listen and read. Then note down the quiz answers for Thomas. (1–4)**

Ta maison idéale

1 Plus tard, je voudrais habiter dans …

a un château ancien à la campagne.
b une petite maison en bois à la montagne.
c un bel appartement récent.
d une vieille maison comme dans les films d'horreur!

2 Je voudrais avoir …

a une cuisine propre et moderne.
b un bon accès pour les personnes handicapées avec un fauteuil roulant.
c ma propre chambre calme et confortable.
d de grandes fenêtres.

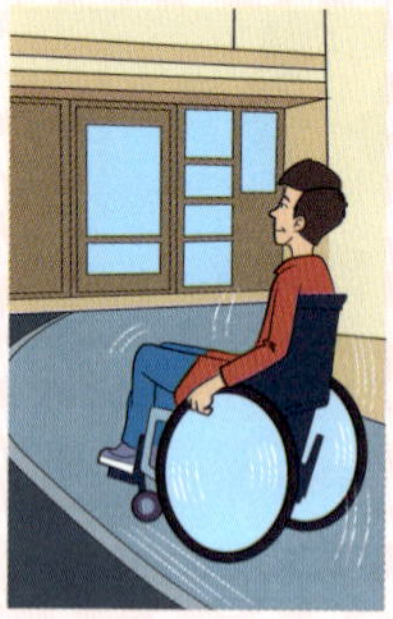

3 C'est moins important pour moi d'avoir …

a beaucoup d'espace.
b une salle de sport.
c un joli jardin.
d des voisins sympa.

4 Si j'étais riche, je voudrais avoir …

a une télévision à grand écran dans ma chambre.
b un cinéma privé pour regarder les derniers films.
c une piscine pour moi tout(e) seul(e).
d un sauna ou un jacuzzi.

le bois	*wood*

Parler 2 **In pairs, do the quiz.**

- *Question numéro un. Plus tard, je voudrais habiter dans un bel appartement récent. Et toi?*
- *Moi, je voudrais habiter …*

Most adjectives (including colours) go <u>after</u> the noun.
However, the following usually go <u>in front</u> of the noun: *grand, petit, joli, beau, vieux.*
A noun can have adjectives before and after it, e.g. *une <u>grande</u> et <u>belle</u> maison <u>moderne</u>.*

Écouter 3 **Listen to Lucie talking about her ideal home. Then write out the sentences, correcting the information.**

1 Lucie would like to live in a small apartment in the town centre when she's older.
2 She would like to have a pretty garden and a dining room.
3 It's less important for her to have nice neighbours.
4 If she were rich, she would like to have an ancient castle in the countryside.

Lire 4 **Re-read the quiz in exercise 1. Find and note down in French:**

- <u>two</u> phrases with an adjective/adjectives <u>after</u> the noun only
- <u>two</u> phrases with an adjective/adjectives <u>before</u> the noun only
- <u>two</u> phrases with adjectives before <u>and</u> after the noun.

G Some adjectives have a different meaning before and after the noun.

une maison <u>ancienne</u>	an ancient house
une <u>ancienne</u> amie	a former friend
une chambre <u>propre</u>	a clean bedroom
ma <u>propre</u> chambre	my own bedroom
un appartement <u>cher</u>	an expensive flat
un <u>cher</u> oncle	a dear uncle

Page 172

Lire 5 **In pairs, take turns to choose a number (1–4) and a letter (a–d) from the quiz, and to translate the full sentence.**

- *2d*
- *I would like to have big windows.*

Écouter 6 **Listen and write down in English what each person's dream or wish is. (1–4)**

Example: 1 *To buy a new flat in the city centre.*

Lire 7 **Read the text. What do the five words or phrases in blue mean in English?**

J'habite avec ma mère et ma sœur dans un appartement. C'est moderne et confortable, mais il y a **peu d'espace** et je dois partager ma chambre avec ma sœur. Si j'avais le choix, je voudrais habiter dans une grande maison, avec ma propre chambre.

En face de notre appart, il y a un vieux bâtiment. Il n'y a personne dans ce bâtiment – il est **vide**. Si j'étais riche, je voudrais acheter ce grand bâtiment.

Je rêve d'avoir une chambre avec une belle vue sur la ville. Je n'ai pas besoin d'un sauna mais, pour moi, c'est essentiel d'avoir **des chambres d'amis**. Je voudrais aussi avoir une grande cuisine et **une salle à manger**. Enfin, je voudrais avoir **une salle de jeux** pour jouer au tennis de table et à des jeux vidéo.

Voilà la maison de mes rêves!

Eva

Sometimes, you can work out the meaning of unfamiliar words from the context.

What do you think the missing word is in the English translation?

Il n'y a personne dans ce bâtiment – il est vide.

There is no one in this building – it is ...

Compound words can also give you clues:

la salle = room

manger = to eat

la salle à manger = ...

G You can use *si* ('if') with a verb in the imperfect tense, followed by ***je voudrais*** (the conditional of *vouloir*) to express your dreams and wishes:

Si j'étais riche, ***je voudrais*** *avoir une grande maison.*

If I were rich, I **would like** to have a big house.

Page 173

Lire 8 **Re-read the text. Then answer the questions in English.**

1. What does Eva say about her flat? Give two details.
2. What is the main thing she dislikes about living there?
3. Where would Eva live if she had the choice? Give two details.
4. Where is the old building she would like to buy?
5. What would Eva do in her games room?

Écrire 9 **Write a description of your ideal or fantasy home. Include:**

- what type of building it would be, and the location
- what rooms you would have
- what would be less important for you.

Include at least one sentence using *si*.

Je voudrais habiter dans	un grand appartement au centre-ville. une vieille maison à la campagne.	
Si j'étais riche, je voudrais acheter un château ancien.		
Je voudrais	avoir	un cinéma privé. un joli jardin. ma propre chambre. une piscine. une salle de jeux. de grandes fenêtres.
Je rêve C'est essentiel pour moi C'est moins important pour moi J'ai besoin / Je n'ai pas besoin	d'avoir	

5 As-tu déjà visité Paris?

- Talking about visiting another town or city
- Translating questions in different tenses
- Spotting different tenses from verb endings

Lire 1 **Read the questions. Then write the tense: present, perfect, near future or conditional. Translate each question into English.**

a Quand est-ce que tu vas aller à Londres?

b As-tu déjà visité le Royaume-Uni ou un autre pays d'Europe?

c Pourquoi veux-tu visiter ce pays?

d Comment est-ce que tu vas voyager et avec qui?

e Quel pays ou quelle ville voudrais-tu visiter un jour?

f Qu'est-ce que tu vas faire pendant ta visite?

To spot tenses, look at the verb endings:

- *-e*, *-es*, *-e*, *-ons*, *-ez*, *-ent* = present tense
- *aller* + infinitive = near future: *je vais visiter, nous allons visiter*
- *je voudrais, tu voudrais, il/elle voudrait* = conditional.

The perfect tense is in two parts: *tu as visité; tu es allé(e)*

Lire 2 **Read the interview. Write the letter of the correct question from exercise 1 for each gap.**

Le voyage de mes rêves!

Bonjour, Raphaël. Je crois que tu as reçu de bonnes nouvelles?

Oui, j'ai gagné un concours et je vais bientôt aller à Londres!

1 ________

Non, je ne suis jamais allé à Londres, mais j'ai toujours rêvé de visiter le Royaume-Uni.

2 ________

Je veux aller à Londres parce que c'est une belle ville historique et culturelle. Je voudrais voir tous les bâtiments célèbres et visiter quelques musées.

3 ________

Je vais aller à Londres le week-end prochain!

4 ________

Je vais voyager en bateau. Ensuite, je vais aller à la capitale en train. Je vais faire le voyage avec mon père.

5 ________

Je vais visiter la Tour de Londres et le musée de Madame Tussaud. Je vais faire un tour de la capitale en autobus de tourisme.

6 ________

Si j'avais de l'argent, je voudrais visiter New York.

The word '*tour*' has two meanings, depending on the gender:

le *tour* tour

la *tour* tower

les nouvelles *(f)*	*news*
avoir toujours rêvé de	*to have always dreamed of*

Écouter 3 **Listen and check. In pairs, take turns to read out Raphaël's answers. Give feedback on each other's pronunciation.**

Lire 4 **Re-read the interview. Is each statement below true or false?**

1 Raphaël received bad news.
2 He has never been to London before.
3 He wants to go to London for its history and culture.
4 He is going to London next month.
5 He is flying to London.
6 If he had money, he'd like to go to New York.

Écouter 5 **Listen to the interview with Zoé and answer the questions in English. (1–6)**

1 Has Zoé visited France before?
2 Why does she want to visit Paris?
3 When is she going to go?
4 What is she going to do during the visit?
5 What other European countries has she visited?
6 If she had money, what other town would she like to visit?

Écrire 6 **Translate the questions into French. There may be more than one way of writing some of the questions.**

1 Have you ever been to France?
2 Why do you want to visit Paris?
3 When are you going to go to Paris?
4 What are you going to do in Paris?

G

The simplest way to ask a question in any tense is to use est-ce que …?
Est-ce que tu es déjà allé(e) en Angleterre?

Or you can use inversion:
Es-tu déjà allé(e) en Angleterre?

The following question words can be used with *est-ce que …?* or with inversion:
Avec qui? Comment? Quand? Où? Pourquoi?
e.g. *Où est-ce que tu es allé(e)? / Où es-tu allé(e)?*

Qu'est-ce que …? cannot be used with inversion.

Quel/Quelle/Quels/Quelles is an adjective and must agree with the noun.

Page 173

Parler 7 **Read the advert below with your partner. Imagine that one of you has won the competition. Do an interview like the one in exercise 2.**

- *Je crois que tu as reçu de bonnes nouvelles?*
- *Oui! J'ai gagné un concours et je vais bientôt aller à Paris!*
- *Quand est-ce que … ?*

Tu as gagné un week-end à Paris!	Oui, je suis (très) heureux/heureuse / content(e).
Quand est-ce que tu vas aller à Paris?	Je vais aller …
Es-tu déjà allé(e) à Paris?	Oui, je suis déjà allé(e) à Paris. Non, je ne suis jamais allé(e) à Paris.
Pourquoi veux-tu visiter Paris?	Je veux visiter Paris parce que …
Comment est-ce que tu vas voyager et avec qui?	Je vais aller à Paris en …
Qu'est-ce que tu vas faire pendant ta visite?	Je vais faire … Je vais visiter …
Ça va être comment?	Cela va être génial!

- Use information from the advert and make up any additional information (e.g. time, place).
- Make sure you answer in the correct tense!

Gagnez un week-end à Paris

- Deux nuits (pour deux personnes) dans un hôtel
- Voyage aller-retour en avion ou en train (première classe)
- Tour de la ville en bateau
- Visite de la tour Eiffel et du musée du Louvre
- Samedi soir: spectacle devant la cathédrale Notre-Dame de Paris

Grammaire 1

Demonstrative adjectives (Culture, page 159)

Écrire 1

Re-read the grammar box on page 159. Copy and complete the sentences, filling in the gaps with the correct form of the demonstrative adjective (*ce*/*cet*/*cette*/*ces*).

1 Qu'est-ce que tu penses de ___ chaussures?
2 J'ai acheté une robe bleue pour aller à la fête ___ soir.
3 ___ week-end, je vais porter ___ chemise.
4 J'ai trouvé ___ baskets sur Vinted.
5 ___ maison est jolie.
6 Tu vas mettre un pantalon pour sortir ___ après-midi?

> If you are not sure which demonstrative adjective to choose, check whether the noun after each gap is masculine or feminine, singular or plural.

Parler 2

In pairs, talk about how to pronounce each *c* or *ç* in the sentences. Take turns to read out the sentences. Then listen and check.

1 Dans cet appartement, il y a cinq chambres.
2 Il y a un cinéma dans ce quartier.
3 Mon cousin français, Camille, est très célèbre.
4 - Tu as reçu mon cadeau d'anniversaire?
- Oui, il est ici, merci.
5 - Comment ça va ce matin?
- Ça va bien, merci.

> The letter **c** is pronounced as a soft sound ('ss') rather than a hard sound ('k')
> - before *e* and *i* – *c'est, ici*
> - when it has a cedilla (*ç*) – *ça va.*
>
> Listen and repeat the words.
> ***c****'est* *i****c****i* ***ç****a va*

Indefinite adjectives (Unit 1, page 160)

Écrire 3

Copy and complete the sentences using a word from the box.

toutes tous toute tout chaque

1 ___ les bâtiments du centre-ville sont vieux.
2 ___ ma famille habite en Martinique.
3 Le samedi, je sors ___ le temps avec mes amis.
4 ___ jour, beaucoup de gens vont à Paris.
5 J'ai visité ___ les grandes villes du nord de la France.

> An article (word for 'a'/'an' or 'the') is needed after *tout* but not after *chaque*.

Écrire 4

Copy and complete the parallel translations.

1 ___ année, nous allons en Algérie.	Every ___, we ___ to Algeria.
2 Tous les habitants ___ au centre-ville.	___ the inhabitants work in the ___.
3 Je suis resté à la maison ___ le mois d'août.	I stayed at ___ the whole ___ of August.
4 ___ la classe aime habiter en ville.	The whole ___ likes ___ in town.

Using *à* and *de* with the definite article (Unit 2, page 162)

Lire 5 **Select the correct form of *de* to complete each sentence.**

1 La banque est à côté **de la / du / de l'** supermarché.
2 Tournez à droite au coin **de la / du / des** rue.
3 Elle joue **de l' / du / de la** piano.
4 Mon frère fait **du / de la / des** cuisine.
5 J'habite près **du / de la / des** magasins.

Remember:
à + le = ***au*** à + les = ***aux***
de + le = ***du*** de + les = ***des***

- *à* can mean 'at' or 'to':
  On va au musée. (We are going to the museum.)
- *de* often means 'of' or 'from', but this doesn't always translate into English, e.g.
  loin de = far from; *près de* = near (to); *en face de* = opposite.

Remember, *à* and *de* are also used with *jouer* and *faire* to refer to sports, musical instruments and other activities:
*jouer **au** football*
*jouer **de la** guitare*
*faire **du** vélo*
*faire **de la** cuisine*
*faire **des** sorties*

Écrire 6 **Copy and complete the sentences, filling in the gaps with the correct form of *à* (*au*, *à la*, *à l'* or *aux*).**

1 Le week-end, on joue ___ cartes.
2 Pour aller ___ cinéma, s'il vous plaît?
3 Tournez à gauche ___ feux.
4 Je dois aller ___ poste.
5 Vous êtes arrivés ___ hôpital.

Écrire 7 **Translate the sentences into French.**

1 I am going to the shops.
2 The bank is next to the café.
3 Do you want to go to the sports centre?
4 We are going to play football.
5 Sometimes, I like to go cycling.

Negatives (Unit 2, page 163)

Écouter 8 **Look at the gapped sentences. Predict the second part of each negative expression. Then listen and fill in the gaps.**

1 Dans ma rue, il n'y a ___ de cafés.
2 Je ne suis ___ allé au Canada.
3 Le soir, dans mon village, il n'y a ___ dans les rues.
4 En ville, il n'y a ___ pour les jeunes.
5 Dans notre quartier, il n'y a ___ de poste.

The following negatives are in two parts that go **around** the verb:

ne ... pas	not
ne ... rien	nothing
ne ... jamais	never
ne ... personne	nobody

Remember that *ne* shortens to *n'* before a vowel.

Écrire 9 **Translate the sentences into French.**

1 I never go food shopping.
2 In my street, there is no bakery.
3 There is no one of my age in my village.
4 In my district, there is nothing for young people.

Grammaire 2

Using *de* to indicate possession (Unit 3, page 164)

Parler 1 **Read the tip on the right. Then, in pairs, take turns to ask and answer the questions below using the information in brackets.**

Example: 1

- *C'est ton tee-shirt?*
- *Non, c'est <u>le tee-shirt de mon père</u>.*

1 C'est ton tee-shirt? (mon père)
2 C'est ton sac? (ma sœur)
3 Ce sont tes baskets? (mon meilleur ami)
4 C'est ton appartement? (mes grands-parents)
5 C'est ton anniversaire demain? (ma mère)
6 Le gâteau, c'est pour ta fête? (mes voisins)

Remember, you cannot say 'my brother's shirt' in French. You have to say, 'the shirt of my brother' ('*la chemise de mon frère*').

Adjectives which can go before or after the noun (Unit 4, page 166)

Some adjectives can have different meanings, depending on whether they are before or after the noun.

Adjective	Meaning before the noun	Meaning after the noun
ancien/ancienne	former	ancient
cher/chère	dear (beloved)	expensive
grand/grande	big, great	tall
propre	own	clean
seul/seule	only	alone, lonely

Lire 2 **Decide whether the adjectives should come before or after the noun in the French translations.**

1 We live in the ancient district of town.	1 Nous habitons dans **l'ancien quartier / le quartier ancien** de la ville.
2 Look at the big house on the left.	2 Regarde **la grande maison / la maison grande** à gauche.
3 My dear auntie lives in Switzerland.	3 Ma **chère tante / ma tante chère** habite en Suisse.
4 He's our only neighbour.	4 Il est notre **seul voisin / voisin seul**.

Lire 3 **Translate each sentence into English. Refer to the grammar box to make sure you use the correct translation of the <u>underlined</u> adjectives.**

1 La maison de gauche est notre <u>ancienne</u> maison.
2 J'aime avoir une chambre <u>propre</u>.
3 Ma sœur a un appartement dans un quartier <u>cher</u>.
4 Tu vois l'homme <u>grand</u> avec les cheveux noirs?

Si clauses (Unit 4, page 167)

In sentences starting with *si*, the imperfect comes first and then the **conditional**.
*Si j'étais riche, je **voudrais** acheter un château.*

Écrire 4 **Copy and complete each sentence using the correct word/words from the box.**

1 Si j'étais riche, je ___ un bel appartement.
2 Si j'___ le temps, je voudrais faire de la natation tous les jours.
3 Si j'avais le choix, je ___ dans une vieille maison.
4 Si je ___ un concours, je voudrais aller en Afrique.
5 Si j'___ célèbre, je voudrais avoir un cinéma dans ma maison.

étais
voudrais habiter
avais
gagnais
voudrais acheter

Lire 5 **Translate the sentences in exercise 4 into English.**

Forming questions in different tenses (Unit 5, page 169)

Écrire 6 **Re-read the grammar box on page 169 about forming questions in different tenses. Then copy and complete the question you would need to ask to get each answer. Make sure you match the tense of each question to the tense in each answer.**

Example: 1 *Pourquoi veux-tu aller à Paris?*

1 Pourquoi ___ aller à Paris? — Je veux aller à Paris parce que c'est une belle ville.
2 Tu ___ déjà ___ la France? — Non, je n'ai jamais visité la France.
3 Quand ___ à Paris et avec qui? — Je vais aller à Paris le week-end prochain avec ma famille.
4 Qu'est-ce que ___ à Paris? — Je vais visiter les musées.
5 Quels autres pays ___ un jour? — Je voudrais visiter le Royaume-Uni et le Canada.

Écrire 7 **Translate the questions into French. There may be more than one way of writing some of the questions.**

a When did you go to Paris?
b Are you going to visit Canada?
c Why would you like to visit Morocco?
d How do you travel and with whom?
e Which museum did you visit?
f What would you like to do during your visit?

C'est parti!

Parler 8 **In pairs, take turns to read out the text. Give feedback on each other's pronunciation. Then listen and check.**

J'habite dans une vieille ville dans le sud-ouest du pays. J'habite avec ma famille dans un bel appartement. Si j'avais le choix, je voudrais habiter dans une jolie petite maison à la campagne. Dans ma ville, il n'y a rien pour les jeunes. Mais je vais sortir ce soir! Pour aller à la fête d'anniversaire de ma meilleure amie, je vais mettre ces chaussures grises.

Module 7

Contrôle de lecture et d'écoute

Reading

Lire 1

My ideal place to live. **You read Alessandro's blog about where he would love to live.**

Salut tout le monde!

Plus tard, je voudrais habiter en Asie ou en Afrique. Il y a deux avantages à vivre à l'étranger: les cultures sont vraiment différentes et apprendre une autre langue est excellent pour mon avenir.

Ensuite, je voudrais être dans une région où il ne fait pas trop froid et où il ne pleut pas tout le temps! Il y a des inconvénients quand le temps est humide: il faut aimer l'eau et on ne peut pas aller au travail à pied. Je n'aime pas être ***mouillé***.

Alessandro

1 Answer the following questions in **English**.

a According to Alessandro, what are two advantages of living abroad?

b According to Alessandro, what are two disadvantages of rainy weather?

Find all the negatives in the text. They are going to be useful to work out the answers.

You only need to give one detail for each advantage or disadvantage.

2 Read the last sentence again. What would you be if you were ***mouillé***? Write the correct letter, **A**, **B** or **C**.

A exhausted **B** wet **C** very hot

To work out the meaning, look at the vocabulary in the sentences just before that word.

Lire 2

Translation. **Translate these sentences into English.**

These words look very similar to some English words. Make sure you check their meaning in French if you are not sure.

Think about how you are going to translate these structures.

Don't forget to translate the negatives.

1 J'aime habiter dans mon quartier.

2 Les logements modernes ne sont pas beaux.

3 Je voudrais vivre dans une vieille maison.

4 Avoir une piscine chez moi ne m'intéresse pas.

5 Il faut aller à gauche pour arriver au château.

Listening

Écouter 3

Buying presents. **You hear Marie and Louis talking about buying presents. Choose the correct answer and write A, B or C for each question.**

> You will hear all three days mentioned. Concentrate on when Marie is going to go.

1 Marie is going to the shops on ...
A Sunday. **B** Tuesday. **C** Wednesday.

2 Marie is going shopping ...
A in town. **B** in another village. **C** where she lives.

3 Louis bought a ... bag for his dad.
A white **B** blue **C** brown

> You will hear all the colours mentioned. Listen out for what Louis actually bought.

4 When he paid, Louis realised that ...
A he didn't have any money.
B the bag was too expensive.
C he didn't have his card.

Écouter 4

Happy homes. **You hear this online news item about happiness at home. What makes French people happy where they live? Write the correct letters (A–F) for the four reasons given.**

A	living in town
B	living somewhere quiet
C	having a big house
D	living near friends
E	living near family
F	having a big garden

Écouter 5

Dictation. **You will now hear four short sentences. Listen carefully and, using your knowledge of French sounds, write in French exactly what you hear for each sentence.**

Contrôle oral

Role-play

Parler **1** **Look at the role-play card and prepare what you are going to say.**

- You are talking to your French friend.
- Your teacher will play the part of your friend and will speak first.
- You should address your friend as *tu*.
- When you see this – **?** – you will have to ask a question.

In order to score full marks, you must include a verb in your response to each task.

1 Describe the area where you live. (Give **one** detail.)
2 Say what you do in your area. (Give **one** detail.)
3 Say **one** thing you would like to have where you live.
4 Give **one** opinion of your area.
? 5 Ask your friend a question about where they live.

You could say it is a town, a village, near the sea, quiet, modern, old ...

You could start with *Je vais ...* or *Je fais ...*

Use *Je voudrais avoir ...*

You could say that you do or don't like the shops, or that it is a small or a good town.

You could start with *Qu'est-ce que tu penses de ...?*, *Qu'est-ce qu'il y a ...?* or *Est-ce qu'il y a ...?*

Parler **2** **Practise what you have prepared. Then, using your notes, listen and respond to the teacher.**

Écouter **3** **Now listen to Zoé doing the role-play task. In English, note down (a) how she answers the questions for tasks 1, 2, 3 and 4, and (b) what question she asks for task 5.**

Reading aloud

Parler **4** **Look at this task. With a partner, take turns to read out the text below, paying attention to the underlined letters.**

Read aloud the following text **in French**.

J'aime habiter dans cette vi<u>ll</u>e.
Le week-end, je trava<u>ill</u>e dans un <u>h</u>ôtel.
Dans ma <u>r</u>égion, il y a beaucoup de tou<u>r</u>istes.
L'<u>h</u>istoi<u>r</u>e de cet endroit est très inté<u>r</u>essante!
Avant, il y avait moins de pollution ici.

Take extra care with how you pronounce the underlined sounds:
- ***r*** makes a raspy sound in the back of your throat
- *vi**ll**e* and *trava**ill**e* sound different; you need the French ***i*** sound in *ville* but the English 'y' sound in *travaille*
- ***h*** is silent.

Take extra care with how you pronounce cognates.

Remember your liaisons!

Écouter **5** **Listen and check your pronunciation.**

Parler **6** **Listen to the teacher asking <u>four</u> questions that relate to the topic of The environment and where people live. Translate each question into English and prepare your own answers in French. Then listen again and respond to the teacher.**

Use the specific vocabulary you have learned in module 7 in your answers.

Photo card task

Écouter 7 **Look at the exam card below and read the first part of the task. Then listen to Zoé describing the two photos.**

1 Who is Zoé describing in the first photo?
2 Where are they, according to Zoé?
3 What does she say about the town in the second photo? Do you agree?

Photo 1

Photo 2

You will be asked to talk about the content of these photos. You must say at least one thing about each photo.

After you have spoken about the content of the photos, you will be asked questions related to any of the topics within the theme of **Communication and the world around us**.

Your responses should be as **full and detailed** as possible.

Parler 8 **Prepare your own description of the two photos. You could mention, for example, the people, the location and what they are doing. Then, with a partner, take turns to describe the photos.**

Sur la première photo, il y a …

Describe what people are doing using the present tense: *elle regarde* ('she is watching'), *elle parle* ('she is talking').

Écouter 9 **Read the second part of the task. Listen to Zoé answering the question: *Le week-end, qu'est-ce que tu fais dans ta ville ou ton village?* Copy out the table below and complete it in English.**

What activity	When

Écouter 10 **Now listen to Zoé answering the question: *Où est-ce que tu voudrais habiter plus tard et pourquoi?* Give two reasons why she would like to live in China (*en Chine*).**

Parler 11 **Prepare your own answers to the module 7 questions on page 227. Your responses should be as full and detailed as possible. Then practise with a partner.**

Remember to use opinion phrases, time phrases and connectives.

Contrôle écrit

Grammar task

Lire 1

Choose the correct form of the verb in the French sentences to match the English translations.

1 **J'aime / J'aimais / J'ai aimé** ma ville.	*I like my town.*
2 Mon quartier **était / est / va être** assez calme.	*My district is quite calm.*
3 Hier, **je vais / je vais aller / je suis allé** à la campagne.	*Yesterday, I went to the countryside.*
4 Avant, **je déteste / je vais détester / je détestais** aller dans les magasins.	*Before, I used to hate going to the shops.*
5 Le week-end **va être / est / était** très agréable.	*The weekend is going to be very pleasant.*
6 Avant, **j'habite / j'ai habité / j'habitais** dans un autre pays.	*Before, I used to live in another country.*

Translation

Écrire 2

Translate the following sentences into French.

Think carefully about each time frame. It might be useful to look back at exercise 1.

1 I don't like my village.
2 I like living here because it is pleasant.
3 Last weekend was very good.
4 Before, my town used to be cleaner.
5 The festival is going to be great.

Use the infinitive form after 'I like'.

Remember to say 'more clean'.

Look out for complex grammatical structures such as different tenses, impersonal structures and negatives.

90-word writing task

Écrire 3

Look at this writing exam task and then, <u>for each bullet point</u>:

1 think about what vocabulary you have learned that you could use in your answer. For example:
- **nouns** and **verbs** to talk about where you live
- **verbs of opinion** and **adjectives** to explain your point of view
- language for **narrating a story** about what you did recently in your area
- language to refer to a **future** outing.

2 write down <u>three or four</u> ideas for what you could write about.
3 write down which tense(s) you will need to use in your answer.

You are writing an email to your Belgian friend about where you live.

Write approximately **90** words in **French**.

You must write something about each bullet point.

Describe:
- the area where you live
- a recent visit in your area
- a future outing with your friends in your area.

Look at the vocabulary you have noted to give you ideas for what to write.

Lire 4 **Read Sam's answer to the exam task in exercise 3. Answer questions 1–5 in the coloured shapes.**

1 This word shows a **variety of vocabulary**. What does it mean? Find two more examples.

2 This is an example of **complex language**. What does it mean? Find three more examples from the text.

3 Which **tense** is this? What other examples of this tense can you find? What other tenses does Sam use?

4 How could he **avoid repetition** by using another word or phrase?

5 How could you form an **extended sentence** here? What other extended sentences does he include?

Salut!

J'aime habiter dans cette ville parce qu'il y a beaucoup de choses pour les jeunes. Ce n'est jamais nul ici. Avant, c'était plus ennuyeux. Le week-end, on peut aller au cinéma, au centre commercial ou dans la forêt.

Récemment, avec mon groupe d'amis, je suis allé dans un café car c'était l'anniversaire de mon meilleur ami, Augustin. Après, nous avons regardé un film chez Augustin. Tout le monde était content!

Le mois prochain, on va aller au festival de musique au centre-ville. C'est un festival très populaire. Ça va être génial.

Sam

Lire 5 **Read Sam's answer again. Answer the questions in English.**

1. Why does Sam like where he lives?
2. What was his town like before?
3. What can he do at the weekend in his town?
4. Why did he go out recently?
5. What does he say about the festival he is going to go to?

Écrire 6 **Prepare your own answer to the 90-word writing task in exercise 3.**

- Think about how you can develop your answer for each bullet point.
- Look back at your notes from exercises 3 and 4.
- Look at the 'Challenge checklist' and consider how you can show off your French!
- Write a **brief** plan and organise your answer into paragraphs.
- Write your answer and then carefully check the accuracy of what you have written.

Challenge checklist

1 chilli	✓ Past, present and future time frames ✓ *Je voudrais* ... ✓ Connectives, time phrases, sequencers ✓ Opinion phrases
2 chillies	✓ Some extended sentences ✓ A variety of adjectives ✓ Some interesting vocabulary ✓ Avoid repetition
3 chillies	✓ Impersonal phrases (e.g. *il faut* ...) ✓ Complex language (e.g. *on peut* ..., *si* clauses, *chez* ..., comparatives (*plus*/*moins*)) ✓ Negatives (e.g. *ne ... jamais, ne ... rien*) ✓ A variety of connectives ✓ Different persons of the verbs ✓ The imperfect tense (*Avant, c'était* ...)

Vocabulaire

Key:
bold = this word will appear in higher exams only
* = this word is not on the vocabulary list, but you may use it in your own sentences

C'est combien? (pages 158–159)

Qu'est-ce que tu penses de cet appartement?	*What do you think of this apartment?*
Il est grand?	*Is it big?*
Il y a ...	*There is ...*
un *accès pour les personnes handicapées.	*access for disabled people.*
un jardin.	*a garden.*
une chambre / une cuisine.	*a bedroom / a kitchen.*
une entrée.	*a hall / an entrance.*
une *salle de bains.	*a bathroom.*
Est-ce qu'il y a un jardin?	*Is there a garden?*
Oui, il y a un jardin.	*Yes, there is a garden.*
Non, il n'y a pas de jardin.	*No, there is no garden.*
Qu'est-ce que tu vas acheter?	*What are you going to buy?*
Qu'est-ce que tu vas porter pour aller ...	*What are you going to wear to go ...*
à la fête / au mariage de ...?	*to the party / the wedding of ...?*
Je vais acheter / porter ...	*I'm going to buy / wear ...*
ce *tee-shirt / pantalon.	*this t-shirt / these trousers.*
cette *chemise / *robe.	*this shirt / dress.*
ces *baskets / *chaussures.	*these trainers / shoes.*
Je voudrais acheter cette *chemise, mais ...	*I would like to buy this shirt, but ...*
c'est trop cher pour moi.	*it's too expensive for me.*
je n'ai pas assez d'argent.	*I do not have enough money.*
Qu'est-ce que tu penses de ...	*What do you think of ...*
ce pantalon noir / blanc / *marron?	*these black / white / brown trousers?*
cette *robe noire / blanche / *marron?	*this black / white / brown dress?*
ces *chaussures noires / blanches / *marron?	*these black / white / brown shoes?*

Là où j'habite (pages 160–161)

Est-ce que tu habites dans une ville ou un village?	*Do you live in a town or a village?*
Où se trouve ta ville / ton village?	*Where is your town / village?*
Comment est ta ville / ton village?	*What is your town / village like?*
Est-ce que tu aimes habiter dans cette ville / ce village? Pourquoi?	*Do you like living in this town / village? Why?*
J'habite dans un petit village / une grande ville.	*I live in a small village / large town.*
Il/Elle se trouve dans ...	*It is in ...*
le nord / l'est / le nord-est	*the north / the east / the northeast*
le sud-est / le sud	*the southeast / the south*
le sud-ouest / l'ouest	*the southwest / the west*
le nord-ouest ...	*the northwest ...*
de l'Angleterre.	*of England.*
de la France.	*of France.*
du Canada.	*of Canada.*
près de la capitale	*near the capital city*
Il y a une partie historique / moderne, avec ...	*There is a historic / modern part, with ...*
des petites rues.	*little streets.*
beaucoup de beaux / vieux bâtiments.	*lots of beautiful / old buildings.*
beaucoup d'entreprises.	*lots of businesses.*
Vivre à la campagne / en ville est parfait pour moi, car ...	*Living in the countryside / town is perfect for me, as ...*
il y a toujours quelque chose à faire.	*there is always something to do.*
je peux faire tout le temps les magasins.	*I can go shopping all the time.*
je peux sortir avec tous mes ami(e)s.	*I can go out with all my friends.*
Je suis très content(e) d'habiter ici.	*I am very happy to live here.*
Un jour, je voudrais ...	*One day, I would like to ...*
habiter à la campagne / en ville.	*live in the countryside / town.*
passer plus de temps à *Lyon.	*spend more time in Lyon.*

Sur la bonne route (pages 162–163)

Pour aller au supermarché / à la boulangerie, s'il vous plaît?	*How do you get to the supermarket / bakery, please?*
Allez / Continuez tout droit.	*Go / Continue straight ahead.*
Tournez à gauche / à droite (aux *feux).	*Turn left / right (at the traffic lights).*
Traversez la place / le pont.	*Cross the square / bridge.*
Prenez la première / la troisième rue à gauche / à droite.	*Take the first / third road on the left / right.*
C'est à côté / en face ...	*It's next to / opposite ...*
du jardin public.	*the public garden.*
de la banque.	*the bank.*
des magasins.	*the shops.*
C'est devant / derrière ...	*It's in front of / behind ...*
le parc.	*the park.*
la *pharmacie.	*the pharmacy.*
les toilettes.	*the toilets.*
C'est entre le cinéma et la boulangerie.	*It's between the cinema and the bakery.*
Et voilà, vous êtes arrivé(e)(s)!	*And there it is; you've arrived!*
C'est loin / près d'ici?	*Is it far from / near here?*
Ma ville est grande / petite.	*My town/city is large / small.*
Ma ville est vieille / belle.	*My town is old / beautiful.*
Mon village est grand / petit.	*My village is large / small.*
Mon village est vieux / beau.	*My village is old / beautiful.*
Il y a ...	*There is/are ...*
un hôpital / hôtel.	*a hospital / hotel.*
une banque / gare / poste.	*a bank / railway station / post office.*
beaucoup de / quelques cafés / magasins.	*a lot of / some cafés / shops.*

Malheureusement, / Mais ...	*Unfortunately, / But ...*
il n'y a personne de mon âge.	*there is no one of my age.*
il n'y a rien à faire.	*there is nothing to do.*
il n'y a pas de cinéma.	*there is no cinema.*
ce n'est jamais calme.	*it is never quiet.*
la pollution est terrible.	*the pollution is terrible.*

Mode et shopping (pages 164–165)

Qu'est-ce que vous cherchez?	*What are you looking for?*
C'est pour vous?	*Is it for you?*
Vous aimez cette *chemise?	*Do you like this shirt?*
Elle coûte combien?	*How much does it cost?*
Je peux l'*échanger s'il y a un problème?	*Can I exchange it if there is a problem?*
Bien sûr. Vous devez la *rapporter à la caisse.	*Of course. You have to bring it back to the checkout.*
Bonjour. Je peux vous aider?	*Hello. Can I help you?*
Quel est le problème?	*What is the problem?*
Avez-vous la même chose en noir?	*Do you have the same thing in black?*
Ça va comme ça?	*How's that?*
Je peux l'/les essayer, s'il vous plaît?	*Can I try it/them on, please?*
J'ai acheté ...	*I bought ...*
ce pantalon noir ...	*these black trousers ...*
ce **manteau** / sac (à main) ...	*this coat / (hand)bag ...*
cette *jupe bleue ...	*this blue skirt ...*
ces *chaussures blanches ...	*these white shoes ...*
pour l'anniversaire de mon frère / ma sœur.	*for my brother's / sister's birthday.*
J'ai trouvé ça dans un magasin de mode / en ligne.	*I found that in a fashion shop / online.*
Il/Elle a coûté ...	*It cost ...*
Ils/Elles ont coûté ...	*They cost ...*
quarante euros.	*forty euros.*
beaucoup d'argent.	*a lot of money.*
peu d'argent.	*not much money.*
cher / pas cher	*expensive / not expensive*
Il/Elle n'a pas coûté cher.	*It was not expensive.*
Mais il/elle est trop petit(e) / grand(e).	*But it is too small / big.*
Malheureusement, ils/elles sont trop petit(e)s / grand(e)s.	*Unfortunately, they are too small / big.*

La maison de mes rêves (pages 166–167)

Plus tard, je voudrais habiter dans ...	*Later, I would like to live in ...*
un château **ancien** à la campagne.	*an ancient castle in the countryside.*
une petite maison en bois à la montagne.	*a little wooden house in the mountains.*
un bel appartement récent.	*a beautiful, recently built apartment.*
une vieille maison comme dans les films d'*horreur!	*an old house like in horror films!*
Je voudrais avoir ...	*I would like to have ...*
Je rêve d'avoir ...	*I dream of having ...*
C'est essentiel / moins important pour moi d'avoir ...	*It is essential / less important for me to have ...*
J'ai besoin de ... / Je n'ai pas besoin de ...	*I need ... / I don't need ...*
Si j'étais riche, / Si j'avais le choix, je voudrais avoir ...	*If I were rich, / If I had the choice, I would like to have ...*
une cuisine propre et moderne.	*a clean, modern kitchen.*
un bon *accès pour les personnes handicapées avec un *fauteuil roulant.	*good access for disabled people with a wheelchair.*
ma propre chambre calme et *confortable.	*my own calm/quiet and comfortable bedroom.*
de grandes fenêtres.	*big windows.*
beaucoup d'espace.	*lots of space.*
une salle de sport / jeux.	*a sports / games room.*
une salle à manger.	*a dining room.*
des chambres d'amis.	*guest bedrooms.*
un joli jardin.	*a pretty garden.*
des voisins sympa.	*nice neighbours.*
une télévision à grand écran dans ma chambre.	*a wide-screen TV in my bedroom.*
un cinéma *privé pour regarder les derniers films.	*a private cinema to watch the latest films.*
une piscine pour moi tout(e) seul(e).	*a swimming pool just for me.*
Il y a peu d'espace.	*There is little space.*
Je dois partager ma chambre.	*I have to share my bedroom.*
une maison **ancienne** / une **ancienne** amie	*an ancient house / a former friend*
une chambre propre / ma propre chambre	*a clean bedroom / my own bedroom*
un appartement cher / un *cher oncle	*an expensive apartment / a dear uncle*

As-tu déjà visité Paris? (pages 168–169)

As-tu déjà visité le *Royaume-Uni ou un autre pays d'**Europe**?	*Have you ever visited the UK or another European country?*
Pourquoi veux-tu visiter ce pays?	*Why do you want to visit this country?*
Quand est-ce que tu vas aller à **Londres**?	*When are you going to go to London?*
Comment est-ce que tu vas voyager et avec qui?	*How are you going to travel and who with?*
Qu'est-ce que tu vas faire pendant ta visite?	*What are you going to do during your visit?*
Ça va être comment?	*What is it going to be like?*
Quel pays ou quelle ville voudrais-tu visiter un jour?	*Which country or town would you like to visit one day?*
Je vais ...	*I am going to ...*
bientôt aller à Paris.	*go to Paris soon.*
aller à Paris le week-end prochain.	*go to Paris next weekend.*
Je vais voyager en avion / en train.	*I am going to travel by plane / by train.*
Je vais faire le voyage avec mon père.	*I am going to make the trip with my father.*
Je vais faire ...	*I am going to do ...*
une visite de la tour Eiffel.	*a visit to the Eiffel Tower.*
un tour de la capitale en bateau / en autobus de *tourisme.	*a tour of the capital by boat / by tourist bus.*
Cela va être génial!	*It's going to be great!*

Module 8

Mes projets d'avenir

Mon été de rêve

- Talking about summer plans
- Using two different tenses to express the future

Parler 1 **Listen and repeat these words. Pay special attention to the pronunciation of *ill/ille* and *ail/aill*.**

la fam**ille** · une f**ille** · un b**ill**et · un trav**ail** · trav**aill**er · Vers**aill**es

The double 'll' in ***-ill-/-ille*** and in ***-ail/-aill-*** sounds like the 'y' sound in English, rather than the English 'l'.

Lire 2 **Read the text. Put the images of different summer jobs (a–f) in the order in which they appear in the text.**

Quel travail peut-on faire à 16 ans?

Beaucoup d'emplois sont ouverts aux jeunes. Voici quelques idées:

- Vous pouvez travailler dans une ferme: vous pouvez, par exemple, cueillir des fruits.
- Vous pouvez servir les clients. Vous pouvez travailler dans une boulangerie ou dans un supermarché.
- Vous pouvez faire du babysitting ou promener des chiens.
- Vous pouvez devenir animateur de vacances ou aider dans un centre sportif.

l'emploi (m)	*job*
cueillir	*to pick (fruit)*
promener	*to (take for a) walk*

a

b

c

d

e

f

Summer camps (*des colonies de vacances*) are popular in France. Children go to them to learn new skills, do sports, play games and work in teams. Older teenagers often work as an *animateur* (m) or *animatrice* (f) to look after the children and organise the activities. You can even do a qualification called the BAFA to become an *animateur*.

Écouter 3 **Listen to the teenagers talking about potential summer jobs. Then copy and complete the grid in English. (1–5)**

	Job	Positive or negative opinion?	Reason
1	Babysitting		

Je voudrais Je ne voudrais pas	travailler dans	une ferme une usine une boulangerie un supermarché	parce que car	c'est	intéressant. génial. dur. ennuyeux.
	faire du babysitting			j'aime j'adore je n'aime pas	les animaux. les enfants. le sport.
	promener des chiens				
	être animateur ou animatrice				
	aider dans un centre sportif				

Parler 4 **In pairs, take turns to ask and answer questions about the summer jobs suggested in exercise 2.**

- *Est-ce que tu voudrais travailler dans un supermarché?*
- *Non, je ne voudrais pas travailler dans un supermarché car c'est dur. Et toi, est-ce que tu voudrais faire du babysitting?*

Écouter 5 **Listen to and read the text about interrailing. With a partner, work out the significance of each of the numbers below.**

Allez partout en Europe avec le Pass Interrail. Explorez en train plus de 30 000 destinations et 33 pays.

Vous avez 27 ans ou moins?
Achetez votre Interrail Pass Jeune!
Réduction de 25% sur vos voyages en train et sur vos activités et vos visites.

Idées de voyage

Je vais visiter l'est de l'Europe – on va visiter la Pologne.

Je vais voir le château de Versailles. On va voyager partout en France!

Ce week-end, je vais à Bruxelles avec ma sœur. Samedi matin, on visite la Grand-Place.

la Pologne	*Poland*
Bruxelles	*Brussels*

Le château de Versailles

La Grand-Place à Bruxelles

1 25 **2** 27 **3** 33 **4** 30,000

Lire 6 **Translate the sentences in the speech bubbles in exercise 5 into English.**

Écouter 7 **Listen to the statements expressing future plans. (1–5) Which tense is each one in? Write:**

a for the near future tense
b for the present tense with a future time adverb.
Example: 1 *a*

G

To express the future, you usually use the **near future tense** (*aller* + an infinitive), e.g.
Je vais visiter l'Italie.
I am going to visit / will visit Italy.

However, sometimes the present tense is used with a time adverb to express the future, e.g.
Ce week-end, je visite Paris avec mes amis.
This weekend, I am visiting Paris with my friends.

Page 192

1 Mes passions et mon avenir

- Talking about future plans and hopes
- Using a range of structures followed by the infinitive
- Using sequencers

Écouter 1 **Read the grammar box. Then listen and, for each speaker (1–8), note down:**

- the French phrase they use from the grammar box
- the letter of the correct picture.

G

You can use any of these phrases, followed by **an infinitive**, to talk about your future plans and wishes:

Je veux	I want to	*Mon objectif est de*	My objective is to
Je voudrais	I would like to	*Mon but est de*	My aim is to
J'espère	I hope to		

Page 192

a

avoir des enfants

b

réussir à mes examens

c

voyager et travailler à l'étranger

d

aller à l'université

e

faire un apprentissage

f

me marier

g

gagner beaucoup d'argent

h

avoir ma propre entreprise

Écouter 2 **Listen and read. Then answer the questions in English.**

Pour commencer, je veux continuer mes études.
J'espère réussir à mes examens l'année prochaine.
Ensuite, mon but est d'aller à l'université.
Après, j'espère visiter d'autres pays et être bénévole pour un projet vert à l'étranger.
Puis je voudrais entrer dans le monde du travail.
Mon but est de travailler dans les médias.
Plus tard, mon objectif personnel est de vivre avec ma copine. Je ne veux pas me marier.
Un jour, j'espère avoir des enfants.
Sophie

1 What does Sophie hope to do next year?
2 What two things does she want to do between finishing university and finding a job?
3 In which sector is she aiming to work?
4 What is her personal objective?
5 What does she hope to do one day?

Use sequencers to extend your sentences and order your ideas.

pour commencer	first of all, to start with
ensuite	next
puis	then
après	after
plus tard	later
un jour	one day

Parler **3** **In pairs, talk about your future plans.**

- *Qu'est-ce que tu veux faire à l'avenir?*
- *Pour commencer, je voudrais …*
  Après, j'espère …
  Puis …
  Et toi?

Lire **4** **Read the article. Find the French for the phrases below.**

Université ou apprentissage?

À mon avis, pour trouver un bon travail, il faut aller à l'université.

Moi, je vais certainement aller à l'université pour étudier les maths. Plus tard, je vais choisir une carrière. Après plusieurs années d'études, il y a beaucoup de possibilités!

En plus, à l'université, on peut devenir plus indépendant. On peut aussi se faire de nouveaux amis.

Après l'université, je voudrais être bénévole. Un jour, je voudrais habiter à la campagne avec mon chien!

Anna

Je ne suis pas d'accord. On peut trouver un bon emploi sans aller à l'université.

Je voudrais travailler dans le tourisme parce que je veux habiter et travailler à l'étranger.

Mon but est de faire un apprentissage pour développer des compétences pratiques.

En plus, je veux gagner de l'argent sans faire de longues études!

Plus tard, j'espère me marier et avoir des enfants.

Habib

1 You can find a good job without going to university.
2 You can become more independent.
3 I want to earn money without doing long studies.
4 In order to find a good job, you have to go to university.
5 Later, I am going to choose a career.
6 My aim is to do an apprenticeship in order to develop practical skills.
7 After several years of studies, there are lots of possibilities.

G

sans + infinitive means 'without (doing something)', e.g.
sans aller à l'université without going to university

pour + infinitive means 'in order to (do something)'. e.g.
pour gagner de l'argent in order to earn money

Page 192

Écouter **5** **Listen. Then copy and complete the grid in English. (1–3)**

	University or apprenticeship?	Reason	Other plans / details
1			

Écrire **6** **Write a blog post about what you want to do in the future, including whether you want to go to university and why / why not. Include:**

- different phrases to introduce future plans
- sequencers
- one sentence using *pour* + infinitive or *sans* + infinitive.

2 Célébrités à l'écran

- Talking about reality TV and influencers
- Using verbs that take *être* in the perfect tense
- Expressing opinions on reality TV and influencers

Écouter **1** **Listen and read. Then answer the questions in English.**

L'Amour à la ferme

Julien, agriculteur de 33 ans, est candidat à *L'Amour à la ferme*, l'émission de télé-réalité qui aide les fermiers et les fermières à trouver l'amour. Originaire d'Amiens, Julien est parti faire ses études à Paris quand il avait 18 ans. Il est revenu à Amiens pour reprendre la ferme de ses parents quand il avait 20 ans. Son rêve, c'est de trouver l'amour.

Deux femmes, Emma (influenceuse de 29 ans) et Rébecca (femme politique de 32 ans), sont venues passer une semaine à la ferme pour découvrir la vie de Julien. Le premier jour, Rébecca n'a pas hésité à aider Julien, mais Emma est allée dans sa chambre pour se relaxer.

Le deuxième jour, Emma est rentrée chez elle car il n'y avait rien pour ses vidéos de réseaux sociaux. Rébecca est restée, et Julien est tombé amoureux d'elle.

Regardez la prochaine émission pour découvrir si Rébecca partage ses sentiments ...

l'agriculteur *(m)* / ***l'agricultrice*** *(f)*	*farmer*
originaire de	*native of, originally from*

1 What is Julien's job?
2 What did he do in Paris?
3 What is his dream?
4 What are the jobs of the two candidates? (Give two details.)
5 What did they do on the first day? (Give two details.)
6 Why did Emma go home?

Lire **2** **Read the text again and list the seven verbs in the perfect tense that use the auxiliary *être*. Then translate them into English.**

G Remember that some verbs, for example, *aller*, *partir*, *arriver* and *rester*, form the perfect tense with *être*, not *avoir*. For verbs that take *être*, the past participle must agree with the subject.

Écouter **3** **Listen to Emma's TikTok video. Then copy and complete the sentences in English.**

1 Emma went on *L'Amour à la ferme* because ... .
2 Emma went to her room because ... .
3 Emma went home because ... . She also thought the farm was very ... .
4 Emma says that farm life ... .

Parler **4** **In pairs, take turns to read the text out. Give feedback to your partner on their pronunciation.**

L'Agence est une émission de télé-réalité qui suit la famille Kretz. Ils vendent des maisons et des appartements de luxe à Paris et à l'étranger. Ce n'est pas une compétition, cependant l'émission parle de belles maisons et des liens familiaux.

les liens *(m)* ***familiaux*** *family links*

Lire **5** **Translate the text from exercise 4 into English.**

A lot of reality shows in the UK have a francophone adaptation. Can you work out the English titles of these shows? *Danse avec les stars, Mariés au premier regard, Frenchie Shore, La France a un incroyable talent, Le Meilleur Pâtissier.*

Lire **6** **Read the conversation about HugoDécrypte. Write the correct letter for each missing question. Listen and check.**

1 ___ Il s'appelle Hugo Travers, mais il est plus connu sous le nom de HugoDécrypte.

2 ___ Il utilise principalement YouTube, Instagram et TikTok.

3 ___ Il est surtout connu pour ses vidéos courtes qui expliquent la politique et l'actualité aux jeunes.

4 ___ Pour lui, l'important, c'est de parler de ses passions: la politique, l'actualité … En plus, il peut rencontrer beaucoup de personnes très intéressantes.

5 ___ Oui, il y a les insultes et la cyberintimidation. C'est un problème quotidien et c'est parfois difficile pour lui.

6 ___ Il a eu la chance d'interviewer des célébrités comme Bill Gates, Angèle et Stromae. Récemment, il a discuté de l'éducation avec le président de la République française.

a Comment s'appelle ton influenceur preféré?
b De quoi est-il fier?
c Il y a des inconvénients pour lui?
d Il est connu pour quoi?
e Quelles plateformes utilise-t-il?
f Selon lui, quel est l'avantage d'être influenceur?

Écouter **7** **Listen to the portraits of these two influencers. Then copy and complete the grid in English.**

Name	**Marc Long (@ModeALaFrancaise98)**	**Maude Robert (@Secret2Beauté2004)**
Age		
Platform(s)		
Areas of influence		
Advantage(s) of job of influencer		
Disadvantage(s) of job of influencer		
Any other details?		

Parler **8** **In pairs, talk about the advantages and disadvantages of being an influencer.**

- *Quels sont les avantages d'être influenceur?*
- *On peut être créatif et bien payé.*
- *Quels sont les inconvénients d'être influenceur?*
- *Il faut toujours être en ligne.*

L'avantage, c'est qu'on peut L'important, c'est de/d'			devenir célèbre / riche (rapidement). gagner beaucoup d'argent. être créatif/créative / bien payé(e).
L'inconvénient, Le pire,	c'est que/qu'	on peut	recevoir des messages / des commentaires méchants. être victime de cyberintimidation.
		il faut	poster du contenu (régulièrement). être toujours en ligne.
		ça peut	être dangereux / difficile pour la santé mentale.

Écrire **9** **Imagine you are an influencer. Write an article about your work. Describe:**

- the sort of content you make and why
- the advantages of being an influencer
- the disadvantages of being an influencer.

3 Quelles sont tes compétences?

- Talking about possible future career paths
- Forming feminine nouns
- Looking up words for possible future jobs

Écouter 1 **Listen to the careers interviews. Write down the five correct letters for each speaker. (1–4)**

Quelles sont tes passions?

a Ma passion, c'est la mode.
b Moi, j'adore les sciences.
c Ma passion, c'est voyager.
d Aider les autres, c'est ma passion.

Comment es-tu?

e Je suis travailleur/travailleuse.
f Je suis sympa et patient(e).
g Je suis responsable et indépendant(e).
h Je suis créatif/créative.

Avec qui voudrais-tu travailler?

i Je voudrais travailler seul(e).
j Je veux travailler avec des enfants.
k Je voudrais travailler avec des gens.
l Je veux travailler avec des animaux.

Qu'est-ce que tu trouves important dans un travail?

m Être responsable, c'est important pour moi.
n Avoir un travail intéressant, c'est essentiel.
o Être actif/active, c'est très important pour moi.
p Pour moi, un bon salaire est essentiel.

Quelles sont tes compétences?

q Mon point fort, c'est la communication.
r Je suis très organisé(e).
s J'ai une attitude positive.
t Je m'entends bien avec tout le monde.

G

Sometimes we can use infinitives as nouns in French. When they are used this way, we translate them as '-ing' in English. For example:

Aider les autres, c'est ma passion.	Helping other people is my passion.
Avoir un travail intéressant, c'est essentiel.	Having an interesting job is essential.

Page 194

Parler 2 **In pairs, take turns to ask and answer the questions in exercise 1.**

- *Quelles sont tes passions?*
- *Ma passion, c'est l'environnement.*
- *Comment es-tu?*
- *Je suis travailleuse et gentille.*

Ma passion, c'est ...	le sport / le théâtre. la lecture / l'environnement. les films / les ordinateurs.
Je suis ...	amusant(e) / calme. sérieux/sérieuse. sportif/sportive. gentil/gentille.

You can change some of the answers to make them true for you. In the table are some ideas, but you can also come up with your own, using vocabulary you have learned in earlier modules.

Use connectives to create extended sentences: ***et***, ***donc***, ***car*** ...

Lire 3 **Read the texts. Select the correct job word to complete each one. Then listen and check.**

1 Je suis créative et responsable et j'aime travailler en équipe. La cuisine, c'est ma passion. Je voudrais travailler comme ____. ***Camille***

2 Ma passion, c'est la musique. Être créatif, c'est important pour moi. Je m'entends bien avec tout le monde et j'ai une attitude positive. J'espère être célèbre. Je voudrais être ____. ***Jack***

3 Je suis patiente et travailleuse. Un bon salaire est assez important pour moi, mais ma passion, c'est la santé. Je veux aider les autres. Je vais être ____. ***Anna***

G

Job nouns often change according to gender:

- -*eur* → -*euse* *influenceur/influenceuse* (influencer)
- -*teur* → -*trice* *acteur/actrice* (actor)
- -*en* → -*enne* *mécanicien/mécanicienne* (mechanic)
- \- → -*e* *ingénieur/ingénieure* (engineer)

Note that *chanteur* → *chanteuse* is an exception.

Some nouns do not change, e.g. *médecin* (doctor).

People who identify as non-binary may prefer to use the following structures:
Je suis mécanicien•ne. Je suis ingénieur•e.

When referring to jobs, you do not need the word for 'a' in French:
Je voudrais être joueuse de basket.
I would like to be a basketball player.

Page 194

médecin

directeur/directrice

joueur/joueuse de foot

chef/cheffe

chanteur/chanteuse

Parler 4 **In pairs, take turns to choose one text from exercise 3 and read it out.**

Écrire 5 **Write a paragraph to explain why you would like to do a particular job and what makes you suitable for it.**

Je voudrais être ...

Je voudrais être	acteur / joueuse de basket ...
... parce que ma passion, c'est	le cinéma / le sport.
Je suis	travailleur/travailleuse / actif/active.
Je veux travailler	seule(e) / avec des enfants.
Les films, / Être en forme,	c'est important pour moi.
En plus,	je m'entends bien avec tout le monde. un bon salaire est essentiel.

Look up in a dictionary any new job words you need.

noun, masculine and feminine

vet *vétérinaire* nmf
nurse *infirmier* nm, *infirmière* nf

noun, masculine — noun, feminine

Écouter 6 **Listen to Antoine. For each of his family members, write down in English (a) the job, and (b) the <u>two</u> reasons why it's suitable for them.**

1 his mum **2** his dad **3** his brother **4** his aunt

Écrire 7 **Imagine that you know these people. Write a few sentences about each person and their job.**

- What job do they do? *Il/Elle est / travaille comme ...*
- What is their passion? *Il/Elle adore ... / Sa passion, c'est ...*
- What sort of person are they? *Il/Elle est ...*

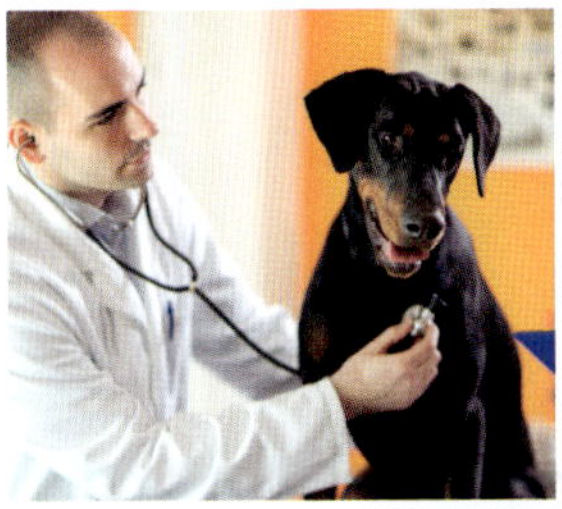

4 Bien payé, mais difficile!

- Discussing different jobs
- Using verbs followed by *à* or *de*
- Translating into French using a range of time frames

Écouter **1** **Listen and write down the letters of the two correct pictures for each speaker. (1–4)**

Les points positifs 😀

a

Le travail est bien payé.

b

Les gens sont sympa.

c

Le travail est intéressant.

d

On peut prendre ses propres décisions.

Les points négatifs ☹

e

Ça peut être dangereux.

f

Les heures sont longues et c'est difficile.

g

La formation dure longtemps.

h

On ne gagne pas beaucoup d'argent.

la formation *training*

Lire **2** **Read the texts and answer the questions.**

Je travaille dans une banque. Un point positif, c'est que mon travail est bien payé. Cependant, c'est embêtant. Il faut travailler dur et les heures sont longues. **Logan**

Je suis architecte et j'ai ma propre entreprise. Je peux prendre mes propres décisions et j'adore ça. Cependant, un point négatif, c'est que la formation dure longtemps. **Lily**

Je suis journaliste. Le point négatif, c'est que ça peut être dangereux. Mais j'aime le travail parce que c'est passionnant et parce que j'apprends beaucoup. **Harry**

Je travaille dans un hôtel. Je trouve le travail difficile et je ne gagne pas beaucoup d'argent. Mais je m'entends bien avec les gens. Ils sont très sympa. Mes collègues m'aident beaucoup. **Joëlle**

Who ...

1 says that they get help at work?
2 has their own business?
3 thinks that they are well paid?
4 thinks that their work is exciting?
5 finds their work hard?
6 says that they learn a lot?

Parler **3** **In pairs, talk about what you think the positive and negative aspects are of the jobs pictured below.**

- Être policier ou policière. Quels sont les points positifs?
- *Un point positif, c'est que le travail est intéressant.*
- *Quels sont les points négatifs?*
- *Un point négatif, c'est que ça peut être dangereux.*

policier/policière

scientifique

joueur/joueuse de tennis

Écouter 4

Listen and read. Then find the French for the phrases below.

Après l'université, je suis devenu influenceur. Ma passion était la mode, mais en ligne, c'était souvent très négatif.
Il y a deux ans, j'ai décidé de faire quelque chose de différent.
J'ai réussi à créer ma propre entreprise en informatique et maintenant je suis plus heureux.
Les heures sont longues, mais je peux prendre mes propres décisions.
À l'avenir, je vais continuer de travailler dur. ***Alexis***

Après le collège, j'ai travaillé comme actrice, mais je n'étais pas très heureuse.
Aider les autres, c'est ma passion. Donc, il y a trois ans, j'ai commencé à étudier la politique à l'université.
Maintenant, je suis femme politique! J'essaye de travailler contre le changement climatique.
Le mois prochain, je vais parler à une conférence. Je rêve d'être présidente un jour! ***Manon***

1 I decided to do something different.
2 I succeeded in creating my own business.
3 I will continue to work hard.
4 I started to study politics.
5 I try to work against climate change.
6 I dream of being president one day.

il y a (deux ans) *(two years) ago*

G Some verbs are followed by *à* or *de* + the infinitive:

commencer à	to start to
réussir à	to succeed in
continuer de	to continue to
décider de	to decide to
essayer de	to try to
rêver de	to dream of

Page 195

Lire 5

Re-read the texts in exercise 4. Select the correct option to complete each sentence.

1 Alexis stopped being an influencer because of **bad pay / negativity online**.
2 He changed career **last year / two years ago**.
3 His business is in the **IT / fashion** sector.
4 Manon became an actress after **school / university**.
5 Her passion is **studying / helping others**.
6 Soon, she is going to **attend an event / become a politician**

Écouter 6

Listen to the people talking about their careers. Then copy and complete the grid in English. (1–2)

	Job they used to do	What they didn't like about it	Job they do now	What they like about it
1				

Écrire 7

Translate the sentences into French.

Use the imperfect tense. Take care with the verb endings and remember to put 'ne' and 'pas' around the verbs.

You don't need the French word for 'a'.

Use the perfect tense.

1 After school, I worked in a hotel.
2 I was not very happy and it was not well paid.
3 I decided to go to university.
4 Now I am a scientist. The work is interesting.
5 In the future, I will try to do something different.

Do you need *à* or *de* after the verb?

Use the near future tense. Don't forget the *de* after this verb.

Grammaire 1

Expressing the future using two different tenses (Culture, page 183)

Lire 1 **Read the grammar box on page 183. Then read the sentences below. Which tense is used? Write 'near future' or 'present + future time adverb'. Then translate the sentences into English.**

Example: 1 near future – We are going to work in a factory.

1 Nous allons travailler dans une usine.
2 Elles vont voyager avec leurs parents.
3 Ce week-end, je vais à Paris avec mes amis.
4 À l'avenir, je vais travailler avec des animaux.
5 Demain, elle joue au foot.
6 Il va faire du babysitting.

Remember that the near future tense is formed using the present tense of *aller* + **an infinitive**.

je vais **voyager**
tu vas **travailler**
il/elle/on va **voir**
nous allons **visiter**
vous allez **jouer**
ils/elles vont **faire**

In each sentence in exercise 2, do you hear a part of *aller* + an infinitive, or just a verb in the present tense (e.g. *je travaille, je vais*) **without** an infinitive?

Écouter 2 **Listen and fill in the gaps with the missing verbs. Some are in the near future and some are in the present tense (but express the future). (1–6)**

Example: 1 vais visiter

1 Je ____ l'Allemagne avec mes parents.
2 Cet été, Aurélie ____ en Espagne.
3 Demain, je ____ dans une ferme.
4 Il ____ la tour Eiffel.
5 Est-ce que tu ____ en Europe?
6 Ce soir, je ____ au tennis avec ma sœur.

Using different structures followed by the infinitive to talk about future plans and wishes (Unit 1, page 184)

Parler 3 **Read the grammar box on page 184. Then, in pairs, take turns to choose a letter from each of the boxes. Your partner says the sentence in French.**

- *b, f*
- *Je voudrais avoir ma propre entreprise. c, j*
- *J'espère ...*

a I want to ...
b I would like to ...
c I hope to ...
d My objective is to ...
e My aim is to ...

f

g

h

i

j

Écrire 4 **Copy and complete the parallel translations.**

Example: 1 Je voudrais organiser une fête. I would like to organise a party.

1 ____ ____ organiser une fête.	I would like ____ ____ ____ ____.
2 Je veux ____ ____ d'argent.	____ ____ to earn lots of money.
3 ____ ____ est d'aller à l'université.	My objective is ____ ____ ____ university.
4 ____ ____ devenir plus patient.	I would like ____ ____ ____ ____.
5 Je veux ____ ____ ____ ____.	____ ____ to travel abroad.
6 ____ ____ ____ ____ ____ dans un autre pays.	My aim is to work ____ ____ ____.

Using *sans* and *pour* followed by an infinitive (Unit 1, page 185)

Écrire 5

Read the grammar box on page 185. Write out the phrases below in the correct order to form sentences using *sans* or *pour* + an infinitive. Then translate them into English.

1 pour | en Espagne | Je voudrais habiter | apprendre l'espagnol
2 pour | Je voudrais faire | développer des compétences pratiques | un apprentissage
3 des enfants | sans | On peut avoir | se marier
4 à l'université | Je veux aller | devenir professeur | pour
5 aller à l'université | beaucoup d'argent | On peut gagner | sans

The perfect tense (Unit 2, page 186)

Lire 6

Translate these sentences into English. Then look at the underlined perfect-tense verbs. Is the auxiliary verb *avoir* or *être* in each case?

1 Nous sommes allés à l'université à l'âge de 18 ans.
2 J'ai eu la chance de rencontrer beaucoup de personnes intéressantes et j'ai discuté de foot avec Sadio Mané.
3 On a travaillé dans une agence et on a vendu de belles maisons à Londres.
4 Elles sont parties à 9 heures et elles sont revenues à midi.

Lire 7

Copy and complete the sentences by selecting the correct auxiliary verb.

1 Ils **ont / sont** partagé des vidéos au sujet de la politique.
2 Nous **avons / sommes** venues passer une semaine à la ferme.
3 Il **a / est** expliqué l'actualité aux jeunes.
4 Ils **ont / sont** partis à 20 heures.
5 **J'ai / Je suis** allée dans ma chambre.
6 Nous **avons / sommes** voyagé à l'étranger.
7 Est-ce que tu **as / es** trouvé l'amour?
8 Vous **avez / êtes** utilisé quelle plateforme?

Remember, the perfect tense is made up of two parts:

1 the auxiliary verb (part of ***avoir*** or ***être***)
2 the past participle.

Here is a list of some key verbs that form the perfect tense with *être*, and their past participles.

aller (to go) → *allé*
arriver (to arrive) → *arrivé*
partir (to leave) → *parti*
rester (to stay) → *resté*
venir (to come) → *venu*

Remember that for verbs which take *être*, the past participle must agree with the subject:
*Sophie est parti**e** en vacances.*
*Nous sommes allé**s** en France.*
*Elles sont arrivé**es** à 10 heures.*

Parler 8

Imagine that you worked as an influencer for your last job. In pairs, take turns to ask and answer the questions below.

- *Comment tu t'appelles?*
- *Je m'appelle ...*
- *Tu as utilisé quelles plateformes?*
- *J'ai utilisé ...*
- *De quoi as-tu parlé?*
- *J'ai parlé de ...*
- *Qui as-tu rencontré?*
- *J'ai rencontré ...*

Grammaire 2

Using infinitives as nouns (Unit 3, page 188)

Parler 1 **Read the grammar box on page 188. In pairs, take turns to make up sentences containing a phrase from each box. Take care with your pronunciation. Your partner then translates your sentence into English.**

Aider les autres,	c'est ma passion.
Protéger l'environnement,	c'est important pour moi.
Gagner un bon salaire,	ce n'est pas important pour moi.
Travailler avec des animaux,	ça ne m'intéresse pas.
Voyager et travailler à l'étranger,	

Masculine, feminine and plural nouns (Unit 3, page 189)

Lire 2 **Read the sentences. Select the correct option to complete each sentence.**

1. Mon père est **chanteur / chanteuse**.
2. Ma mère est **acteur / actrice**.
3. Mon frère est **policier / policière**.
4. Ma sœur veut être **président / présidente**.
5. Ma tante est **chef / cheffe**.

Some nouns have different masculine and feminine forms. The key patterns you need to know are:

-eur	→	-euse	*influenceur/influenceuse* (influencer)
-teur	→	-trice	*directeur/directrice* (director/boss)
-en	→	-enne	*mécanicien/mécanicienne* (mechanic)
-	→	-e	*président/présidente* (president)

There are some other patterns too, e.g.
chef/cheffe (chef)
policier/policière (police officer)

Some nouns do not change, e.g. *médecin* (doctor), *artiste* (artist).

People who identify as non-binary may prefer to use the following structures:
Je suis infirmier•ière. *Je suis influenceur•euse.*

Most nouns add -s to form the plural. However, there are some exceptions:

- Masculine nouns ending in *au*, *eau* or *eu* add -*x*:
  - *un bâteau, des bâteaux* — one boat, (some) boats
  - *un jeu, des jeux* — one game, (some) games
- Nouns that already end in -*x* or -*s* do not change:
  - *un choix, des choix* — one choice, (some) choices
  - *un fils, des fils* — one son, (some) sons

Écrire 3 **Fill in the gaps with the correct form of the noun in bold.**

Example: 1 *joueur*

1. Sarah est **joueuse** de foot professionnelle. Son petit frère voudrait aussi être ___ de foot.
2. Mon père était **mécanicien** et ma cousine veut aussi travailler comme ___.
3. Joseph est **médecin**. Sa femme est aussi ___.
4. Ma cousine Zahra est très connue comme **influenceuse**. Mon frère veut aussi être ___.
5. Mon meilleur ami voudrait être **président** un jour. À l'avenir, ma sœur espère aussi être ___.
6. Ma tante est **professeure** mais mon cousin ne veut pas être ___!

Écrire 4 **Write the plural forms of each of the nouns below.**

Example: 1 *des châteaux*

1. un château (*a castle*)
2. un ami (*a friend*)
3. un virus (*a virus*)
4. un feu (*a fire*)
5. un joueur (*a player*)
6. un prix (*a price*)
7. un bureau (*an office*)
8. un film (*a film*)
9. un pays (*a country*)
10. un réseau (*a network*)

Verbs followed by *à* or *de* + an infinitive (Unit 4, page 191)

Écrire 5

Copy and complete each sentence with *à* or *de/d'*. Then translate the sentences into English. Take care with the tenses!

Example: 1 *J'ai réussi à trouver un travail. I (have) succeeded in finding a job.*

1 J'ai réussi ___ trouver un travail.
2 Elle a décidé ___ quitter son emploi.
3 Lise a commencé ___ jouer au foot le samedi.
4 Mon grand-père va continuer ___ faire du babysitting pour ma sœur.
5 Je vais essayer ___ aller à l'université.
6 Je rêve ___ devenir mécanicien•ne.
7 Elle n'arrive pas ___ trouver un travail à l'étranger.
8 J'ai fini ___ travailler dans le magasin du village.

Some verbs are followed by **à** or **de** + the infinitive, e.g.

arriver à	to manage to	*décider de*	to decide to
commencer à	to start to	*essayer de*	to try to
réussir à	to succeed in	*finir de*	to finish
arrêter de	to stop	*rêver de*	to dream of
continuer de	to continue to		

*Je n'arrive pas **à** faire mes devoirs.* I can't manage to do my homework.
*J'arrête **de** travailler le samedi!* I'm stopping working on Saturdays!

C'est parti!

Écouter 6

Listen and write down the missing words.

J'ai décidé **1** devenir **2**.

Un jour, **3** avoir mon propre restaurant! Je voudrais aussi **4** beaucoup d'argent.

Je pense qu'on peut avoir un bon travail **5** aller à l'université.

L'année prochaine, je **6** faire un apprentissage.

7, c'est très important pour moi.

L'été dernier, je **8** allé en Angleterre et j'ai **9** dans un hôtel.

There are lots of infinitives in this exercise. These often end in *-er*. However, the final sentence is in the perfect tense and, for gap 9, you need a past participle.

Lire 7

Read the text. Look for and note down examples of each of the grammar points below.

J'ai décidé d'aller à l'université pour continuer mes études.

Mon but est de devenir médecin.

Aider les autres, c'est ma passion!

À l'avenir, je vais me marier mais je ne vais pas avoir d'enfants.

Je voudrais aussi voyager un peu pour apprendre des langues.

L'année dernière, je suis allée en Suisse et j'ai visité des villages traditionnels.

- The near future tense
- Different structures followed by an infinitive to express hopes/plans
- *Pour* + an infinitive
- Using an infinitive as a noun
- The perfect tense with *avoir*
- The perfect tense with *être*
- A verb followed by *à* or *de* + the infinitive

Parler 8

In pairs, take turns to read out the text from exercise 7. Give feedback on each other's pronunciation.

Module 8

Contrôle de lecture et d'écoute

Reading

Lire 1 ***Job adverts.*** **You see some job adverts. Which advert matches each job? Write the correct letter (A–E) for each job.**

A	Notre collège est moderne et nos élèves sont excellents!
B	Les animaux sont votre passion, alors ce travail est pour vous!
C	Vous aimez lire? Venez travailler dans notre bibliothèque.
D	Notre club a besoin de vous pour aider notre président.
E	Notre centre médical a besoin de vous!

1 vet **2** teacher **3** doctor

Lire 2 ***A gap year.*** **Read Rachid's blog about his plans. Answer the questions in English.**

#RachidMaroc

J'ai décidé de prendre une année sabbatique* après le lycée et avant l'université.

Je voudrais voyager et aider des gens dans des pays qui ont besoin de nous.

Plus tard, mon but est de chercher un travail pour un journal en ligne. Dans ma famille, il n'y a personne qui travaille comme journaliste. Cependant, le père de mon meilleur ami est directeur d'un journal et je lui ai parlé. Je pense que son métier est vraiment intéressant.

l'année** (f) **sabbatique *gap year*

1 When has Rachid decided to take a gap year? — Read the time phrases carefully.
2 What would he like to do while on his gap year?
3 What type of career would he like? — Beware of the false friend *journal*!
4 Who has influenced his ambition? — Read the last two sentences carefully. Read until the end.

Lire 3 ***Translation.*** **Translate these sentences into English.**

These words are different ways to express quantities.

What is this tense?

Look back at your notes to find these verbs.

1 Il y a trop de choix.
2 Je m'intéresse à beaucoup de choses.
3 Je suis allé à un événement qui s'appelle 'Mon avenir'.
4 Je voudrais travailler dans le monde des affaires.
5 Je rêve d'être dans la politique.

Listening

Écouter 4

Voice messages. **Your French friend has sent you some voice messages. What is each message about? Write the correct letter (A–F) for each message. (1–4)**

A	gap year plan
B	past work experience
C	social media
D	ambitions
E	qualities
F	interests

Écouter 5

Celebrities. **You hear Fathia's interview about celebrities. Choose the correct answer and write A, B or C for each question.**

1 Fathia ...
- **A** would like to be an influencer.
- **B** wouldn't like to be an influencer.
- **C** doesn't know if she would like to be an influencer.

2 According to Fathia, the worst aspect of being an influencer is that ...
- **A** you can't go out.
- **B** everybody knows you.
- **C** you can have problems on social media.

3 Fathia thinks that the best thing about being an influencer is ...
- **A** the money.
- **B** the free clothes.
- **C** going to concerts.

4 Fathia's friend Salima ...
- **A** is already an influencer.
- **B** was an influencer before.
- **C** will soon start to be an influencer.

Écouter 6

Careers advice. **Alex is talking to a career advisor about his future plans. What does he say? Listen to the recording and make notes in English under the following headings. You do not need to write in full sentences.**

1 The industry Alex would like to work in
2 What isn't important for him
3 What he plans to do after sixth form

Écouter 7

Dictation. **You will now hear <u>four</u> short sentences. Listen carefully and, using your knowledge of French sounds, write in French exactly what you hear for each sentence.**

Module 8 Contrôle oral

Role-play

Parler 1

Look at the role-play card and prepare what you are going to say.

You could talk about a particular job or a job in an area such as business or politics. Start with *Je voudrais être …* or *Je voudrais travailler dans …*

- You are talking to your French friend.
- Your teacher will play the part of your friend and will speak first.
- You should address your friend as *tu*.
- When you see this – **?** – you will have to ask a question.

In order to score full marks, you must include a verb in your response to each task.

1. Describe the type of job you would like. (Give **one** detail.)
2. Say **one** thing you want to do after secondary school.
? 3. Ask your friend a question about university.
4. Give **one** opinion of working abroad.
5. Say what languages you speak.

You could say that you want to work or continue to study …

You could ask if they want to go to university, or what they think of it.

Parler 2

Practise what you have prepared. Then, using your notes, listen and respond to the teacher.

Écouter 3

Now listen to Logan doing the role-play task. In English, note down (a) how he answers the questions for tasks 1, 2, 4 and 5, and (b) what question he asks for task 3.

Reading aloud

Parler 4

Look at this task. With a partner, take turns to read out the text below, paying attention to the underlined letters.

Read aloud the following text **in French**.

Je n'aime pas le collège.
Je ne veux pas continuer à étudier.
J'espère trouver un travail avec un bon salaire.
Il est important d'avoir un boulot intéressant.
Je voudrais un emploi dans le monde des affaires.

Take extra care with how you pronounce the underlined sounds:
- ***ail***
- sounds made of two vowels: ***eu***, ***ai***, ***ou***, ***oi***
- silent final consonants.

Take extra care with how you pronounce cognates.

Remember your liaisons!

Écouter 5

Listen and check your pronunciation.

Parler 6

Listen to the teacher asking four questions that relate to the topic of Education and work. Translate each question into English and prepare your own answers in French. Then listen again and respond to the teacher.

You need to develop your answers as much as possible, using a variety of nouns, verbs and opinions.

Photo card task

Écouter **7** **Look at the exam card below and read the first part of the task. Then listen to Logan describing the two photos.**

1 What does Logan say about the people in the first photo? Do you agree?
2 What does he say about what each person is doing in the first photo?
3 What does he say about the location of the first photo? Do you agree?
4 What does he say about the second photo?

Photo 1

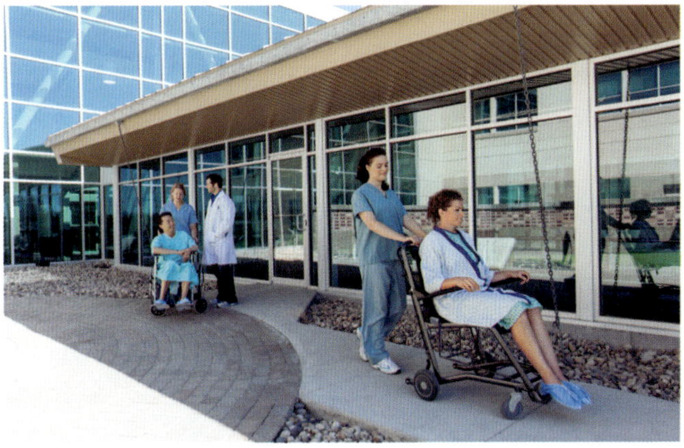

Photo 2

You will be asked to talk about the content of these photos. You must say at least one thing about each photo.

After you have spoken about the content of the photos, you will be asked questions related to any of the topics within the theme of **People and lifestyle**.

Your responses should be as **full and detailed** as possible.

Parler **8** **Prepare your own description of the two photos. You could mention, for example, the people, the location and what they are doing. Then, with a partner, take turns to describe the photos.**

Sur la première photo, il y a ...

If you are not sure, you can say *peut-être* ('maybe') or *je pense que* ... ('I think that ...').

Écouter **9** **Read the second part of the task. Listen to Logan answering the question: *Qu'est-ce que tu voudrais faire plus tard?* Write the letters (a–c) in the order that he hopes to do these things.**

a earn money **b** travel **c** do an apprenticeship

Écouter **10** **Now listen to Logan answering the question: *Est-ce que tu as déjà travaillé?* Make notes in English under the following headings:**

When? How long for? Where? Opinion?

Parler **11** **Prepare your own answers to the module 8 questions on page 227. Your responses should be as full and detailed as possible. Then practise with a partner.**

Remember to use a range of structures in order to improve your answers, e.g. 'I want', 'I hope', 'my aim is to'.

Contrôle écrit

Translation

Lire 1

Match the French phrases (1–8) to the English ones (a–h).

1 je voudrais
2 je veux
3 j'espère
4 mon but est de
5 j'ai décidé de
6 je rêve de
7 je vais chercher
8 avoir un travail est

a my aim is to
b I am going to look for
c I dream of
d I would like
e I want
f having a job is
g I hope
h I have decided to

Écrire 2

Translate the following sentences into French.

Remember to use some of the structures you covered in exercise 1.

Can you think of three different words to say 'job'?

1 I want to live abroad.
2 I hope to work this summer.
3 I would like a job with a good salary.
4 I have decided to look for a job in politics.
5 I am going to have a job in my dad's company.

You will need the infinitive form of the verbs.

Remember to translate this as 'the company of my dad'.

90-word writing task

Écrire 3

Look at this writing exam task and then, <u>for each bullet point</u>:

1 think about what vocabulary you have learned that you could use in your answer. For example:
- **nouns** and **verbs** to talk about your future plans and volunteering
- **verbs of opinion** and **adjectives** to explain your point of view and describe your personality
- language for **narrating a story** about a recent volunteering experience
- how to explain what you ideally **are going to do** in the future.

2 write down <u>three or four</u> ideas for what you could write about.
3 write down which tense(s) you will need to use in your answer.

You are writing a post about future plans for a French careers forum.

Write approximately **90** words in **French**.

You must write something about each bullet point.

Describe:
- the type of person you are
- a past volunteering experience
- your plans for the future.

Look at the vocabulary you have noted to give you ideas for what to write.

Lire 4 **Read Madison's answer to the exam task. Answer questions 1–5 in the coloured shapes.**

1 This is an example of **complex language**. What does it mean? Find <u>three</u> more examples from the text.

> Salut!
>
> J'aime aider les gens et je pense que je suis travailleuse. Avant, j'étais plus timide mais maintenant je travaille bien en équipe.
>
> Cette année, j'ai fait beaucoup de choses comme bénévole. D'abord, j'ai aidé dans mon église, ensuite j'ai fait un projet vert avec mon collège, et puis j'ai lu des livres à des enfants à la bibliothèque locale. J'ai trouvé toutes ces expériences très utiles.
>
> Plus tard, je veux aller au lycée. Après, j'espère aller à l'université. Puis je voudrais entrer dans le monde du travail. Mon objectif est de travailler dans les médias.
>
> **Madison**

2 This word shows a **variety of vocabulary**. What does it mean? Find <u>two</u> more examples.

3 Which **tense** is this? What other examples of this tense can you find? Does Madison use any other tenses?

4 How could she **avoid repetition** by using another word?

5 How could you form an **extended sentence** here? What other extended sentences does Madison include?

Lire 5 **Read Madison's answer again. Make notes in English about the following points:**

1 how Madison describes herself and how she has changed
2 <u>two</u> things she has done as a volunteer
3 what she thought of her experience as a volunteer
4 <u>two</u> things she wants to do in the future.

Écrire 6 **Prepare your own answer to the 90-word writing task in exercise 3.**

- Think about how you can develop your answer for each bullet point.
- Look back at your notes from exercises 3 and 4.
- Look at the 'Challenge checklist' and consider how you can show off your French!
- Write a **brief** plan and organise your answer into paragraphs.
- Write your answer and then carefully check the accuracy of what you have written.

Challenge checklist

	✓ Past, present and future time frames ✓ Connectives, time phrases, sequencers ✓ Some extended sentences ✓ Different opinion phrases
	✓ A wide range of tenses ✓ Different persons of the verb ✓ A variety of adjectives ✓ A wide range of interesting vocabulary
	✓ Phrases with more than one tense ✓ Range of expressions (e.g. *mon but / objectif est de …, j'ai l'intention de …, j'espère …*) ✓ Complex language (e.g. *sans / pour* + infinitive, *si* clauses) ✓ A variety of connectives

Module 8 Vocabulaire

Key:
bold = this word will appear in higher exams only
* = this word is not on the vocabulary list, but you may use it in your own sentences

Mon été de rêve (pages 182–183)

Est-ce que tu voudrais …	*Would you like to …*
travailler dans une ferme / une boulangerie / une usine?	*work in a farm / a bakery / a factory?*
faire du *babysitting?	*do babysitting?*
*promener des chiens?	*walk dogs?*
être *animateur ou *animatrice de vacances?	*be a holiday camp leader?*
aider dans un centre sportif?	*help in a sports centre?*
Je voudrais / Je ne voudrais pas (*promener des chiens) parce que / car …	*I would like / I would not like to (walk dogs), because / as …*
c'est …	*it is …*
intéressant / génial.	*interesting / great.*
dur / ennuyeux.	*hard / boring.*
j'aime / j'adore / je n'aime pas …	*I like / I love / I don't like …*
les animaux / les enfants.	*animals / children.*
Je vais visiter l'*Italie.	*I am going to visit / will visit Italy.*
Ce week-end, je visite Paris.	*This weekend, I am visiting Paris.*

Mes passions et mon avenir (pages 184–185)

Qu'est-ce que tu veux faire à l'avenir?	*What do you want to do in the future?*
Pour commencer, …	*To start with, …*
Ensuite, …	*Next, …*
Puis …	*Then …*
Après, …	*After, …*
Plus tard, …	*Later, …*
Un jour, …	*One day, …*
je veux …	*I want to …*
je voudrais …	*I would like to …*
j'espère …	*I hope to …*
mon **objectif** est de/d' …	*my objective is to …*
mon but est de/d' …	*my aim is to …*
réussir à mes examens.	*pass my exams.*
voyager à l'étranger et travailler.	*travel abroad and work.*
être bénévole.	*volunteer.*
aller à l'université.	*go to university.*
continuer mes études.	*continue my studies.*
choisir une carrière.	*choose a career.*
entrer dans le monde du travail.	*enter the world of work.*
faire un apprentissage.	*do an apprenticeship.*
développer des compétences pratiques.	*develop practical skills.*
gagner beaucoup d'argent.	*earn lots of money.*
avoir ma propre entreprise.	*have my own business.*
vivre avec mon copain / ma copine.	*live with my (boy)friend / (girl)friend.*
me marier.	*get married.*
avoir des enfants.	*have children.*
sans aller à l'université	*without going to university*
sans faire de longues études	*without doing long studies*
pour gagner de l'argent	*in order to earn money*

Célébrités à l'écran (pages 186–187)

Il/Elle est allé(e) …	*He/She went …*
Il/Elle est parti(e).	*He/She left.*
Il/Elle est rentré(e) (chez lui/elle).	*He/She went home.*
Il/Elle est resté(e).	*He/She stayed.*
Il/Elle est revenu(e).	*He/She came back.*
Il/Elle est tombé(e).	*He/She fell.*
Il/Elle est venu(e).	*He/She came.*
Quels sont les avantages / inconvénients d'être influenceur?	*What are the pros / cons of being an influencer?*
L'avantage, c'est qu'on peut …	*The advantage is that you can …*
L'important, c'est de/d'…	*The important thing is to …*
devenir célèbre / riche (rapidement).	*become famous / rich (quickly).*
être *créatif/créative / bien payé(e).	*be creative / well paid.*
gagner beaucoup d'argent.	*earn a lot of money.*
*interviewer des célébrités.	*interview celebrities.*
parler de ses/mes passions.	*talk about your/my passions.*
L'inconvénient / **Le pire**, c'est que/qu'…	*The downside / The worst thing is that …*
on peut recevoir des messages / des **commentaires** méchants.	*you can receive nasty messages / comments.*
on peut être **victime** de *cyberintimidation.	*you can be a victim of cyber-bullying.*
il faut poster du *contenu (régulièrement).	*you have to post content regularly.*
il faut être toujours en ligne.	*you have to always be online.*
ça peut être dangereux / difficile pour la santé *mentale.	*it can be dangerous / difficult for your mental health.*

Quelles sont tes compétences? (pages 188–189)

Quelles sont tes **passions**?	*What are your passions?*
Ma **passion**, c'est …	*My passion is …*
le sport / le théâtre.	*sport / drama.*
la lecture / l'environnement.	*reading / the environment.*
les films / les ordinateurs.	*films / computers.*
voyager.	*travelling.*
Aider les autres, c'est ma **passion**.	*Helping others is my passion.*
Comment es-tu?	*What are you like?*
Je suis …	*I am …*
amusant(e).	*fun.*
calme.	*calm.*
*créatif/créative.	*creative.*
gentil/gentille.	*kind.*
indépendant(e).	*independent.*
patient(e).	*patient.*
responsable.	*responsible.*
sérieux/sérieuse.	*serious.*
sportif/sportive.	*sporty.*
travailleur/travailleuse.	*hard-working.*
Avec qui voudrais-tu travailler?	*Who would you like to work with?*
Je voudrais travailler …	*I would like to work …*
seul(e) / avec des gens.	*alone / with people.*
avec des animaux / des enfants.	*with animals / children.*
Qu'est-ce que tu trouves important dans un emploi?	*What do you find important in a job?*
Être actif/active, c'est (très) important pour moi.	*Being active is (very) important for me.*
Avoir un travail intéressant, c'est essentiel.	*Having an interesting job is essential.*
Pour moi, un bon salaire est essentiel.	*For me, a good salary is essential.*
Quelles sont tes compétences?	*What are your skills?*
Mon *point fort, c'est la communication.	*My strong point is communication.*
Je suis très organisé(e).	*I am very organised.*
J'ai une **attitude** positive.	*I have a positive attitude.*
Je m'entends bien avec tout le monde.	*I get on well with everyone.*
En plus, j'aime travailler en équipe.	*Also, I like working in a team.*
Je voudrais être …	*I would like to be …*
Il/Elle travaille comme …	*He/She works as …*
acteur/actrice.	*an actor.*
chanteur/chanteuse.	*a singer.*
chef/cheffe (de cuisine).	*a chef.*
directeur/directrice.	*a manager.*
influenceur/influenceuse.	*an influencer.*
*ingénieur/*ingénieure.	*an engineer.*
joueur/joueuse de foot.	*a football player.*
*mécanicien/*mécanicienne.	*a mechanic.*
médecin.	*a doctor.*

Bien payé, mais difficile! (pages 190–191)

Être … Quels sont les *points positifs/négatifs?	*What are the positive/negative points of being a/an …?*
*architecte	*architect*
journaliste	*journalist*
policier/policière	*police officer*
*homme/femme politique	*politician*
scientifique	*scientist*
Un *point positif/négatif, c'est que/qu' …	*A positive/negative point is that …*
le travail est bien payé / intéressant.	*the work is well paid / interesting.*
les gens sont sympa.	*the people are nice.*
on peut prendre ses propres décisions.	*you can make your own decisions.*
ça peut être dangereux.	*it can be dangerous.*
les heures sont longues.	*the hours are long.*
c'est embêtant.	*it's annoying.*
la **formation** dure longtemps.	*the training lasts a long time.*
on ne gagne pas beaucoup d'argent.	*you don't earn much money.*
Après le collège, …	*After school, …*
j'ai travaillé comme …	*I worked as …*
je suis devenu(e) …	*I became …*
Je n'étais pas très content(e) et ce n'était pas bien payé.	*I was not very happy and it was not well paid.*
Il y a cinq ans, j'ai décidé d'aller à l'université.	*Five years ago, I decided to go to university.*
J'ai commencé à étudier …	*I started to study …*
J'ai réussi à créer ma propre entreprise.	*I succeeded in creating my own business.*
À l'avenir, je vais essayer de faire quelque chose de différent.	*In the future, I am going to try to do something different.*
Je vais continuer de travailler dur.	*I am going to continue to work hard.*
Je rêve d'être président(e) un jour.	*I dream of being president one day.*

Révisions de grammaire 1

Prepositions (Pages 163, 164, 171, 191 and 195)

The prepositions *à* and *de* have several uses:
- *à* often means 'to' and *de* often means 'from'
- *de* can be used to indicate possession
- *à* can be used with places to mean 'in' or 'to'
- *de* features in location prepositions such as *en face de* (opposite), *près de* (near to) and *à côté de* (next to).

Note that *à* changes to *au, à la, à l'* or *aux* depending on the noun that follows.
Similarly, *de* changes to *du, de la, de l'* or *des* depending on the noun that follows.

Écrire 1 **Copy and complete the sentences with *à, au, à la, à l'* or *aux*.**

Example: 1 *Elle aime aller au musée.*

1 Elle aime aller ___ musée.
2 Tu voyageais ___ New York.
3 Nous voulons aller ___ université.
4 Je vais commencer ___ jouer au basket.
5 Il faut aller ___ magasins.
6 Tu veux aller ___ fête de ma sœur?

Écrire 2 **Copy and complete the sentences with *de, du, de la, de l'* or *des*.**

Example: 1 *Je suis en face du cinéma.*

1 Je suis en face ___ cinéma.
2 C'est la maison ___ mes grands-parents.
3 La poste est à côté ___ banque.
4 Il vient ___ États-Unis.
5 La protection ___ environnement est ma passion.
6 Tu as vu le portable ___ mon ami Louis?

Lire 3 **Translate the sentences into English.**

1 Mon frère est allé à Paris le week-end dernier.
2 C'est le livre de ma copine Jade.
3 Je vais continuer de travailler dur au collège.
4 Elle vient de Madrid mais elle habite à Barcelone.
5 Le café est en face du grand château.
6 Mon prof a commencé à chanter assez souvent!

When some verbs are followed by an infinitive, the preposition *à* or *de* is required. These include:

aider à	to help to
apprendre à	to learn to
arrêter de	to stop
choisir de	to choose
oublier de	to forget to

For more verbs followed by the infinitive, see pages 190, 191 and 195.

Écrire 4 **Put the words into the correct order to translate the English sentences.**

1 Are you going to learn to sing next year?
Tu vas | à | apprendre | l'année prochaine | chanter

2 My uncle continues to go to the cinema every weekend.
continue | au cinéma | tous les week-ends | d'aller | Mon oncle

3 Have you seen my friend Alessandro's new car?
la nouvelle voiture | mon ami | de | Alessandro | Tu as vu

4 I forgot to do my English homework last night.
hier soir | mes devoirs | faire | J'ai oublié | de | d'anglais

5 The cinema used to be next to the shopping centre.
centre commercial | à côté du | Le cinéma | était

6 She comes from Leeds but she lives in Halifax.
de | mais | Leeds | Halifax | Elle vient | elle habite | à

Demonstrative adjectives (Pages 159 and 170)

Écrire 5 **Copy the French nouns, adding *ce, cet, cette* or *ces*.**

1 ____ livre (m)
2 ____ table (f)
3 ____ maisons (pl)
4 ____ baguette (f)
5 ____ hôtel (m)
6 ____ chien (m)
7 ____ table (f)
8 ____ appartement (m)

Remember that before a masculine noun that starts with a vowel or a silent *h*, you use *cet*.

Écrire 6 **Copy out the parallel translations, completing the missing words.**

Example: 1 *This bed is too small for me. Ce lit est trop petit pour moi.*

1	This bed is too ____ for ____.	____ lit est trop petit pour moi.
2	I saw this house ____ ____.	J'ai vu ____ maison hier soir.
3	____ don't ____ this idea.	Je n'aime pas ____ idée.
4	Have ____ ____ these chairs?	Tu as vu ____ chaises?
5	She doesn't ____ these ____.	Elle n'aime pas ____ voitures.
6	____ ____ these blue trainers.	Je préfère ____ baskets bleues.

Pronouns (Pages 34, 40, 44, 46, 67 and 72)

Lire 7 **Read the sentences. Note down if the underlined pronoun is subject, reflexive, direct object or indirect object. Then translate the sentences into English using the sentence starters in the box.**

Example: 1 *Subject – I am going to start buying recycled paper.*

1 <u>Je</u> vais commencer à acheter du papier recyclé.
2 Je <u>l'</u>adore depuis trois ans.
3 Elle <u>me</u> donne des fruits et légumes.
4 Il <u>se</u> demande quand sa sœur arrive.
5 Je vais <u>te</u> parler après les vacances.
6 Nous <u>l'</u>achetons tous les week-ends.
7 <u>Ils</u> n'ont jamais vendu de vêtements sur Vinted.
8 Je <u>me</u> lave avant le petit-déjeuner.

She gives me …
We buy it …
They have never …
I am going to start …
He wonders …
I have loved him …
I get washed …
I am going to talk …

Écrire 8 **Copy and complete the sentences with the correct subject or reflexive pronoun.**

1 ____ suis allée au centre commercial hier. (*subject*)
2 Il ____ entend bien avec tous les profs. (*reflexive*)
3 ____ avons une nouvelle voiture noire. (*subject*)
4 Normalement je ____ lève à huit heures. (*reflexive*)

Écrire 9 **Copy and complete the sentences with the correct direct or indirect object pronoun given in brackets.**

1 Je ____ ai donné un ordinateur. (*indirect – 'to her'*)
2 Je ____ aime depuis deux ans. (*direct – 'him'*)
3 Il ne ____ parle pas souvent. (*indirect – 'to me'*)
4 Nous allons ____ chercher. (*direct – 'you'*)

Modules 1–8

Révisions de grammaire 2

Negatives (Pages 69, 92, 114, 163 and 171)

Lire 1 **Read the French sentences. Write the letter of the correct English translation for each sentence.**

1 Elle n'était pas timide.
2 Je ne suis jamais allé à Nice.
3 Tu n'as vu personne au collège?
4 Il ne va rien acheter au marché.

a I have never been to Nice.
b You didn't see anyone at school?
c She didn't use to be shy.
d He is not going to buy anything at the market.

Écrire 2 **Re-write the sentences in the negative, using the expression given in brackets.**

1 J'aime les légumes verts. (*ne ... pas*)
2 Tu es allé au stade de rugby? (*ne ... jamais*)
3 Il jouait de la guitare tous les jours. (*ne ... pas*)
4 J'ai acheté sur Vinted. (*ne ... rien*)
5 Elle est allée au centre commercial. (*ne ... jamais*)
6 Nous aimons regarder la télévision ensemble. (*ne ... pas*)

Remember, *ne* shortens to *n'* before a vowel or silent *h*.

Écrire 3 **Put the words into the correct order to make sentences. Then translate them into English.**

1 regarder / aime / de films romantiques / n' / je / pas
2 jamais / au centre commercial / elle / n' / allée / est
3 n' / as / au musée / rien / hier? / tu / acheté
4 à la réception / ne / vois / personne / je / de l'hôtel

Asking questions (Pages 12, 18–19, 111 and 169)

There are several ways of forming questions.

a Intonation (making your voice go up at the end)	*Tu es heureux?*
b Using *est-ce que* for a yes/no question	***Est-ce que*** *tu regardes des vidéos sur YouTube?*
c Using *est-ce que* after a question word	*Quand* ***est-ce que*** *tu joues au basket?*
d Using *quel, quelle, quels, quelles* (*what/which*)	***Quelle*** *est ta matière préférée?*
e Inverting the subject and the verb	*Que* ***fais-tu*** *pour protéger l'environnement?*
f Using *qu'est-ce que*	***Qu'est-ce que*** *tu as fait le week-end dernier?*

The most useful question words are:

combien → how much / how many
comment → how
où → where
pourquoi → why
quand → when
quel(le)(s) → which/what
qui → who
que/quoi → what

Lire 4 **Read the questions. Write the letter (a–f) of the correct question style from the grammar box for each question. Then translate the sentences into English.**

Example: 1 *c – Why is he speaking to me?*

1 Pourquoi est-ce qu'il me parle?
2 Où vas-tu avec ta famille ce week-end?
3 Quelle est la date de ton anniversaire?
4 Qu'est-ce que tu as mangé au restaurant?
5 Tu veux aller au cinéma demain?
6 Est-ce que ton frère joue au basket?
7 Comment peut-on protéger l'environnement?
8 Qu'est-ce que tu as fait la semaine dernière?

Écrire **5** **Write a question to go with each answer, using a sentence starter from the box.**

1 Le week-end prochain, je vais aller au cinéma avec mes amis.
2 Le voyage en train était très long.
3 J'habitais à Reims quand j'étais plus jeune.
4 Parce que c'est mon équipe préférée.
5 Non, je ne veux pas aller dans les Pyrénées.
6 J'aime aller au bord de la mer.

Pourquoi est-ce que …?
Tu vas aller où?
Tu veux aller …?
Comment était …?
Tu habitais où …?
Qu'est-ce que tu aimes faire …?

Infinitive expressions (Pages 62, 87, 107, 184 and 185)

Écrire **6** **Copy and complete the sentences with an infinitive from the box.**

1 Un jour, je veux ___ au Canada.
2 Mon ambition est d'___ à l'université.
3 Elle peut ___ la télé avec ses parents.
4 Je ne peux pas ___ sans rêver d'argent!
5 Mon but est de ___ tous les matchs.
6 J'espère ___ à mes examens cette année.

aller réussir habiter regarder dormir gagner

Écrire **7** **Put the words into the correct order to translate the English sentences.**

1 I would like to organise a party. — voudrais / je / une fête / organiser
2 She knows how to play the piano. — sait / elle / du piano / jouer
3 My ambition is to open a shop. — un magasin / mon ambition / d'ouvrir / est
4 You must drink lots of water. — beaucoup / boire / il faut / d'eau
5 I hope to study maths at university. — à l'université / les maths / j'espère / étudier
6 You can choose without seeing the cakes. — sans / choisir / voir / tu peux / les gâteaux

Past participles (Pages 16, 85, 141, 186 and 193)

Lire **8** **Match up the correct past participle to each infinitive. Write them out in a list.**

1 choisir (*to choose*)
2 rester (*to stay*)
3 mettre (*to put*)
4 partir (*to leave*)
5 écouter (*to listen*)
6 faire (*to do/make*)
7 arriver (*to arrive*)
8 attendre (*to wait*)

fait écouté mis attendu
parti arrivé resté choisi

Écrire **9** **Copy and complete the sentences with the past participle of the verb in brackets.**

1 Je suis ___ au lycée hier. (*aller*)
2 Elle a ___ la porte deux fois. (*ouvrir*)
3 Vous avez ___ de recycler? (*finir*)
4 Nous n'avons pas ___ de gâteau. (*faire*)
5 Ils ont ___ les chaises sur les tables. (*mettre*)
6 Elles n'ont pas ___ de billets à la gare. (*acheter*)
7 Tu as ___ le même article que moi? (*lire*)
8 J'ai ___ à jouer au basket il y a trois ans. (*commencer*)

Révisions de grammaire 3

Present tense verbs (Pages 8, 10, 11, 20–21, 141 and 144)

Écrire 1 **Copy and complete the sentences with the correct choice of present tense verb in brackets. Then translate the sentences into English.**

Example: 1 *habitent – They live in Spain.*

1 Ils **regardent / habitent** en Espagne.
2 Elle **va / prend** au cinéma demain.
3 Je ne **vends / écoute** plus mes vêtements.
4 Nous **portons / attendons** le bus.
5 Il **écrit / mange** un deuxième livre.
6 Je **joue / bois** au basket tous les jours.

Écrire 2 **Copy and complete the sentences with the present tense form of the verb in brackets.**

1 Elle ___ du lait. (*boire*)
2 Ils n'___ pas faim? (*avoir*)
3 On ___ à la plage. (*aller*)
4 Je ne ___ jamais le train. (*prendre*)
5 Nous ___ nos devoirs. (*faire*)
6 Elles ___ de Paris. (*venir*)
7 Je ___ en vacances. (*partir*)
8 Vous ___ près de l'hôtel. (*être*)

Past tense verbs (Pages 16, 22, 89, 113, 114, 119, 141, 143 and 148)

Lire 3 **Read the sentences and match up the correct halves. Then translate them into English.**

1 Ce matin, il y avait du soleil et ...
2 Je mangeais à la cantine quand ...
3 Le week-end dernier, il faisait froid et ...
4 Ma mère regardait la télé quand ...

a mon copain a pris mes frites!
b elle a fait du snowboard à la montagne.
c je suis arrivé à la maison.
d j'ai joué au volley sur la plage.

Écrire 4 **Copy and complete the sentences, putting the verbs in brackets into the perfect or imperfect tense.**

Example: 1 *J'allais au collège quand j'ai vu la nouvelle prof.*

1 J'___ (*aller*) au collège quand j'___ (*voir*) la nouvelle prof.
2 Je ___ (*regarder*) un film romantique quand Enzo ___ (*arriver*).
3 J'___ (*être*) en vacances quand j'___ (*manger*) au restaurant.
4 Il ___ (*faire*) très froid quand j'___ (*faire*) du ski à la montagne.

Remember, for perfect tense verbs, you will need a part of the auxiliary verb (*avoir* or *être*) and then the past participle.

You will often see the imperfect tense giving some background information before something then happens in the perfect tense.

Elle jouait au tennis quand elle est tombée. She was playing tennis (imperfect) when she fell over (perfect).

Lire 5 **Find five perfect tense and four imperfect tense verbs in the text. List them, write whether they are perfect or imperfect tense verbs and then translate them into English.**

Example: *c'était – imperfect – it was*

Samedi dernier, c'était l'anniversaire de ma mère. Le matin, elle a joué au golf avec ses amies pendant trois heures. Il faisait beau donc elle s'est beaucoup amusée! Ensuite, elle est arrivée à la maison à midi. Mon frère a fait un grand gâteau, mais nous n'avons pas chanté! L'après-midi, elle a dormi un peu, car elle était assez fatiguée. Moi, pendant l'après-midi, je jouais aux cartes en ligne avec des copains, et j'ai gagné!

Talking about the future (Pages 14, 90, 96, 183 and 192)

There are two ways to talk about the future:

a Present tense verbs with a future time expression — *Je **fais** mes devoirs ce soir.*

b Near future tense verbs ('going to' do something) — *Je **vais** faire mes devoirs ce soir.*

Lire 6 **Read the sentences. Find all the verbs used to express the future and note down which form of the future tense is used (a or b in the grammar box above). Write the verbs out in both French and English.**

Example: 1 *on va aller – b – we are going to go ...*

1 L'année prochaine, on va aller en France et je vais voir la tour Eiffel.
2 Après les examens, je vais aller au lycée et je vais étudier les sciences.
3 Malheureusement, je ne fais pas de baby-sitting ce soir.
4 Mes parents vont partir en vacances samedi prochain.
5 Tu portes des baskets au festival samedi soir?
6 Il passe le week-end chez un ami et ils font du camping.

Combining tenses with *si* phrases (Pages 92, 108 and 167)

You can use *si* (if) with a verb in the imperfect tense, followed by ***je voudrais*** (the conditional of vouloir), to express your dreams and wishes:

*Si j'étais riche, **je voudrais** avoir une grande maison.* — If I were rich, I **would like** to have a big house.

Écrire 7 **Copy out the parallel translations, completing the missing words.**

1	Si j'étais ___, je voudrais ___ une belle voiture.	If I ___ rich, I would like to buy a ___ car.
2	Si j'avais le temps, je ___ faire la ___ tous les soirs.	If I had the ___, I would like to do the cooking every ___.
3	Si j'___ célèbre, je voudrais ___ à Londres.	___ I were famous, I ___ like to live in London.
4	Si j'___ le choix, je voudrais ___ moins de devoirs.	If I had the ___, I would like to do less ___.

Using tenses together (Pages 8–11, 14–15, 16–17, 144 and 163)

Écrire 8 **Write an article about your local area for your French friend's school magazine.**

You must include the following points:

- what you usually do at the weekend
- the advantages and disadvantages of your town/village
- what you did during the last school holidays
- what you are going to do with your friends next weekend.

Write your answer in **French**. You should aim to write between 80 and 90 words.

- The bullet points prompt you to use a variety of tenses. In this task you will need to use the present tense (first two bullet points), perfect tense (third bullet point), and the future tense (last bullet point).
- Try to use connective words ('but', 'however', 'also', etc.) to make longer sentences.
- Also include some negative expressions and object pronouns to show your range of language.

Module 1

Révisions

Parler **1** ***Refresh your memory!*** **In pairs, tell each other what you like to do each day of the week. There are suggested activities in the box below.**

- *Le lundi, j'aime ... Et toi?*
- *Moi, le lundi, j'adore ...*
- *Le mardi, ...*

Make sure you vary the way you express your opinion. Don't repeat *j'aime* too often.

acheter des vêtements en ligne   aller à un concert   télécharger des chansons
aller au cinéma   regarder une émission de télé-réalité   suivre des influenceurs

Écouter **2** ***Refresh your memory!*** **Listen to Zoé talking about a past event. Make notes in English under the following headings.**

- When (was it)?
- Who (did she go) with?
- What (did she do)?
- What (did she like)?

Écrire **3** ***Refresh your memory!*** **Look at the vocabulary list on pages 30–31 and make a list of ten words that you have not used a lot or at all in your work in this module. Then, with the ten words, write sentences relating to the topic of Free-time activities.**

Lire **4** ***In my free time.*** **Read Ahmed's blog about his free time. What does he say about the activities below? Write P for an activity he did in the past, N for an activity he does now, or F for an activity he is going to do in the future.**

Mes amis et moi

Avec mes amis, le week-end, j'aime aller au centre commercial et au centre sportif. On adore aussi aller au cinéma. C'est génial pour réduire le stress du collège.

Demain, je vais aller à un magasin de vêtements car c'est la fête d'anniversaire de mon ami. Je vais acheter un nouveau tee-shirt.

Mes amis et moi, on aime aussi la musique. On joue et chante dans un groupe. Hier, on a joué pour le concert du collège.

Ahmed

1 Going to the sports centre
2 Going to the cinema
3 Going to a clothes shop
4 Playing at a concert

Look out for key phrases that will help you work out the time frames.
- What do these time words/phrases mean?
- Look carefully at the tense of each verb.

Lire 5

Translation. Translate these sentences into English.

1 Il y a un festival de musique.
2 J'aime regarder des films sur mon portable.
3 Je passe beaucoup de temps sur les réseaux sociaux.
4 Je pense que je vais commencer un nouveau sport.
5 À la fête, j'ai chanté la chanson de ma chanteuse préférée.

Écouter 6

New apps. You hear some adverts promoting new apps. What is each app for? Write down the correct letter. (1–4)

A	downloading songs	D	doing homework
B	sharing photos	E	sending messages
C	expressing what you think	F	young people

Parler 7

Reading aloud. With a partner, read out the text, paying attention to the underlined letters. Listen and check your pronunciation.

Read aloud the following text **in French**.

Je fais beaucoup de choses.
Le sport, c'est génial pour la santé.
Je préfère rester dans ma chambre.
Je regarde des vidéos sur Internet.
J'adore être actif et faire partie d'une équipe.

Take extra care with how you pronounce the underlined sounds:
- ***é*** and ***er*** sound the same
- final ***e*** is silent
- the final consonants ***p***, ***s*** and ***t*** are silent, except in *Internet*.

Make sure you use French pronunciation when saying these words.

Parler 8

With a partner, take turns to ask and answer the following four questions that relate to the topic of Free-time activities.

- Qu'est-ce que tu fais pendant ton temps libre?
- Tu aimes regarder le sport à la télé?
- Qu'est-ce que tu fais sur Internet?
- Qu'est-ce que tu penses de la musique?

Make sure you learn key opinion phrases such as *je pense que*, *je trouve que*, *j'aime* and *je n'aime pas*. Use connectives such as *car* and *parce que* ('because').
Every time you give an opinion, also give a reason: 'I like ... because it is ...'

Parler 9

Role-play. Prepare this role-play. Then listen and respond.

You are talking to your French friend.
Your teacher will play the part of your friend and will speak first.
You should address your friend as *tu*.
When you see this – **?** – you will have to ask a question.

1 Say **one** type of programme you like watching on TV.
2 Say when you watch TV. (Give **one** detail.)
3 Say why you like watching TV. (Give **one** detail.)
4 Say **one** type of programme you do **not** like watching.
? 5 Ask your friend about their favourite TV programmes.

You need to include a **verb** in each sentence.

You could start with *Qu'est-ce que tu ...?*

Module 2

Révisions

Parler 1

Refresh your memory! **In pairs, play 'adjective tennis'. Take turns to say an adjective that could describe someone and give the English translation.**

- *Gentil, gentille*
- *Kind. Embêtant, embêtante*

Try to give both the masculine and feminine forms if they are different, e.g. *paresseux/paresseuse*.

Écrire 2

Refresh your memory! **Describe at least three people, real or imaginary. Use the sentence starters below.**

- Il/Elle s'appelle ...
- Il/Elle a les yeux / cheveux ...
- Je pense qu'il/elle est ...

Écrire 3

Refresh your memory! **Here are some notes about famous people. Write sentences about each one using the information provided.**

Name	Yanis Marshall
Occupation	dancer
Family	Nadia Marshall = mother no children

Name	Mentissa
Occupation	singer
Family	boyfriend

Remember that you don't need to add *un/une* in front of a job in French, e.g. *Ma sœur est prof.*

Lire 4

My family. **You read an email that Lucie wrote to her French friend. Write the correct letter to complete each sentence.**

Coucou Lola!

Alors, le week-end dernier, qu'est-ce que tu as fait avec ta famille ou tes amis?

C'était l'anniversaire de ma belle-mère, alors je suis allée au restaurant avec mon père, mes sœurs et ma belle-mère. Mon petit frère n'était pas avec nous. Il était avec ses copains.

Ma sœur Jade était avec sa copine Inès: elles vont bientôt se marier! C'est génial!

1 Lucie went to the restaurant with her ...
 A brother only.
 B family.
 C friends.

The three options for question 1 all appear in the text, so it is important that you read very closely to find the answer.

2 Lucie's brother ...
 A was at the restaurant. **B** didn't celebrate with them. **C** is older than her.

3 Lucie's sister Jade ...
 A is married. **B** doesn't want to get married. **C** isn't married.

Lire 5

Best friends. **Read Enzo's email about friendship. Answer the following questions in English.**

1 How does Alex's age compare to Enzo's?
2 How did Alex and Enzo become best friends?
3 What do Alex and Enzo have in common? Give one detail.
4 How does Enzo know Louise?

Salut Morgane,

J'ai deux meilleurs amis: Alex et Louise. Alex a mon âge. Louise habite dans une autre ville. Alex ne connaît pas Louise.

Je connais Alex parce qu'on était dans le même club de foot. On aime la même sorte de musique et on joue de la guitare.

Louise, je la connais car ses parents sont les voisins de mes grands-parents.

Enzo

Écouter 6

My step-family. **You hear Hugo talking about his step-family.**

1 What are the qualities of his step-mother? Give two details in **English**.
2 How old are his step-brothers? Write down the letters of the two correct answers.

A	2
B	4
C	12
D	14

Écouter 7

Dictation. **You will now hear four short sentences. Listen carefully and, using your knowledge of French sounds, write in French exactly what you hear for each sentence.**

Parler 8

Photo card task. **Look at the photo and prepare what you are going to say.**

Describe this photo. Your description could cover the **people**, **where they are** and **what they are doing**.

When you have finished your description, you will be asked **questions** relating to the **overall theme**. Remember that you won't know the questions in advance. Here are two questions for you to answer that could be part of the conversation. Your answers must be as full as possible.

1 Qu'est-ce que tu aimes faire quand tu as du temps libre?
2 Qu'est-ce que tu as fait le week-end dernier?

Écrire 9

Translation. **Translate the following sentences into French.**

Think carefully about how you are going to translate 'my'. Is it *mon*, *ma* or *mes*?

What tense is this?

1 I live with my family.
2 My mother is very intelligent.
3 I don't get on well with my sisters.
4 My friends are very important for me.
5 Yesterday, I met my favourite celebrity.

Remember to make your adjectives agree with the noun they describe. Are you going to add an *e*? An *s*?

Module 3

Révisions

Parler 1

Refresh your memory! **In pairs, look at the school vocabulary on pages 80–81. Then play 'opinion tennis'. Take turns to say a subject and give an opinion on it.**

- *Le français*
- *C'est utile!*

When you give your opinion, start with *C'est ...*, *Je pense que c'est ...* or any other opinion phrase that you know.

Lire 2

Refresh your memory! **Rearrange each set of words to create a sentence and then translate the sentences into English.**

1 porter / faut / Il / uniforme / un
2 importantes / du / Les / collège / sont / règles
3 Il / pas / faut / ne / manger / en classe
4 pas / en / utiliser / portable / ne / Il / son / faut / classe
5 le / faut / professeur / écouter / Il

Look out for each infinitive to follow *il faut* or *il ne faut pas*.

Écouter 3

Refresh your memory! **Listen and make notes in English on each question below.**

1 Qu'est-ce que tu penses de ton uniforme?
2 Qu'est-ce que tu penses de ton collège?
3 Quel est ton avis sur tes cours?
4 Quelle est ton opinion sur les devoirs?

Lire 4

Learning languages. **You read Rafa's blog about learning languages. Write the letter of the correct option to complete each sentence.**

#RAFA

Salut, moi c'est Rafa!

Je pense qu'il est essentiel de parler deux langues. On peut aller en vacances à l'étranger. En plus, quand on parle une autre langue, c'est bien pour le CV quand on cherche un travail!

Cependant, tout le monde parle anglais dans le monde alors beaucoup de jeunes ne veulent pas apprendre une autre langue. Ils pensent que l'anglais est plus important que le français ou l'espagnol! Moi, je pense que toutes les langues sont importantes. Si on considère une autre langue, pourquoi pas l'espagnol ou le chinois?

1 Rafa thinks it is important to speak ...
  A only one language.
  B two languages.
  C three languages.

2 If you speak another language, ...
  A you can get a better job.
  B it is good for your CV.
  C you can live abroad.

3 According to Rafa, a lot of young people ...
  A are not interested in learning a language.
  B think French is more important than English.
  C can speak Spanish well.

4 Rafa thinks that ...
  A Spanish is better than French.
  B Chinese is more important than English.
  C all languages are equal.

Lire 5

Translation. **Translate these sentences into English.**

This looks like an English word, but be careful! Think of the school subject!

1 Je n'aime pas le théâtre.
2 Les langues sont importantes.
3 Je vais choisir mes matières.
4 Hier, j'ai beaucoup travaillé.
5 En France, les élèves ne portent pas d'uniforme.

What tenses are these?

Don't forget the negative.

Écrire 6

90-word writing task

You are emailing your French friend about the activities your school offers.

Write approximately **90** words in **French**.

You must write something about each bullet point.

Describe:

- clubs and activities at your school
- an activity you took part in at school recently
- what clubs or activities you would like to try.

Read the bullet points carefully to make sure you cover all of them in your answer.

You could start with *Il y a* or *Nous avons* ...

Write about a few things that you did and give your opinion.

Écrire 7

Grammar task. **Using your knowledge of grammar, copy and complete the following sentences in French. Choose the correct word from the three options.**

1	Les règles du collège sont ___.	**strict / strictes / stricte**
2	Ma matière ___, c'est l'histoire.	**préférée / préfère / préférées**
3	Est-ce que tu ___ un uniforme?	**porte / portes / portent**
4	Avant, dans mon collège, mon prof de maths ___ bien.	**expliquer / expliquait / explique**
5	Le lundi, ___ allons au club de maths.	**nous / elle / je**

Parler 8

Reading aloud. **With a partner, read out the text, paying attention to the underlined letters. Listen and check your pronunciation.**

Read aloud the following text **in French**.

Dans mon collège, il y a vingt clubs.

Après les cours, je vais au club de musique.

Il commence à seize heures.

Le soir, je fais mes devoirs et c'est long.

Parfois, j'utilise Internet pour mon travail scolaire.

Remember that these words are cognates. Don't say them with English pronunciation!

Remember the liaison here and that the ***h*** is silent.

Take extra care with how you pronounce the underlined sounds:

- ***oi***
- ***-s-***.

What are the endings that you are not going to say?

Parler 9

With a partner, take turns to ask and answer the following four questions that relate to the topic of Education and work.

- Qu'est-ce que tu aimes utiliser pour faire tes devoirs?
- Qu'est-ce que tu penses des devoirs?
- Parle-moi des clubs dans ton collège.
- Qu'est-ce que tu aimes faire après les cours?

- Remember that you won't see the questions. Your teacher will ask you questions when you have finished reading out the text.
- Always justify your opinion with a reason.

Module 4

Révisions

Parler **1** ***Refresh your memory!*** **Spend five minutes looking back at the vocabulary on pages 104–105. Then, in pairs, take turns to say in French:**

- eight things that you like to eat and drink
- five things that are good for your wellbeing
- five things that are bad for your wellbeing.

Écrire **2** ***Refresh your memory!*** **Look again at the vocabulary on pages 104–105 and make a list of at least six adjectives you can use to talk about healthy living. Write the adjectives in the masculine and feminine forms.**

masculine	feminine
sain	saine

Refer to the grammar section on page 45 to revise adjective rules.

Écrire **3** ***Refresh your memory!*** **Copy and complete the following sentences. Choose from the verbs in the box. Then translate the sentences into English.**

commencer vapoter faire boire manger

1 Il faut ___ du sport.
2 Tu ne dois pas ___ trop de fast-food.
3 Je veux ___ une nouvelle activité.
4 Il ne faut pas ___ beaucoup d'alcool.
5 Il ne faut pas ___.

Lire **4** ***Technology and mental health.*** **You see this online forum. Some French students are discussing the impact of technology on mental health. Match the correct person with each question. Write A for Amadou, M for Malika and D for Dorian.**

Amadou Les portables créent des problèmes pour tout le monde mais les jeunes ont plus de problèmes avec Internet.

Malika Il est important de choisir avec soin les sites qu'on regarde. Certains sites peuvent avoir un impact négatif sur notre santé mentale.

Dorian Il faut passer moins de temps devant nos écrans. Il faut aussi aller au lit tôt pour bien dormir. C'est essentiel.

1 Who says that having a good night's sleep is important?
2 Who thinks that young people are more at risk on the internet?
3 Who says that we must reduce our screen time?
4 Who mentions the bad effects of some websites?
5 Who says that everyone can be affected by the negative effects of mobile phones?

Some words in the text are cognates, which means they look like English words. How many can you find and what do they mean?

Some words in the questions will be in the texts, but don't assume that where they are will give you the answer. Read carefully!

Écouter 5 ***Daily routine.*** **You hear some French students talking about their daily routine. What is the opinion of the students on the following aspects? Write P for a positive opinion, N for a negative opinion or P+N for a positive and negative opinion.**

1. breakfast
2. journey to school
3. meals at school
4. activities

Écouter 6 ***Healthy school.*** **Axel is talking about what their school does to promote healthy living. What do they say? Complete the sentences in English.**

1. a Axel's school organises a special event which lasts …
   b Axel's friends think the event …
2. a Axel thinks that this event …
   b During the event, Axel usually …

Écouter 7 ***Dictation.*** **You will now hear four short sentences. Listen carefully and, using your knowledge of French sounds, write in French exactly what you hear for each sentence.**

Parler 8 ***Photo card task.*** **Look at the photo and prepare what you are going to say.**

Remember that in the exam:
- there will be two photos
- you won't see the questions.

Describe this photo. Your description could cover the **people**, **where they are** and **what they are doing**.

When you have finished your description, you will be asked **questions** relating to the **overall theme**. Remember that you won't know the questions in advance. Here are two questions for you to answer that could be part of the follow-up conversation. Your answers must be as full as possible.

1. Qu'est-ce que tu aimes faire pour être en forme?
2. Qu'est-ce que tu as mangé récemment?

Parler 9 **With a partner, take turns to ask and answer the two questions in exercise 8.**

Écrire 10 ***Translation.*** **Translate the following sentences into French.**

1. I don't like chips.
2. For breakfast, I eat fruit.
3. We must drink a lot of water.
4. I am going to eat more vegetables.
5. I would like to be in good health because it is important.

Remember to say '*the* chips'.

The phrase is *il faut*.

What are these two key verbs?

You need to say 'I eat some fruit'. Remember that 'fruit' is plural in French ('some fruits').

You need *de* after a quantifier (e.g. *beaucoup de …*, *trop de …*).

You need to use the infinitive form (e.g. *manger*).

Module 5

Révisions

Parler 1

Refresh your memory! **In pairs, take turns to name a means of transport using the words and phrases below. Give one reason why you like travelling that way and one reason why you don't.**

- *La voiture*
- *Pratique mais cher*

voiture | train | métro | bateau | avion | bus | car
pas cher | confortable | pratique | direct | bon pour l'environnement
rapide | lent | cher | mauvais pour l'environnement

Écouter 2

Refresh your memory! **Listen. Then copy and complete the grid in English. (1–6)**

	What they complain about	What's wrong with it/them
1		

Listen out for adjectives.

Écrire 3

Refresh your memory! **Write a sentence in French about each holiday feature below.**

Use intensifiers like *très* and *assez* to modify your adjectives. Can you think of any different adjectives to use?

l'hôtel | la vue | la nourriture
la ville | les activités | les transports

You could write what something is like or what you think of it.

Lire 4

Technology and holiday booking. **You read this text that Toni wrote about the impact of technology on holiday bookings. Answer the questions in English.**

Beaucoup de personnes pensent qu'Internet a un impact négatif sur le tourisme. À mon avis, la technologie a changé notre façon de réserver nos vacances et c'est positif.

Maintenant, on peut réserver nos vacances avec des applis. C'est vraiment pratique. On peut comparer la qualité des hôtels et décider rapidement. L'avantage d'Internet, c'est qu'on peut voir les meilleurs prix et réserver un hôtel moins cher.

1 Who thinks that the internet has negative effects on tourism? — Read the start of the text.
2 According to Toni, how has technology changed tourism?
3 How can we book holidays now?
4 What is an advantage of the internet when booking holidays? — You may find several advantages, but you should give only one.

Lire 5

Translation. **Translate these sentences into English.**

1 Le château est près de la mer.
2 Pendant les vacances, je voudrais aller à la campagne.
3 Il faut essayer la nourriture locale.
4 Le festival se passe en juin et il dure une semaine.
5 L'année dernière, on a passé quinze jours à la montagne.

Do you remember these verbs?

How are you going to translate *on*?

How are you going to translate *à la*?

Écouter 6

Camping Beau Séjour. **You hear this advert about a new campsite. Which aspects of the campsite are mentioned? For each question, write the two correct letters. (1–2)**

A	campsite size	**D**	access
B	shopping facilities	**E**	facilities
C	price	**F**	location

Écouter 7

Lottery win. **You hear this interview with two lottery winners, Maxence and Louise.**

1 What will Maxence spend the money on? Give two details in **English**.

2 What will Louise do with the money? Write the two correct letters.

A	book a trip for herself in the mountains
B	book a holiday for her parents
C	go abroad
D	go away with her friends

Écrire 8

Describing a photo. **Look at the photo and prepare a description. Write five sentences in French.**

You could mention, for example, where it is, who the people are, what they are doing or what they are wearing.

Écrire 9

50-word writing task

You are sending an email to your French friend about where you are on holiday.

Write approximately **50** words in **French**.

You must write something about each bullet point.

Mention:
- the location
- who you are with
- the accommodation
- the weather
- the attractions.

Set out your answer using a separate paragraph for each bullet point. This shows clearly that you have answered each one.

Écrire 10

Grammar task. **Using your knowledge of grammar, copy and complete the following sentences in French. Choose the correct French word from the three options.**

1	Je voudrais des vacances ___.	**actif / actives / active**
2	J'aime ___ en avion.	**voyager / voyage / voyagent**
3	Nous allons ___ plage.	**en / au / à la**
4	L'année dernière, je ___ en France.	**vais / suis allé / aller**
5	___ peux réserver une table.	**On / Nous / Je**

Module 6

Révisions

Parler 1

***Refresh your memory!* With a partner, look at the weather forecast below. Take turns to ask and answer questions about what the weather will be like on a particular day.**

- *Il va faire quel temps lundi matin?*
- *Lundi matin, il va faire beau.*

> To talk about the weather in the future, you can use:
> *Il va faire ... beau / chaud / mauvais.*
> *Il va y avoir du soleil.*
> *Il y aura du vent.*

	lundi	**mardi**	**mercredi**	**jeudi**	**vendredi**
matin		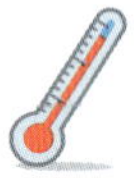	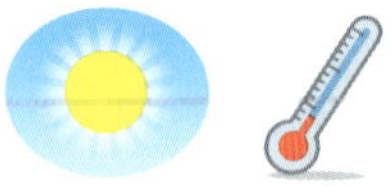		
après-midi					

Écrire 2

***Refresh your memory!* Complete the gap in each sentence using a word from the box. There are more words than gaps.**

1. Ici, il y a des ____. On peut faire du ski.
2. J'aime marcher dans la ____. J'adore voir les grands arbres.
3. La ____ n'est pas loin de chez moi.
4. Dans ma ville, il y a beaucoup d'____ verts.

espaces   forêt   montagnes   mer   paysage   vue

> Look at the article or pronoun before each gap and at other words in the sentence to help you choose the correct word.

Écouter 3

***A new campsite.* You hear these short adverts for a new campsite. What is each advert about? Write the correct letter. (1–4)**

A	meals
B	recycling facilities
C	geographical features
D	the weather
E	seasons
F	children's activities

> What key words would you hear if recycling was mentioned?

> What weather phrases do you know?

> What geographical features do you know?

> What are the four seasons in French?

Lire 4

***Translation.* Translate these sentences into English.**

1. Dans ma ville, il y a beaucoup de choses à faire.
2. En été, la mer est idéale pour les familles.
3. Les montagnes sont très belles.
4. Récemment, j'ai vu des déchets dans le parc.
5. Il faut protéger notre planète.

> What is this season?

> What is this structure?

> What tense is this?

Lire **5** ***A protest in my town.*** **You read this online article about a recent protest. Write the correct letter, A, B or C, to complete each sentence.**

Récemment, dans ma ville, il y a eu une grande manifestation qui a duré au moins trois heures. Elle a commencé à une heure.

La police a dit qu'il y avait quatre cents jeunes mais les organisateurs* ont compté plus de cinq cents ados. À la fin de la journée, il y avait six cents jeunes!

Ces jeunes ont marché en groupes, dans le calme, sans bruit. Ils n'ont pas parlé.

Tous ces ados étaient contre la pollution qui détruit notre planète et ils portaient des banderoles* comme «Protégez la nature!» ou «Il faut arrêter de polluer!»

***l'organisateur** (m)	*organiser*
***la banderole**	*banner*

1 The protest lasted …
A one hour. **B** several hours. **C** two hours.

There are two times or lengths of time in the first two sentences. Which one refers to the duration of the protest?

2 At the end of the day, there were about … young people at the protest.
A 400 **B** 500 **C** 600

What does each number refer to?

3 During the protest, the young people were …
A quiet. **B** noisy. **C** angry.

Beware of negatives when completing this sentence. Read the third paragraph carefully. What does each highlighted section mean?

4 On some banners they had written …
A We must not pollute! **B** Too much pollution! **C** We must stop polluting!

Parler **6** ***Photo card task.*** **Look at the photo and prepare what you are going to say.**

Describe this photo. Your description could cover the **people**, **where they are** and **what they are doing**.

When you have finished your description, you will be asked **questions** relating to the **overall theme**. Remember that you won't know the questions in advance. Here are two questions for you to answer that could be part of the follow-up conversation. Your answers must be as full as possible.

1 Parle-moi des problèmes de l'environnement dans ta ville ou dans ton village.
2 Qu'est-ce que tu fais pour protéger l'environnement?

You could say that you think they are a family. Say who is in front and who is behind. Describe what they are wearing, what they look like and if they look happy or not. You could use prepositions to describe where people are: *près de, à gauche, à droite*.

You could say that they are in a park, and that there are trees and buildings behind them. Don't forget to mention the weather.

Try to mention a few activities. Who is running? Who is walking? Who is talking? Remember to use the **present tense** to say what people are doing: *il/elle / l'homme / la femme …* ***court*** ('is running') / ***marche*** ('is walking') / ***parle*** ('is talking').

Écouter **7** ***Dictation.*** **You will now hear four short sentences. Listen carefully and, using your knowledge of French sounds, write in French exactly what you hear for each sentence.**

Module 7

Révisions

Parler 1

Refresh your memory! **In pairs, take turns to say the following words.**

une maison | un appartement | un jardin | un bâtiment | un pont | un endroit | un coin | mon quartier | un magasin | une rue

Remember your silent final consonants and your nasal sounds.

Écrire 2

Refresh your memory! **Make these sentences negative, using the negative expression in brackets. Then translate each sentence into English.**

1 J'ai ma propre chambre. (*ne … pas*)
2 Mon village est calme. (*ne … jamais*)
3 Dans mon quartier, je connais tout le monde. (*ne … personne*)
4 Il y a beaucoup de choses pour les touristes. (*ne … pas*)
5 Il y a une piscine. (*ne … pas*)
6 Je voudrais tout changer. (*ne … rien*)

Remember that *ne* shortens to *n'* before a vowel, an *h* or a *y*.

In questions 3-6, be aware that you will have to remove some words to make the sentences negative.

Écouter 3

Asking for directions. **Listen. Copy and complete the grid in English. (1–4)**

	Where they want to go	Directions	Distance / Time
1			

Écouter 4

Shopping trip. **You hear Rachid talking about a recent trip to the shops. Complete the sentences in English.**

1 Rachid went shopping with …
2 Rachid bought something for his …
3 He didn't have help to choose …
4 The bag was …

Lire 5

My dream bedroom. **You read this blog that Mathis has written about his ideal bedroom. Write the correct letter, A, B or C, for each question.**

Dans la chambre de mes rêves, je ne voudrais pas un lit avec un matelas* traditionnel mais un grand matelas avec de l'eau! Je ne voudrais pas de bureau car je n'aime pas travailler dans ma chambre. Si possible, je voudrais un coin de jeux pour mettre ma console. Je n'ai pas besoin d'une nouvelle console mais d'une partie de ma chambre juste pour jouer. Enfin, ce n'est pas necessaire d'avoir ma propre chambre! Je voudrais partager avec mon frère.

***le matelas** *mattress*

1 Mathis would like …
A a traditional bed. B a different bed. C a smaller bed.

2 Mathis would also like …
A a table. B a desk. C an area for gaming.

3 Mathis would like …
A a new games console. B a bigger space to play. C new gaming equipment.

4 Mathis would like to …
A share his room with his brother. B have a room for himself. C continue to have his own room.

Écrire 6

90-word writing task

You are emailing your French friend about shopping.

Write approximately **90** words in **French**.

You must write something about each bullet point.

Describe:
- what shops you like in your area
- a recent shopping experience
- what you would like to buy soon.

This is in the past. Talk about where you went and what you bought. You may also mention what other things you did, like eating.

Is there a particular occasion coming up (a birthday or a party)? Don't forget to include adjectives!

Parler 7

Role-play. **Prepare this role-play. Then listen and respond.**

You need to say 'I prefer shops of clothes / shoes / technology ...'.

You could say that you need to buy something for you, for a special occasion ...

You could say what it is and its size, colour, price ...

You could ask them if they like it or what they buy online.

You are talking to your French friend.

Your teacher will play the part of your friend and will speak first.

You should address your friend as *tu*.

When you see this – **?** – you will have to ask a question.

In order to score full marks, you must include a verb in your response to each task.

1. Say the type of shops you prefer. (Give **one** detail).
2. Say why you would like to go shopping today. (Give **one** detail.)
3. Describe what you would like to buy. (Give **one** detail.)
4. Give **one** opinion of shopping centres.

? 5. Ask your friend something about shopping online.

Écrire 8

Translation. **Translate the following sentences into French.**

Remember the negative *ne ... pas*.

Remember that you need the perfect tense here.

1. I like my town.
2. It is not far from Paris.
3. Our house is near the station.
4. Recently, I went shopping with my dad.
5. I would like to stay here in the future.

There are two ways you can translate 'shopping': one for food and one for other things.

Parler 9

Reading aloud. **With a partner, take turns to read out the text below, paying attention to the underlined letters. Then listen and check your pronunciation.**

Take extra care with how you pronounce cognates.

J'habite dans un village.

Il y a un petit théâtre et un hôtel très sympa.

Ici, il n'y a pas de centre commercial.

C'est très calme et tout le monde est gentil.

Il est important de protéger les traditions.

Once you have read the text, answer the four follow-up questions below.

1. Parle-moi de ta ville ou de ton village.
2. Qu'est-ce qu'il y a dans ta ville ou dans ton village?
3. Quel est ton avis sur les centres commerciaux?
4. Où est-ce que tu voudrais habiter plus tard?

Révisions

Parler 1

Refresh your memory! **With a partner, look at the career options below. Take turns to say whether you would want that type of career or not.**

- *Tu voudrais travailler avec des enfants?*
- *Oui, je voudrais travailler avec des enfants. Et toi, tu veux aider les gens?*

Use verbs and structures such as *je voudrais, j'espère, je ne veux pas, je veux.*

travailler avec des enfants | devenir professeur | être médecin | travailler dans le monde des affaires | travailler dans un hôpital | aider les gens | avoir un boulot bien payé | être actif/active

Écouter 2

Careers event. **You hear this advert for an event called *Journée avenir*. Answer the following questions in English.**

1 When should the pupils go to the event?

2 Name one career option that is represented at the event.

3 Why is the event suitable for everyone?

4 At the event, what is going to help pupils choose their career options?

Écrire 3

Refresh your memory! **Write sentences about your future plans. Use words such as *d'abord* ('first'), *ensuite* ('next') and *après* ('afterwards'). You can use the ideas below to help you or use your own.**

Example: ***D'abord****, je veux voyager et* ***après****, je veux trouver un boulot.*

You can use different verbs here such as 'I want', 'I hope', 'I would like' and their negative forms.

voyager | travailler sans gagner d'argent | trouver un boulot | acheter une maison | avoir des enfants | aller à l'étranger | étudier à l'université | apprendre un métier | me marier

Écouter 4

My future. **You hear this interview about careers with Yasmina and Hugo.**

1 Answer the following questions in **English**.

a In which area does Yasmina want to work?

b What does Yasmina think of money?

2 What would Hugo like to do? Write the two correct letters.

A	have his own company
B	work in his parents' company
C	work abroad
D	travel

Lire 5 ***My dream job.*** **You read Théo's school blog.**

Mon rêve dans la vie, c'est de visiter beaucoup d'endroits. J'adore passer du temps à l'étranger et j'ai beaucoup voyagé avec ma famille. Nous sommes allés dans beaucoup de pays très intéressants. Alors, je pense que ma carrière va être dans le tourisme.

Dans le tourisme, il y a un grand choix de boulots, et ça, c'est bien. On peut aussi rencontrer de nouvelles personnes de cultures différentes. Je sais que le tourisme n'est pas bien ***rémunéré*** mais l'argent n'est pas une priorité pour moi. Je veux d'abord être heureux dans mon travail!

1 Answer the following questions in **English**.
   a Why does Théo want to work in tourism? Give two details.
   b What are the benefits of working in tourism? Give two details.

2 Read the last but one sentence again. What is the best translation of the word ***rémunéré***? Write the correct letter, **A**, **B** or **C**.
   A considered **B** paid **C** advertised

Read the whole sentence carefully to work out the meaning.

Parler 6 ***Photo card task.*** **Look at the two photos and prepare a description of each one.**

For the first photo, you can say that the people are at a café. You can describe what they are doing. For example, they are sitting outside, in the street; they are laughing and drinking coffee. Remember to use the **present tense** to say what people are doing.

For the second photo, you can say that they are making a video, that a career online interests them, that they want to be influencers, etc.

Parler 7 **After you have spoken about the photos in exercise 6, you will be asked questions related to the overall theme. Remember that you won't know the questions in advance.**

Here are two questions for you to answer that could be part of the conversation.
Respond to them as fully as possible.

1 Qu'est-ce que tu voudrais faire comme carrière?
2 Qu'est-ce que tu as fait récemment au collège pour t'aider avec ton avenir?

Here you could mention what you would like to be and why.
You could use phrases such as:
XX m'intéresse
mon choix de carrière, c'est ...
je rêve de ...
mon rêve, c'est ...

Make sure you use the perfect tense in your answer. You could say that you talked to your teachers or that you watched a video on jobs.

Lire 8 ***Translation.*** **Translate these sentences into English.**

1 J'aime la musique.
2 Je veux avoir une carrière dans les affaires.
3 Je voudrais pouvoir chanter et être actif dans mon boulot.
4 Pendant mon stage, j'espère gagner de l'expérience.
5 Après le lycée, j'ai l'intention de partir à l'étranger.

Écouter 9 ***Dictation.*** **You will now hear four short sentences. Listen carefully and, using your knowledge of French sounds, write in French exactly what you hear for each sentence.**

Conversation questions

You can use these questions to help you prepare for two different sections of the speaking exam:

- the short unprepared conversation which follows on from the **reading aloud task**
- the unprepared conversation which follows the description of the photos during the **photo card task**.

In the **reading aloud task**, there are four conversation questions. All four questions are in the present tense and relate to the topic of the reading aloud text.

In the **photo card task**, there is an unprepared conversation relating to the theme of the photo in which you have the opportunity to show the examiner that you know a range of structures and tenses in French.

Module 1 (pages 6–31)

Theme 3: Communication and the world around us

1 Qu'est-ce que tu fais en ligne?
2 Est-ce que tu fais ça souvent?
3 Quels sont les dangers d'Internet? Et les avantages?

Theme 2: Popular culture

4 Quel est ton avis sur la musique?
5 Qu'est-ce que tu aimes regarder?
6 Tu vas souvent au cinéma? Pourquoi / Pourquoi pas?
7 Est-ce que tu as une vie active?
8 Pourquoi aimes-tu ces activités?
9 Qu'est-ce que tu vas faire le week-end prochain?
10 Qu'est-ce que tu as fait récemment avec tes amis? C'était comment?

Module 2 (pages 32–55)

Theme 1: People and lifestyle

1 Qu'est-ce qui fait ton identité?
2 Décris ta famille.
3 Qu'est-ce que tu fais le week-end, en famille?
4 Tu t'entends toujours bien avec tes amis? Pourquoi / Pourquoi pas?
5 Qu'est-ce que c'est, un bon ami, pour toi?
6 Qui est ton modèle dans la vie? Pourquoi?

Theme 2: Popular culture

7 Tu as un chanteur préféré ou une chanteuse préférée?
8 Qu'est-ce que tu as fait pour ton dernier anniversaire?
9 Comment vas-tu fêter ton anniversaire l'année prochaine?
10 Parle-moi d'une occasion spéciale avec ta famille ou tes amis.

Module 3 (pages 58–81)

Theme 1: People and lifestyle

1 Quelle est ta matière préférée? Pourquoi?
2 Tu n'aimes pas quelles matières? Pourquoi?
3 Quel est ton avis sur les langues?
4 Comment sont tes profs?
5 Quelles matières voudrais-tu étudier à l'avenir?
6 Parle-moi de ton collège et de ta routine scolaire.
7 Qu'est-ce que tu penses des règles du collège?
8 Quel est ton avis sur l'uniforme scolaire?
9 Qu'est-ce que tu as fait au collège récemment?
10 L'école primaire, c'était comment pour toi?

Module 4 (pages 82–105)

Theme 1: People and lifestyle

1 Qu'est-ce qu'il faut faire pour être en bonne santé?
2 Qu'est-ce que tu manges et bois pour le petit-déjeuner? le midi? après les cours? le soir?
3 Qu'est-ce que tu as mangé pour le dîner hier soir?
4 Qu'est-ce que tu vas manger demain et pourquoi?
5 Quelle nourriture est-ce que tu aimes bien acheter?
6 Quel est ton avis sur les restaurants fastfood?
7 Qu'est-ce que tu fais pour être en forme?
8 À l'avenir, qu'est-ce que tu vas faire pour avoir une vie plus saine?
9 Quand tu étais plus jeune, ta vie était comment?
10 Décris ta vie maintenant.

How to prepare:

- Read through the questions to check you understand them. Focus on the question words, like *Quel …?, Comment …?, Quand …?*, etc.
- Check the verbs and time phrases to understand which time frame the question is about.
- Then practise answering the questions using full sentences.
- Think about how you could extend your answers using more complex structures, particularly for answering questions during the **photo card task** conversation.

Ways to extend your answers:

- Join together ideas with connectives: *et, mais, aussi …*
- Add in opinions and justify them: *J'aime / Je déteste … parce que …*
- Use opposing arguments: *D'un côté … d'un autre côté … / Cependant …*
- Add in examples of recent activities in the past tenses.
- Add in examples of future plans using a future tense.

Module 5 (pages 106–129)

Theme 3: Communication and the world around us

1. Est-ce que tu penses que les vacances sont importantes? Pourquoi / Pourquoi pas?
2. Tu voudrais voyager? Pourquoi / Pourquoi pas?
3. Parle-moi de tes vacances de rêve.
4. Qu'est-ce qu'on peut visiter dans ta région?
5. Décris-moi tes dernières vacances.
6. Parle-moi d'un problème que tu as eu en vacances.
7. Tu préfères rester chez toi ou partir en vacances? Pourquoi?
8. Quels sont les avantages et les inconvénients des vacances entre amis?
9. Qu'est-ce que tu vas faire cet été, pendant les vacances?

Theme 2: Popular culture

10. Tu es déjà allé(e) à un festival?

Module 6 (pages 134–157)

Theme 3: Communication and the world around us

1. Que penses-tu du recyclage?
2. Décris-moi un problème dans ta région.
3. Qu'est-ce qu'il faut faire pour protéger l'environnement, à ton avis?
4. Qu'est-ce que tu fais pour protéger l'environnement?
5. Quand tu étais plus jeune, qu'est-ce que tu faisais pour protéger l'environnement?
6. À l'avenir, qu'est-ce que tu vas faire pour protéger l'environnement?
7. Quel transport public préfères-tu et pourquoi?
8. Quels moyens de transport as-tu utilisés récemment?
9. Qu'est-ce que tu penses des voitures?
10. Qu'est-ce que le gouvernement doit faire pour encourager les gens à faire plus pour protéger l'environnement?

Module 7 (pages 158–181)

Theme 3: Communication and the world around us

1. Parle-moi de ta ville.
2. Qu'est-ce qu'il faut visiter dans ta ville?
3. Quels sont les avantages et les inconvénients de ta région?
4. Quelle est l'importance du tourisme pour une région, à ton avis?
5. Qu'est-ce que tu veux changer dans ta ville pour l'améliorer et pourquoi?
6. Décris-moi ta maison idéale.
7. Est-ce que tu es déjà allé(e) en France?
8. Dans quel pays est-ce que tu voudrais habiter plus tard et pourquoi?

Theme 2: Popular culture

9. Qu'est-ce que tu as acheté la dernière fois que tu es sorti(e) dans ta ville?
10. Qu'est-ce que tu vas acheter comme vêtements bientôt?
11. Où préfères-tu acheter tes vêtements et pourquoi?

Module 8 (pages 182–203)

Theme 1: People and lifestyle

1. Est-ce que tu voudrais un job d'été?
2. Quels sont tes projets pour le futur?
3. Quel métier voudrais-tu faire à l'avenir?
4. Quelles sont tes passions?
5. Quelle sorte de personne es-tu?
6. Avec qui voudrais-tu travailler?
7. Qu'est-ce que tu trouves important dans un emploi?
8. Quelles sont tes compétences?

Theme 2: Popular culture

9. Quels sont les avantages et les inconvénients d'être influenceur?
10. La télé-réalité, c'est une bonne idée, selon toi? Pourquoi / Pourquoi pas?

French phonics

Here is a list of all the sounds that you need to understand and produce.
The **SSCs** (Sound Symbol Correspondences) will be assessed in the **reading aloud** and **dictation** tasks.

The **reading aloud** task will be the second task in your oral exam. You will have **15** minutes' preparation time for the whole oral. The task will contain a short text of **a minimum of 35 words** based on a specific topic.

The **dictation** task will form part of your listening paper. You will have to transcribe a minimum of **20 words** (in four sentences). Some of the words will not be on the vocabulary lists. Practising the sounds on these pages will help with both the **reading aloud** and **dictation** tasks.

Sounds	Key word and other examples	Pages with a focus on this sound	Further examples to practise
1 silent final consonant	**tout** dan**s**, e**st**, deu**x**, tro**p**, tar**d**	pages 7, 9, 47	Il n'e**st** pa**s** tro**p** tar**d**. Le magasi**n** e**st** fermé. J'ai troi**s** frère**s**.
2 a	**aller** t**a**ble, m**a**g**a**sin, soci**a**l	page 158	Il y **a** un centre soci**a**l. Le voy**a**ge était agré**a**ble. Le festiv**a**l est géni**a**l.
3 i/y	**il/stylo** **i**déal, ut**i**le, s**y**stème	'*i*' page 20 both page 161	C'est mon st**y**le **i**déal. Il **y** a le wif**i** **i**c**i**? Ce s**i**te est très ut**i**le.
4 eu	**peu** bl**eu**, f**eu**, mi**eu**x	pages 87, 95	Il a les y**eu**x bl**eu**s. Il est un p**eu** séri**eu**x. Je v**eu**x d**eu**x j**eu**x.
5 e	**je** l**e**, m**e**, t**e**, s**e**	page 23	J**e** l**e** veux en rouge.
6 au/eau/ closed o/ô	**autre/eau/nos/tôt** **au**, b**eau**, vidé**o**s, bient**ô**t	page 107	Je vais voir le b**eau** chât**eau**. La vidé**o** est m**au**vaise. N**o**s **au**tres amis sont **au** rest**au**rant.
7 ou	**vous** **ou**, r**ou**ge, tr**ou**ver	pages 20, 95	**Où** se tr**ou**ve la c**ou**r? P**ou**vez-v**ou**s n**ou**s aider, s'il v**ou**s plaît? Je v**ou**drais j**ou**er dans un gr**ou**pe.
8 u	**tu** b**u**s, pl**u**s, s**u**r	page 20	Le b**u**s est pl**u**s **u**tile. Le déb**u**t est dans **u**ne min**u**te. La v**u**e est **u**nique.
9 silent final e	**elle** petit**e**, bell**e**, group**e**	page 9	Elle achèt**e** une nouvell**e** voitur**e**.
10 é/-er/-ez	**été/parler/avez** mang**é**, dans**er**, ch**ez**	*é* only – page 7 Revisited: *é/-er/-ez* page 16	Le week-end derni**er**, j'ai mang**é** ch**ez** mes amis. Pouv**ez**-vous r**é**p**é**t**er**? Vous av**ez** regard**é** la t**é**l**é**.
11 en/an/em/ am	**entendre/dans/temps/jambe** comm**en**t, **an**s, ex**em**ple, ch**am**bre	pages 84, 115	Il porte un p**an**talon bl**an**c. Elle a tr**en**te **an**s. L'**en**vironnem**en**t est vraim**en**t **en** d**an**ger.
12 on/om	**mon/combien** t**on**, opini**on**, n**om**bre	page 110	C'est m**on** opini**on**. Il y a c**om**bien de p**on**ts? Le n**om**bre est l**on**g.
13 ain/in/aim/im	**pain/fin/faim/important** cert**ain**, mat**in**, **im**possible	page 84	Le mat**in**, je mange du p**ain**. Mon cop**ain** a f**aim**. La f**in** est **im**possible.
14 è/ê/ai	**collège/être/faire** tr**è**s, f**ê**te, r**ê**ve, m**ai**son	page 34	C'est la m**ai**son de mes r**ê**ves. J'**ai**me f**ai**re la f**ê**te. Mon coll**è**ge est tr**è**s moderne.
15 oi/oy	**moi/moyen** tr**oi**s, b**oi**re, empl**oy**er, envoyer	page 64 Revisited: *oi* page 95	J'ai env**oy**é tr**oi**s messages. B**oi**re de l'eau est un bon m**oy**en d'être en forme. M**oi**, je b**oi**s beaucoup.

Sounds	Key word and other examples	Pages with a focus on this sound	Further examples to practise
16 ch	**cher** gau**ch**e, **ch**anter, blan**ch**e	page 38	Je **ch**ante **ch**aque diman**ch**e. J'aime mar**ch**er avec mon **ch**ien. Mes **ch**aises sont blan**ch**es.
17 ç/soft 'c'	**reçu/cette** fran**ç**ais, **ç**a, **c**inq, pla**c**e	page 170	Le fran**ç**ais est fa**c**ile. J'ai re**çu** **c**inq lettres. **Ç**a va bien.
18 qu	**qui** **qu**atre, **qu**and, pour**qu**oi	page 12	**Qu**'est-ce **qu**'on peut faire? J'ai **qu**atre chats. Mon **qu**artier est tran**qu**ille.
19 j	**jouer** **j**aune, **j**eudi, **j**anvier	pages 20, 23	**Je** **j**oue au tennis chaque **j**eudi. **J**'aime le mois de **j**anvier. **J**e n'aime pas le **j**aune.
20 -tion	**pollution** ac**tion**, inten**tion**, rela**tion**	page 135	Il y a des solu**tion**s pour lutter contre la pollu**tion**. J'ai l'inten**tion** de commencer la nata**tion**. J'aime les films d'ac**tion**.
21 -ien	**bien** ch**ien**, r**ien**, b**ien**tôt	page 69	Mon ch**ien** aime b**ien** manger végétar**ien**. Je n'ai r**ien** acheté. Je vais b**ien**tôt partir.
22 s-liaison	**vous avez** troi**s** ans, me**s** amis, de**s** heures	page 7	Me**s** amis sont trè**s** actifs. J'aime les petit**s** animaux. J'ai passé de**s** heures au centre commercial.
23 t-liaison	**il faut aller** ce**t** été, tou**t** est bien	page 7	Ce**t** été, je vais en France. À l'hôtel, tou**t** était bien. Le film es**t** amusant.
24 n-liaison	**on a** mo**n** amie, so**n** école	page 7	À mo**n** avis, so**n** animal est gentil. Mo**n** école est grande.
25 x-liaison	**deux heures** di**x** amis, deu**x** ans	page 7	J'ai deu**x** amis. Il est di**x** heures.
26 h	**hôtel** **h**eure, **h**eureux, **h**istoire	page 107	Je suis **h**eureux où j'**h**abite. Il est **h**uit **h**eures. L'**h**istoire de l'**h**ôtel est intéressante.
27 un	**un** l**un**di, empr**un**ter	page 115	Je cours **un** l**un**di par semaine. J'empr**un**te des livres.
28 -gn-	**gagner** monta**gn**e, campa**gn**e, li**gn**e	page 108	J'habite à la campa**gn**e près de la monta**gn**e. J'ai ga**gn**é à un jeu en li**gn**e. Il ensei**gn**e l'espa**gn**ol.
29 r	**rien** **r**ester, févr**i**er, pa**r**c	page 162	Je **r**este ici pendant deux heu**r**es. J'ado**r**e ma**r**cher dans le pa**r**c avec mes pa**r**ents. Il n'est pas t**r**op ta**r**d pou**r** a**rr**êter les p**r**oblèmes.
30 open eu/œu	**leur/sœur** s**eu**l, j**eu**ne, c**œu**r	page 34	L**eu**r s**œu**r est j**eu**ne. Je n'ai fait qu'une s**eu**le err**eu**r. Il y a n**euf** jou**eu**rs.
31 open o	**notre** dr**o**gue, sp**o**rt	page 138	Le sp**o**rt est n**o**tre passion. La dr**o**gue est un danger.
32 -s-	**faisons** amu**s**ant, cho**s**e, rai**s**on	page 67	C'est une cho**s**e amu**s**ante. Nous fai**s**ons de la mu**s**ique. Ils ont rai**s**on.
33 th	**théâtre** **th**ème, ma**th**s	page 162	J'adore les ma**th**s et le **th**éâtre. Je bois du **th**é. Le ry**th**me est passionnant.
34 -ill-/-ille	**billet/famille** f**ille**, gent**ille**, brou**ill**ard	page 183	La f**ille** est gent**ille**. Je voudrais un b**ill**et pour le mois de ju**ill**et. Il y a du brou**ill**ard.
35 -aill-/-ail	**travailler** trav**aill**eur, trav**ail**, t**aill**e	page 183	C'est ma t**aill**e. Il trav**aill**e. Je suis très trav**aill**euse.

Écouter **1** **Listen to each key sound or key word and repeat the sounds or words. Make a list of the sounds or words you find most challenging and keep practising them. Then, find other words for each key sound to test your pronunciation skills.**

Role-play skills

What do I need to know about the role-play?

- It is the first part of the speaking exam (before **reading aloud**).
- It is an imagined **conversation** with a friend on a variety of topics.
- The teacher speaks first.
- You will say something for each of the **five** numbered items.
- Speak in the present tense.
- You will need to ask **one** question.
- You should refer to your teacher as *tu* in the role-play, including when you ask a question.

Themes and topics

There are three themes, each with three topics. The table below shows which themes are covered in each module. There are example role-play cards on the exam pages at the end of each module, in the revision module and on this page.

Themes and topics	Module
Theme 1 – People and lifestyle	
1 Identity and relationships with others	Module 2
2 Healthy living and lifestyle	Module 4
3 Education and work	Modules 3 and 8
Theme 2 – Popular culture	
1 Free-time activities	Modules 1 and 7
2 Customs, festivals and celebrations	Modules 1, 2 and 7
3 Celebrity culture	Modules 2, 4 and 8
Theme 3 – Communication and the world around us	
1 Travel and tourism (and places of interest)	Modules 5 and 7
2 Media and technology	Modules 1 and 8
3 The environment and where people live	Modules 5, 6 and 7

Although there are **nine** possible topics, you can use vocabulary from any module. Use some of the preparation time to look at each numbered item and work out what you know you can say. Look at the example numbered item below and a suggested answer.

1 Describe your town. (Give **one** detail.) →

In English, you might think of a reply such as 'My town is polluted,' or 'There is an ice rink.' However, you might not remember how to say 'polluted', or how to say 'ice rink'. Therefore, keep it simple.

Ma ville est petite.
or
Il y a un cinéma.

Useful vocabulary

J'aime ...	*I like ...*
Je n'aime pas ...	*I don't like ...*
C'est ... / Ce n'est pas ...	*It is ... / It is not ...*
Il y a ... / Il n'y a pas ...	*There is/are ... / There isn't/aren't ...*
Je vais ...	*I go ...*
Je fais ...	*I do ...*
Il/Elle est ...	*He/She is ...*

Tu peux répéter la question?	*Can you repeat the question?*
Tu as ...?	*Do you have ...?*
Tu aimes ...?	*Do you like ...?*

Remember that you can ask the teacher to repeat if you have not understood.

Question

This is a key part of role-plays. You will need to ask **one question**. When it comes to your numbered item telling you to ask a question, it will be indicated with a **?** in front of it. Here are some examples of role-play questions.

Learn these key question words and phrases:

À quelle heure?	At what time?	*Que?*	What?
Comment?	How?	*Qui?*	Who?
Combien?	How many/much?	*Quel(le)(s)?*	Which?
Quand?	When?		
Où?	Where?		

Role-play question item	Example questions
Ask your friend a question about where they live	**Il y a** une piscine dans ta ville?
Ask your friend a question about school	**Tu aimes** ton collège / le sport?
Ask your friend a question about food	**À quelle heure** est-ce que tu manges?
Ask your friend a question about celebrations	**Que** fais-tu pour célébrer Noël?
Ask your friend a question about free time	**Quel** est ton sport préféré?
Ask your friend a question about social media	Tu suis **quelles** célébrités?
Ask your friend a question about the environment	**Qu'est-ce que** tu fais pour protéger l'environnement?

Remember that you can add ***est-ce que*** to ask a question in French:
Est-ce qu'*il y a …?* Is/Are there …?
Est-ce que *tu as …?* Do you have …?

Example role-plays

Look at the first role-play card and the model conversation next to it. Then look at the second role-play card and prepare what you are going to say.

You are talking to your French friend.
Your teacher will play the part of your friend and will speak first.
You should address your friend as *tu*.
When you see this – **?** – you will have to ask a question.

In order to score full marks, you must include at least one verb in your response to each task.

1 Say **one** subject you like at school.
2 Give **one** opinion about this subject.
? 3 Ask your friend a question about maths.
4 Describe your favourite teacher. (Give **one** detail.)
5 Say what you do at lunchtime at school.

Teacher: Quelle est ta matière préférée?
Student: J'adore le français.
Teacher: Qu'est-ce que tu penses de cette matière?
Student: Le français, c'est facile.
Tu aimes les maths?
Teacher: Oui, j'adore les maths!
Comment est ton ou ta prof préféré(e)?
Student: Ma prof préférée est très gentille.
Teacher: Qu'est-ce que tu fais à midi au collège?
Student: Je fais du sport avec mes amis.

You are talking to your French friend.
Your teacher will play the part of your friend and will speak first.
You should address your friend as *tu*.
When you see this – **?** – you will have to ask a question.

In order to score full marks, you must include at least one verb in your response to each task.

1 Describe what you do to stay healthy. (Give **one** detail.)
2 Give **one** opinion about fast food.
3 Describe your favourite meal. (Give **one** detail.)
4 Give **one** opinion about eating out.
? 5 Ask your friend something about food.

You can say what you eat (*je mange*), you do (*je fais*) or you drink (*je bois*).

You could say that it is good or expensive.

Start with *C'est …*

Start with *J'adore / J'aime manger …*

You could ask what they like to eat.

Photo card task

The **photo card task** is the final part of your speaking exam and is made up of **two** parts.

The photo card contains two photos relating to one of the three themes:

- Theme 1 – People and lifestyle
- Theme 2 – Popular culture
- Theme 3 – Communication and the world around us

Each theme includes three topics (see page 230).

1 Response to the two photos
(one minute)
Give a detailed description of both photos on the photo card.

→

2 Unprepared conversation
(three to four minutes)
Take part in a conversation on any or all of the topics from the theme specified on the photo card.

Response to the two photos

During your preparation time, **PLAN** how you are going to describe the two photos.

People
Who can you see?

Location
Where are they?

Activity
What are they doing?

Now check your accuracy carefully.

Sur la photo, Au premier plan, Derrière, Au centre, À droite, / À gauche, Ici,	il y a je vois	un garçon / une fille. un homme / une femme. des personnes / gens / jeunes / touristes. beaucoup de monde.
Je pense que	c'est une famille / un groupe de ...	
L'homme / La femme Il/Elle	**est** grand/grande et il/elle **a les yeux** ... et **les cheveux** ...	
Ils/Elles	sont ... / ont ...	
L'homme / La femme Il/Elle	**porte** (un pantalon ...) et ...	
Ils/Elles	portent ...	

À mon avis, Je pense que/qu'	ils sont elles sont	**dans**	un restaurant / un hôtel / un collège. une école / un magasin. un centre commercial. un centre sportif / un parc.
		en vacances. **sur** la plage. **à la** montagne / campagne / maison. **chez** des amis.	
	c'est l'été/hiver car (il fait beau / il y a du soleil / il fait froid / ils portent des tee-shirts ...).		

La fille (ici) L'homme (au centre)	mange / achète / joue / parle / écoute / marche ...
Les personnes à droite Les touristes	mang**ent** / achèt**ent** / jou**ent** ... parl**ent** / écout**ent** / march**ent** ...

Check:

- verbs
  - regular / irregular?
  - 'he/she' / 'they'?
- indefinite articles (**un**/**une**/**des**)
- definite articles (**le**/**la**/**les**)
- adjective agreements.

To say what people **are** doing, use the present tense. Remember that *ils mangent* means both 'they eat' and 'they are eating'.

Remember that the ***-ent*** verb ending is silent.

Example photo card task (Theme 3: Communication and the world around us)

Photo 1

Photo 2

During your preparation time, look at the two photos. You may make as many notes as you wish and use these notes during the test.

- Your teacher will ask you to talk about the content of these photos. The recommended time is approximately **one minute**. **You must say at least one thing about each photo**.
- After you have spoken about the content of the photos, your teacher will then ask you questions related to **any** of the topics within the theme of **Communication and the world around us**.

Unprepared conversation

After you have finished talking about the photos, you will take part in an unprepared conversation about any or all of the three topics from the theme on the photo card.

Listen carefully to the questions that your teacher asks and take care with how you start each answer. Are you using the correct tense?

If you make a mistake, just correct yourself. If you want the teacher to repeat a question, ask *Vous pouvez répéter, s'il vous plaît?*

Use the example questions on pages 226–227 to practise answers to questions you might be asked. This is an opportunity to show off your French!

How can I do my best in the unprepared conversation?

Do I give lots of information clearly?

Do I always try to give details in my answers?

Is my pronunciation accurate and easy to understand?

Do I use a range of vocabulary and structures?

Do I avoid repeating the same words?

Is my language always accurate?

Do I use verbs and tenses accurately?

Keep answers relevant.

Refer to past, present and future events.

Give detailed and varied answers.

Avoid grammar mistakes.

Use a range of nouns, verbs and adjectives.

Give clear answers.

Use a range of grammar and structures.

Derivational morphology

In the reading exam, you may need to understand and use variations of words which you have learned, for example:

participer (to participate) → *la participation* (participation) *cinq* (five) → *cinquième* (fifth)

Prefixes

Écrire **1** **Write words which have the opposite meaning to the ones below, adding the prefix *in-* or *im-*.**

1 égal (*equal*)
2 connu (*known*)
3 possible (*possible*)
4 moral (*moral*)

Adding ***in-*** or ***im-*** to a word can give it the opposite meaning:
actif (active) → ***in**actif* (inactive)
l'égalité (equality) → *l'**in**égalité* (inequality)
parfait (perfect) → ***im**parfait* (imperfect)

Lire **2** **Translate the underlined words into English.**

1 Elle est incapable de choisir une nouvelle voiture.
2 Les règles scolaires sont injustes!
3 L'ordinateur que tu veux acheter est indisponible.
4 Mon portable est inutile pour prendre des photos.

Suffixes

Écrire **3** **Write the ordinal numbers in words in French.**

1 5th
2 14th
3 20th
4 100th

Cardinal numbers (1, 2, 3, etc.) become ordinal numbers (1st, 2nd, 3rd, etc.) by adding *-ième* (or by dropping *-e* and adding *-ième*).
deux (two) → *deux**ième*** (second) *quinze* (fifteen) → *quinz**ième*** (fifteenth)

There are two exceptions:
un (one) → ***premier/première*** (first) *cinq* (five) → *cinq**uième***

Lire **4** **Translate the adjectives into English.**

1 comparable
2 aimable
3 jouable
4 mangeable

Some verbs can become adjectives by adding *-able* or *-eable* to the verb stem.
accepter (to accept) → *accept**able*** (acceptable)
télécharger (to download) → *télécharg**eable*** (downloadable)

Lire **5** **Translate the adverbs into English.**

1 exactement
2 premièrement
3 traditionnellement
4 uniquement

Some adjectives can become adverbs by adding *-ment*, or by dropping *-ant/-ent* and adding *-amment/-emment*.
libre (free) → *libre**ment*** (freely)
patient (patient) → *pati**emment*** (patiently)

Écrire **6** **Write nouns using the stem of the verbs below and adding the suffix *-ation* or *-ion*.**

1 accepter
2 progresser
3 participer
4 réserver

Some verbs can become nouns by adding *-ation* to the verb stem.
préparer (to prepare) → *prépar**ation*** (preparation)

Some verbs ending in *-ser* can become nouns by adding *-ion* to the verb stem.
réviser (to revise) → *révis**ion*** (revision)

Lire **7** **Translate the sentences into English.**

1 Les chiens ne sont pas tous adorables.
2 La participation est importante en classe de musique.
3 Mon père lave la voiture quotidiennement.
4 Son portable est vraiment introuvable!
5 La huitième page du livre est intéressante.
6 La vieille maison n'est pas habitable.

Useful verb tables

Key:
* = this verb form won't appear in exams, but you may use it in your own work

Regular verbs

INFINITIVE	PRESENT TENSE (stem + present tense endings)	PERFECT TENSE (auxiliary + past participle)	FUTURE TENSE (aller + infinitive)	IMPERFECT TENSE (stem + imperfect endings)
regarder to watch	je regard**e** tu regard**es** il regard**e** nous regard**ons** vous regard**ez** ils regard**ent**	j'ai regard**é** tu as regardé il a regardé nous avons regardé vous avez regardé ils ont regardé	je vais regarder tu vas regarder il va regarder nous allons regarder vous allez regarder ils vont regarder	je regard**ais** tu regard**ais** il regard**ait** *nous regard**ions** *vous regard**iez** *ils regard**aient**
finir to finish	je fin**is** tu fin**is** il fin**it** nous fin**issons** vous fin**issez** ils fin**issent**	j'ai fin**i** tu as fini il a fini nous avons fini vous avez fini ils ont fini	je vais finir tu vas finir il va finir nous allons finir vous allez finir ils vont finir	je finissais tu finissais il finissait *nous finissions *vous finissiez *ils finissaient
entendre to hear	j'entend**s** tu entend**s** il entend nous entend**ons** vous entend**ez** ils entend**ent**	j'ai entend**u** tu as entendu il a entendu nous avons entendu vous avez entendu ils ont entendu	je vais entendre tu vas entendre il va entendre nous allons entendre vous allez entendre ils vont entendre	j'entendais tu entendais il entendait *nous entendions *vous entendiez *ils entendaient
s'amuser to have fun	je **m'**amuse tu **t'**amuses il **s'**amuse *nous **nous** amusons *vous **vous** amusez *ils **s'**amusent	je me suis amusé(e) tu t'es amusé(e) il s'est amusé *nous nous sommes amusé(e)s *vous vous êtes amusé(e)(s) *ils se sont amusés	je vais m'amuser tu vas t'amuser il va s'amuser *nous allons nous amuser *vous allez vous amuser *ils vont s'amuser	je m'amusais tu t'amusais il s'amusait *nous nous amusions *vous vous amusiez *ils s'amusaient

These verbs have some spelling changes that affect pronunciation.

INFINITIVE	PRESENT TENSE (watch out for the change of stems)	PERFECT TENSE (auxiliary + past participle)	FUTURE TENSE (aller + infinitive)	IMPERFECT TENSE (stem + imperfect endings)
acheter to buy	j'ach**è**te ils ach**è**tent	j'ai acheté ils ont acheté	je vais acheter ils vont acheter	j'achetais *ils achetaient
commencer to start	je commence nous commen**ç**ons	j'ai commencé nous avons commencé	je vais commencer nous allons commencer	je commençais *nous commencions
jeter to throw	je je**tt**e nous jetons	j'ai jeté nous avons jeté	je vais jeter nous allons jeter	je jetais *nous jetions
manger to eat	je mange nous mang**e**ons	j'ai mangé nous avons mangé	je vais manger nous allons manger	je mang**e**ais *nous mangions
mener to lead	je m**è**ne nous menons	j'ai mené nous avons mené	je vais mener nous allons mener	je menais *nous menions
préférer to prefer	je préf**è**re ils préf**è**rent	j'ai préféré ils ont préféré	je vais préférer ils vont préférer	je préférais *ils préféraient
se lever to get up	je me l**è**ve *ils se l**è**vent	je me suis levé(e) *ils se sont levés	je vais me lever *ils vont se lever	je me levais *ils se levaient

Useful verb tables

Key:
* = this verb form won't appear in exams, but you may use it in your own work

Key irregular verbs

INFINITIVE	PRESENT TENSE (watch out for the change of stems)	PERFECT TENSE (auxiliary + past participle)	FUTURE TENSE (aller + infinitive)	IMPERFECT TENSE (stem + imperfect endings)
aller to go	je **vais** tu **vas** il **va** nous **allons** vous **allez** ils **vont**	je **suis** allé(e) tu **es** allé(e) il **est** allé nous **sommes** allé(e)s vous **êtes** allé(e)(s) ils **sont** allés	je vais aller tu vas aller il va aller nous allons aller vous allez aller ils vont aller	j'allais tu allais il allait *nous allions *vous alliez *ils allaient
avoir to have	j'**ai** tu **as** il **a** nous **avons** vous **avez** ils **ont**	j'ai **eu** tu as eu il a eu nous avons eu vous avez eu ils ont eu	je vais avoir tu vas avoir il va avoir nous allons avoir vous allez avoir ils vont avoir	j'avais tu avais il avait *nous avions *vous aviez *ils avaient
être to be	je **suis** tu **es** il **est** nous **sommes** vous **êtes** ils **sont**	j'ai **été** tu as été il a été nous avons été vous avez été ils ont été	je vais être tu vas être il va être nous allons être vous allez être ils vont être	j'**ét**ais tu étais il était *nous étions *vous étiez *ils étaient
faire to do/make	je **fais** tu **fais** il **fait** nous **faisons** vous **faites** ils **font**	j'ai **fait** tu as fait il a fait nous avons fait vous avez fait ils ont fait	je vais faire tu vas faire il va faire nous allons faire vous allez faire ils vont faire	je faisais tu faisais il faisait *nous faisions *vous faisiez *ils faisaient
prendre to take (**apprendre**, **comprendre** follow the same pattern)	je **prends** tu **prends** il **prend** nous **prenons** vous **prenez** ils **prennent**	j'ai **pris** tu as pris il a pris nous avons pris vous avez pris ils ont pris	je vais prendre tu vas prendre il va prendre nous allons prendre vous allez prendre ils vont prendre	je prenais tu prenais il prenait *nous prenions *vous preniez *ils prenaient

Modal verbs

INFINITIVE	PRESENT TENSE (watch out for the change of stems)	PERFECT TENSE (auxiliary + past participle)	FUTURE TENSE (aller + infinitive)	IMPERFECT TENSE (stem + imperfect endings)
devoir to have to (must)	je **dois** tu **dois** il **doit** nous **devons** vous **devez** ils **doivent**	*j'ai **dû** *tu as dû *il a dû *nous avons dû *vous avez dû *ils ont dû	je vais devoir tu vas devoir il va devoir nous allons devoir vous allez devoir ils vont devoir	*je devais *tu devais *il devait *nous devions *vous deviez *ils devaient
pouvoir to be able to (can)	je **peux** tu **peux** il **peut** nous **pouvons** vous **pouvez** ils **peuvent**	*j'ai **pu** *tu as pu *il a pu *nous avons pu *vous avez pu *ils ont pu	je vais pouvoir tu vas pouvoir il va pouvoir nous allons pouvoir vous allez pouvoir ils vont pouvoir	*je pouvais *tu pouvais *il pouvait *nous pouvions *vous pouviez *ils pouvaient

INFINITIVE	PRESENT TENSE (watch out for the change of stems)	PERFECT TENSE (auxiliary + past participle)	FUTURE TENSE (aller + infinitive)	IMPERFECT TENSE (stem + imperfect endings)
savoir to know	je **sais** tu **sais** il **sait** nous **savons** vous **savez** ils **savent**	*j'ai **su** *tu as su *il a su *nous avons su *vous avez su *ils ont su	je vais savoir tu vas savoir il va savoir nous allons savoir vous allez savoir ils vont savoir	*je savais *tu savais *il savait *nous savions *vous saviez *ils savaient
vouloir to want (to)	je **veux** tu **veux** il **veut** nous **voulons** vous **voulez** ils **veulent**	*j'ai **voulu** *tu as voulu *il a voulu *nous avons voulu *vous avez voulu *ils ont voulu	je vais vouloir tu vas vouloir il va vouloir nous allons vouloir vous allez vouloir ils vont vouloir	*je voulais *tu voulais *il voulait *nous voulions *vous vouliez *ils voulaient

Other useful irregular verbs

INFINITIVE	PRESENT TENSE (watch out for the change of stems)	PERFECT TENSE (auxiliary + past participle)	FUTURE TENSE (aller + infinitive)	IMPERFECT TENSE (stem + imperfect endings)
boire to drink	je **bois** tu bois il boit *nous **buv**ons *vous buvez *ils **boiv**ent	j'ai **bu** tu as bu il a bu nous avons bu vous avez bu ils ont bu	je vais boire tu vas boire il va boire nous allons boire vous allez boire ils vont boire	*je buvais *tu buvais *il buvait *nous buvions *vous buviez *ils buvaient
connaître to know (also applies to **reconnaître**)	je **connai**s tu connais il connaît *nous **connaiss**ons *vous connaissez *ils connaissent	j'ai **connu** tu as connu il a connu nous avons connu vous avez connu ils ont connu	je vais connaître tu vas connaître il va connaître nous allons connaître vous allez connaître ils vont connaître	*je connaissais *tu connaissais *il connaissait *nous connaissions *vous connaissiez *ils connaissaient
courir to run	je cours tu cours il court *nous courons *vous courez *ils courent	j'ai **couru** tu as couru il a couru nous avons couru vous avez couru ils ont couru	je vais courir tu vas courir il va courir nous allons courir vous allez courir ils vont courir	*je courais *tu courais *il courait *nous courions *vous couriez *ils couraient
croire to believe	je **croi**s tu crois il croit *nous **croy**ons *vous croyez *ils **croi**ent	j'ai **cru** tu as cru il a cru nous avons cru vous avez cru ils ont cru	je vais croire tu vas croire il va croire nous allons croire vous allez croire ils vont croire	*je **croy**ais *tu croyais *il croyait *nous croyions *vous croyiez *ils croyaient
dire to say	je **di**s tu dis il dit nous **dis**ons vous **dites** ils **dis**ent	j'ai **dit** tu as dit il a dit nous avons dit vous avez dit ils ont dit	je vais dire tu vas dire il va dire nous allons dire vous allez dire ils vont dire	je disais tu disais il disait *nous disions *vous disiez *ils disaient

Useful verb tables

Key:
* = this verb form won't appear in exams, but you may use it in your own work

INFINITIVE	PRESENT TENSE (watch out for the change of stems)	PERFECT TENSE (auxiliary + past participle)	FUTURE TENSE (aller + infinitive)	IMPERFECT TENSE (stem + imperfect endings)
écrire to write	j'**écris** tu écris il écrit *nous **écriv**ons *vous écrivez *ils écrivent	j'ai **écrit** tu as écrit il a écrit nous avons écrit vous avez écrit ils ont écrit	je vais écrire tu vas écrire il va écrire nous allons écrire vous allez écrire ils vont écrire	*j'écrivais *tu écrivais *il écrivait *nous écrivions *vous écriviez *ils écrivaient
lire to read	je **li**s tu lis il lit nous **lis**ons vous lisez ils lisent	j'ai **lu** tu as lu il a lu nous avons lu vous avez lu ils ont lu	je vais lire tu vas lire il va lire nous allons lire vous allez lire ils vont lire	je lisais tu lisais il lisait *nous lisions *vous lisiez *ils lisaient
mettre to put (in, on)	je **met**s tu mets il met nous **mett**ons vous mettez ils mettent	j'ai **mis** tu as mis il a mis nous avons mis vous avez mis ils ont mis	je vais mettre tu vas mettre il va mettre nous allons mettre vous allez mettre ils vont mettre	*je mettais *tu mettais *il mettait *nous mettions *vous mettiez *ils mettaient
ouvrir to open	j'ouvr**e** tu ouvr**es** il ouvr**e** nous ouvr**ons** vous ouvr**ez** ils ouvr**ent**	j'ai **ouvert** tu as ouvert il a ouvert nous avons ouvert vous avez ouvert ils ont ouvert	je vais ouvrir tu vas ouvrir il va ouvrir nous allons ouvrir vous allez ouvrir ils vont ouvrir	j'ouvrais tu ouvrais il ouvrait *nous ouvrions *vous ouvriez *ils ouvraient
partir to leave	je **par**s tu pars il part nous **part**ons vous partez ils partent	je **suis** parti(e) tu **es** parti(e) il **est** parti nous **sommes** parti(e)s vous **êtes** parti(e)(s) ils **sont** partis	je vais partir tu vas partir il va partir nous allons partir vous allez partir ils vont partir	je partais tu partais il partait *nous partions *vous partiez *ils partaient
recevoir to receive	je **reçoi**s tu reçois il reçoit *nous **recev**ons *vous recevez *ils **reçoi**vent	j'ai **reçu** tu as reçu il a reçu nous avons reçu vous avez reçu ils ont reçu	je vais recevoir tu vas recevoir il va recevoir nous allons recevoir vous allez recevoir ils vont recevoir	*je recevais *tu recevais *il recevait *nous recevions *vous receviez *ils recevaient

INFINITIVE	PRESENT TENSE (watch out for the change of stems)	PERFECT TENSE (auxiliary + past participle)	FUTURE TENSE (aller + infinitive)	IMPERFECT TENSE (stem + imperfect endings)
rire to laugh	je **ri**s tu ris il rit *nous **ri**ons *vous riez *ils rient	j'ai **ri** tu as ri il a ri nous avons ri vous avez ri ils ont ri	je vais rire tu vas rire il va rire nous allons rire vous allez rire ils vont rire	*je riais *tu riais *il riait *nous r**ii**ons *vous riiez *ils riaient
sortir to go out, leave	je **sor**s tu sors il sort nous s**ort**ons vous sortez ils sortent	je **suis** sorti(e) tu **es** sorti(e) il **est** sorti nous **sommes** sorti(e)s vous **êtes** sorti(e)(s) ils **sont** sortis	je vais sortir tu vas sortir il va sortir nous allons sortir vous allez sortir ils vont sortir	je sortais tu sortais il sortait *nous sortions *vous sortiez *ils sortaient
suivre to follow	je **sui**s tu suis il suit *nous **suiv**ons *vous suivez *ils suivent	j'ai **suivi** tu as suivi il a suivi nous avons suivi vous avez suivi ils ont suivi	je vais suivre tu vas suivre il va suivre nous allons suivre vous allez suivre ils vont suivre	*je suivais *tu suivais *il suivait *nous suivions *vous suiviez *ils suivaient
traduire to translate	je **tradui**s tu traduis il traduit nous **traduis**ons vous traduisez ils traduisent	j'ai **traduit** tu as traduit il a traduit nous avons traduit vous avez traduit ils ont traduit	je vais traduire tu vas traduire il va traduire nous allons traduire vous allez traduire ils vont traduire	je traduisais tu traduisais il traduisait *nous traduisions *vous traduisiez *ils traduisaient
venir to come (also applies to **devenir**)	je **vien**s tu viens il vient nous **ven**ons vous venez ils **vienn**ent	je **suis venu**(e) tu **es** venu(e) il **est** venu nous **sommes** venu(e)s vous **êtes** venu(e)(s) ils **sont** venus	je vais venir tu vas venir il va venir nous allons venir vous allez venir ils vont venir	je venais tu venais il venait *nous venions *vous veniez *ils venaient
voir to see	je **voi**s tu vois il voit *nous **voy**ons *vous voyez *ils **voi**ent	j'ai **vu** tu as vu il a vu nous avons vu vous avez vu ils ont vu	je vais voir tu vas voir il va voir nous allons voir vous allez voir ils vont voir	*je **voy**ais *tu voyais *il voyait *nous voyions *vous voyiez *ils voyaient

The verb **pleuvoir** (to rain) is only used in the *il* form.

INFINITIVE	PRESENT TENSE	PERFECT TENSE	FUTURE TENSE	IMPERFECT TENSE
pleuvoir to rain	il **pleu**t	*il a **plu**	*il va pleuvoir	*il pleuvait